National Ideology Under Socialism

1. Jan Jozef Lipski, *KOR: A History of the Workers' Defense Committee in Poland, 1976–1981,* translated by Olga Amsterdamska and Gene M. Moore
2. Adam Michnik, *Letters from Prison and Other Essays,* translated by Maya Latynski
3. Maciej Łopiński, Marcin Moskit, and Mariusz Wilk, *Konspira: Solidarity Underground,* translated by Jane Cave
4. Alfred Erich Senn, *Lithuania Awakening*
5. Jaff Schatz, *The Rise and Fall of the Generation of Jewish Communists of Poland*
6. Jadwiga Staniszkis, *The Dynamics of the Breakthrough in Eastern Europe,* translated by Chester A. Kisiel
7. Katherine Verdery, *National Ideology Under Socialism: Identity and Cultural Politics in Ceauşescu's Romania*

National Ideology
Under Socialism

Identity and Cultural Politics in
Ceauşescu's Romania

Katherine Verdery

UNIVERSITY OF CALIFORNIA PRESS

Berkeley / Los Angeles / Oxford

University of California Press
Berkeley and Los Angeles, California

University of California Press
Oxford, England

Copyright © 1991 by The Regents of the University of California

Library of Congress Cataloging-in-Publication Data

Verdery, Katherine.
  National ideology under socialism : identity and cultural
politics in Ceauşescu's Romania / Katherine Verdery.
      p.   cm. — (Societies and culture in East-Central Europe)
  Includes bibliographical references and index.
  ISBN 0-520-07216-2 (alk. paper)
  1. Romania—Cultural policy. 2. Romania—Politics and
government—1944–1989. 3. Intellectuals—Romania.
4. Ceauşescu, Nicolae. I. Title. II. Series.
DR267.V47   1991
306'.09498—dc20   90-47727
                                                                            CIP

Printed in the United States of America

1 2 3 4 5 6 7 8 9

Lui David Prodan
şi tuturor celorlalţi care, împreună cu el,
au spus "Nu!" chiar cu preţul vieţii.

To David Prodan
And to all those who, like him,
Said "No!"—some even with their lives.

Whoever would take the measure of intellectual life in the countries of Central or Eastern Europe from the monotonous articles appearing in the press or the stereotyped speeches pronounced there, would be making a grave error. Just as theologians in periods of strict orthodoxy expressed their views in the rigorous language of the Church, so the writers of the people's democracies make use of an accepted style, terminology, and linguistic ritual. What is important is not what someone said but what he wanted to say, disguising his thought by removing a comma, inserting an "and," establishing this rather than another sequence in the problems discussed. Unless one has lived there one cannot know how many titanic battles are being fought . . .

—Czesław Miłosz

Contents

Figures

Preface

The manuscript of this book was sent to the press on November 8, 1989; on November 9 the Berlin Wall was opened, marking the beginning of the end of "actually existing socialism" in Eastern Europe. Six weeks later the last unreformed regime in the region was overthrown, with the flight and execution of Romanian dictator Nicolae Ceaușescu.

These events changed not only the face of Eastern Europe but, more modestly, the significance of this book. From being an analysis of how cultural production and national ideology are intertwined in a socialist society, it became a recent history of a now-very-different future cultural and national politics, in the transition from socialism to whatever will come after it. As my open-ended analysis suddenly became self-contained, I could change my tenses and close the dossier on cultural politics in what I call (with irony) "Ceaușescu's Romania." I have resisted the urge to update the text with events of the moment, summarizing in the Conclusion those events related to my narrative—particularly what happened to persons mentioned in these pages after December 22, 1989.

The present form of my study came into existence in 1988 as the concluding chapter of another book, on how Romanian intellectuals developed the idea of the nation over three centuries. As that "chapter" lengthened to become its own book, I set aside the work that ought logically to have preceded it. I mention this history because a number of Romanian scholars and institutions that supported my research on the original project, and whom I did not inform of my belated change in direction, will be amazed to see this as its result. It is important for me to affirm that my original project proposal was made in good faith and will eventually, I hope, bear its intended fruit. The motivation for that project was suited to this one as well: to understand a phenomenon many Romanians regard as of the utmost importance—their national identity and ideas concerning it—as a way of repaying their patience with my earlier research, which had addressed my own interests rather than theirs. Needless to say, what began as their topic was soon transmuted by its contact with American social science and may no longer be wholly recognizable to them.

If, as I claim in this study, all intellectual activity is rooted in social life and implements values even when it claims neutrality, then I should lay my own values on the line as explicitly as did those who are its subjects and from whom I have learned that scholarship is politics. On one level, my scholarly politics include an effort to utilize analytic terms crafted for the systems in question, rather than political models derived from western political systems; to examine in a relatively distanced manner the terms employed by all participants in an argument and not to adopt straightaway the affects, meanings, or justifications offered by either side; and to insist that the activity of cultural production is permeated with politics and that culture itself is best seen as a form of practice, rather than as a set of meanings to be explicated. These "political" values place me in a certain relation to theories and methodologies in other disciplines and within my own. I believe that implementing these values enables both fuller understanding of the situation of Romanian intellectuals, passionately defining their nation's identity while struggling for their livelihood, and an enlarged capacity to learn from them, toward clarifying the conditions of intellectual activity at home.

Beyond this, however, I found myself compelled to evaluate the positions of my research subjects, as well, which required imposing my own set of "ideological" values. I had at first intended to present conflicts among intellectuals in Ceauşescu's Romania from a completely neutral stance, resisting the powerful temptation to adopt the values of my closest associates, who belonged chiefly to one faction. I hoped to avoid what all my associates described as their own experience of being inexorably pushed in the direction of one or other "camp." Nonetheless, I too succumbed to the pressures. Even though I attempt to maintain a fair degree of objectivity in these pages, and even though I criticize *all* parties for reinforcing an ideology basic to reproducing their problematic social order, I too have taken sides. Life in Ceauşescu's Romania was so unpleasant that I simply could not remain neutral in the face of evidence that one or another faction was contributing dispropor-tionately to the misery. Before the fall of the regime, my role would have been to support those whose voices were being silenced by the ap-paratus of repression, but as it happened, they soon gained their own platforms. I now see the political utility of my analysis as drawing atten-tion to certain groups and, especially, certain tactics that I expect will feed demagogy and intolerance in Romania after Ceauşescu. In decid-ing which side to take, I chose to defend not "truth" or "expertise" but, rather, those very American values that champion a pluralist resistance to the totalization of social life. If to choose sides on the basis of these values is to reinforce a certain ideology basic to reproducing our own problematic social order, so be it.

Acknowledgments

A number of Romanian scholars read parts of this book in manuscript; several were good enough to disagree—often violently—with its arguments. For most, their names (along with those of other colleagues) appear in a footnote to the specific chapters they helped to improve. A few, however, played so important a part in the whole work that I wish to salute and thank them here as well. One name appears with disproportionate frequency in these pages, that of Mihai Dinu Gheorghiu; this brilliant Romanian sociologist contributed so much to my treatment of Romanian culture that I sometimes think he should be co-author. My efforts were stimulated and encouraged also by historian Alexandru Zub, who not only gave me hours of conversation and passed on to me innumerable bibliographic references but, together with Sorin Antohi and Mihai Gherman, also verified a number of titles and quotations I was unable to confirm at home. Pavel Campeanu and Ştefana Steriade, in the United States on a Fulbright grant while I was writing the book, read most of the chapters and offered extensive criticism. Andrei and Delia Marga provided me with not just excellent intellectual advice but memorable friendship and hospitality. Finally, Academician David Prodan, who knew nothing about this book while it was being written and may well not like it, inspired it in two respects: by making me realize how deeply Romanian intellectuals feel the matter of their national identity and how central it is to the best works of Romanian culture, and by his intransigent example, which made me want to study scholarly resistance to Romanian party rule. I remain his deeply grateful admirer.

Friends and colleagues in the United States helped make this book possible in other ways. Gail Kligman read the entire manuscript and provided constant assistance and criticism; *mulțam fain, dragă*! My colleagues in anthropology at Johns Hopkins—Sidney Mintz, Emily Martin, Gillian Feeley-Harnik, Michel-Rolph Trouillot, and Ashraf Ghani—not only improved specific chapters but have literally shaped my vision as a scholar in ways too thorough-going to acknowledge. I owe a special debt to Emily Martin, who as department chair created many opportunities supportive of my writing, and to Ashraf Ghani, for his gift of pointing out that one's achievements are greater than one might have thought. All scholars should be as fortunate in their collegial environment as I. Others whose encouragement or suggestions made an important difference include David W. Cohen, Jane F. Collier, Keith Hitchins, Norman Manea, Erica Schoenberger, and, more personally, Dori, Jo, Sido, my parents and siblings, and my favorite sociologist.

I am thankful for the assistance of several institutions. Grants from the International Research and Exchanges Board (IREX), through funds provided by the National Endowment for the Humanities and the United States Information Agency, supported most of my research. A fellowship at the Woodrow Wilson International Center for Scholars, Washington, D.C., enabled me to write two chapters free of other chores and provided me with the excellent company of, among others, Martin Meisel, Maria Todorova, Anne-Marie Esche, Barbara Jo Lantz, and John Lampe. Neither of these organizations, of course, is responsible for the results of their generosity. In Romania, my research was organized by the Academy of Social and Political Sciences and took me to the Institutes of History in Cluj, Iași, and Bucharest, as well as to the University and Academy Libraries in the same three cities; my thanks to Dan Ghibernea and to the directors of those institutions for their cordial welcome, and to Prof. Pompiliu Teodor, my research sponsor early in the project (before it took on its present coloration). The American Embassy in Bucharest provided crucial logistic support—mail and food.

My work on this project aroused my great respect for the commitment, sophistication, and talent of many Romanian intellectuals. May the end of Ceaușescu's rule permit these qualities to flourish as they deserve.

Introduction: Ideology, Cultural Politics, Intellectuals

The identity of a people and of a civilization is reflected and concentrated in what has been created by the mind—in what is known as "culture." If this identity is threatened with extinction, cultural life grows correspondingly more intense, more important, until cultural life itself becomes the living value around which all people rally.

—Milan Kundera

Culture is the arena in which there occurs the political struggle to obtain identity and legitimacy.

—Mihai Dinu Gheorghiu

In March of 1989, six former officials of the Romanian Communist Party wrote an open letter to Romanian President Nicolae Ceauşescu protesting his policies.[1] Among their accusations was this: "Romania is and remains a European country. . . . You have begun to change the geography of the rural areas, but you cannot move Romania into Africa." An emigré Romanian writer echoed this image, lamenting the shift from "ideocracy" to "idiocracy" in his native land and the "offensive against competence, intelligence, talent, in a word, against culture" and decrying Ceauşescu's personality cult as "worthy of an African state." Other writers, too, despaired at the thought that Romania had ceased to be a European society, and they begged assistance from the "European family" to restore Romania to the "civilizing principles" of the French Revolution: "Romania must once again assume its place in Europe." A literary critic at war with a highly placed writer opened his book of essays with an anti-European quotation from his opponent ("I hate French for its much-vaunted cartesianism") and then, calling such an attitude "barbarian," launched a defense of European culture against it. All over Romania, during and after the violence that over-threw Ceauşescu's "barbarian" rule, demonstrating students chanted "Europe is with us!" and newspapers and jubilant Romanians writing their friends abroad exclaimed, "We are returning at last to Europe!"[2]

Illustrating quite the contrary attitude, a sociologist insisted: "[Our culture] cannot keep limping along behind European civilization, fix-ated on a peripheral identity. . . . [Ours] is not a subaltern culture and the road to our values does not pass through the West." He was joined by others who railed against European influence as an "intellectual dic-tatorship" and "an attack on Romanian cultural tradition." One critic condemned the intolerable "boycott of our values," complaining that "we have translated the fourth book by [French anthropologist] Lévi-Strauss but not one by [Chicago-based Romanian emigré] Mircea Eliade." Still more graphic illustration of these people's point of view was the board game "Dacians and Romans" being sold in Romanian toy stores in 1987, which cast the ("European") Romans as the game's villains against the ("native") Dacians.[3]

Europe and Africa, culture and barbarism, colonial exploitation and western dictatorship: these images ricocheted through the space of Ro-mania's cultural and political life in the 1970s and 1980s. As is evident from the exultant Europeanism of the anti-Ceauşescu forces, such im-ages were the distilled expression of fierce and passionate sentiments, the emblems of diametrically opposed political positions. To be against the regime had become synonymous with being pro-European, whereas Ceauşescu and those in factions more or less allied with him ranted against western imperialism and the Europeanizing obliteration of the national soul.

Although these highly charged symbols adorned political speeches often enough, it was in a somewhat different domain that they formed the very essence of political discourse: in the world of Romanian cul-ture. They were the currency of life-and-death struggles in intellectual life under Ceauşescu. They flowed easily, however, between intellectual and political domains, for two reasons, one historical and one contemporary. Different political options had been intertwined for over three centuries with alternative definitions or representations of Romanian identity (as European, as eastern, as something different from both); and the relations established between Romanian intellectuals and the Communist party ensured that cultural life would be entangled with politics.

This book is about how images of Romanian identity entered into battle with one another in the politicized world of Romanian culture and, in so doing, perpetuated a Romanian national ideology within an order claiming to be socialist. It is about the relations among those who created such images (different groups of intellectuals or, more broadly, producers of culture), and between them and the leadership of the Romanian Communist Party. These various groups, producers of culture and of rule, wrote and talked about "the nation," constructing it as a politically relevant field of discourse. Their words coexisted with words on other themes and with a larger set of strategies that included subtle coercion and outright violence. Together, these formed the system of "legitimation" or "consent" in Ceaușescu's Romania, as well as the elements of its transformation. The following chapters discuss intellectuals' contribution to these processes, asking how philosophers, artists, writers, historians, journalists, and others created and recreated a national ideology, and what difference it made that this was occurring in a "socialist" system rather than one of another kind. Underlying these are larger questions: What was there about twentieth-century Soviet-type socialism that brought politics and culture together in mutually informing ways? What was there about the idea of "the nation" that made it so apt a junction for culture and politics? And what consequences, finally, did the discourse on the nation have for the socialist order that sought to appropriate it?

Most of this book deals with apparently esoteric matters—arguments among sociologists, literary critics, historians, and philosophers. Its significance, however, goes far beyond these. To begin with, it is precisely the nexus between politics and culture which enables us to understand why the new government that emerged in late December 1989 included not only communist reformers but several poets (such as Mircea Dinescu and Ana Blândiana), literary critics (Aurel Dragoș Munteanu), philosophers and aestheticians (Mihai Șora, Andrei Pleșu), and a teacher of French (Doina Cornea). The Romanian example can thereby enlighten even more striking instances of the same thing, such as Václav Havel's extraordinary transformation from jailed playwright to president of Czechoslovakia.

More important, I believe, is the relevance of the material in this book to what will surely be a prominent feature of Eastern Europe in its transition from socialism: national ideologies and the mobilization of national sentiments in the new "democratic" politics. Some commentators attribute a possible "new nationalism" to the resuscitation of interwar politics, as if everything that had intervened was inconsequential. In contrast, I see national ideology as having been built up in Romania throughout the communist period—and not just by the Party's recourse to it, but by intellectuals' continued elaboration of the national idea, which was also highly functional within Romania's socialist political economy (see chapters 3 and 5). Moreover, I suggest, this national ideology disrupted the Marxist discourse and thus—despite the Communist party's apparent appropriation of it—was a major element in destroying the Party's legitimacy. The analysis in these chapters, then, not only offers the history of how a national identity was reproduced within a particular Eastern European socialism and how it contributed to undermining that social order, but also illuminates the context for politics in the 1990s and the place national ideologies will occupy in them.

My analysis presupposes that intellectual activity is complexly related to power and may construct empowering ideologies even when intellectuals intend otherwise. In addition, I presuppose that intellectual activity is *situated*: that it does not emanate from a neutral zone of ideas floating freely above and indifferent to social conflict, order, and interest but that it is, rather, one of several instruments for realizing these. Intellectual arguments about identity are sometimes seen as expressing the dilemmas of those from subaltern cultures (see, e.g., Herzfeld 1984, 1987; Jowitt 1978; Sugar et al. 1985), and contradictory images of national "selves"—as eastern, as western, and so forth—are sometimes read as evidence of confusion about identity, resulting from interstitial placement between dominating imperial powers (Herzfeld 1987: 112, 114; McNeill 1964: 209). Although I, too, recognize that the overwhelming crosscurrents of influence from powerful "cores" have profoundly disorienting effects on intellectuals in "peripheries," I take a different approach in this book. I attempt to show how various groups, variously situated in Romanian society, have taken advantage of these crosscurrents to produce rival images of their nation while competing with one another to be the nation's acknowledged cultural representatives. It is for this reason that I see questions of identity as wrapped up in a *politics* of culture, whose result is to strengthen the national ideology.

My analysis has several different audiences concerned with diverse literatures and conceptual issues. Anthropologists, sociologists, political scientists, and historians have pursued either theoretically or empirically one or another of the themes I explore. These include the politics of culture (especially in socialist societies); the social role of intellectuals and their relation to power; the theoretical analysis of socialist-type systems; and processes whereby hegemony, ideology, and legitimating discourses—specifically national ones—are formed. Different facets of the book will recommend it to different audiences. From an anthropological point of view, it contributes to writings on the political economy of cultural production and on culture as practice ("culture" understood here in the sense of "high culture," which is also, of course, a form of culture as anthropologists usually treat it). The book also addresses literature in social theory—especially the work of Foucault, Gramsci, Raymond Williams, and Pierre Bourdieu—on the nature of discourse, of intellectual work, and of the relation of these to power. Among other things, I seek to modify Bourdieu's notions of "cultural capital" and "symbolic markets," which I see as inappropriate for socialist systems, where "capital" and "markets" do not work as in the systems he describes. Political scientists interested in questions of legitimation, especially in the very precarious regimes of the formerly socialist Eastern Europe, may find my treatment of this issue useful, along with my account of politicking in Romanian culture. Students of historical and contemporary national ideologies may benefit from my somewhat unusual definition of "ideology" and my atypical account of nationalism, as compared with the modalities common to intellectual history and political analysis.

An investigation of these subjects might do or ought to do many things that this one does not; I should state its limitations at the outset. First, and most alarmingly to many of my Romanian friends, this book does not pretend to be a study of Romania's cultural life under Ceauşescu and of the works of value it produced. Of the several Romanian colleagues who read parts of this book in draft, nearly all complained that it tells too little about the excellent things that appeared in Romanian art, letters, and scholarship. I agree with them that much of value was created, but to describe it and its contribution to Romanian

civilization is not my aim. The entire orientation of this work prob-
lematizes the notion of "value" their urgings took for granted. In short,
persons coming to the book for a taste of Romania's cultural achievements will leave it hungry. Although I have, certainly, my preferences in
Romanian culture and scholarship, I view my own evaluations as situated, just like those of Romanians. I see my task in these chapters not
primarily as upholding one or another of their definitions of cultural
value but as inquiring into the total field in which different definitions
of value conflicted with each other. If in the end I nevertheless take
sides, I do so not from unquestioned attachment to values of "truth" or
"creative freedom" but because, in an irredeemably American way, I
prefer pluralism to centralization. Despite the self-serving quality of intellectual invocations of truth and creative freedom, I support the actions of any group that tends to slow the absorption of values into the
political center and to maintain an environment of alternative
possibilities.

An analysis of elite discourse or ideology might be expected to ask
how these shape the subjectivities, or the consciousness, of persons in
society. Some scholars would phrase the entire problem in this way:
rather than talking about how domination is ideologically organized,
they would investigate the aspects of power relations in which the identity of groups and individuals is at stake, creating in people an experience or a consciousness that makes them *subjects* (Foucault 1982: 212;
Corrigan and Sayer 1985: 1–13). Scholarship has only just begun to
scratch the surface of this fascinating problem; the present book will
not carve into it more deeply. As for the more general relation of intellectual discourse to "the masses" (the "is-anyone-listening" problem),
the circumstances of my research made it difficult for me to answer this
question.[4] More important, I do not think that *every* interest in public
discourse must be treated in a whole-societal way. It is legitimate to ask
how communities of culture-producers were engaged with the Communist party without also asking what peasants and workers thought of
it all. I proceed, therefore, to look primarily at activities within the elite,
seeing there a process of ideological construction whose consequences
for the masses can and should be studied in their own right. I refer readers interested in the latter problem to Gail Kligman's work on the Romanian party's attempt to create a mass culture, eliminating altogether
the distinction—central to the phenomena I write about here—between mass and elite culture (Kligman MS).[5]

A final set of limitations has to do with my sources and the way I treat them. This book is chiefly about various forms of speech acts, mostly printed. (For my interpretations I also rely upon extensive conversations with Romanian intellectuals, but I do not directly cite them.) I am not trained in discourse analysis and interpret these texts differently from those who are. I do not attend adequately, for example, to questions of genre, such as the difference between things published as books or as articles in periodicals. To some extent, that difference was often moot for the material I discuss, because articles were collected into books and books were often serialized in periodicals (sometimes in quite significant ways, as chapter 7 will show). I am attentive to the *kind* of periodical a piece appeared in, but do not ask if the form in which it was published is significant.

Moreover, I do not attend much in this book to *silences*. Although I do indicate a few significant silences, on the whole this book concerns what was said more than what was suppressed. This is a limitation, because the centralization of discourse under the control of the Romanian party conferred ever greater value upon silence. Silence became a way of resisting totalization. Nevertheless, one could fight only so far with silence: for people struggling to obtain the resources necessary to produce culture, speech became essential. One could not make a claim or justify one's rights to an allocation silently. Thus, given how Romania's socialist bureaucracy worked (see chapter 2), power forced speech: producers of culture could not hold their ground if they refused to speak up.[6] For this reason, I believe that despite the significance of silence, we can still learn something valuable about cultural politics by attending to speech.

Concepts and Terms

Nearly every term in the title of this book is imprecise and its definition contested. Although there is a certain rudimentary agreement on what "national" and "identity" mean (not, however, on the processes that generate national and ethnic identities), the same cannot be said of "ideology," which has multiple and contradictory uses. "Socialism" has changed radically in a very short time. "Culture" is both vague and specific, a lay notion and a specialist one. It will be easier to follow my discussion if I explain how I understand such terms. Because my ambition in this book falls short of theoretically advancing these

concepts, I have dispensed with an extended critical review of the literature concerning them and have restricted myself to what is necessary to
locate my conceptual point of departure. In the remainder of this introduction I will discuss "ideology," "cultural politics," and "intellectuals," reserving my somewhat lengthier treatment of "socialism" for
chapter 2.

IDEOLOGY, LEGITIMACY, HEGEMONY

I begin with "ideology" because some notion of its meaning will be necessary for discussing the other terms treated below. Any
author who puts the word "ideology" in a book title is asking for
trouble. I do so partly because some of this book's possible readers
would never even pick it up if the title contained the word "discourse,"
which in some ways might serve my purposes better (though not by
definitional simplification). Other terms that one occasionally finds
tangled up with these two include "consciousness," "legitimation," and
"hegemony." How do I understand these terms and what place do they
have in this book?

The easiest to dispose of is "consciousness," for it is largely extra-
neous to my interests in this analysis. Consciousness is, naturally, an element of any social experience involving national values, and the formation of a consciousness that feels itself to be national is a complex and
fascinating problem; but it is not my problem in these chapters, except
indirectly (some form of consciousness being implicated in the actions
of persons I discuss). As stated above, I am also not much concerned
with the extent to which the national ideology being formed and reproduced through elite discourses has entered into the consciousness of
"the masses." This choice is particularly defensible for the present case,
in which most of the action occurred between intellectuals and the
Party bureaucracy, action to which the broader public was fairly
irrelevant.

I am less interested in questions of consciousness than in questions
of representation: how was Romanian identity represented, what images of the nation were proposed and fought over, and how are we to
understand the social space from which these images were generated?
Owing to the sources I employ, these images are largely *discursive*,
offered in politically relevant public discourse. I do not use the term
"discourse" in its strictly Foucauldian sense (as something independent
of the subjects who are its agents), yet I follow Foucault in assuming

that it is not necessarily about "consciousness." Moreover, like him I assume that discourse acquires its own properties and autonomies beyond the utterances that bear it. Specifically, in the situations I discuss, it is obvious that Romanian intellectuals' capacity to act was limited by their participating in discursive fields, in which no one effectively controlled what was said: as people's words entered into a discursive field, they were instantly available for reinterpretation, to be seized and turned against their speakers.

Discourse is, for the cases I examine, the most common form of signifying practice through which ideological processes occurred. I speak, whenever possible, of "ideological processes" rather than "ideology" because the reification seems to me—as so often happens—to violate the phenomenon of interest. Nonetheless, it is impossible, this being English and not some other language, to avoid the reifying noun. By "ideology" I do not intend the generally pejorative sense that has clung to the word since its early days, and in particular I intend neither the "false consciousness" nor the "propaganda" meanings common to fundamentalists of Marxist or sovietological persuasion. Ideological processes are not just a form of blinding, and they are not well exemplified by their official Soviet version (in Fehér's words, "Soviet ideology is not an ideology but a dogma"; see Fehér et al. 1983: 188). Nor do I understand this concept as referring simply to a system of thought, or to ideas or beliefs held. Rather, it means the systemically structured processes and the experienced social relations through which human subjectivities are constituted and through which humans act upon the world. Ideologies—and I employ the plural because there are always more than one, forming ideological and discursive fields—are beliefs or ideas materialized in action, often in political conflict (for which ideology constitutes an arena), and often in discursive form.[7]

To the extent that "ideologies" thus conceived shape consciousness, the emphasis is upon their doing so through *experience and action within* social relations, rather than through *thinking or hearing about* such relations. To ask whether ideology "reflects" social and economic relations is less useful than to see it as a means for enforcing and contesting them. Ideological processes are contests in which alternative conceptions of the world enter into conflict and, through their encounter, acceptance of or resistance to the existing order of domination is furthered. In talking of ideology that is national, I refer to discursive struggles in which the concept of "the nation" or "the Romanian people" has formed a central preoccupation, sometimes intersecting with other sorts of discursive struggles (about development, for example, or socialism, or the state) not treated here. (I do not see national ideology as synonymous with "nationalism," a word that rarely appears in this book since it has, for some East Europeans, a negative connotation I wish to avoid.)

Ideological processes are among the most basic to any mode of domination, for through them are formed what Gramsci calls hegemony: the inscription of consent into various forms of coercion, through which subordinate groups accept their subordination. Hall expresses well the relation between the two notions:

[I]deology provides the "cement" in a social formation, . . . not because the dominant classes can prescribe and proscribe, in detail, the mental content of the lives of subordinate classes (they too, "live" in their own ideologies), but because they strive and to a degree succeed in *framing* all competing definitions of reality *within their range*, bringing all alternatives within their horizon of thought. . . . Gramsci makes it plain that ideological hegemony must be won and sustained through the existing ideologies, and that at any time this will represent a complex *field* (Hall 1979: 333, original emphases).

Hegemony suggests a society-wide regularization of discursive productions and practices that elicit minimal contestation from the subjugated. It is provisional, a matter of degree, and is not present at all times in all societies.

Among those from which it was wholly absent are those of East European socialism.[8] To discuss these cases, I prefer a perhaps idiosyncratic use of the more limited concept of legitimacy.[9] In Weber's formulation, this concept does not mean that all major groups in a society accept the system of domination; it means only the assent of a part of the population, with the remainder *not* adhering to some alternative image of a possible social order.[10] In short, it is the nonorganization of an effective counterimage. Legitimacy is not necessarily the opposite of force, for if a segment of the population sees a regime as having effective force they may fail to organize against it for that reason, which makes it "legitimate." A similar point is made by Corrigan and Sayer (1985: 198): "Integration [of persons into a polity] needs to be understood at least as much in terms of rendering the subordinated speechless—striking them dumb—as in terms of the active securing of assent." From a different angle, legitimacy in this sense may intersect with Bourdieu's notion of "doxa," that which is taken for granted, which goes without saying and is therefore unquestioned (Bourdieu 1977: 166); this is rather different, however, from consent. One should proceed with caution, then, in assuming that consent is necessary to legitimation.

I would argue that like Gramsci's hegemony, legitimacy is always in process and is linked with ideology and ideological struggle. Particularly important in both processes is *debate*, which constructs hegemonies or legitimating ideologies by obscuring the premises upon which the debate occurs. To the extent that debate thereby promotes unspoken agreement—howsoever circumscribed—on certain fundamental premises, then one can speak of this as a "legitimating outcome" or "legitimating moment." The importance of debate in generating such outcomes suggests that ideological fields are preeminently fields of *disagreement* (Ghani 1987), rather than of conscious, consenting belief. The basis for understanding legitimating moments and the larger ideological processes they participate in is thus to look at language as a realm of disagreement that is, simultaneously, a realm of agreement—on premises such as the existence of "the nation," for instance.[11] (My wording should not suggest that discursive fields are always unified. The extent to which people engage in loosely coexisting, overlapping, fragmented fields of discourse as opposed to fairly unitary ones varies from case to case. For the Romanian case, Party control made the discursive field more unified than most.)

If there was an ideology in Ceauşescu's Romania that had potentially hegemonic force, it was national ideology. Virtually all Romanians accepted and still accept the importance of the national idea, with its accompanying unification of the social world (and its implied blurring of internal social divisions). Lefort argues that a peculiar characteristic of what he calls "totalitarian" ideologies is the production of a unified discourse that explicitly asserts the homogeneity of the social domain (Lefort 1986: 284); this would make national ideology a candidate for hegemony in socialist Romania. However, Romanians who agreed that something called "the nation" exists were far from agreed on how to define and protect it. Some argued to me, moreover, that the Party's effort to preempt the discourse on the nation threatened to evacuate national ideology of the element of consent the regime was seeking. For these reasons, then, I see struggles over "the nation" in Romania as part of processes I would call ideological and potentially legitimating, but not hegemonic.[12] Alternatively, one could argue that in this case—and perhaps more generally—legitimation and hegemony are *nothing but* processes of struggle, rather than achieved conditions: in other words, struggle is all there is.[13]

The process of contention did not involve only individuals and groups, however, but also discourses. As I suggest in chapters 3 and 4, the years between 1947 and 1989 were the locus of a battle between two powerful discourses: Marxism, and the discourse on the nation. "The nation" entered into this battle fortified by many decades of work that had given it an institutionalized base (see chapter 1). In its encounter with Marxism, it proved itself capable of subordinating the latter and subverting its terms. Thus, "the nation" as a kind of master symbol can be seen to have *structuring properties*: discourses concerning it had the capacity to interrupt other discourses (see Laclau MS) and redefine them. A discourse about unity and continuity—the nation—overwhelmed one about differentiation and change—Marxism. This outcome shows another aspect of the ideological construction in which Romanian intellectuals were taking part.

THE POLITICS OF CULTURE

In this book, I do not use the word "culture" in the specialist sense typical of most anthropologists, although the way in which I treat my subject is very much part of contemporary anthropological reconsiderations of what "culture" is or means.[14] Instead, I employ the word in something like its lay sense, and particularly its meaning as "high culture"—that is, what artists, writers, musicians, and scholars produce, sometimes for fairly narrow specialist audiences and sometimes for broader publics. I use the expression "politics of culture" to refer to the processes of conflict and maneuvering that go on both internal to communities of this kind of cultural producer and between them and the political sphere "proper," dominated by the Communist party, as it sought to manage and shape the culture being produced.

Research into the politics of culture proceeds, in its most general form, along a path opened by Milan Kundera's celebrated remark in *The Book of Laughter and Forgetting*, "All man's life among men is nothing but a battle for the ears of others." My inquiry into cultural politics in Romania follows the part of this battle that was waged by different groups in the political and intellectual elite, as they strove through discourse to suppress alternative messages and capture "ears," crucial to gaining the resources that would facilitate a broader hearing for their message. (Cultural politics occurred at many other sites besides the elite level, such as the Party's selective encouragement or suppression of various forms of popular culture;[15] these forms do not figure in my discussion, however.) Not all human speech is fraught with contention, not every word uttered is political; but in Romania (and other highly centralized systems), the politicization of culture made contention pervasive. This affected how culture was produced and how its texts should be read. My investigation concentrates on specific instances of politicized cultural production in literary criticism, history, philosophy, and sociology, suggesting how we might read some of their texts.

Cultural politics occurs in societies of all types, as writers and scholars form and reform the canons that define their fields, for example, or create and break reputations (see, e.g., Rodden's [1989] excellent study of the reputation of George Orwell). The subject has been of particular interest, however, to students of socialist systems, for whom the principal form of politics to be analyzed has generally been that between intellectuals and the Party. Much of the extensive corpus on socialist cultural politics comes from emigré artists and scholars, having firsthand experience of the battle between writer and censor or historian and Party.[16] Indeed, emigrés have been the best source of detailed information of this kind, even though their unpleasant personal experiences tend to give their narratives the form of heroes' tales of the beleaguered intellectuals defending Truth and Art from assault by Power (e.g., Hruby 1980; Georgescu 1981; Shlapentokh 1987). Most of these writings give details on the relation between scholarly or other activity in some domain, such as history or literature, and "the Party," often presented as monolithic. Processes examined include the purging or rehabilitation of one or another writer or thinker, the "game" of censorship, politically motivated shifts in subjects of research or themes in fiction, and so on. The best studies differentiate both within the community of producers (e.g., different kinds of historians or sociologists) and within the bureaucracy (e.g., reformist vs. conservative factions), and acknowledge that political processes are more complicated than the simple manipulation of cultural production by Party leaders (cf. Heer 1971: 92–94).

To clarify what distinguishes the present study from others on this topic, I might briefly compare my approach with that of a few exemplary works. Nancy Heer's (1971) book on the politics of Soviet historiography—which, despite its age, is conceptually more sophisticated than many more recent works—admirably refuses a simple dichotomy between Party and scholars and does not see the latter as passive instruments in Party hands. She insists on the complexity both of these interactions and of the politicking within Party circles, which produces contradictory messages for historians and facilitates struggles internal to the profession. She also views historiographic methods as an active force, not simply the malleable tools of a capricious power. Heer is less helpful on what the stakes might be for scholars who debate each other, and she tends to see the "scholars" as the "good guys" in the story without explicating adequately the social or moral grounds upon which such an evaluation should rest: she takes for granted that people defending canons of "truth" or "science" are doing the right thing. In contrast, I do not take this for granted. I seek to show in greater detail than Heer what kind of political claim it is to defend "truth" and what social positions and stakes in struggle such a claim reveals. As already stated, my partisanship of one or another group does not rest on automatic adherence to "science" or "truth" as values.

A similar bias toward "professionalism" and "scholarly values" (unexamined as claims) characterizes Shlapentokh's study of the politics of Soviet sociology. This work is more sophisticated than Heer's in its sociology of the field of contenders—its treatment of disciplinary definitions and of sociology's birth from philosophy, for example, is particularly illuminating (Shlapentokh 1987: 24–29, 74–75). Nevertheless, although Shlapentokh mentions in passing that the development of sociology shows the effects of its socialist environment, he does not explain what it is about command systems that creates a special environment for cultural production. The same conceptual absence appears in another of the best studies, Gabanyi's (1975) detailed examination of relations between writers and Party in Romania. Gabanyi is relatively more neutral toward the claims of the participants than are Heer and Shlapentokh, and like them, she gives a nuanced presentation of a complex field of cultural-political interaction; she too, however, does not make explicit the nature of the socialist milieu or of the competition taking place.

My analysis differs from these in proposing a model of the dynamics of socialist society and of their implications for cultural production. In this respect, it is closest formally to that of Kagarlitsky (1988), who also theorizes the field of intellectual activity, using a model of socialism somewhat different, however, from mine. The conceptualization employed by Shafir (1983b), although less fully articulated and using other terms, resembles mine more closely. The claims I make for the present study, then, are that it places its examples within an explicit model of socialist systems and within an explicit understanding of intellectual activity, as other treatments of cultural politics in socialist settings do not. My hope is that this will facilitate further scholarly analysis that might either refine the conceptualization, which is still rough, or offer a better one.[17]

INTELLECTUALS

Many, though not all, of those engaged in Romania's cultural politics are persons we might loosely call "intellectuals." The operative word here is "loosely"; there are so many definitions of intellectuals and of the related but distinct term "intelligentsia" that any invocation of either can hardly be motivated by a quest for precision.[18] Intellectuals and their social role are a topic of wide interest, as scholars (creating their own genealogies and charters) examine the quest of intellectuals for power or autonomy, their role in promoting revolution, their prospects for transforming socialism, their contributions to state-building, and so on.[19] Most scholars who use the term "intellectuals" comment on the definitional morass in which it is mired (see, e.g., Camp 1985: 33–49).

I would call the bulk of definitions functional, behavioral, or self-ascriptive—that is, they define intellectuals as persons playing a particular role in society, as advisers to or critics of power, shapers of values, legitimators of social order, guardians of morality, self-appointed defenders of their nations. For example: "In every society there are social groups whose special task it is to provide an interpretation of the world for that society" (Mannheim 1955: 10). They are defined as "liv[ing] for rather than off ideas" (Coser 1965: viii) or as filling occupations that produce ideas and knowledge (Brym 1980: 12), or they "create, evaluate, and analyze transcendental symbols, values, ideas, and interpretations" (Camp 1985: 38). For some, they ought to be concerned with "purely disinterested activity of the mind" as "officiants of abstract justice sullied with no passion for a worldly object" (Benda 1969: 44, 51). Self-ascriptive definitions emphasize communities of educated persons united by "a charismatic sense of calling and a certain set of values and manners" (Gella 1989: 132); some such definitions underscore a subjective sense of alienation from and criticism of power as basic to the "calling" of intellectuals. The literature is full of unanswered questions as to whether intellectuals constitute a class, a stratum, or a category; whether they are spokesmen for a class interest, and for which one; and whether in the contemporary era "intellectuals" have been superseded by professionals and technicians.

In my view, Bauman is right to see all such "trait" and "role" definitions as part of an exercise whereby the persons offering them draw a boundary between themselves and everyone else. He observes that all definitions of intellectuals are self-definitions; their most important property is the creation of in- and out-groups, a second social space being implicitly created by the act of characterizing the space proper to intellectuals:

What most definitions refuse to admit is that the separation of the two spaces (and the legislating of a specific relationship between them) is the purpose and *raison d'être* of the definitional exercise . . . . The specifically intellectual form of the operation—self-definition—masks its universal content, which is the reproduction and reinforcement of a given social configuration, and—within it—a given (or claimed) status for the group (Bauman 1987*b*: 8–9).

For Bauman, the point of "trait" definitions and of their accompanying anxiety about who is and who is not an intellectual is to legitimate separate status for knowledge as a societal value, enthroning this central element of intellectual praxis at the heart of social superiority (p. 18). With this, he joins social theorists such as Foucault, Bourdieu, and Elias in identifying intellectuals by the kinds of claims and resources they employ in social struggles—claims to a monopoly on knowledge, competence, and truth (Foucault 1980: 128), or possession of a specific form of "capital" (symbolic, or cultural) upon which their social position rests (Bourdieu 1988: 285, n. 1). To invoke "culture," "science," "truth," and related values, then, is a form of boundary-maintenance by which a certain segment of the privileged classes sets itself off from those around it—including (perhaps especially) others in the elite (cf. Elias 1978: 1–50). All these theorists understand such knowledge claims, or the legitimation of social position through values of "culture," as bearing a relation to power and reproducing the system of domination, but they leave the nature of that relationship an open question, to be answered differently for each case.[20]

The present book adopts a version of this perspective on intellectuals. I do not seek a precise definition of who is in or out but include anyone whose social practice invokes claims to knowledge or to the creation and maintenance of cultural values and whose claim is at least partly acknowledged by others.[21] That is, to "be" an intellectual means to make knowledge/value claims, to gain some degree of social recognition for them, and to participate in social relations on the basis of this exchange of claims and recognition. If possible, I would altogether avoid the term "intellectuals" (which, when it does not individualize, inaptly suggests a bounded collectivity), speaking instead of a structural or relational space. Bauman offers something of this sort:

[W]e will confine our search to the task of locating the category of the intellectual within the structure of the larger society as a "spot," a "territory" within such a structure; a territory inhabited by a shifting population, and open to invasions, conquests and legal claims as all ordinary territories are. We will treat the category of the intellectual as a structural element within the societal figuration, an element defined not by its intrinsic qualities, but by the place it occupies within the system of dependencies which such a figuration represents . . . (Bauman 1987b: 19).

Following Bauman's lead, I treat "intellectuals" as sometime occupants of a site that is privileged in forming and transmitting discourses, in constituting thereby the means through which society is "thought" by its members, and in forming human subjectivities. The site they occupy is therefore part of the space of ideology and legitimation, distinguished from other sites within that space by its coordinates: recognized specialist claims to knowledge or symbolic capital, as opposed, for instance, to occupancy of formal political positions. (Occupants of political positions may themselves invade the intellectual "site" with knowledge claims of their own.) This "space of legitimation" does not always serve the existing system of power but may be a locus for forming alternative consciousnesses or images of social reality. One cannot assume, however, that all seemingly oppositional activity will have this consequence, for argument and debate often congeal the legitimating premises of rule even when their participants intend otherwise (see chapter 6).

To clarify what sorts of activity take place in this "space of legitimation" I make use of the writings of Pierre Bourdieu (e.g., 1977, 1984, 1985, 1988), although I do not import his conceptual apparatus wholesale, with all its talk of cultural "capital," symbolic "markets," "investments," and "profits." For Bourdieu, the domain of culture contains processes absolutely vital to political order. Political struggles are quintessentially about "the very representation of the social world . . . [which] can be uttered and constructed in different ways" (Bourdieu 1985: 723, 726):

Knowledge of the social world and, more precisely, the categories that make it possible, are the stakes, par excellence, of political struggle, the inextricably theoretical and practical struggle for the power to conserve or transform the social world by conserving or transforming the categories through which it is perceived (ibid., 729).

The social reality that human beings perceive and experience, including its relations of power, are constructed through social practice. Although *all* social actors engage in this practice and thereby make social meanings constantly, a central element of orders of domination is that some

persons enjoy privileged access to the means for constructing and disseminating a particular view of reality. Their privileged placement rests
on what Bourdieu calls "symbolic (or cultural) capital": those who possess more of it are more likely to have their version of reality recognized
and accepted. To give a specific example, a scientist who gains a professional reputation accumulates symbolic capital in the form of scientific
authority, and the weight of that authority makes it more likely that in a
scientific dispute, his version of what is happening will prevail over the
version of someone lacking such authority.[22] Similarly, writers, artists,
scholars, and so forth, accumulate symbolic capital enabling them to
produce and impose cultural meanings, which may generalize more
widely to become part of the legitimate vision of the social world (ibid.,
730–731).

Any mobilization of symbolic capital in such disputes is relative,
however, to recognition of it: that is, one's version of reality will not be
accepted by people who have not learned the distinctions upon which
one's claim to status, or one's authority, rests. This means that any claim
to competence, to scientific authority, to stature in the cultural world
requires a corresponding recognition somewhere else in society—first
by other "intellectuals" accepting or contesting one's claims, but beyond this by holders of power, who thereby authorize the view presented, or by others in the broader public. Bourdieu's research on these
questions in France assumes that stable, class-differentiated publics already exist, socialized into certain patterns of recognition of the entitlements of others. This assumption is clearly wrong for East European
socialist societies, in which a situation of stably socialized groups ori-
enting to a more or less secure set of values was precisely what the political authorities had hoped to achieve but did not. Thus, I argue,
much of the cultural politicking in socialist Eastern Europe involved defending prior definitions of cultural value (and grounds for authority)
that had not yet been wholly eroded and working to form what I call
"cognizant publics," who would recognize and support the values being
defended. (This notion will be further explicated in chapter 4.) Processes of this sort are absent from Bourdieu's account of the activity of
those holding "symbolic capital"—one of several ways in which his
ideas about culture and its production must be respecified for socialist
societies (see chapter 2).

Seen in this light, then, intellectuals engage in contests over different
definitions of cultural value, competence, and authority; they strive to
impose their definitions of value and to gain recognition for their version of social reality. To see cultural politics in this way is to emphasize

the inextricable connections between social definitions of what is valuable—authenticity, first-rate scholarship, artistic excellence, what have you—and the politics through which these judgments, evaluations, and discriminations are produced. It is also to emphasize not questions of meaning but questions of action: how culture is an instrument for social action becomes a more important issue than what a particular cultural text or performance means.

This set of assumptions will be offensive to those who see in them a reduction of fine sensibilities and noble motives (the quest for truth, the creation of the beautiful) to some base quest for power.[23] It is important to answer this objection. The point of view expressed above does not assume that *underlying* people's attachment to values, their aesthetic preferences, their standards of scholarly work, and so on is a quest for power. It assumes that people "become intellectuals" for any of a variety of reasons, that they may form a genuine attachment to certain values, preferences, and standards as against other ones, and that because values, preferences, and standards are multiple, under certain circumstances one's own will be forced into competition with other standards. Although the participants perhaps do not *experience* their activity as one of "struggle" or "competition," this is no proof that their activities are not bringing alternative values into competitive relation. The investigator's task is to specify the circumstances under which this competition will occur and the forms it might take. It is wholly true that sincere attachments may motivate defense of one or another standard of taste or evaluation. Nevertheless, analysis should not stop there: it must also recognize that knowledge and cultural values play a central part in maintaining and transforming social orders, and that defense of one or another value participates in this. As a result, culture and intellectual activity are *inherently* political (not *underlain* by politics, but *interwoven* with it), at two different levels: that of their encounter with alternative values within their own sphere, and that of their place in reproducing society.[24]

Methods[25]

Finally, a word about the methods I employ. Although this book focuses on the analysis of texts, it does so through an anthropological method that supplements a reading of texts with fieldwork. "Supplements" is perhaps the wrong term, for what an ethnographic approach to textual analysis entails is a thorough-going revision of the idea of reading. Fieldwork places the texts themselves within the context of sets of social relations. It substitutes for the relation "text: reader [analyst]" a whole nexus of relations among producers of texts—who are also readers for one another—and the institutions they inhabit; all of these also bear a relation to the world of the "reader [analyst]," as I show clearly in these pages. Instead of having the unit of analysis be texts, then, it becomes the field of social relations within which texts are generated, consumed, and commented upon in still other texts. The possibility of ethnographically exploring these fields of social relations changes the reading one might otherwise give the texts produced within them. As a method, the ethnography of textual production requires reformulating what it means to "give a reading." At the same time, it enables us to see more clearly, as in the case at hand, the ways in which textualized discourses both constitute and alter the nature of power and its exercise.

Science, says Claude Lévi-Strauss, does not consist of simplifying the complex but of making complexity more intelligible without sacrificing its complexity (1966: 248). Although I would not want to claim "scientific" status for the method I employ in this analysis, I believe it has the effect Lévi-Strauss sees as desirable. Neither political science nor literary analysis, with their customary methods, reveals the complexities that surface when an investigator can interrogate not only written works but those who wrote them. These complexities make more intelligible and more interesting a world that western scholars have mostly managed to render grey and unpleasant: the "communist" world. They also animate lifeless texts. Even if (as in my case) the possibilities for interrogation are constrained—very few people on the "indigenist" side of cultural arguments would make themselves available for interviewing, a limitation that should be kept in mind—they nonetheless permit us to link the realm of the "symbolic" with the activities within which symbols have their social life. To separate these spheres (symbols, and action within fields of social relations) simplifies and distorts complicated processes to which a different method does more justice.

Organization of the Book

An empirical investigation based in the above assumptions about knowledge, cultural values, and the intellectual "space" could, in principle, center on any subject in which knowledge or creativity is at issue—scientific research (Latour and Woolgar 1979), the professions (Abbott 1988), or history-writing (Novick 1988), among others. The present study focuses on intellectual politics around the idea of Romanian identity. This focus is not idly chosen: decades of intellectual activity in Romania have centered on the idea of the nation—defining its nature, winning allies for it, gaining its independence, protecting its interests. All of these were pursued through the creation of philosophies, histories, literatures, musics, ethnographies, even biologies and geographies suitable for an authentic and valuable Romanian being-in-the-world. For centuries, much of Romanian politics has been conducted precisely through representing Romanian identity. Representations of Romanianness were simultaneously products of cultural striving and means of politics, elements of a relation to the peoples both within and beyond Romania's borders. To be a producer of culture, in Romania, to be an intellectual, has long meant having a central role in defining the Romanian nation to itself and to the world.

Subsequent chapters show some of the ways in which this occurred in recent times. The first three chapters give the historical, theoretical, and political context for the arguments discussed in chapters 4 to 7. I begin with an overview of the politics of identity prior to World War II, an overview necessary to understanding the meanings and claims evident in struggles of the 1970s and 1980s. In addition to this, chapter 1 shows that specifically in the realm of scholarship and letters, arguments about national identity were instrumental in forming an institutional infrastructure built on "the nation." This fact had important consequences for both intellectual life and the national discourse once the Communist party came to power. Chapter 2 provides a theoretical discussion of the nature of socialist systems and the place of intellectual activity in them. This discussion might have fallen in the Introduction, but its length and its stronger relation to the material in chapters 3 through 7 suggested separating it from the conceptual issues I have raised here. In chapter 3 I describe how the Party initially sought to suppress the entire subject of "the nation," which nonetheless insistently reasserted itself in hidden arenas and at length reappeared within public discourse.

Following these three chapters are four others on cultural politics in Romania under Ceaușescu. Each of them focuses on a different domain of cultural life and suggests different aspects of the reproduction of national ideology. Chapter 4 provides a sort of dynamic glossary for some of the terms employed in arguments within cultural politics, and it describes a few techniques through which Romanian intellectuals sought to build up their own cultural authority and undermine that of others. Unlike chapters 5 to 7, this one does not revolve around a central debate and does not explain the organization of the contests whose means of struggle it describes; the full significance of its examples will be clear only after subsequent chapters, the exposition of which it is intended to smooth. The more important burden of chapter 4 is to raise the question of how Marxism was related to the national discourse. It asks, how was a discourse that nearly all Romanians perceived as alien brought into relation with the native discourse on nationality, so highly developed prior to the installation of a Marxist-Leninist regime? I describe how the unification of these two discourses and the subordination of one to the other proceeded through conflicts in which opponents strove to excommunicate each other and deny one another access to political favor.

In chapter 5, I show these factional struggles for recognition and for access to bureaucratic resources in greater detail, as they appeared through an innovation in the sphere of literary criticism. Persons differently situated in the community of literary criticism tried to outdo each other in claiming that their version of Romanian identity was more representative of the values on which the nation's cultural life should be founded. Literature proved a complicated domain for the Party to control, for it sits atop an immense reserve of prior symbolic accumulations, arguably the largest of any area of culture; the destruction and reappropriation of those values was a complex process into which I hope to provide some insight.

Chapter 6 shows an intellectual debate in historiography, a field even closer to the heart of the Party leadership than literature. Owing to its ideological centrality, it was somewhat more subject to direct political control and at the same time less influenced than literature was by market forces. These differences made competition among individuals, which I emphasize in chapter 5, somewhat less important than competition between institutions. Although the discussion centers on a debate between two persons, it uses this to explore relations between institutional sites for producing history and between history-producers and Party control. I argue that the debate strengthened national ideology, even though some participants believed they were opposing the center, but I also suggest ways in which opposition among historians served to diminish central control.

Chapter 7 looks at a development within a corner of philosophy, a discipline once central to the Party's legitimation but subsequently less so. Whereas literature had a wide audience, and history—depending on how it was written—an only slightly narrower one, the audience for philosophy was potentially the narrowest of all, and its prior accumulations were smaller than those of the other two domains. In this quiet sphere, however, I find the highest potential for an alternative vision of reality, one that raised a challenge to the Party leadership and gained the adherence of some in the more powerful literary community. The chapter attempts to show how this opposition constituted itself discursively and sought to bring its message to a wider public.

In all the domains considered, much more was going on than disputes in which national identity and its definitions were implicated. Yet in my opinion, by placing the matter of identity at the center and seeking to understand the arguments that developed around and through it, I believe we have an especially fruitful vantage point for understanding the relation of culture to power in socialist Romania: through the ideological constitution of identity and its use in intellectual contests.

PART I:

Frameworks

CHAPTER ONE

Antecedents: National Ideology and Cultural Politics in Presocialist Romania

There is no first or last discourse, and dialogical context knows no limits . . . . Even past meanings, that is those that have arisen in the dialogue of past centuries, can never be stable (completed once and for all, finished), they will always change (renewing themselves) in the course of the dialogue's subsequent development, and yet to come. At every moment of the dialogue, there are immense and unlimited masses of forgotten meanings, but, in some subsequent moments, as the dialogue moves forward, they will return to memory and live in renewed form (in a new context). Nothing is absolutely dead: every meaning will celebrate its rebirth.

—Mikhail Bakhtin

National identity as an element in Romanian cultural politics, the subject of this book, did not come into being with socialism but has a long history, stretching back to at least the mid-1700s. In the present chapter[1] I outline that history, whose themes and personages are essential to understanding Romanian cultural politics in the 1970s and 1980s. Because the most important context of the present is the series of debates on Romanian identity during the period between

27

the two World Wars, I concentrate on that period, with briefer treatment of what preceded it.[2]

I insist at such length on this history because I believe my theme cannot be addressed properly without it—and in this I depart from other studies of intellectual life under socialism. The national ideology so often evident in cultural politics was historically produced; its history informs its present. The symbols that provoked heated argument in the 1980s—symbols that include writers and thinkers of earlier times— draw upon multiple significances established by the use or the actions of such symbols in the past. One can best see how these multiple meanings have sedimented by examining debates in which different sides to an argument attribute contrasting values to an idea or a person's work. Interwar Romanian philosopher Lucian Blaga, for example, was the object of attack and defense even as his books appeared (e.g., Băncilă 1937; Stăniloae 1942; Stahl 1937, 1938), and he continued to be throughout the 1980s, within terms partly indebted to the interwar years in which he wrote (see Mihu 1988a; Bugnariu n.d.; and chapter 4). The ongoing relevance of interwar figures like Blaga is evident in the space given over to them in 1980s publications and seminars, in the number of works from the interwar period republished in the 1970s and 1980s, and in anthologies of the debates on identity that span the divide between socialist and presocialist times (e.g., Bucur et al. 1984; Marcea 1975; F. Mihăilescu 1981).

Many of the arguments concerning national identity were specialist matters in literature and the humanities: what sort of novel is the best, should aesthetic criteria be independent of social concerns or embrace them, how can Romanian cultural products enter international cultural circuits, what is the status of folk culture and how should it be preserved, and so forth. They had implications, however—which indeed often motivated them—for economy and politics. (What began as a literary movement, for instance, became the Peasant party; see Roberts 1951: 89.) Nowhere is this more visible than in arguments about the so-called "national essence" of Romanians as a people.[3] These arguments arose with the nineteenth-century Romantics and continued, with modifications, into the interwar period, resurfacing once again as of the 1960s. By incessantly probing the question of Romanians' true nature, contributors to the pool of writings that made up these debates produced and reproduced a major element in the national ideology.

The people who argued about national identity did so in a multidisciplinary field of discourse that overlapped with talk on other themes:

on the nature of the state, the parlous situation of politics, the role of religion in the life of the people, the class composition of Romania, the history of its economic backwardness, and, above all, the proper course of development Romania should follow—a path toward industrialization and parliamentary democracy, or something else. These arguments were not well insulated from one another. As an anthology of the 1980s put it, "The struggles among literary ideas are also struggles with social and political implications" (Bucur et al. 1984: 4).[4] For example, one writer who opened the question of Romania's class structure found himself accused of destroying the Nation * (a charge he had invited by claiming that the upper class had "sold out" the masses and abandoned their national interests; see Tăslăuanu 1908a and b; Popovici 1908a and b). Similar formulations surfaced in discussing the nature of the Romanian state. Proposals for and against reform of the countryside were tied up with definitions of the peasantry as the repository of the national spirit. Religion, too, overflowed into debates on the national essence, as certain participants held that Eastern Orthodoxy was basic to the soul and essence of the Romanian people. And writers defended or decried political programs for development according to whether they encouraged or violated the fundamental character of Romanians. Partisans of a peasant-based, ahistorical national essence objected strenuously, for instance, to proposals for industrializing Romania.

The overlap among these domains shows the political significance of debates on national identity and justifies examining such debates, even if I cannot cover fully their political and economic context. Not only did positions in the debates entail prescriptions for politics, not only did they establish a language of political argument, but the entire field of discourse, with its overlapping domains of "state," "development," "religion," and so forth, continually created and recreated the Nation in relationship to those other elements. These were not, then, "merely" intellectual arguments: they formed the rhetoric and laid down the premises of political discourse. They reproduced a hegemonic ideology in which the Nation occupied a central place.

The present chapter presumes something that does not yet exist: a sociohistorical analysis of the formation of Romania's national ideology. My broader goals in this book limit me to offering here only a fragment of such a history, fitted to my investigation of the politics of identity in Ceauşescu's Romania. I rarely seek to explain why particular

---

*The upper-case N (Nation) is explained in note 3.

kinds of persons took particular stances toward defining Romanian identity, even though I am convinced that alternative images of Romanianness are systematically linked to political choices and social positions, rather than reflecting confusion about identity. I begin with a brief history of the central images defining Romanian identity in the seventeenth through nineteenth centuries, move on to some of the debates of the twentieth century, and conclude by suggesting how, through these arguments, social actors affected the balance of social forces and transformed institutional structures.

Seventeenth through Nineteenth Centuries[5]

The context of early efforts by Romanians to define their national identity was the fierce competition for empire-building among the Habsburgs, Romanovs, and Ottomans (see McNeill 1964). Each empire bordered one of the three regions—Transylvania and the Principalities of Moldavia and Wallachia—that were eventually joined to form contemporary Romania. Their competition drove them collectively to centralize and consolidate their rule (a project that in the Habsburg case entailed attempting religious homogenization) in hopes of prevailing over the other two empires in the southeast European buffer zone. The impetus to centralize culminated in one or another eighteenth-century "enlightened absolutism." In all three Romanian lands, agents of an external imperial power worked to centralize imperial rule, thus undermining provincial nobilities. The result differed in the Ottoman and the Habsburg dependencies: in the former, a Romanian nobility lost power to agents of the Ottoman sultan (known as "Phanariots"), whereas in multiethnic Transylvania, Habsburg centralization undermined a nobility that was Hungarian, thereby favoring the rise of a new elite among the Romanians (see Verdery 1983: 113–123).

In the fate of the Romanian lands one could see the progress of interimperial rivalries as the Ottomans lost Transylvania to the Habsburgs and the Principalities entered a Russian orbit (though formally under Turkish rule until 1877/1878). Yet many changes of fortune interrupted this secular trend. Despite substantial differences in their environments, Romanian elites in the three regions were challenged in similar ways and responded similarly also: they appealed to or allied themselves with stronger external powers against their tyrannical overlords. This often involved siding with one of the three contending empires against another, a strategy pursued by each region's elite as a whole or, sometimes, by one fraction of it against another. Representations of Romanianness came to play an important part in these alliances.

HOW ROMANIAN IDENTITY WAS REPRESENTED: THE QUESTION OF ORIGINS

From the outset, Romanian elites couched their appeals for assistance in terms of an image of themselves that was rooted in the past.[6] This established at the very beginning that Romanian identity was to be linked with history as a field of knowledge and with historical truth as a site of representations for pursuing the truth about the Nation (cf. Foucault 1977: 143), understood as a question of *origins*. A highly speculative question, this matter has been disputed and revised continually for centuries, with opinions falling into three main camps. One, the "Latinist" camp, argues that Romanians are the lineal descendants of the legions of Roman Emperor Trajan and of colonists he brought from Rome, after he conquered the area (105–106 A.D.) and incorporated it into his empire as the province of Dacia. A second, the "Dacianist" camp, holds in its most extreme version that Romanians are descendants of the original inhabitants (known as the Dacians), who adopted the Latin language and some elements of Roman civilization but otherwise transmitted their own customs and bloodline down into the present. The third, "Daco-Roman," view—the one most widely held in the twentieth century—regards Romanians as the descendants of intermingled Roman colonists and survivors of the Dacian indigenes. Some "dacianizing" variants of this view place greater weight on Dacian ancestry without, however, denying the Roman element. The three views are situated, as is clear, between pro-westernism and indigenism, with no one offering a purely eastern ancestry.[7]

The question of origins produced the first and perhaps most durable representation of Romanian identity that had openly political intentions: early Latinism. Its authors, and the forerunners of what emerged during the eighteenth century as the discourse on Romanian national identity, were a handful of seventeenth-century writers known as the Chroniclers (*cronicarii*), attached to one or another noble faction in the courts of the Moldavian and Wallachian princes (Oțetea et al. 1964: 282–284, 540–541). It was the Chroniclers from Moldavia,[8] writing in a province more and more heavily burdened by tribute to the Ottomans, who provided the first Latinist argument. Seeking to make their people known to Europeans "misled by calumnies from abroad,"[9] as they claimed, these early historians urged Europeans to show proper reverence for their own Roman ancestors by coming to the rescue of Trajan's Romanian heirs. The argument for Roman or predominantly Roman origins meant for them not just an image of Romanians as bold, courageous, cultured, free, and so forth: it meant a claim upon the attention and interest of "Europe," to help liberate the sons of Rome from Turkish or Hungarian or Austrian oppression. These same associations were to motivate the Latinism of later writers, including the would-be founders of a Romanian state in the 1840s and 1850s.

The writings of the Chroniclers influenced a much more extensive quest into the matter of origins, a quest that again had political aims and produced a major representation of Romanian identity. This was the effort of Transylvanian clerics[10] (the "Transylvanian School") to secure political gains for Transylvania's Romanians, who lacked basic rights within an aristocratic order dominated by Hungarians and Germans (see Verdery 1983: 79–125). Their argument was that Romanians too were of noble status by virtue of their descent from Rome. By claiming nobility (and the glory of conquest) in an empire itself descended from the Holy Roman Empire, these clerics hoped to win the same rights enjoyed by other nobles.[11]

Their Latinist argument gained overwhelming but not universal acceptance among Romanians. One voice that resisted it was part of a larger resistance by the Romanian Orthodox population against the Habsburg efforts to unify the empire by catholicizing Transylvania, via the Greek-Catholic or Uniate Church (created 1699) to which the "Transylvanian School" belonged. For every effort by Transylvania's Uniate priests to gain Habsburg support and assistance, Orthodox Romanians were likely to solicit support from the Czar, the Serbian Orthodox hierarchy, or the Orthodox in the Principalities (Blaga 1966: 55). In the early 1760s, one of several anti-Uniate uprisings of Orthodox peasants reportedly culminated in a letter to Hungarian authorities, its signers averring that Romanians are older than Hungarians in the region "for we are the descendants of the old Dacians" (Prodan 1971: 212). Those struggling to oppose the incursions of the "Roman" faith did not, it seems, find a Roman origin wholly convenient. (It later became useful, however, once aggression began from an expansionist Orthodox Russia, to emphasize the Roman rather than Byzantine sources of Romanian Christianity so as to underscore differences from the East; see Zub 1981: 95.)

This example shows how groups within the emerging Romanian national movement selected different emphases in defining Romanian identity: those who wished to use the institutions held out by the Habsburg centralizers touted a Roman (therefore western) Romanian, whereas those more firmly rooted in the institutions of the Orthodox faith discovered a Romanian of mixed or even indigenous character. The split neatly represents the competition for Romanian territory on the part of western (Austrian) and eastern (Russian) empires, both of which might be invited to resolve disputes among Transylvania's inhabitants.

Similar defection from the Latinist position on origins came from some elites in the two Principalities. Their chief concern was not to gain equal rights with other groups but to achieve independent rule, which would return to them the privileged access to high office that they had lost with Ottoman absolutism. Toward this end, they too found, nevertheless, that the proper origins could help justify their right to independence. Some leaders argued for this right as descendants of the Roman masters of the world, and especially in the 1800s, the common Latin origin of all Romanians was seen as an important weapon in the fight for political unification (Georgescu 1971: 171). But a few others preferred to emphasize the Dacian ancestry, a preference Georgescu links to the *alienness* of the Romans, foreigners who had come from abroad to subjugate the indigenes and who should be given no quarter. Dacian ancestry had the further advantage of pushing a "Romanian" presence back another millennium in time and of implying a larger territory than the Roman Dacia of Trajan (ibid., 165, 172).[12] Although it would be misleading to present Dacian imagery as a major alternative to Latinism at this point in Romanian history, it is important to register the appearance of a counterimage to Latinism, for subsequent political argument would invoke now one, now the other of the two possible ancestors.

The difference between the views of these Romanian elites, one view associated with pro-western groups, the other with "indigenist" ones, loosely represents at this point a regional division between the (European) Habsburg dependency and the (Oriental) Turkish one, with their divergent political exigencies: seeking a place within the existing system of rule versus explicitly rejecting foreign rule so as to reestablish native control over the machinery of state. But even within this latter situation, by the mid-1800s factions within the elite regularly couched their political strategies in terms of divergent references to Significant Others—westerners, indigenes, or easterners[13]—neatly captured by historical arguments about origin. This established the pattern wherein talk about national identity was the idiom for intra-elite struggles over access to power (with accusations of "foreignness" serving as the ultimate disqualification for rule), indicating alliances with groups outside. And through the medium of such talk, these struggles—despite the differing environments in which they occurred—made the Nation a reality. The next step was to create a state within which this Nation would live.

STATE FORMATION AND WESTERNISM

In the nineteenth century, the fates of Transylvania and the two Principalities diverged sharply. The Principalities, on the one hand, achieved independent statehood as the Romanian Kingdom (1881), having first united into a single political entity (1859) within the Ottoman empire. The groups internally responsible for these outcomes were the large and smaller nobility and the developing "bourgeoisie" (with their loosely associated intelligentsia), who had recovered the exercise of local rule from the Sultan's Phanariots in 1821. After this date, few non-Romanians occupied positions of political importance in the Principalities; only in the limited commercial and trading sectors did one find a significant number of Jews and other "aliens." This contrasted with the situation in Transylvania, where the Romanian elite of businessmen and intellectuals (chiefly lawyers, teachers, and clergy) remained politically subject to local rule by Hungarians and Habsburgs. While elites in the Principalities were beginning to run their own affairs, Transylvanian Romanians continued to plead vainly for political rights within a Habsburg and, after the Austro-Hungarian compromise of 1867, a Hungarian Transylvania. This political struggle consumed their energies and bore little fruit until 1918.

Acquiring their own state was a major boon to elites in the Principalities, for without it many would have had no livelihood. During the mid-1800s, high western demand had made East European grain farming uncommonly prosperous. Prices of Romanian cereals had shot upward during these years, bringing hefty incomes to owners of large estates. Sons had been sent abroad to school (there being no advanced education in their homeland), whence they had returned to translate the demands of western bourgeoisies for freedom, equal representation, and so forth, into a language suited to their own lands: calls for eliminating distinctions within the elite, for uniting to form a national state, and for freeing it from control by foreigners. Scarcely had the foundations of the new state been laid than the grain market collapsed, bringing ruin to some and hard times to many, who sought shelter in the state bureaucracy. This produced intense competition for revenue-bearing political office and for expanding the bureaucratic opportunities that promised more than did the market.[14] The winning of independence in 1877/1878 coincided, then, with the ascendancy of a Romanian state apparatus over market-based economic change;[15] henceforth, in Romania as elsewhere in Eastern Europe, the state (and its occupants) would exercise a strong hand in directing economic growth,[16] and arguments about the direction of such growth would become integral to political discourse.

The process whereby Romanians created a state and achieved independence involved even more resolute manipulation of allies in "Europe" than before and even more determined representations of Romanians' western nature. History-writing continued to bear the burden of this, the writers of history having learned firsthand from such French thinkers as Michelet and Quinet how a nation's identity should look and how its history should be written (see Cristian 1985; Durandin 1989: 89–153).[17] That a foreign audience was intended for many of their historical arguments is obvious, since several major works were first published in French or German. But representations of Romanianness went beyond history-writing into everyday political discourse, as in the following statement from politician and historian Kogălniceanu, an architect of the Romanian state and a manipulator of Romania's western identity:

Europe gives its sympathies and support only to countries that aspire to align their institutions with those of the civilized world. . . . [T]o show Europe our desire to europeanize our country will be to attract the sympathies and support of the Great Powers and of foreign public opinion (Kogălniceanu 1940: 287).[18]

The culmination of pro-western statements came in 1859, when the Latin alphabet officially replaced cyrillic characters for writing the Romanian language and a massive campaign was begun to "restore" lapsed Latinisms into Romanian.

Emulation of European social, political, and cultural forms produced a backlash, however, as some Romanians derided the aping of foreign manners and criticized resort to foreign solutions. As had occurred in Ottoman times, political argumentation often invoked patriotism versus foreignness, with critics of the "modernizers" accusing them of betraying Romania's uniqueness, whereas the pro-western faction defended itself as serving the country's best interests. They were as quick to label the Conservative landowners russophile as the latter were to label them francophile. With this, we see continued the earlier practice by which groups form alliances across the country's borders and accuse each other of destroying the Nation through such alliances.

ROMANTICISM, DACIANISM, AND THE "NATIONAL ESSENCE" [19]

Although Latinizers had played the preeminent role in the Romanian upheavals of 1848 and in founding the Romanian state, alternative representations increased in frequency and in force thereafter. The Dacians in the Romanian past were to acquire ever more numerous enthusiasts as the century progressed, culminating in the work of B. P. Hasdeu, the "father" of scientific folklore in Romania. By the turn of the century, Hasdeu's influence brought general acceptance of the Daco-Roman position on origins, widely held ever since, although to rectify earlier overemphasis on the Romans, Hasdeu himself promoted greater attention to the Dacians within the mix. It is to this new emphasis on Dacians (i.e., *not* exclusive of Romans) that I refer in the following paragraphs.

Babu-Buznea observes (1979: 8) that because militant Dacianism was more obviously useful inside the Romanian polity than for audiences abroad, the theory made greater headway once the creation of a Romanian state had diminished the need to gain European support for independence. Nonetheless, the Dacians had political meanings that were useful on the international stage as well as the internal one. To begin with, incorporating them into the lineage meant bringing in a people who represented a spirited opposition to imperial expansion, a fight-to-the-death for liberty against external conquest (the Dacian ruler, Decebal, being believed to have drunk poison rather than fall into Trajan's hands alive). Unlike Latinism, Dacianism meant *independence* in politics, for pre-Roman Dacia had been powerful within its region

and had even exacted tribute for a time from Rome. Rebuking the Latinist allegiances that would permit Romania to be engulfed by French
interests, one commentator observed that since the Dacians were not
Russians or Austrians, Russia and Austria would have no claim to them
(ibid., 77).[20] For a public long exercised by the rigors of foreign domination, this was heady stuff.

To emphasize Dacia also strengthened Romanian claims to continuity on the territory they inhabited, as against some Austrian and Hungarian theories of the Romanian past, for it was thought that half-
Dacian Romanians would be less likely to abandon their homeland during the withdrawal of Roman legions in 271. This enabled a "scientific"
counterargument to Hungarians, who claimed that the territory of
Transylvania had been empty of inhabitants when the Hungarian
nomads entered it in 896 and that Transylvania therefore belonged to
Hungary. A Dacian background meant deeper roots (Zub 1981: 159),
more ancient rights in the region, than did a purely Latin origin. Moreover, it constituted a powerful argument in favor of uniting the three
Romanian lands within a new state that would resurrect the old Dacian
polity within its proper borders, a goal for which even some incorri-
gible Transylvanian Latinists found Dacia a convenient symbol (ibid.,
150). Coupled with Romantic theories that a people's inner nature is
determined by the soil on which it is formed, the Dacian emphasis char-
tered a "manifest destiny" for restoring to Romanians all the soil of
Daco-Roman cohabitation. One scholar ensured foreign recognition of
this point by publishing, in French, his *Topographie de la Roumanie*—on
the eve of the Paris Conference that would decide the political fate of
the Principalities—writing explicitly of the Dacian Empire's territorial
extent and of its people as "free men, or barbarians, as the Romans
called them." (In thus appealing to the western descendants of Rome,
however, he was careful to emphasize that Romanians had Roman forebears as well [ibid., 72–74.)

Beyond representing political objectives and thereby mobilizing political action, the Dacian emphasis had meaning for Romania's economic and political development. This came not only from Romantic
exaltation of the "primitive" but also from Voltaire's idea, reiterated by
Herder, that a people can progress only if they develop in organic continuity with their own nature rather than through forms borrowed or imposed from elsewhere. With this, Dacianists joined forces with the opponents of "gallomania" and of foreign imitation, to which many

Liberal reformers were prone. The combination of Dacianism and Romanticism produced a linked series of antinomies (however questionable their equivalence):

$$\frac{\text{Dacian}}{\text{Roman}} = \frac{\text{primitive}}{\text{civilized}} = \frac{\text{native}}{\text{foreign}} = \frac{\text{natural}}{\text{artificial}} = \frac{\text{organic}}{\text{forced}} = \frac{\text{durable}}{\text{perishable}}$$

(Babu-Buznea 1979: 51). This series associated Dacian ancestry with the virtues of an autochthonous tradition, in contrast to the predatory (if civilized) foreigners, and ended with the conclusion "imitation is unpatriotic"; Dacians would endure, as autochthones, whereas foreign influence meant death. From the typical Romantic eulogizing of the natural, spontaneous, and uncultivated against the corrupting effects of civilization, then, the Dacians became the primary symbols of reaction against all that was perceived as wrong with the present social order (ibid., 57–62, 153). Once again, historically based symbols represented political statements simultaneously about identity, international allegiance, and internal political choices.

Through its emphases, Dacianism stood at the heart of what became a quest to define the "national essence," integral to defining Romania's trajectory. By associating itself with what was unique and original in the Romanian character, rather than with "imports," Dacianism became central to a posited pristine ethnic ego, upon which Romanians' capacity for survival depended and which must be nourished and protected from external corruption. Such ideas had consequences not only for politics but also for literature, since Romanticism held that the most important quality of cultural and especially of literary works is *originality*, which is linked with the national essence (ibid., 50). The traits unique to the Nation will produce a literature rich in the precious quality of originality. Therefore, just as folk literature uncontaminated by foreign sources was viewed as the treasury of the national spirit, Dacian themes—held to represent the natural ethnic traditions harboring Romanian individuality—became major constituents of literary production.

The several elements of this political and aesthetic concatenation were well expressed by Romania's most famous poet, Eminescu, a user of Dacian themes, when he lamented the state of his people in 1881:

[T]errible ignorance and corruption above, black ignorance and deep misery below. And this is the Romanian people? Our people of 50–60 years ago, with its healthy barbarity, rare and god-given quickness of mind, great vigor of spirit; truthful, cheerful, industrious, ironical? . . . And whence all this change? . . . Superimposed upon our people sits a foreign layer without traditions, without a fixed homeland, without fixed nationality, which did away with what is a people's most precious possession, its historical sense, its sense of ongoing and organic development. . . . The true civilization of a people consists not in the wholesale adoption of laws, forms, institutions, etiquette, foreign clothes. It consists in *the natural, organic development* of its own powers and faculties. If there is ever to exist a true civilization on this soil, it will be one that arises from the elements of the ancient [Dacian] civilization. From its own roots, in its own depths, arises the true civilization of a barbarian people; not from the aping of foreign customs, foreign languages, foreign institutions (cited in Babu-Buznea 1979: 154, 155; original emphasis).

This was Eminescu's literary and political program, which he shared with many other Conservatives: a combination of antipathy to all that smacked of foreign impositions, praise for the "barbarian" in the Romanian past, and worship for that past as giving vital indications for the proper future course. All of this was tied to postulates concerning the national essence.

By the late 1800s, then, a Dacian emphasis had arisen in strong counterstatement to the postulate of Roman origins as a definition of Romanian identity; and it posed a criticism of Romania's alliance with the West.[21] This counterstatement had antecedents in earlier times but achieved vigor only late in the century, when state formation and independence provided new room for such a voice. Several things, I believe, were particularly significant about its emergence. First, even though the Dacian emphasis rarely denied the Roman element in the pedigree altogether, it expanded the scope for serious indigenist considerations of identity. This expanded room for an indigenist voice was a significant addition to a politics whose referents had long been overwhelmingly *external*. The shift accompanies the formation of a Romanian polity aspiring to act *for itself*, in terms of an identity symbol that was not "alien." Second, the Dacian alternative perpetuated argument about Romanian identity on grounds that were, still, historical. Third, on that historical ground Dacianism staked out an alternative, enlarging the terms in which identity might be argued. When there was only one fortified position on this historical terrain—the Latinist one—statements could be emitted, but they could not be adequately contested and, thereby, deepened. Now the terrain had become fully two-dimensional. Argument could occur upon it, and regardless of the outcome, intensive interaction would strengthen the premises upon which the argument rested: the existence of an entity called "the Romanian people," having an identity that could be specified in large part through scholarly and historical investigation.

The concept around which much of this investigation would revolve was the "national essence." Although the notion was not new, it received explicit attention only in the latter part of the 1800s. Generally credited with having introduced it into discussion is philosopher and critic T. Maiorescu, a leading ideologue of the Conservative party. Maiorescu articulated one of the most trenchant critiques of the Liberal/pro-western program of development, the theory of "form without substance," which argued that the Liberal program imposed on Romania a set of forms unsuited to the substance of Romanian society. To make such an argument required, of course, some idea of what the substance or essence of Romanianness might be, and it was with this problem that an increasing number of thinkers and writers came to occupy themselves.[22]

The question engaged intellectual domains that had participated less actively in defining the Nation hitherto. When the problem of definition had been regarded as primarily historical, it had been the preserve largely of historians, philologists, and folklorists. Now these were joined by philosophers, literati, psychologists, and aestheticians, whose domains were beginning to develop sharper disciplinary profiles and firmer professional standards as fields like ethnopsychology, folklore, and literature distanced themselves somewhat from history and from one another (Zub 1981: 35). As the following section of this chapter will show, much of this differentiation expressed itself through claims about who could offer the best analysis of Romanians' national essence.

RECAPITULATION

Several important developments occurred during the period summarized in this section. In all three Romanian lands, the social structure was transformed from one in which a nobility had considerable power (even while lacking full control over the political mechanism) to one in which its power had been severely curtailed. The cause of this transformation was not only that princes or emperors had centralized their rule at the nobles' expense but that the economy was changing: agriculture was in crisis and manufacturing was on the rise. The consequence was new spaces in the social structure. In Transylvania these were occupied by the non-Romanian nationalities and by a small, growing stratum of educated Romanian professionals and civil servants; in the Principalities, members of the imperiled nobility joined the bourgeois, intellectual, and bureaucratic ranks. These various groups produced national movements in all three lands, movements that from the outset cross-fertilized one another despite significant differences in their regional situations.

From these movements and the traditions they drew upon, in all three regions the precedent was firmly established that persons active in intellectual and political life served as spokesmen for the Nation. They routinely filled political argument with notions about Romanian identity, so as to gain external allies, and represented internal political opponents as Aliens. For most of the period discussed, those who spoke for the Nation did so largely in opposition to the actual holders of power. That is, the Nation as a socio-symbolic construct was produced in a counterdiscourse to the exercise of rule. Only in the third quarter of the 1800s did the two—rule and discourse—come together. At that point indigenism began to appear in the repertoire of identity statements, its tendency represented here by a new Dacian emphasis in the matter of Romanian origins. With heightened indigenism came intensified efforts to define something called a "national essence" so as to advocate policy suited to the people's inner character and to defend Romanians' native endowment against political corruption.

By the turn of the century, the struggle between indigenism and westernism was firmly lodged in representations of identity and political discourse. Scholars of different disciplines were sharpening their disciplinary boundaries by relating their specialties to the national essence, while politicians attacked one another's proposals for "imitation," "foreign borrowing," or "gallophilia." In the next section I show how these arguments were perpetuated under new conditions after World War I, solidifying both the national ideology and the position of intellectuals engaged in constructing it.

1900 to World War II

For the subject of national ideology, it is impossible to divide the nineteenth century cleanly from the twentieth, since currents in national discourse that became visible after 1900 had been gathering force in previous years. One could instead break at 1918, for Romanian politics was dramatically altered by the outcome of World War I; yet even so, many of the post-1918 arguments about the "national essence" merely continued debates from before. There is nonetheless some sense to breaking at the century, for then commenced a reversal of the near-quarter-century of economic stagnation from which the landed classes in Romania never recovered. By the turn of the century the balance of forces in Romanian politics had shifted, together with the country's economic options. The shift is significant for my theme, given how much of the discourse on national identity concerned itself also with arguments about development.

The bulk of this section describes interwar representations of Romanian identity that would influence those of the period after World War II. Without a brief account of the political context, however, one could not comprehend why representations of Romanianness were so frequent and so crucial during the first few decades of the twentieth century, most especially the 1920s and 1930s. This means, in particular, an outline of the changes that occurred in 1918 and that gave entirely new valences to old arguments, otherwise seemingly continuous from the years before the war.

To begin with Romania's international situation, Germany was struggling to support its capitalist development, like France and Britain before it, by creating colonies. Because other Europeans had already colonized most of the regions overseas, much of Germany's expansion was intra-European, particularly in the Balkans and resource-rich Romania. The straitened economic circumstances after the war permitted Romanians few sources of credit for their development plans. Germany, especially during the 1930s, proved a willing lender; as a result, the Romanian economy was tightly secured within the German orbit by 1940, confirming its trajectory as a colony of capitalist powers (see Chirot 1976). An important subtext of the interwar arguments about the proper path for the Nation concerned whether or not Germany was a more desirable protector than other western powers.[23]

Second, postwar Romanian leaders faced difficult decisions concerning the economy: how best to increase domestic capital accumulation without adding to the already huge foreign debt from war reparations. Arguments raged as to whether industrialization was the answer, how to achieve it, and what form to give it. Scarcely were programs for development in place when the Depression resuscitated the arguments all over again. Questions about the "national essence" entered into them: would industry and foreign capital corrupt the national soul, what kind of peasantry should economics promote (one like the French, the

Danish, the Germans? a meditative one, an enterprising one?), and so forth. Naturally, the economic solutions also influenced culture and its images of identity. For example, the Liberal party, which argued for only selective capital import, had trouble generating enough revenue to promote cultural interests adequately. In the prevailing climate, competition for funding among cultural interests took the form of arguing over whose definition of culture best suited Romanians' true soul—that is, of contesting over and over again the definition of Romanian identity. That the government tended to support science over the humanities should be borne in mind in analyzing the "cultural protectionism" of those humanists who promoted the "national essence" in art.

Third, perhaps the most overwhelming problems for interwar Romania came from the territorial changes of the peace treaties. To the Romanian Kingdom—known as the "Regat"—were added Transylvania (taken from Hungarian control), Austrian Bucovina, and Bessarabia (disputed with Russia for a century). The result was a near doubling of Romania's population and land mass. Although these changes fulfilled nationalist dreams, they also brought tremendous problems of reorganization and unification. Higher levels of development in Transylvania set off a scramble among Regat-based financial and political interests to secure these new resources, alienating many Transylvanians. Political organizations with largely regional bases now had to broaden their appeal; parties proliferated and competition increased. The task of unifying the administrative, fiscal, jural, and religious apparatuses proved arduous because Romania now contained sizable national minorities: 28 percent, as opposed to 8 percent in prewar Romania, all making claims and looking to outside powers. Hungarians, the largest minority (8 percent), impatiently awaited restitution of the old borders and deliverance from Romanian rule. Romanian representations of national and territorial unity therefore took place against the constant threat of territorial dismemberment, a threat actually realized in 1940, when the Soviet Union annexed Bessarabia and Hitler gave northern Transylvania back to Hungary.

The new national diversity (to say nothing of widespread anti-Hungarian feeling) motivated a determined effort by the state to mobilize Romanian national sentiment behind unity, for not all in the new territories were convinced that membership in united Romania was serving them well.[24] Unification began with the very means of cultural production and transmission: spelling and the lexicon were standardized, as they had also been when the two Principalities united in 1859.

Bureaucrats concerned about urban ethnic imbalances sought to encourage Romanians' social advancement into elite status, as well as to
raise their cultural level and thereby encourage the minorities to assimilate (Janos 1978: 98). In addition, new cadres had to be created for the
newly Romanian state bureaucracy and educational apparatus in the
provinces, hitherto staffed by other nationalities. Perhaps these concerns underlay the growth in the budget for education—10 percent before the war and 16.2 percent after it (ibid., 98)—and the remarkable
rise in the numbers of students in higher education during these years.
Between 1921 and 1929, for example, enrollments in the university of
Bucharest increased by almost two-and-a-half, from 8,911 students to
20,985, and university enrollments nationwide during the 1930s stood
at 2.2 students per 1,000 population—a higher ratio than in any other
European country (Kiriţescu 1935: 3–7).

Fourth, politics and discourse changed considerably in interwar Romania because of the 1917 Bolshevik Revolution. Fear of the spread of
Bolshevism became a permanent undercurrent of interwar political life.
The revolution sharpened anti-Russian sentiment, always strong in
Moldavia, and strengthened pro-western identifications. But perhaps
most important for the future of Romanian national ideology was the
position taken by the Communist International in the years between
1922 and 1928, when it openly supported minority struggles for national liberation even where these jeopardized the integrity of already-
constituted states. Romania itself was labeled an imperialist creation
and an oppressor of its newly acquired minorities. Because of this challenge to the country's political integrity, the government banned the
newly formed Romanian Communist Party in 1924, driving underground both it and its potential contributions to defining the national
soul. Thenceforth, arguments about socialism and efforts to come to
terms with it, in part through national means, were tacitly interwoven
with Romania's interwar national discourse. The discussion was truncated, however, and as chapter 3 will show, this had fundamental consequences for the fate of nationalism and Marxist ideology after 1945.

A final important postwar change was the altered status of two
groups that would become central to representations of Romanian
identity: the peasants and the Jews. A massive peasant uprising in 1907,
together with what the Bolshevik Revolution implied for peasant consciousness, caused the Romanian Parliament to pass a major land reform and to extend universal male suffrage to peasants. These changes
required incorporating the peasantry—in rhetoric, if nothing else—

into political platforms, which now might also advocate a previously unrealistic small-holder economy. The land reform eliminated from the political scene the last vestiges of the Conservative (large landowners') party, leaving a clear field to the Liberals until an ostensibly Peasantist coalition was cemented in the late 1920s. The changed status of the peasantry is one reason why peasants now figured even more centrally than before in representations of Romanian identity—and from a variety of political angles. Another reason was the high level of urbanization of the national minorities in the new provinces, which lowered from 74 percent to 59 percent the proportion of the urban population that was ethnically Romanian. With this, peasants literally became the common denominator of (ethnically) Romanian society (Livezeanu 1986: 17–18). Although the peasants' changed status reverberated in countless positive images of the Nation, the changed status of Jews affected their image adversely. Their enfranchisement and the removal of all constraints on their economic activities made them a threat to the aspirations of the expanding Romanian bourgeoisie; in consequence, they became even more important as a principal "Other" (often under the guise of antiurban representations) against whom Romanian identity would be defined. An association between "Jew" and "Bolshevik" exacerbated the problems Jews now faced in Romania and augmented the currents of antisemitism already flowing prior to World War I.

For all these reasons, the preoccupation with defining the Nation increased after the war, even over its already-high level of before, and contributed to forming an all-embracing national discourse that structured the language of politics and culture (see also Livezeanu 1986: 3). The tensions of localism and centralism, the fragility of the new borders, the efforts of the left to create an international working-class movement hostile to the Romanian state, the disproportions of national minorities in occupations of high reward, and all the other exigencies of nation-building gave preeminence to the idiom of the Nation. Those who utilized this idiom were members of political, religious, and intellectual elites, having diverse social origins and affiliations.[25] Since social actors circulated in and out of formal political office, "intellectuals" were not categorically separate from "politicians"[26] (and even the archbishop of Transylvania served for a time as regent). Politicians and intellectuals were equally active in developing the national discourse, rehearsing a variety of themes that referred overtly or implicitly to the identity of Romanians. Through them, the interwar years became a concerted period for making national ideology hegemonic, the basis for a broad consent that incorporated the attachments of Romanian peasants freed from national oppression in the newly acquired provinces. Only 20 percent of the population failed to find this ideology attractive.

This leads to one final point concerning the difference in Romanian national ideology before and after World War I. Before, there had always been Romanians outside the state borders whose interests had to be defended against discrimination by other national groups (Hungarians, Russians, Austrians, and so forth). Now, virtually all Romanians were contained in a single state within which they, along with a sizable number of non-Romanians, were oppressed by their own. An ideology that had been developed for several centuries as a way of gaining rights for Romanians now became the ideology of a social system that had its own fundamental inequalities.[27] Although by focusing on intellectuals my discussion underemphasizes class difference, it should not be forgotten that those intellectuals who argued about the national essence were constructing the means for ideological subjection of their countrymen, Romanian and non-Romanian, within the new state.

DEFINING THE NATION BETWEEN EAST AND WEST

By the turn of the century, concern with the "national essence" had spread into virtually all political and intellectual discourse. Not everyone who participated in the debates used the term "national essence," nor was it the explicit agenda for all who contributed to it; but from 1900 on, there was scarcely a politician, regardless of party, and scarcely a thinker, whether in economics, psychology, sociology, ethnography, philosophy, literature, or art, who did not directly or indirectly have something to say about Romanians' essential character.[28] For nearly all of them, the objective was to create a strong national polity, economy, and culture. Much of this writing took off from the "form without substance" theory of Maiorescu, mentioned earlier, which criticized the corrosive effects of "cosmopolitan borrowings" and aimed to promote the organic development of a Romanian culture and society, suited to the people's innate character. His solutions (which included advocating a literature built upon ethnic and rural themes) were picked up and widely debated throughout the next several decades, as participants worried whether to keep the old social and literary structures within which Romanian forms had developed or to alter them, and how or how much (Ornea 1980: 349).

The various positions in these debates have been classified in several ways, nearly all of which employ the terms used by the participants.[29] No one has yet proposed a comprehensive analysis that avoids "native" terms and identifies locations in the field of discourse by entirely other criteria; the present chapter is no exception. In keeping with my interest in representations of identity, I will speak primarily of "westernizers," "indigenists," and "pro-orientals." Indigenists came in great variety; some of them leaned ever so slightly eastward or westward, while still emphasizing qualities they thought peculiar to Romanians and wished to protect from the corrupting effects of imported civilizations, particularly the western one. The bulk of argument took place between the westernizers and the indigenists, but the pro-orientals were significant disproportionate to their numbers, owing to their success in keeping the question on the agenda and to their association with the fascist currents that gradually prevailed in Romanian politics.

Clustered within each participant's views were not only ideas about Romania's relation with the West or East but proposals for or against industrialization, an agrarian or peasant state, parliamentary democracy, religion in the national soul, populist or peasant themes in literature, the positive or negative social value of groups such as the peasantry or the urban bourgeoisie, and so on. Disagreement persisted over such points as what were the primary and what the secondary defining traits of the national essence; whether its diacritica are customs and language and territory or, rather, matters of tonality or intensity of affect; whether it is subject to alteration under changed environmental conditions; to what extent history has a part in producing it; whether it is lodged in the blood. The questions came to be phrased in such a way that almost every academic discipline, as well as every position on the political spectrum, could have something to say about them.

The positions are best illustrated through the words of some of the participants themselves. Our survey is necessarily brief, and it oversimplifies because it can give voice to only a few of the best-known contributors. First, the pro-orientals (known at the time as the "Orthodoxists"):

If the mission of the Romanian people is to create a culture after its image and likeness, this implies as well how its orientation must be resolved. Whoever recommends an orientation toward the West speaks nonsense. *Orientation* contains within itself the notion of *Orient* and means directing ourselves toward the Orient, in accord with the Orient. Altars face toward the Orient; the icons of the hearth face us from the Orient; the peasant who kneels in his field faces the Orient. Everywhere it is said that light comes from the East. And for us, who find ourselves geographically in the Orient and who, through our Orthodox religion, hold to the truths of the eastern world, there can be no other orientation than toward the Orient, that is, toward ourselves . . . . Westernization means the negation of our orientalness; Europeanizing nihilism means the negation of our creative potential. Which means to negate in principle a Romanian culture, to negate a destiny proper to Romanians, and to accept the destiny of a people born dead (Crainic 1929: 3).

A great river of orientalness, then, flowed in the riverbed of our people's soul. Byzantium and Kiev took their toll of it as it passed by, flowing underneath Orthodoxy—that import, which in time dissolved into the reservoir of our primitive forces. [Orthodoxy] thus forms part of our people's wealth and constitutes yet another power by which our patriarchal mentality, our native genius, differentiates itself from and resists the currents of European civilization, so fresh in their historical origin (Crainic 1936: 90).

Nichifor Crainic, theologian and professor of mysticism in the Bucharest Faculty of Theology, held down the "easternmost" corner of debates on the national essence, largely through journalistic pieces in the magazine he edited, *Thought* (*Gândirea*).[30] For him, the essential Romanian was a peasant, a contemplative who disdained material concerns and was therefore unsuited to industrial work, and whose soul was formed by adherence to the Orthodox faith. Crainic and another influential Orthodoxist, philosophy professor Nae Ionescu, opposed all western forms, including democracy; their program was for a peasant state free of industrial artifice. As Ionescu put it:

What state politics do we now propose? . . . A wholly revolutionary politics, . . . [which] recommends: decoupling us from world politics; closing us up in our own borders as completely as possible; taking into consideration what is realistic for Romania; provisionally reducing our standard of living to a realistic level; and laying the foundations for a Romanian State of peasant structure, the only form in which we can truly live according to the indications of our nature and the only one we can implant that will enable the powers of our race truly and completely to bear fruit (Ionescu 1937: 286–287).

As this quotation makes clear, even these extreme pro-oriental voices spoke for a kind of indigenism, rather than for union with the Orient (irredeemably tainted now with Bolshevism), and this is evident also in their preferring the Dacians to some more oriental ancestor. Both these men are generally regarded as major ideologues of Romanian fascism, admirers of Hitler and Mussolini despite their anti-western talk, and antisemites. A charismatic figure, Ionescu exerted tremendous influence on his students at university, among whom were Mircea Eliade and Constantin Noica (see chapter 7).

Associated with the Orthodoxists for a time but gradually parting company with them were eastward-leaning indigenists such as Transylvanian philosopher/poet Lucian Blaga.[31] Here is an early formulation of his idea of Romanianness, before the growing fascist danger caused him to reconsider:

We think ourselves merely Latins—lucid, rational, temperate, lovers of classical form—but willy-nilly we are more than that. [A] significant percent of Slavic and Thracian blood seethes in our veins. The Romanian spirit may be dominated by Latinity, a peaceful and cultured force, but we have also a rich latent Thraco-Slavic foundation, exuberant and vital, which, no matter how much we oppose it, sometimes detaches itself from the nether realms and rises up powerfully in our consciousness. Our Latin symmetry and harmony are often battered by a storm that rages in the Romanian spirit at near-metaphysical depths; and this storm is the revolt of our non-Latin soul . . . Why should we violate our true nature, corset ourselves in a formula of Latin clarity, when so many other possibilities for development lie within us in that barbarian unconscious? (Blaga 1921: 181–182).

A sizable part of Blaga's opus went to defining the metaphysical basis for Romanian identity, in terms that owed much to Frobenius, Freud, and Jung. Of roughly similar indigenism, despite great differences in their theoretical systems and their approaches to questions of the day, were people such as the famous historians Vasile Pârvan and Nicolae Iorga. The latter, like Blaga, emphasized now the Thracians, now Rome (and sometimes Byzantium), while parting company with the Orthodoxists. All these thinkers agreed in ruralizing and indigenizing the national essence.

Close to them in indigenist representations but resolutely opposed to eastern affiliations as well as to western influence, was philosopher-psychologist Constantin Rădulescu-Motru:

Our whole social life is shot through with illusions. We have adopted civil and political laws unsuited to our traditions; we have organized a public education useless to the large majority of the people; we have imitated the bourgeois technique of economic production in which neither the qualities of our people nor the wealth of our country can bear fruit; we have done everything in our power to falsify the traditions and the aptitudes given us by nature . . . [thinking] ourselves obligated to be to Europe's taste. . . . For better than a century, the Romanian people has not been faithful to itself. Let us have an end to experiments with laws for the [so-called] "Belgium of the Orient" (Rădulescu-Motru 1936: 31, 118, 35).

A student of Maiorescu's with advanced degrees from France and Germany, Rădulescu-Motru worked to develop a philosophy and psychology suited to the Romanian character and to create a form of ethnic consciousness different from western-style nationalism.[32] His indigenism emphasized autonomously based cultural and political development but not complete isolation: the very title of the publication he founded, *The European Idea*, indicated his desire for Romania's communication with and integration into Europe, but only on Romanian terms. His ideal Romanian was, like that of all the writers mentioned so far, a peasant unsuited to industrial work. Unlike many indigenists, however, he saw ethnic traits not as bred in the genes but as environmentally conditioned.

In contrast to indigenists such as these (and there were many others) were moderate westernizers such as Moldavian literary critic Garabet Ibrăileanu:

In the twentieth century, history has set Romanians the following problem: will Romania continue to be a semi-asiatic, oriental country or will it enter the ranks of European peoples and European culture. This problem has been answered by history. For various reasons, Romania could not exempt itself from the European influence [that] penetrated into our country. It penetrated through the very fact of its superiority (Ibrăileanu 1909: 261).

Ibrăileanu and the publication he edited from 1906 to 1933, *Romanian Life*, were associated with the Populist movement founded in 1893–1895 by the Bessarabian C. Stere. It accepted a certain amount of western influence and innovation as necessary to catalyzing Romania's social and artistic development, which should nonetheless give priority to ethnic values. The qualified pro-westernism of the Stere-Ibrăileanu group was unexpectedly combined with such emphases as the peasantry *qua* heart of the Nation,[33] an agrarianist politicoeconomic program, a generally center-left political orientation, an ethnicist aesthetic ideal (art based on ethnic themes), and cultural protectionism (see below). Despite having early socialist sympathies, they insisted that the Nation took precedence over its class divisions, criticized the socialists for not attending to the national essence, and refused to encourage revolutionary peasant action on the grounds that it would produce civil war. Stere rejected a class analysis of Romanian society thus:

Germany can afford to be divided into antagonistic classes in a state of struggle, for its existence as a country is not thereby imperiled. But the structure of Romania is feeble. She has not the possibility to throw herself into a struggle of classes. We must place the interests of our country above everything else (Stere, cited in Durandin 1987: 86).

His subordination of a class program to the "national interest" led him to merge his Populists with the Liberal party in 1899.

In contrast to Stere's and Ibrăileanu's grudging acceptance of western influence were those enthusiastic westernizers who eagerly embraced it:

Under the banner of Orthodoxy and tradition some persons flourish the ideal—static and immobilized in hieratic byzantine-muscovite forms—of a primitive [Romanian] culture without development or prospects. *Our* cultural ideal [in contrast] is dynamic, eager for growth, renewal and fructification. . . . We mean to propagate a sense of culture that is European. Our light comes from the West. We see our deliverance in the occidentalization of this country, many of whose vital organs are putrefying even before it has reached maturity. Balkanism, our cherished and idealized orientalness . . . now shelters all the brigands who have impeded political purification and opposed uplifting the people from the cultural cesspool in which they flounder. . . . [We seek] the affirmation of our genius and specific character in the forms of European culture, in the harmonious and shining framework of the culture of the West. . . . We have faith that soap, comfort and urbanism, the telegraph and civil law in no way threaten the purity of our race . . . (Filotti 1924: 2–4).

Isolated from the rhythm of Western civilization by its surroundings and its religion, the Romanian people was unable to develop in its own manner and was derouted from the potentialities of its race; for entire centuries it expressed its Latin thought in cumbersome cyrillic letters; descended of those whose unbeaten will and energy conquered the world, our soul was dislocated by infiltrations of oriental fatalism. Is this the definitive formula for our race? . . . Time is on our side and, after ages of alienation and deformation, new prospects have arisen for the creation of a truly Romanian soul. If we seem to some historians melancholy stepchildren of a Romanian-Byzantine-Slavic-Turkish-Phanariot tradition, let us hope that in the eyes of future generations, we will seem venerable forefathers of a true Romanian tradition [through the influence of Europe] (Lovinescu 1972: 458–459).[34]

Westernizers such as literary critics Filotti and Lovinescu, together with others like Zeletin and Voinea in political economy, sat at the opposite end of the spectrum from Crainic's pro-oriental extreme. They saw contact with the West as liberating even while they worked for a "truly Romanian tradition" as a result of such contact. Stalwarts of the Liberal party, like most of the associates of *Romanian Life*, they nonetheless differed from the latter in advocating industrial and urban development and in rejecting the rural world as the epitome of the Romanian essence or the model for Romanian art. Peasants do not represent purity, Lovinescu argued, since they have absorbed as many heterogeneous elements as the bourgeoisie.

Lovinescu's centrality to some of the debates of the 1970s and 1980s, particularly those discussed in chapter 5, requires a brief summary of his most important ideas.[35] The principal work in which he joined debates about the national essence was his three-volume *History of Modern Romanian Civilization* (1972 [1924–1926]). This work engaged in open and vigorous polemic with virtually every other view about the proper interpretation of Romania's prior development, prospects, and essence; his main opponents, however, were the "traditionalists," whom he attacked with the notion of *synchronism* (*sincronism*). By this he meant "interdependence, . . . that is the tendency for all forms of life in modern societies that are solidary with one another to become uniform" (ibid., 395). He raised this notion to the status of a sociological law: given that all European countries are interdependent, ideas and developments in one will necessarily have repercussions in the others, as the less-developed societies imitate the more advanced. This principle of imitation obtained in all realms, he said, from the technical through the sociopolitical and on into literary and artistic forms, and it held the promise of progress in all of them.

At bottom, Lovinescu strove to demonstrate that modern capitalist society and all its entailments were sociological necessities for Romania and had already brought it benefits. This was in no way intended, however, to negate the idea of the national essence, as latter-day "traditionalists" would sometimes charge. At no point did he question whether such an essence existed but adhered fully to the idea of a "national soul"—which, however, he saw relativistically, as subject to change. He encouraged borrowing of western forms in the belief that they would contribute to developing what was best in indigenous social and cultural life:

On account of the vicissitudes of history, the artistic sensibilities of our people could manifest themselves only in inferior forms and genres, which cannot serve as points of departure for an art subject to the imperatives of world-wide synchronism. . . . From the fusion of all foreign influences with the molding spirit of our race will emerge the art of the future, *with sufficient particularities to constitute a Romanian style* (Lovinescu 1927: 133, emphasis added).

That is, synchronism with the West would help to affirm a Romanian identity with its own special characteristics. Lovinescu resisted not the idea of a national essence but its dogmatization, accepting the idea if it was not used to create straitjackets for literary production. He was relentless in his opposition to whatever created such straitjackets—mysticism, Orthodoxism, Romantic sentimentalism, and exaltations of a primitive rural spirit, which he regarded as anachronistic. To minimize the constraints on literary creation, he advocated that aesthetic judgments be autonomous of all other considerations (this position would reappear in the 1960s). That he was spitting into the wind of his time is evident in the defeat of his nominations for membership in the Romanian Academy and for a university post.

This brief survey of representations of Romanianness from East to West has coincided in part with a passage from the far right of the political spectrum to the center-left (though these two axes—East/West and right/left—do not superimpose perfectly). It remains to consider what the far left—the socialists and communists—contributed to defining the national essence. Some people with socialist sympathies (such as Ralea of *Romanian Life*) were westernizers with reservations; others, although they rejected Lovinescu's "idealist" analysis of Romania's political and economic development, shared his embrace of the West and of a bourgeois/capitalist trajectory for Romania, which could lead to socialism; still others resisted the entire discourse of a national essence, in which they saw the obfuscating intent of a bourgeoisie aiming to disarm the class consciousness of the masses. This last point of view is well illustrated by leftist P. Pandrea,[36] who insisted that any nation contains huge differences within it, persons of the same class position from different nations sometimes having more in common than different classes within a single nation. "We neither find useful nor accept the idea of 'national' cultures," he said, claiming that the theory of national cultures marks the ascension of national bourgeoisies, who use it to suppress the class struggle: peasants and proletarians, unlike bourgeoisies, have theories that are *international* (Pandrea 1931: 1). An even bolder statement comes from the founder of Romanian socialism, C. Dobrogeanu-Gherea, who asserted, "The nation is a sentimental ideological-utopian fantasy that does not exist" (1976: 134). Ideas such as these reflect the internationalism of the world socialist movement of the time and show why the ideology of the Nation could become the preserve of the political right.

This is not to suggest, however, that no one on the left was prepared

to defend the Nation, though under the conditions set by the Communist International it was not easy. An example of such a defense comes
from one of the few early Romanian communists with a solid reputation as both a genuine Marxist and a patriot, L. Pătrășcanu:

The right monopolized the nationalist formula for itself. But this was an outrageous lie. . . . How to explain otherwise the fact that it was precisely the far
right . . . that stood by impassively when the body of Transylvania was being
torn to shreds? [i.e., Hitler's award of northern Transylvania to Hungary in
1940—k.v.] Were they nationalists? No! They were reactionaries, and they borrowed nationalist phrases so as to capture the minds of the naive.

We [communists] struggle to resolve the problems of democracy within the
framework of our nation. In our solutions nationalism will not mean chauvinism or antisemitism; we will tie the national idea to the idea of the masses,
realizing the national idea in truth by raising the masses to a conscious life. Between our political faith as communists and the national idea thus understood
there is no contradiction (Pătrășcanu 1946: 14).

With this, he adopts the widespread tactic of accusing his opponents—
the far right—of serving "foreign interests" (Hitlerism) and identifies
the essence of the Nation with "the masses." In his writings Pătrășcanu
does not go to the lengths of the writers considered above, however, to
define what identity the Romanian Nation should have, other than a
mass base. Thus, although not abdicating national questions altogether,
he and other communists contributed minimally to forging national
ideology because they refused to argue its specifics and thereby to consolidate its unspoken premises.

THE SOCIAL EFFICACY OF DEBATES
ON THE NATION

The preceding section has introduced some themes and
personages that will recur in subsequent chapters. My intention now is
not to offer an extended analysis of these arguments, their symbolic
content, or their links to the political field in which they were occurring[37] but to suggest provisionally how this discourse was socially efficacious: what did it accomplish socially that might have consequences
for the resumption of talk about the Nation after the 1950s. I argue,
following Gheorghiu, that much of this talk about the Nation was
creating a space for intellectual production, and I suggest in particular
that talk about national identity during the interwar years became literally constitutive of academic disciplines and their associated practices.
One sees these processes in action especially in the intellectuals' pro-

liferating talk to and about themselves and their self-mobilization in defense of the Nation; one sees it as well in their invocations of the national essence as their disciplines became more specialized. I will first illustrate these two points with some quotations and then consider why they might have taken this particular form.

Intellectuals Defend the Nation and Construct Themselves.
Georgescu observes (1983: 135) that the excesses of interwar nationalism came from the desire to preserve Romania's gains in World War I. There is no doubt that territorial anxieties provided a major conscious motivation for many people. Perhaps less consciously, intellectuals in each province were struggling to preserve and even expand the space for intellectual activity, in a society in which the technical requirements of economic development were displacing humanists from center stage. In the interwar cultural press there appeared numerous articles appealing to Romanian intellectuals to help build the state, to defend national unity, to organize against corrupt politicians, to engage in projects for reform, and many other things.[38] Here are three statements drawn from articles of this type, to show what they propose.

[T]he role intellectuals deserve [is] giving directives and establishing the new basis for organizing and leading our state, tasks that to this point have been entrusted only to people made rich through commerce and corrupt politics. Only an intellectual reform will bring about the necessary change in habits and the moral reform needed to heal our state organism of its many sins . . . . Organized intellectuals will be called upon to give directives and to reorganize on a firm basis all that the war disorganized and broke apart. . . . We have much need of greater wisdom and honor in the leadership of our land (Raul-Teodorescu 1919: 2).

The obligation of intellectuals is to consolidate peace and to offer their labors toward resolving our moral and material difficulties. Intellectuals cannot continue to remain indifferent to the gravity of the current situation, which threatens the very foundations of the Romanian state. . . . Their purpose should be to organize with foresight for state leadership. To this end, [we] appeal to intellectuals to form an Association, having a program more general than those of the associations organized to defend professional interests. In addition to spreading through all social strata enlightenment, ideas of justice, and scientific truth—indispensable for resolving the problems faced in organizing our state—this Association will present, whenever necessary, specific proposals drawn up by competent persons free of party prejudice. . . . Above all other matters . . . [the Association will occupy itself with] consolidating our national unity, through laying down a Constitution for United Romania . . . (Rădulescu-Motru 1921: 2).

Intellectuals . . . represent the only invincible force of a nation. . . . A nation enters into eternity not through its politicians, nor its army, nor its peasants or proletarians—but only through what is thought, discovered, and created within it. . . . The forces that sustain a country's history and feed its mission have nothing to do with the political, the economic, or the social. They are borne and magnified *only* by "intellectuals." . . . *This*, then, is what "intellectuals" represent: the struggle against non-being, against death; the permanent affirmation of their nation's genius, virility, and power to create (Eliade 1934: 2, original emphases).

These and many other articles call upon intellectuals to clean up the mess that corrupt politics has created, to raise the consciousness and cultural level of the rest of the Nation, and to defend it or the integrity of the state.

In this part of their talk about the Nation, intellectuals were constructing—among other things—the separation of themselves from manual labor. The implications underlying much of the rhetoric about "the peasantry" show this well. As mentioned above, changes after the war made the "peasant problem" a major concern of the period, apparent in the central role accorded the peasantry in interwar debates. The problem was not, of course, only Romanian: Hobsbawm observes (1983: 265–266) that states face problems whenever the franchise is extended, and these problems are eased if a segment of the populace can be identified as "traditional," that is, obedient. This was surely the role assigned to Romania's peasantry, along with many other peasants in the world of the twentieth century. Organizations and projects for rural reform abounded in the plans of elites across the whole spectrum of representations and political persuasions.

In addition, peasants provided fertile ground for conflicts within the elite, as different parties defended their programs by identifying them with the peasants and the Nation. Groups accused one another of betraying the Nation, its national mission, and/or its peasant masses (e.g., Dobridor 1935; Madgearu 1921). Politicians and philosophers alike spoke for and against the idea of a "peasant state" and uplifting the village, and writers insisted that the national essence was to be found in the purity of peasant souls. Common to many of these arguments was the distance created between the peasantry and its elite spokesmen—a denial of "coevalness" between peasants and the persons writing about them (see Fabian 1983). For example, peasants were seen as inhabiting a space untouched by time:

The village has not let itself be tempted and drawn into the "history" made by others over our heads. It has preserved itself chastely, untouched in the autonomy with which poverty and mythology have endowed it, and awaits the time when it will serve as the sure foundation of an authentically Romanian history (Blaga 1980 [1937]: 258).

[The peasant remains] on the same patch of soil, generation after generation, confined in the immobility of the same destiny, while outside his radius everything is in perpetual change. . . . Peasant life has no history. It absorbs itself in nature. But like the seeds that lie in nature's breast, like the minerals hidden in the folds of the earth, the embers of possibility smoulder in this primitive life (Crainic 1936: 89).

Alternatively, peasants were rendered "backward," "ignorant," in need of culture:

[The changes of World War I] brought about the conditions for transforming serfs into citizens. It remains to give them the culture necessary for them to become Europeans. From now on this must be the task of those who aspire to raising Romania up to the level of the western countries (Ibrăileanu 1933: 8).

The culture peasants required would, of course, enlarge the educational apparatus and employ more intellectuals,[39] who would by their educational activities further intensify the bases of their own legitimation: acceptance of the central value of knowledge (Bauman 1987b: 18).

This discursive interest in the peasantry accomplished several things, I suggest, akin to discursive interests in women, in other times and places (see, for example, Poovey 1986; Scott 1988): it distanced and silenced them, and it rendered them an open field for intellectuals and the state to colonize. The distancing and silencing are eminently visible in those quotations that remove peasants from time, as well as in a sociologist's angry accusation that some writers, so eloquent on the peasantry's "boycott" of history, had never done research in a village to find out what real peasants actually thought about anything.[40] The forms of distancing varied from one group to another, but nearly all had the effect of inviting the state in and giving it work to do, and of widening the chasm between the peasants and those who claimed to speak in their defense. Some critics on the left chose to point this out:

The intellectual elite seeks to have entrusted to them the fate of our people (political power, therefore) because (1) they are superior, (2) they are benevolent, (3) the masses are incapable of leading themselves on their own or through their own representatives (Păun 1935: 4).

Behind the celebrations of peasant innocence, the many proposals for reform of the countryside, and the rhetoric of disinterested concern, then, lies a celebration of the peasantry's elite patrons, set firmly apart on the far side of a class barrier.[41]

It would be unwise to argue that all parties to the debates on identity were playing the same role, for each was somewhat differently positioned in the cultural/political field and therefore offered its own special nuance to the national ideology-in-formation. With the help of two astute analyses of Populism and its publication, *Romanian Life* (Alexandrescu 1987; Gheorghiu 1985*a*), we gain a glimpse into how general ideological processes were proceeding in very particular ways.

The Populist movement, together with the related Peasantists, was the most important of several groups that centered their political program on the peasantry. Alexandrescu (1987) contends, however, that Stere's Populists, although arguing about the situation of and best policies for the peasantry, were speaking with the voice of the "*petite robe*"— small functionaries, local bureaucrats, village priests and teachers (as opposed to the *grande robe* of high functionaries, magistrates, university professors, and so forth). Their program defended, under another guise, the space within which a rural and urban petite bourgeoisie ought to form. Their concern with obstacles to the social advancement of the peasantry aptly symbolized the obstacles to their own exercise of power within the existing electoral system and, more generally, of the obstacles to the formation of a middle class between the peasant masses and the rich (ibid., 23)—particularly in Moldavia, where the movement began. They spoke of "the peasantry," yet their programs promoted the differentiation of peasants into a wealthier stratum and a still-impoverished mass. Thus, Alexandrescu argues, they defended small or medium peasant *property*, rather than general peasant interests.

Alexandrescu also points to an interesting feature of Stere's Populism, its proposal that the "third estate" to be created between peasant masses and the powerful should have the function not of creating riches but of *social communication*—of creating Romanian literature and culture (Alexandrescu 1987: 27–28). Here Alexandrescu's analysis joins with that of Gheorghiu (1985*a*), who argues that the entire strategy pursued by *Romanian Life* suggests a program for autonomizing the cultural sphere and promoting the "primitive accumulation" of Romanian cultural capital within a protected internal market. Basic to this were arguments that separated *culture* from *politics*, making intellectuals the guardians of morality that a corrupt politics had abandoned (Gheorghiu 1985*a*: 134). This constituted a form of capital to which Ibrăileanu, on behalf of a certain disposition within the intelligentsia as a whole, laid claim and which he sought to protect by arguing for an aesthetic that privileged an art based on ethnic themes.

Ibrăileanu and *Romanian Life* pursued this argument in various ways. One was to join the critique of Romania's dichotomized class structure with an account of why Romania's contact with western culture had brought so few benefits. The editorial statement in the journal's first issue, justifying its program, did this as follows:

Our situation is not just backward, which would be bad enough; it is abnormal, which is worse. The upper classes are suspended in the air, without contact with the people below, which is in our country the only *positive* class and which has preserved a cleaner *Romanian soul*. Between the upper classes and the people is a deep abyss, which in our case separates what are effectively *two nations*. The upper classes aspire only to western culture, with which the people have no contact, and because they are divorced from the Romanian people the upper classes do not *assimilate* [that culture] . . . [F]oreign culture, instead of *being absorbed by us, absorbs us, assimilates* us. This is the reason for the inimical stance of some people to foreign culture (*Viaţa românească* 1906: 5–6, original emphases).

What Romanian culture needs, this editorial implies, is a new class so organically tied to its people that it can assimilate the benefits of western civilization without being overwhelmed. Among the prescriptions for forging such a tie is to promote ethnic themes in art. This prescription is culturally "protectionist" precisely in the audience it presupposes and the indigenous cultural production it thereby protects. Instead of furthering the circulation on Romania's internal market of the foreign cultural products that already dominate it, instead of *imitating* western culture, say these cultural populists, we must *create our own*. Gheorghiu's translation of this program: we must move from a simple to an expanded reproduction of cultural capital, nationalizing it and its production rather than getting capital from abroad by theft (Gheorghiu 1985*a*: 134). In this respect, the group was in perfect consonance with the protectionism of the Liberal party with which Stere's Populists had merged in 1899.

It was not only *Romanian Life* that advocated such a course: most of the indigenist arguments about the national essence did so as well. Everywhere one finds articles from this period arguing that Romanians must have their *own* intellectual production, must educate the peasants with things *Romanians* produce rather than with the products of cultural imperialism. Crainic, complaining that pro-western "intellectualists" (he contests their claim to intellectual status) are advocating cultural consumption, observes:

It is an attitude different from ours. Traditionalism demands a culture creative of autochthonous values, our own cultural creation. This does not exclude cultural consumption but implies it, according it the subordinate status it ought to have. . . . A people's purpose in this world is not to [consume] but to create, to create what others have not because no other people has that particular creation in its nature (Crainic 1929: 2).

Other indigenist groups campaigned to have a tax placed on all foreign books (Vrancea 1965: 104). This was, indeed, the common denominator linking indigenists with the westernizing *Romanian Life*: to protect the conditions for cultural production. Just as the basic problem for political economy was, What conditions should govern Romania's industrial and agricultural production?, the basic problem for literati, philosophers, and other thinkers was, What conditions should govern the production of culture?

The circumstances in which such argument was occurring were, of course, the circumstances of a small and undercapitalized country trying to create the instruments for its advancement (Saizu 1981: 816), while groups differently placed in society argued over how that might best be done. It was a society whose weak tax base virtually necessitated foreign borrowing to support the cost of a state bureaucracy, "oversized" because state employment gave more certain livelihood than economic activity (Janos 1978: 107–108). Even so, the bureaucracy could not absorb all the people its educational system produced, nor pay them adequately despite disbursing 56 percent of the total budget for the salaries of state employees (ibid., 108). The result was a struggle for the positions and the resources that existed, efforts by producers of culture to protect themselves from the vagaries of market competition, and continued calls upon the state to do more for culture (see, e.g., Antipa 1923: 3–4; Livezeanu 1986: 206; Saizu 1981).

For humanist intellectuals, the struggle was all the more intense given that in the years after the war there was a general drift of state funds toward science and economics, which could contribute to rationalizing the economy that politicians had determined to industrialize. Saizu (1981) describes this context, in which resources for literati, philosophers, theologians, perhaps even ethnographers and historians, began losing ground to those for economics, sociology, chemistry, and other hard and applied sciences. Between 1922 and 1927 the Romanian Society of Science reorganized all its hard-science sections; several proposals were floated for reorganizing the Romanian Academy to direct all scientific research at the national level. In 1934 it was proposed that the mission of the Academy until that time—encouraging cultural activity—be reduced to simply rewarding works of high quality with prizes, and that the Academy's more active guidance go to directing scientific work (Saizu 1981: 814). The new emphasis on progress in science led to the founding of research institutes separate from university teaching, intended (in one scholar's words) to be "the most powerful fortifications for defending the nation and for undreamed-of increases in the forces of endurance of our nation and state" (Antipa 1940: 7).

Also struggling for a share in resources were spokesmen for the Orthodox Church. This includes not just Crainic (a theologian, it should be remembered) but other clerics, spiritual descendants of the eighteenth-century "fathers" of Romanian national ideology. Interwar conditions subjected the church, too, that self-proclaimed ancient bastion of Romanian identity, to greater strains on its well-being. Not only did it undergo internal upheaval from the union with differently organized Orthodox churches in the new provinces, but it and the conditions of its financing were placed more firmly under state control. The landed properties and levels of funding set for Romania's major creeds were relatively more advantageous for other faiths than for Orthodoxy (Nistor 1935: 11–12),[42] as were the salaries fixed for priests and the subventions allotted for specific purposes (ibid., 25–26; Editura Institutului Biblic 1957: 606). Protestant denominations were making a concerted evangelizing effort in Romania during these same years. Arguments arose in Parliament between Orthodox bishops and the Minister of Religion, the former complaining about the level of church funds from the state—seen as evidence of insufficient love for the Nation, inattention to the people's soul, and a threat to Romanian civilization—whereas the latter pointed to the state's exhausted budget and the numerous claims on its finances, inadequate to the bishops' requests.[43] Under these circumstances, it is scarcely surprising that persons such as theology professors Crainic and Stăniloae (another Orthodoxist) defended the church by inserting it into the heart of the Nation.

Secular intellectuals, feeding in part from the same state trough, logically rejoined that because Orthodoxy was not restricted to Romanians, it could not define their national identity. Some directly attacked the claims of churchmen and their allies that the church had preserved Romanian identity through centuries of deculturating foreign rule:

The Orthodox Church is and has been perpetuated as foreign. Faith manifests itself in acts; the Orthodox faith is not represented by a single Romanian Orthodox act in a single domain of religious application: miracles, proselytism, oratory, writing, propaganda, sacrifices. Not a single initiative begun under the sign of a religious sentiment [has been Romanian in its character] (Arghezi 1928).

In a similar vein, see also the comments of Constantinescu (below). Such writers sought to capture the Nation from the grip of the church with the familiar accusation of "foreign borrowing." Others went so far as to claim that the actions of the church had impoverished the people and impeded the national mission (e.g., Ghibu 1924). They accused the church of fostering the people's ignorance through mystical and irrational practices. Clerics might have founded the national ideology, these critics argued, but only their secular offspring—intellectuals, the builders of science and knowledge—could be entrusted with the Nation's interests in the modern world where Reason, not superstition, reigns. The Nation's intellectual guardians sometimes even arrogated unto their own projects the language of the church: consider the title and agenda of Rădulescu-Motru's 1936 *Romanianism: Catechism of a New Spirituality*, which aimed to develop a national ideology resting on Reason as against the mysticism of religion.

The language of the competition in which all were locked emphasized different claims to represent the interests and the "proper" cultural values of the Romanian Nation. Indeed, this is precisely what was at issue in arguing over Romanian identity: whose definition would prove the most efficacious in claiming resources, whose cultural program was "really" serving *foreign* interests rather than Romanian interests, whose journals did or did not deserve state subsidies? In 1931, Rădulescu-Motru launched an attack on the mysticoid tendencies of the Orthodoxists and demanded that their journals no longer receive government subventions (Ornea 1980: 299). Positions on the national essence tended to become identified with particular publications, which then promoted the names and work of their contributors; set up meetings and activities; solicited subscriptions, ads, and subsidies—which they sometimes obtained from the government or from banks. The pool of resources to support all this intellectual activity was shallow and the aspirants many. The Nation and its defense were a way of shouldering others aside, as not nationally representative. From all sides, not only from indigenists, accusations of "foreign borrowing" and "imitation" rang out:

The traditionalism of Mr. Crainic takes its nomad's tent toward the Orient and byzantinism, invoking in support of autochthonous traditionalism Keyserling,

Unamuno, and Berdiaeff. Here we see the sophistry of this tradition of imported rhetoric, of imitation through the panslavic apocalypse. . . . [Crainic's]
tradition has excommunicated us for our adherence to the Latin idea, only to
protect us with Unamuno and Berdiaeff; it has strangled our Latin reality only
to suffocate us in orientalist weeds, and it has crucified us for negating the
people, only to affirm the people for us in Byzantium (P. Constantinescu 1929:
134–135).

Taken up thus by different groups, these accusations became permanent
weapons of excommunication in the cultural sphere.

    Intellectuals and the Disciplines. This was the environ-
ment—one of budgetary constraints and competition on the one hand,
and educational expansion on the other—within which members of
various academic disciplines argued over the national essence. In so
doing, they contributed to the institutionalization of their activity in a
way quite different from the protectionism discussed earlier: they
produced the structures within which they might continue to argue,
sometimes defending the Nation against those who claimed to serve its
interests through state politics. That is, the debates actively created part
of the material infrastructure that would sustain talk about the Nation,
and in this way they further solidified the Romanian national ideology.
In part through these arguments, academic disciplines were consolidated and differentiated, university departments and chairs established,
research institutes set up, and publications subsidized. The very material of the discourse on nationality provided a means for disciplinary
proliferation. I do not contend that the national discourse *caused* this
proliferation, for disciplines were being established in all western countries during this period and not always through nationalism. I argue
only that the medium within which this larger process was occurring in
Romania was the language of the Nation (rather than a language of science or of social progress, for example), and this fact had consequences
for subsequent scholarly activity.

  The process of disciplinary growth and differentiation in Romania
included claims and counterclaims that one or another discipline had
superior capacity to treat aspects of the national identity. Typical of
such claims is the following rationale one writer offered to promote a
discipline of ethnopsychology distinct from ethnology: "Ethnology has
to do only with *externalities*: distributions, kinship, migrations, customs; it does not occupy itself with the residues all these changes leave
in the spirit of the people, with the psychological substrate" [impor-

tant matters that a discipline of ethnopsychology would treat—k.v.] (Eminescu, cited in Babu-Buznea 1979: 105 n.2). In making claims of this sort, I must emphasize, scholars were not consciously and intentionally manipulating the national idea in the interests of expanding their turf. If their turf did nonetheless expand, this was most probably unintended and shows the material consequences of the national ideology Romanian intellectuals were producing.

The examples one could adduce to illustrate this process are so numerous that some selection must be made. I will begin by showing how the internal definition and the external boundaries of sociology might involve the Nation, and will then give some additional examples from philosophy and psychology. But I note in advance that virtually *any* academic discipline could lay claim to special resources on the grounds of its relationship to the Nation. Such arguments were as available for biology (the study of the ethnic body), geography (the study of the territory that defines the national soul and influences the national character by its physical forms), or applied science (the particulars of soil, climate, population, etc. which will be necessary to solving the Nation's specific problems [see Antipa 1940: 5]) as for sociology (the science of the Nation), history (the study of the Nation's past), or psychology (the study of the national psyche).

To begin with, the Nation and debates about it could enter into divergent definitions of a given discipline, such as sociology. One observer divides the interwar sociological field into three camps—the national-reformist, the national cultural, and the extreme right—whose leaders argued among themselves from different cities on both scientific and political grounds.

Romanian sociology . . . was the terrain of an implicit and explicit ideological battle centering on the problem not so much of the nation in general as of the Romanian nation confronted with internal social contradictions, tested by the plague of fascism, and threatened by external perils (Mihu 1984*b*: 518).

The exponent of the first camp and interwar Romania's most famous sociologist, D. Gusti, defined his agenda thus:

[Sociology as] a positive science, that is, oriented to facts, cannot fail to consider the hierarchy of problems posed by reality itself. From the moment that the nation reveals itself to us as the most significant form of modern social life, the science of society—sociology—must constitute itself as the science of the nation. . . . The science of the nation will determine for it the ethics and politics through which the people will find its true road to self-realization. . . . This science will enable us to establish, at last, the true national ideal, which will not mean an estrangement, a departure from the historical path of the people but a maximum development toward the fulfillment of all its natural capacities (Gusti 1968 [1937]: 493, 506).

In the name of discovering the exact character of Romanian social reality so as to determine the people's true path and then to press for appropriate social reforms, he developed a complex theoretical and methodological system and set the landscape crawling with sociological researchers.

Gusti's definition of sociology did not go unchallenged. His former student P. Andrei, among others, argued that the science of sociology should be more than simply a descriptive and methodologically narrow sociography, built upon innumerable village monographs and aimed at social reform (Mihu 1984b: 528). It should use the data of Romanian social life toward larger theoretical ends. Andrei was deeply read in philosophy and made a sociophilosophical concern with cultural values a major part of his work, seeing his objective as the general study of sociocultural life. Even within this broader vision of sociology, however, he too settled upon the Nation:

The supreme ideal of culture should refer to the whole of humanity, and should be to bring about a cultured humanity without borders . . . . As a result, the bearer of this supreme ideal of culture would have to be humanity as a whole. But since this is too large, at least for our time, what remains as the real substrate, as the active subject, as the social personality that achieves cultural value is *the nation* (Andrei 1945: 236–237, original emphasis).[44]

Thus, even for Andrei the discipline was to be defined in large part by its relation to the Nation, understood more in the abstract than in the concrete, Romanian, sense.[45]

The Nation and its proper treatment could become the basis for contrasting visions and claims upon resources not simply within the discipline itself but also across the border between sociology and other disciplines (across *any* such borders). Against Gusti's definition of sociology, consider a statement by a partisan of psychology:

If our sociology is relatively far advanced because, thanks to [our best researchers] we know aspects of the formation and functioning of some of our classes—the nobility, the gentry, the peasantry, and the bourgeoisie—, Romanian psychology contains not one single chapter, has gathered material for not one single problem, because no one has yet posed a problem for it. And yet no one would disagree that Romanian psychology is every bit as necessary as Romanian sociology (Ralea 1943: 81).

This scholar then makes clear that the proper object for this sorry discipline is the study of *ethnic* psychology. In his reading, sociology really has little to do with the national essence as such: rather, its proper object is the social structure of the national society. For him, a better claim to treating the national essence adequately is offered by psychology.

Arguing sociology's superiority to ethnography, another scholar noted that the rise of national consciousness brought an interest in folklore, which was expected to "enlighten our understanding of the nature and destiny of the Romanian people" but has produced nothing of scientific importance (Herseni 1941: 5). He explains this by the inadequacy of folklore as a discipline, both methodologically (it is too unsystematic) and scientifically (it lacks rigor):

Collections made at random, by persons full of zeal but lacking scientific training, deepen the national sentiment more than they enhance knowledge of ethnic reality and therefore have more an educational and political than a scientific value (ibid., 5).

For scientific knowledge of ethnic reality, he claims, sociology is vastly preferable to ethnography and folklore: it is more than merely a science of *things*, as ethnography often is, and the assumptions it rests on make it a better tool than other disciplines for researching the Romanian people: "Only in collaboration with sociology can ethnography and folklore satisfactorily fulfill their task" (ibid., 13).

An especially lively dispute concerned the border between sociology/ ethnography and philosophy; its protagonists were sociologist Henri Stahl and philosopher Lucian Blaga. Blaga published in the 1930s a philosophy of culture that theorized the national essence and linked it with peasants, village life, and folklore. In response, Stahl flatly rejected Blaga's proposals and contended that sociologists and ethnographers had offered far more plausible accounts of the elements of folk life that Blaga claimed to interpret. Stahl took particular offense at Blaga's speculating upon the Romanian village without actually studying it by any other than armchair means; he resented Blaga's arrogant assumption that because the "Romanian phenomenon" has nothing to do with real historical time or sociological space, philosophy is the only way to study it. Objecting to the implicit sociology in Blaga's philosophy of culture, Stahl comments sarcastically:

Modern sociology affirms that any fact of social life takes a certain form on account of a series of factors [environmental, biological, psychological, and so forth—k.v.] that determine one another reciprocally . . . Mr. Blaga, on the other hand, finds that social phenomena have only a single law: *style*, which springs from a single series of factors: the unconscious. . . . But we find criticism of Mr. Blaga's sociology not only justified but imperative, for in the present day we have embarked upon systematic research into the history and forms of Romanian popular culture. We have barely crossed the threshold of the most abject ignorance and behold! right in our path lies an unexpected obstacle, put there by the enticing formulas of the philosophy of culture . . . [which wants to make] any further study of the Romanian phenomenon superfluous. Mr. Blaga has given us the key to the problem: the style of any Romanian creation is explained for us by his stylistic matrix. . . . The thoughtless ease . . . [with which] he brushes aside scientific research and all other domains but the philosophy of culture irritates those of us who do scientific field research, and we will fight against it (Stahl 1937: 491).

In later essays, even less polite in tone than those of the 1930s, Stahl objects in so many words to Blaga's claim to "monopolize knowledge of the Romanian cultural phenomenon" (1983a: 78).

Whereas sociologists might entwine their discipline around the Nation, others with an aversion to sociology might pry it loose. Crainic, for example, gave an interview with his opinions on Lovinescu's *History of Modern Romanian Civilization*, which he read as a work of "sociological determinism":

This sociological determinism is nothing less than the obliteration of the ethnic personality. It is a pessimistic and erroneous teaching which the vigor of our young nation, still in search of the original expression of its culture, must reject. . . . I do not believe that sociology is a science with iron-clad laws before which an entire people must submit, as before a grim fatality (Şoimaru 1925: 2).

As we have already seen, Crainic was out to expropriate all but religious and perhaps philosophical cultivators of the national essence. Indeed, to the extent that he accepted philosophy at all, his way of defining the essence reserved that discipline effectively to himself, for most other philosophers worked within a rationalist tradition outlawed by Crainic's would-be Orthodoxism. He criticized the "scientific philosophy" of Rădulescu-Motru, for instance, claiming that Orthodoxy was Romanian philosophy's only chance; and one of his disciples contended that good Romanian philosophy would result only from studying the "soul of the people" in the form of rustic spirituality (see Ornea 1980: 284–285).

Extended arguments entwining the Nation with a different kind of philosophy from Crainic's came from Blaga and Rădulescu-Motru, the latter in particular aiming to develop a philosophy and a psychology of the Nation as his goal. Instead of trying to summarize their lengthy and complex works, however, I will make the same point with the briefer and very unusual argument that philosopher V. Băncilă proposed, in an article entitled "The Autochthonization of Philosophy" (1927). The problem Băncilă poses is how one gets from imitating western forms to creating local values and thereby to the creation of autochthonous traditions in science, literature, and other disciplines. He observes that the first spheres of Romanian culture to be thus "autochthonized" were literature and then history, both of them drawing from the West the models and questions with which they treated Romanian themes. Philosophy was late in this process, for philosophy is the highest expression of self-knowledge (Băncilă 1927: 274), and this requires long experience, accumulation of knowledge, and reflection upon it. Philosophy, he claims, cannot be built on imitation. Once autochthonized, however, philosophy has the most important role in any society's cultural life: to *unify the different branches of culture*, to organize the material other disciplines produce into a general harmony—a super-discipline (ibid., 275–276). For this reason, no development in Romanian culture will be of greater value than the autochthonization of philosophy, for no other field enjoys such unifying authority or enables communication across all of intellectual life.

Having in this way made philosophy the heavy industry of intellectual production—one that uses the raw materials of history, ethnography, literature and so forth, nationalizes their results, and concentrates their cultural capital—Băncilă proceeds to a more stunning set of claims. Only after philosophy is autochthonized will certain other disciplines (e.g., psychology and theology) even become possible, for only once an autochthonous philosophy exists will the Nation be fully formed. That is, only philosophy enables the final unification of the Romanian people. "Just as individual character achieves unity . . . only after lengthy reflection has remade it, so peoples achieve a clear and unitary psychology only after a philosophical culture has remade them" (ibid., 276–277). Philosophy will unify and shape the national psyche, helping to generate a "Romanian spirit," which an indigenous psychology can then study (there having been hitherto no unified object for such a science). Thus, philosophy as "heavy industry" (my term) generates further cultural capital in the form of not just new disciplines but a new object of investigation and social action: the people itself, finally complete. He concludes,

Our philosophy must recognize the responsibility it bears through its singular importance for the future of Romanian culture and society. This culture and society cannot enter a higher phase of its own constitution without an autochthonous philosophy . . . (Băncilă 1927: 279).

It is hard to imagine a more remarkable vindication for a discipline's priority with respect to its Nation and its Nation's cultural future.

A final example, this one from ethnography, shows how the Nation, its defense, and a discipline might be linked with expansionary processes furthered by study of the national essence:

It is amazing how all the disciplines that study the people—history, philology, geography, and so forth—have created special institutes in all the universities; only ethnography has nothing but a university department . . . . [He lists some causes of this dismal state of affairs.] Thus postwar *arrivisme* has led to the perversion of ethnicist sentiment and to ignoring the treasures that lie buried in village life. . . . [W]hen the spiritual equilibrium of intellectuals will be reestablished, when the state will consider it a capital obligation to promote ethnographic research, then . . . ethnography will be able to stand with greater success in the service of one of the loveliest missions of all: knowledge of the nation (Pavelescu 1939: 462).[46]

This complaint indicates what I see as a major consequence of the debates on the national essence: their role in producing an institutional environment, a material infrastructure, that was saturated with ideas about the Nation. Between the late 1890s and World War II but particularly after 1918, Romanian universities expanded the numbers of departments and chairs (see Popescu-Spineni 1932), created research institutes, and established other vantage points for pursuing intellectual activity. These chairs, departments, and institutes were sometimes disciplinarily defined by external criteria (what specialties were needed, what European universities were doing, and so forth), but sometimes they were defined by the specialties of the person whose eminence the new department was rewarding. That is, if a philosophy department split into two new departments, their profiles might depend on the specialty of the incumbent professor or the one being brought in. Conversely, at a professor's departure, his chair might be dissolved or redefined.[47]

In these circumstances, I submit, given the national concerns of Romania's new political bureaucracy, it made sense for scholars to compete for eminence and for the institutionalization of their specialties by claiming to treat the Nation and represent its values better than any

other field or scholar. Romanian practitioners of what became institutionalized disciplinary specialties distinguished themselves materially by
appropriating the Nation as their special object and claiming institutional resources on grounds of their expertise in treating it. By these
means, they secured a stable vantage point in university departments
and institutes.[48] I do not wish to suggest that these intellectuals were
single-mindedly pursuing and serving power by their actions—indeed,
many of them thought they were doing just the opposite. Persons
struggling over values believe in them, just as do the writer and readers
of these lines. But I do insist that values are not wholly innocent of the
positions from which they are articulated, in this case positions of cultural production in a resource-poor environment better disposed to the
sciences that would develop industry than to humanists.

The effect of all this carving up of disciplinary turf on the basis of the
Nation was to embed the Nation permanently in intellectual life, which
came to be shot through with it in every sphere of inquiry and creation,
and to bring into existence a more substantial material grounding for
the national form of discourse.[49] "The nation" and "the people" had become the unquestioned basis for every statement made in the debate:
nowhere was anyone asking the question, "Is there such a thing as 'the
Romanian people'?" Despite sometimes-fierce disagreement on the particulars, these notions had become the basis for interaction across the
whole spectrum of political and cultural life. In this sense, the national
discourse can be said to have become a basic ideological premise of all
argumentation in Romania, the linguistic currency both among intellectuals and between them and others actively engaged in politics. If, as
Foucault says (1972: 224), disciplines constitute a system of control in
the production of discourse that continually reactivates a uniform set of
rules within which statements can be made, then the interwar years continued and completed a process of disciplinary definition that made a
particular form of discourse—the national one—an ineradicable feature
of Romanian scholarly life, governing the forms of statements that
might be produced.

This chapter has examined some debates about Romanian identity,
illuminating means whereby a national ideology was constructed that
became hegemonic. The ideological process involved a combination of
discord and harmony among those engaged in them, which obscured
and therefore deepened fundamental shared premises by suppressing
them in argument. The terms that were used had implications for politi-

cal programs even when these were not made explicit: asserting a "western" or "eastern" character for Romanians, for example, invoked political programs for or against capitalist industrialization. The ideological process also constructed through discourse a relation to the lower classes, especially the peasants, that perpetuated their subjection, setting the masses squarely in another camp from those who spoke for them and precluding a new political relationship among groups. It constructed a unitary symbolic space (the Nation) that denied diversity, even as the actual space was rent by diversity. Finally, it entrenched certain values and practices more firmly within institutional structures. These values and practices concerning the Nation fortified it for the encounter it was soon to have with the discourse of Marxism.

Despite massive changes in the class and political structure after 1945, these consequences of the national discourse continued to be felt even within a Romania ruled by the Communist party. Intellectuals continued to argue among themselves and with the Party leadership about the political programs that would best serve the Nation's interests; the arguments continued to reinforce the ideological premises underlying them; and the fate of "the masses" continued to be ignored except rhetorically. Because the debates embedded the Nation deeply not just in intellectual and political discourse but also in institutions supporting intellectual and political life, continued action within these ideologically saturated institutions reproduced Romanian nationalism further, complicating the attempt of the Marxist alternative to secure an institutional foothold.

CHAPTER TWO

Modeling Socialism and Socialist Cultural Politics

From time to time the state, embarrassed by the increasing demand for positions in its service, is forced to open the sluices of the bureaucratic canals in order to admit thousands of new postulants and thus to transform these from dangerous adversaries into zealous defenders and partisans. There are two classes of intellectuals: those who have succeeded in securing a post at the manger of the state, whilst the others consist of those who . . . have assaulted the fortress without being able to force their way in.

—Robert Michels

The communist revolution explicitly proclaimed and ostensibly practiced the unity of power and knowledge, the innermost core of the intellectual idiom.

—Zygmunt Bauman

In the preceding chapter, I showed how arguments about national identity entrenched the Nation in the rhetoric and institutions of intellectual life, particularly in the years before World War II. Although I did not make an explicit argument linking this national discourse to the specifics of its social environment, my discussion implied

72

that two elements were formative. First, many intellectuals made their living as state employees and expanded their disciplines at state expense. State bureaucrats were the people through whom one might gain ground by showing that one's image of Romanian identity, values for it, and manner of attending to it were better—more representative—than those of others. Second, intellectuals also sold their products on a market. Novelists, literary critics writing for a paying clientele, writers of history books, and so on, had every reason—even if they were also partly covered by subventions and grants—to expand the national market for their works and to protect it from too much "foreign" (i.e., western) influence. Their environment was defined, then, by a combination of state handouts and what Anderson (1983) calls "print capitalism."

Romania's metamorphosis from capitalist colony into socialist satellite altered the framework for intellectual activity. It greatly reduced the role of the market and curtailed western influence, while making the state bureaucracy virtually the sole employer and sustainer of culture. The imposition of socialism did not merely change the values of a few existing variables, however: it brought into being a social order driven by wholly different principles. To understand the cultural struggles that took place in socialist Romania and their relationship to national ideology requires formulating these principles explicitly. This chapter presents, therefore, a theoretical framework for analyzing "real socialism" as a social order.[1]

The framework I offer ceased to characterize the East European socialist bloc during the revolutionary year 1989; indeed, its applicability to some of those countries and to the Soviet Union was already diminishing before that year. (Its continued relevance for understanding the Asian socialist states or others that may yet be formed is a question beyond my competence.) Nevertheless, I believe the model I present is appropriate for analyzing East European socialist systems up to that time and may be profitably used by future students of this period in East European history. It is exceptionally well suited for Romania, in particular, up to the overthrow of Ceaușescu. In what follows I will describe the model employed in subsequent chapters and discuss its implications for the production of culture, for the intersection of culture with power, and for the link between these and Romanian national identity. As is usual in describing abstract models of social systems, I use the present tense even though the reality is largely past.

I offer this framework to facilitate not just explanation but also evaluation. In my introductory comments about cultural politics under socialism, I cautioned against favoring certain intellectuals just because they uphold the values of our own scholarly practice, such as the "search for truth," standards of professional competence, and so forth. On what grounds, then, might one take a position on intellectual/political battles like those in this book? I believe I must establish explicit grounds, for the following reason. Western leftists who have not troubled to live in socialist settings may find in some of the battles I describe an anticolonial rhetoric they would wish to support (as, in other circumstances, might I myself). It is as important for me to explain to them why this is the wrong political choice as it is for me to challenge western liberals' automatic support of "truth" and "science."

Readers who lack the taste for complex and obfuscating jargon will be relieved to know that most of it is concentrated in the present chapter. Although my hope is that this theoretical interlude will enrich the subsequent discussion, some readers may prefer to skip this chapter altogether and get on with the show.

The Dynamics of "Real Socialism"[2]

MAXIMIZATION PRINCIPLES AND BUREAUCRATIC ALLOCATION

I will dispense with a thorough review of literature on the nature of socialism and will simply present an analysis distilled from the works I find the most persuasive.[3] Thus, I eschew questions about whether or not socialism is a class society, what its class structure consists of, and so forth—questions with which the analysis of socialism (as a "new class system") began—and move directly to works analyzing the fundamental mechanisms of socialist systems. My taste in theories of socialism is "indigenist": I find the best theorists to be sophisticated "natives," who have better data than outsiders. The following discussion draws chiefly upon writings of the Romanian scholar Campeanu (1988) and the Hungarians Kornai (1980), Konrád and Szelényi (1979), and Fehér, Heller, and Márkus (henceforth FHM 1983). Even though they were not just analysts but participated very directly in the politics of East European intellectual life and contributed to the downfall of the systems they critically described,[4] I find their models far more informative than anything generated in the West.

The most fruitful beginning on the question of socialism's "laws of motion" came, in my opinion, from Konrád and Szelényi (1979). They rejected the question of *ownership* as a starting point for the analysis of socialism and asked instead how the socialist economy is integrated— what legitimates the appropriation of surplus (Konrád and Szelényi 1979: 48; Szelényi 1982: 290 ff.). Socialism's central legitimating principle, they answered, is "rational redistribution," the ideology through which the bureaucratic apparatus justifies appropriating the surplus product and allocating it by priorities the Party has set. From this they defined the "motor" of socialism as the *drive to maximize redistributive power* (in contrast to that of capitalism: the drive to maximize profit) (Szelényi 1982: 318). I rephrase this as "*allocative power*" and speak of bureaucratic allocation rather than redistribution, so as to avoid confusing socialist redistribution with forms more familiar from economic anthropology.

Fehér, Heller, and Márkus phrase the principle somewhat more cumbersomely: "the maximization of the volume of the material means (as use-values) under the global disposition of the apparatus of power as a whole constitutes the goal-function governing the economic activities of the state" (1983: 65). Their aim is to emphasize that maximizing allocative power does not necessarily mean maximizing the *resources available for allocation*, that is, the social surplus. To the contrary: these scholars argue that the "rationality" specific to socialist economies includes their often *sacrificing* an expanded total output, thereby diminishing the potential pool of resources to allocate. What is more important, systemically, than increasing the pool of resources is having the most important ones—especially the resources that generate *more* resources— *under the apparatus's control* so that as much as possible, resources generated within the society remain within the bureaucratic apparatus rather than falling out of it into consumption (FHM 1983: 67–68). When these systems appear to behave irrationally, they are in fact piling up resources that enhance the capacity of the apparatus to allocate. The best example is the "irrational" emphasis of socialist economies on developing heavy industry (which produces more resources and can be centrally controlled) at the expense of consumer industries, whose products fall out of central control into the hands of consumers. This system emphasis is, of course, one cause of the long queues for consumer goods, so characteristic of unreformed socialist societies, and of the widespread "corruption" and cultivation of personal ties that help people to procure things the bureaucracy's love for heavy industry would otherwise deny them.

Campeanu's phrasing of essentially the same point is the leanest: socialism's fundamental dynamic is to accumulate means of production (1988: 117–118). For this, considerations of salability (i.e., of consumption) are truly an obstacle to accumulation rather than, as in capitalism, a condition of it, which helps to explain why socialist economies make goods of such poor quality: "Stalinist monopoly . . . produces the means of production precisely in order not to sell them. Transmitting their non-value to all the salable objects they produce, these unsellable means of production veritably constitute the extraeconomic base of the Stalinist economy" (ibid., 132). Because power is a function of social ownership of the means of production, that is, enhancing the means of production so owned enhances the dominance of the political apparatus that controls them. Although other theorists rationalize it somewhat differently, the crucial emphasis is the same: socialism's central imperative is to increase the bureaucracy's *capacity* to allocate, which is not the same as increasing the amounts to be allocated.[5]

The obverse of this accumulation of resources within the apparatus is the destruction of resources outside it. Because the allocative capacity of a social actor is *relative to that of other actors*, power at the center will be enhanced to the extent that the resources of other actors can be disabled.[6] Other foci of production must be prevented from posing an alternative to the central monopoly on goods. I draw this idea of disablement from Gross's analysis of how the Soviet state incorporated the Polish Ukraine in 1939 (Gross 1988). Calling this state a "spoiler state," Gross argues that its power came from incapacitating actual or potential loci of organization, thus ensuring that no one else could get things done or associate for purposes other than those of the center.[7] The necessity for these systems to disable all organizations of resources outside the center is apparent from the catastrophic effects (for system maintenance) that resulted when alternative organizations emerged, as in Poland and Hungary during the late 1980s.

This tendency of the center works in contradictory relation, however, with one of the most pervasive features of socialist systems: the formation of "second economies," largely external to the formal economic bureaucracy though integrated with it. Because the command system serves consumers so poorly, informal provisioning of consumer goods and services springs up everywhere. Sometimes, as with the "private plot" of collective farm members, such activity is even legal. A bureaucracy that recognizes its incapacity to provide these goods and that fears the social consequences of their unavailability, such as in Hungary, will restrain its tendency to persecute these independent foci of organization, activity, and resources. A bureaucracy like that of Ceauşescu's Romania, more concerned with threats to its monopoly on allocation and prepared to use force if necessary, will persecute—often to the hilt. In Romania, for example, peasants caught selling above the fixed price or found with more than a month's food supply on hand were liable for as much as five years' imprisonment.

Several observations should be made about this analysis. First, it should not be seen as a version of earlier western theories of "totalitarianism" or confused with such theories. It addresses socialist systems from a completely different theoretical angle, and its implications for the analysis of culture are completely different as well. The second observation concerns conscious intent. Although some Party leaders may indeed consciously intend to increase control over means of production—the express emphasis on heavy industry suggests this, for example—the analysis concerns the conscious intention of socialist bureaucrats less than the systemic effects of their behavior. On the whole, bureaucrats are not consciously striving to increase allocative power (Márkus 1981: 246); they are usually preoccupied with fulfilling planned output targets. It is the cumulative effects of bureaucrats fulfilling plans that generates the system's central tendency—the accumulation of allocative power—not consciously strategized as such by any actor.

To see why this is so requires understanding two basic elements of behavior within these systems: bargaining and shortage, on the one hand, and the logic of allocative bureaucracies, on the other. The mechanisms of bargaining and shortage within centrally planned economies have been illuminated by the Hungarian economists Bauer (1978) and Kornai (1980). Fundamental to their arguments is that socialism's producing units operate within *soft budget constraints*—that is, firms that do poorly will be bailed out, and financial penalties for what capitalists would see as "irrational" and "inefficient" behavior (excess inventory, overemployment, overinvestment) are minimal. In consequence, socialist firms do not develop the internal disciplinary mechanisms more often characteristic of firms under capitalism.[8] Because of this, and because central plans usually overstate productive capacities and ratchet output targets higher each year, firms learn to hoard materials and labor. They overstate their material requirements for production, and they overstate their investment needs, in hopes of having enough to meet or even surpass targets, thus increasing their incomes. Whenever a manager encounters bottlenecks in production or fails to meet targets, he can always claim that he will be successful if he receives more investment. Processes of this sort go on at every level of the system: from small firms up to the largest steel combines and on through progressively more inclusive segments of the economic bureaucracy. At each level, manager-bureaucrats are padding their budgets. Thus, these systems have expansionist tendencies that are not just inherent in growth-oriented central plans but are also *generated from below*.

Soft budget constraints and access to bureaucratic favor are not distributed uniformly throughout the economy. Planners view some sectors (heavy industry, armaments) as more strategic and will therefore protect them more extensively. Knowing this, managers of strategic enterprises often argue for and obtain higher investment so as to *preempt* bottlenecks. Claims like theirs set up a gradient, with smaller, less central firms or bureaucratic segments striving to increase their budgets so as to become more strategic and more likely to receive future investments. Moreover, in times of crisis or in the early phases of certain reforms, less strategic sectors may be released from central subsidy into quasi-market conditions, where they have to fend for themselves under harder budgetary conditions. Variability in the hardness of budget constraints can be felt even within a sphere such as cultural production, as chapters 5 and 6 will show.

The result of bargaining and hoarding by enterprises in relation to the center is an "economy of shortage" (Kornai 1980). Hoarding at all levels freezes in place resources that are needed for production somewhere else; all producing units want more inputs than they can get. Shortages are sometimes relative, as when sufficient quantities of materials and labor for a given level of output actually exist, but not when and where they are needed. Sometimes shortages are absolute, owing to the nonproduction that results from relative shortage (or the export of items needed locally, as in 1980s Romania). Because what is scarce and problematic in socialist systems is *supplies*, rather than *demand*, as in capitalist ones, Kornai calls socialist systems *supply-* or *resource-constrained* (as opposed to *demand-constrained* capitalism). The cause of supply constraints is not some planning error but the investment hunger inherent in socialist planning. The combination of expansionist tendencies and insatiable investment demand is the main reason why the productive forces grew so incessantly during socialism's early phases

(1980: 201–202)—feeding, in this way, the central drive of the system as described above, which is to accumulate means of production and allocative capacity.

Allocation is the business of what nearly all theorists of socialism call the "apparatus" and/or the "bureaucracy" (without always being very explicit about what they mean by this).[9] The apparatus is not, however, a unitary organism. Most theorists of it make a distinction I think is crucial for understanding some of the contradictory tendencies in these systems. Fehér et al. speak of the bureaucratic apparatus—an all-embracing mono-organizational entity—on the one hand, and, on the other, of its "pinnacle," "a small circle of the political elite, the Party leadership, where all the basic-orientative decisions concerning the overall distribution of social surplus are made" (FHM 1983: 51, 70). Kagarlitsky speaks of the "bureaucracy" versus the "statocracy" (1988: 123–124, n. 20), Konrád and Szelényi of the bureaucracy versus the Party elite (1979: 153), and Campeanu (1988: 143–157) of the state bureaucracy versus the "global monopoly" or "supreme entity," whose meaning is somewhat obscure in his analysis but seems to reduce to the topmost handful of the Politburo and the Leader.[10]

Campeanu theorizes this distinction between what I will call bureaucracy and center more explicitly than others: he attributes it to the division characteristic of monopolies of all kinds, including capitalist ones—between *ownership* and *management*. Most *ownership* functions, he argues, are monopolized by the center; the role of the bureaucracy is to *manage*. This division suggests ways of discussing one source of conflicting tendencies within socialism, based in the different interests of the body that owns/controls and the body that manages. The contradictory tendencies have something to do, I think, with "reform"—ideas about decentralization, market socialism, and so forth, which, before they changed the system definitively (and unexpectedly) in the 1980s, had appeared a number of times before.[11] Whereas the central "owners" of socialized means of production can persist in policies whose effect is to accumulate means of production without concern for things like productivity and output, the bureaucratic managers of the allocative process *must* be concerned with such things. There are two sets of reasons for this: processes involving bureaucrats' prestige, and the realities of their role as "allocators."

Behind the bureaucratic expansionism-within-shortage described above are competitive processes perhaps analogous to the dilemmas faced by entrepreneurs in capitalism.[12] Constrained by demand, capitalists strive for ever-greater domestication (predictability) of the demand structure, through such devices as advertising and through softening the budget constraints of consumers via credit and consumer debt.[13] In a supply-constrained system, by contrast, what must be domesticated is supplies: everyone scrambles for access to the pot.[14] At all points in the system, bureaucratic positions or jobs are used as a platform for amassing resources. Personal influence, "corruption," and reciprocal exchanges are some of the major mechanisms. This sort of behavior goes on throughout the society but is especially important for bureaucrats, whose entire reputation and prestige rest upon their capacity to amass resources. Any bureaucrat, any bureaucratic segment, tends to feed the expansion of its own domain, increasing its capacity to give out—whether the "gift" be education, apartments, permission to publish, medical care, social welfare, wages, funds for investments in factory infrastructure, or something else. Throughout the bureaucracy, then, there is rampant competition to increase one's budget at the expense of those roughly equivalent to one on a horizontal scale, so as to have potentially more to disburse to claimants below. That is, what counts most in the competition among social actors within allocative bureaucracies is *inputs to one's segment*, rather than outputs of production (Stark 1988: 48).[15]

In the redistributive systems common to literature in anthropology, chiefs redistribute goods to their followers, just as socialist bureaucrats allocate social rewards. The limits on a chief's power, as on a socialist bureaucrat's, come from the *power of other chiefs* to siphon followers away by giving—or creating the impression that they *can* give—bigger and better feasts or more generous loans. Like chiefs in such redistributive systems, bureaucrats are constantly under pressure not to be outdone by other bureaucrats: they must continue to strive for influence, amass more resources, and raise the standing of their segment of the bureaucracy. The competition characteristic of socialism consists of always trying to get more allocable inputs than others at one's level, so one can move up closer to the privileged circle that always gets whatever it asks for (the Soviet military, for example, until the mid-1980s).

Within this context, social actors at all levels must justify why they, rather than some other actor or unit, should receive allocations. This is true of enterprise managers, local administrative officials, government ministers, editors of publishing houses, individual authors or scholars—that is, the principle is pervasive. Understanding it is fundamental, for only if the basic form of competition is seen in these terms rather than in terms of competing capitals will the various claims upon resources for cultural production, to be discussed later in this book, make any sense.

This discussion of inputs suggests a problem. As I argued earlier, maximizing allocative *capacity* is not the same as maximizing the actual surplus—the concrete disposable resources over which a bureaucrat makes allocative decisions. But at some point, real resources do have to be delivered, and for this a bureaucrat's allocative reputation is not always enough. This is especially true in the domain of economic production, heavy industry above all. Without actual investments and hard material resources, lower-level units cannot produce the means of production upon which both bureaucracy and center rely. Productive activity cannot be so stifled that nothing gets produced, or the prestige of those who supposedly allocate would enter a crisis. Thus, I suggest that when central accumulation of means of production begins to threaten the capacity of lower-level units to produce; when persistent imbalances between investment in heavy industry and in light industry, between allocations for investment and for consumption, and so forth, cause a decline in the accumulation of actual allocable goods; and when the center's attempts to keep enterprises from interfering in the process of appropriation actually obstruct the process of production itself: then pressure arises for a shift of emphasis. The pressure is partly from those in the wider society to whom not enough is being allocated and partly from bureaucrats themselves whose prestige and, increasingly, prospects of retaining power depend on having more goods. One then hears of decentralization, of the *rate of growth*, of *productivity*—in a word, of matters of *output*, rather than the inputs that are the heart of bureaucratic performance. The intrusion of concern with output means, of course, the intrusion of mechanisms inimical to expanding allocative capacity. The most obvious of these is the introduction of freer markets, which socialism as a rule suppresses precisely because they move goods *laterally* rather than—as all redistributive systems require—vertically towards the center.[16]

Inherent in the different demands that management—as opposed to "ownership"—of social resources places on an allocative bureaucracy, then, is the necessity to see to it that resources are actually generated (and not merely by more coercive extraction, as in 1980s Romania): that the centralization of means of production does not stifle production altogether. Thus, quite aside from the so-called "second" or informal economies that flourish at the edges of the command economy, one finds within the apparatus of management itself an interest in mechanisms that subvert the system's central logic. Similarly to capitalism, where, in Marx's view, the goal-function of the economy is to maximize surplus value but the subjective aim of capitalists is to maximize profit (not the same thing)—that is, subjective intention feeds something different from what accumulation objectively requires—so in socialist systems the goal-function of the economy is to maximize allocative capacity and control over means of production, but the subjective aim of at least some bureaucrats and enterprise managers some of the time is to maximize production of a disposable surplus.

This introduces into the system a subordinate rationality not wholly consonant with the overriding logic, a rationality hinting that the center cannot set values with impunity as if there were no such thing as actual production costs. When this subordinate rationality is amplified by events that bind socialism's dynamic with that of capitalism—through international credits and indebtedness to western banks, for example, with the ensuing necessity of hard-currency exports that require a concern with salability—then the tension between the central logic of command and the subordinate "counterrationalities" will intensify. This sharpens the conflict between command and market, centralization and decentralization, investment and consumption (FHM 1983: 270–271).[17] Campeanu summarizes the resulting tensions between center ("supreme entity") and bureaucracy:

Thus a potential for revolt against the supreme entity is inscribed in the genetic code of Stalinist bureaucracy. Actualized in the hidden form of imperceptible but formidable daily pressures, this potential has drawn the bureaucracy into all the major conflicts which, from 1956 to the present, have shaken Stalinist societies. On each of these occasions, its inherent ambiguity has regularly divided its ranks into one segment which defended the supreme entity and another which contested it. . . . This potential for revolt nourishes the organic mistrust the supreme entity has of its bureaucracy, which in turn nourishes their historical tendency to transform their separation into conflict (1988: 148).

From these tensions, I believe, emerged Mikhail Gorbachev's attempt to reform the Soviet system and the East European socialisms along with it. His throwing the weight of his own reformism behind potentially reformist bureaucratic segments in the other socialist states ultimately had the effect of fracturing monolithic Parties, exposing their actual or potential fragility to restive publics, and destroying Communist party rule. The series of progressively more dramatic confrontations through which this came about culminated in the violent overthrow of Nicolae Ceauşescu's communist dictatorship in Romania, its violence fed precisely by the relentlessness with which this Party apparatus, above all others in the bloc, had accumulated social resources in its own hands, devastated productive capacity, and left the public destitute.[18]

WEAK STATES AND THE MODE OF CONTROL

The preceding section has treated socialism's "laws of motion" and some of its bureaucratic politics. In this section I discuss some features of socialist states, particularly their inherent weakness and their principal modes of controlling their populations. The breathtaking speed with which Communist party leadership in Eastern Europe collapsed in the face of public opposition during 1989 makes it gratuitous to argue what would have been regarded, even in September or October of that year, as a rather contentious view: that contrary to their original "totalitarian" image, socialist states were weak. Arguments to this effect had been emerging not only for Eastern European polities but for China as well.[19] Although it is now less necessary to justify this view, I ought nonetheless to suggest why these states proved as weak as they did.

We can conceptualize socialism's weak states from three different angles, each employing a somewhat different definition of power. Jan Gross makes one kind of argument. Implicitly defining power as the capacity to get things done, he contends that "to gain a fresh insight into the essence of the political process under communism we must revise our notions about the monopolization of power by communist parties" (1989: 208). He argues that the power monopoly of socialism's "spoiler" states destroys the state's capacity to get things done and thereby weakens it. "The image of Stalin's Russia as a gigantic, all-powerful, centralized terror machine is wrong": a state that attains its "power" by denying power to any other social actor is not a powerful state, and it crumbles the instant an effective social challenge arises (1988: 232–233). To the extent that Stalin's state appeared all-powerful, the reason was a pervasive "privatization" of the instruments of coercion, which—far from being concentrated somewhere at the top—were made available to everyone, through the mechanism of the *denunciation*: "The real power of a totalitarian state results from its being at the disposal of every inhabitant, available for hire at a moment's notice" (1988: 120).[20] This is a dispersed kind of power, and the kind that remains at the center is purely the vacuum left after all foci of organization around the center have been destroyed: "Hence the perplexing 'weakness' of these all-powerful regimes" (Gross 1989: 209).

A second argument for the weakness of socialist states defines power as a relationship of dependency: any social actor that depends heavily upon another for a crucial resource or performance that cannot be gotten elsewhere is not powerful, no matter how many means of coercion lie at its disposal (Emerson 1962). Bauer (1978) and Rév (1987) argue, for example, that the political center in socialist systems is utterly dependent upon lower-level units for accurate production figures, which exist only at the point of production where the center exercises minimal control. This lack of control debilitates, because without such figures the center cannot plan. But lower-level units *never* deliver reliable figures, either because they fear the consequences of failed targets or because they wish to continue inflating their investment requests (see also Kagarlitsky 1988: 80). Because central agencies have inadequate information, they cannot easily detect excessive investment claims, which makes it impossible for them to resist the expansionist drive from below. A related argument emerges from the implications of the shortage economy for the strength of the political center. Bargaining and hoarding by firms make labor a scarce item within socialist economies; structurally speaking, that is, labor has considerable implicit leverage, as Solidarity and the Soviet miners' strikes made very clear. (Thus, a major analytic problem has been to understand how this implicit leverage has been undercut; see, e.g., Burawoy 1985: ch. 4). Since bureaucratic monopoly over productive resources relies, ultimately, on workers' labor, this source of leverage—even when it is not overtly manifest—is structurally debilitating to the state.

A third kind of argument mixes the two above definitions, seeing power as a capacity (to enact policies) mitigated by the center's dependency (on intermediate and lower-level cadres). Policies may be *made* at the center, but they are *implemented* in local settings, where those entrusted with them may ignore, corrupt, overexecute, or otherwise adulterate them. This sort of argument is especially common in the work of anthropologists, who have observed at close range some of the many ways in which local executors of central policy bend and redefine it in accord with their own styles of leadership, their capabilities for enforcement, and so on (see, e.g., Hann and Sampson MS; Kideckel 1982; also Bialer 1988: 79).

Whatever argument one prefers, each brings to the fore a basic question about socialism's mode of domination: how can such a relatively weak state control its subordinates, particularly the masses (as opposed to the bureaucrats, who, being advantaged by the system, pose less of a threat to its continuity)? Control over the means of production, and power to limit consumption, give socialist leaderships extensive command over labor in the aggregate and do much to keep subordinates passive, but these are not sufficient. Because leaders cannot use labor markets, firings, lockouts, unemployment, bankruptcies, and so forth, the means for disciplining labor under socialism are much less subtle and varied than those available to capitalists. Even in regimes of maximum coercion, such as Romania in the late 1980s, workers do not necessarily perform as the center might wish. Although in some respects the central apparatus is more interested in arousing public *awe* than in building public legitimacy (Jowitt 1983: 282), the bureaucracy responsible for managing society wants not subjects who are awe-struck but subjects who are compliant. This invites us, then, to problematize the notion of "control" and to inquire into the various forms through which socialist regimes have sought to achieve it.

Several scholars have approached this problem by looking specifically at the mechanisms for controlling labor power and the labor process. To the extent that the labor power of working people is what generates the wealth with which these systems operate, control over the labor of others is a crucial component of social power (see, e.g., Böröcz 1989; Humphrey 1983: 124, 300–316, 370). What modes of control can we identify, and how do they relate both to the central dynamic of socialist systems and to the matter of nationalism? In his consideration of the first of these questions, Böröcz suggests that there are two main modes of exercising social control: the market, and "political means" (Böröcz 1989: 289). An alternative possibility comes from Burawoy's discussion of "production regimes," in which he too refers to market forces but also brings in varying political means that include degrees of consent or coercion (Burawoy 1985: 12). His discussion brings to mind Skinner and Winckler's (1969) treatment of "compliance succession" in China, which, although it lacks a model of socialist systems, contains a helpfully differentiated view of social control. Skinner and Winckler suggest that at any given time, a complex organization (including socialist bureaucracies) may be pursuing one or more of three kinds of strategies to secure the compliance of its subordinates. The authors define these strategies, which I will call modes of control, as remunerative (relying on material incentives), coercive (relying on force), and normative (relying on moral imperatives, societal norms, or other ideological appeals). The normative instability of socialist societies leads me to call this third control strategy "symbolic-ideological" rather than normative.

Within socialism's bureaucratic mode of domination, then, I speak of these three modes of control. Remunerative strategies entail giving markets a role in allocating goods and labor; these have formed the heart of most efforts by communist leaderships to reform the system. Coercive strategies entail not just systematic use of police and security forces but an attempt to *minimize* nonofficial or market-derived sources of income, for these reduce people's vulnerability to coercion. Symbolic-ideological strategies entail outright exhortations and also attempts to saturate consciousness with certain symbols and ideological premises to which subsequent exhortations may be addressed.

We might further subdivide symbolic-ideological strategies according to their potential bases of appeal: to norms of kinship and friendship, important in organizing informal networks and local solidarities; to the emancipation of the proletariat and other tenets of Marxism/ Leninism; to standards of living and material comfort. The third of these, sometimes referred to as "the new social contract," was an important auxiliary to the remunerative control strategy used in Hungary during much of the 1970s and early 1980s, as well as at various times in East Germany, Czechoslovakia, and Poland under Gierek. A final form of appeal that symbolic-ideological control strategies can emphasize is to patriotism and sacrifice for the Nation. Here, at last, we see a role for national ideology, as part of a mode of control that is primarily symbolic-ideological and that eschews appeal to standards of living or local solidarities. This was the situation in Romania of the 1970s and 1980s, where leaders made heavy use of symbolic-ideological appeals to the Nation, alongside ineffective appeals to Marxist-Leninist norms.

In Skinner and Winckler's formulation, the three modes are not pure types but constitute a mix, with one or another element predominating at one or another time and reflecting the balance of social forces within the apparatus of leadership. This crucial point must be kept in mind, for in my frequent references to "symbolic-ideological control," in the rest of this book, it would be easy to read a denial of the major role of coercion, in all East European socialist systems but especially in the Romanian one. The manner in which the Czech, East German, and Romanian regimes fell made it obvious that coercion had been their first pillar: as soon as it became clear that those Parties did not fully control the means of destruction—that the Czech and East German leaders could not rely on locally based Soviet troops in order to retain power, and that the Romanian army had sided with the rebels—their rule was over. Perhaps more than any other, the Ceauşescu regime rested on co-ercion, to which symbolic strategies were at best an important supple-ment. Greater or lesser reliance on coercion was part of the mix of con-trol strategies in all these regimes, then, however much more visible remuneration or symbolic appeals may have been.

Socialism and Cultural Production

The above discussion of the nature of socialist systems had as its purpose to clarify the environment in which socialism's cul-tural producers work. On this theme, theories of socialist systems (Konrád and Szelényi excepted) tend toward the inarticulate. They rarely pursue the full implications of their new-class theory or owner-ship theory or goal-function theory for how *meaning* is produced and controlled in socialist systems. Literature on cultural production in other social orders is not much help, for such thinkers as Bourdieu (1984, 1988) and Williams (1982) frame their analyses explicitly in terms of capitalist markets; yet the suppression of the market in socialist systems means that except when reforms reintroduce market mecha-nisms into its sphere, culture ceases to be a commodity. The following arguments must be seen as exploratory, aiming to suggest what the properties of socialist systems might imply for the relation of intellec-tuals to power and for their behavior within socialist society.[21] This does not mean that in other kinds of society, power has no interest in intellectuals or in knowledge production, merely that in socialism the reasons for its interest are particular.

We might begin with a 1988 observation from a Romanian emigré: "Of all the social strata of today's Romania, the only one whose aspira-tions bring it into touch with that domain which power considers in-alienable is the intellectuals" (Solacolu 1988: 28). How is this so? One answer comes from Konrád and Szelényi: the legitimating myth of the system, "rational redistribution," gives the Party a monopoly on "teleo-logical knowledge," the knowledge necessary to setting and implement-ing goals for society, knowledge of the laws of social development and of the path to realizing progress (cf. Szelényi 1982: 306). Yet at the same time, the Party creates educated persons—a larger pool than it requires, so as to permit selection. Some of them specialize precisely in knowledge of society and social values, and not all of these people become (or want to become) apparatchiks. For this very reason, these two theorists see the intellectuals as a class-in-formation: because their form of work'makes them basic to reproducing the inequality on which the allocative bureaucracy rests. By sharing with intellectuals a legitimation resting on claims to knowledge and by creating a stratum of knowledge-empowered persons, the Party reinforces a privileged situation for intellectuals, even as it reinforces its own (Bauman 1987a: 178).[22] One need scarcely look further than the slogans "The Party knows best" or "The Party is always right" to see in their most blatant form knowledge claims that intellectuals can easily contest, having the means to posit alternative values that might influence how resources are allocated and goals set.

Socialism's intellectuals are therefore both necessary and dangerous: necessary because their skills are implied in determining social values, and dangerous because they and the center have potentially different notions of what intellectual practice should consist of. When—as often happens—these notions do not agree, a conflict emerges over who has the authority to define intellectual work: those who *do* it, or those who *order* it. For those who order it, matters are clear. From the heyday of Stalin's culture-czar Zhdanov onward, the apparatus sees cultural production as a minor category of ideological activism and the function of art as indoctrination, providing clear answers to social questions (Condee and Padunov 1987: 13). Romanian writers report endless exchanges with censors, who call into question everything from words used to the artist's judgment in framing a story. For example, "Why does the hero die at the end? What do you mean, he's killed? A crime? But crimes are not representative of our socialist spirit. . . . Hey, you can't hang the fellow, he's the driver for the collective farm!!" (Solacolu 1988: 28). In all this we see the tangled relation between a Party that thinks of itself as directing all aspects of society according to specialized knowledge and the potential revolt of those whom it has created to help in this task.[23]

These examples merely underscore the point made more abstractly in my Introduction: intellectuals are defined as occupying the "space of legitimation," a space of vital concern to a bureaucracy needing performances and compliance from its subjects. All intellectuals work with the symbolic means that form subjectivities; their talents are essential to power, and above all to any leadership or any period in which a sym-bolic-ideological mode of control is important. The nature of intellec-tual work is such that all new regimes must seek to capture its producers and its products; socialist regimes are no exception. To the question of whether socialist systems show a special form of this general truth, I have suggested that the double legitimation of Party and intellectuals via knowledge constitutes one peculiarity in the Party's relation to intel-lectual work. Another comes from socialism's "laws of motion."

I have proposed as socialism's "motor" the systemic drive to accumu-late allocative power, rooted in accumulating means of production. Is there some way in which *culture's* means of production are susceptible also to this tendency? If one asks what constitute the means of cultural production, one immediately thinks (besides such things as printing presses, paper, paints, and the other material means) of certain forms of accumulated knowledge that serve as means of further cultural produc-tion: dictionaries, encyclopedias and other compendia, publication of documentary sources, treatises and works of synthesis—such as the offi-cial four-volume History of Romania published in the 1960s and in-tended as the point of orientation for all subsequent writing in that dis-cipline. In socialist Eastern Europe, all these were produced by large collectives, in public institutions, benefiting from huge allocations of funds for culture. There is every reason to believe that these projects were won for their institutes through the processes of competition and bargaining described above (see also chapter 6). The importance of these cultural equivalents of heavy industry means that they must be produced by "reliable" institutions under the guidance of the Party. To see the apparatus as having a conscious concern with monopoly over such means of production does not seem far-fetched.

There is another means of cultural production, more basic even than the ones just mentioned: language. For a Party bent on transforming consciousness, control over language is one of the most vital require-ments. Gross captures an aspect of this when he writes that communist rule changes language so it no longer reflects or represents reality; metaphor becomes more important than prosaic discourse, and magical words replace descriptive and logical ones (Gross 1988: 236–238). But whereas Gross sees this as an aspect of the destruction of language, I see it as the retooling of language *qua* means of ideological produc-tion. I would develop this thought further with Bakhtin's discussion of authoritative discourse—any religious, moral, political, parental dis-course, which demands that we acknowledge it and make it our own:

"We encounter it with its authority already fused to it" (1981: 342). This discourse is not one to be selected from a range of equivalent possibilities: it imposes itself and demands unconditional allegiance. The semantic structure of such discourse is static, and its terms have been cleansed of all but one meaning; it is often marked by a special language or a different script (ibid., 343).[24] Gross might have said, then, that socialist power seeks to make all language authoritative discourse, to reduce the meanings of words, to straitjacket them into singular intentions, and to preclude any use of language that permits multiple meanings.[25] Although one could argue that all regimes are concerned with language to some extent, I would hold that socialist ones lie at the extreme on this dimension.

As a result of the attempt to create an "authorized" language, *all* language becomes a terrain shaped by power and contested by those who resist the centralization of meanings. Producers of words populate these words with objectives that might be suspect; the center must therefore keep language under constant surveillance. Party officials understand Bakhtin very well:

[I]n the makeup of almost every utterance spoken by a social person—from a brief response in casual dialogue to major verbal-ideological works (literary, scholarly and others)—a significant number of words can be identified that are implicitly or explicitly admitted as someone else's, and that are transmitted by a variety of different means. Within the arena of almost every utterance an intense interaction and struggle between one's own and another's word is being waged, a process in which they oppose or dialogically interanimate each other. The utterance so conceived is a considerably more complex and dynamic organism than it appears when construed simply as a thing that articulates the intention of the person uttering it, which is to see the utterance as a direct, single-voiced vehicle for expression (Bakhtin 1981: 354–355).

What is true of everyday utterance is true in spades for utterances in the "space of legitimation."

This is so because we are not speaking, in the end, of language as merely a means for cultural production, but of both language and cultural products as vehicles for the formation of consciousness and subjectivity: as means of *ideological* production, of producing ideological effects. If, as I argued in the Introduction, characteristic of socialist societies is their nonexistent hegemony and their fragile legitimacy, their constant vulnerability to the persuasiveness of alternative visions, including those that emanate from the West; and if Gramsci is right that any alternative vision undermines the formation of hegemony; then no socialist regime can countenance the production of ideological effects contrary to its purposes, effects that would reveal its nakedness.

Beyond even this, however, the categories of language and of discourse *produce the social world*. Language and discourse are among the *ultimate* means of production. Social objects, consciousness, social life itself, are constituted in discourse, which can create objects formerly "unthinkable" (such as a "patriotic communist") and can undermine the "thinkability" of existing objects (such as a "fascist patriot" [Laclau MS: 12–13]). Although social objects, consciousness, and social life are also constituted through practices that are *not* articulated in discourse (Bourdieu 1977), in socialist systems language takes on special significance as a constitutor of social life precisely because a new order of society-generating practices has not been regularized, does not function reliably.[26] For a political regime such as this, where discourse has a disproportionately productive role, and especially for one whose self-proclaimed task is to change society, the producers of discourse *must* be incorporated within the regime. The argument about socialism's "weak state" makes this even more imperative, for it suggests that only in discourse can the power and unity of such a state be achieved: "The state is at best a fragmented subject that imagines itself a unity. . . . Despite its imaginary basis, however, [it] proves more solid than any other reality and its effects are stronger than any element of the real" (Anagnost 1988: 3).

I have been speaking so far of a struggle to control language between agents of Party rule and intellectuals as a group. But this struggle merely explains why culture is so politicized in socialist societies. What my earlier discussion of socialism's logic suggests, however, and what I hope to show in some of these chapters, is that the more telling arena of conflict is *within* the intellectuals' terrain. The Party sets up an educational system that produces more intellectuals than its "ideological apparatus" can absorb. Those whose thinking is congenial and whose ambitions permit a collaboration with power enter into alliance with it. The remainder, whose preference or unsuitability excludes them, are left with a sense that they are *entitled* to influence—on the basis of their knowledge—but they can achieve it only by claiming that their knowledge or artistic creativity constitutes separate grounds for status. For them, that is, influence depends upon their gaining recognition for their *cultural authority* as something independent of the political status to which the Party wants to restrict the exercise of cultural power.

Such persons are likely to find the route to influence blocked by other intellectuals whose representations to bureaucrats are more convincing; by those with better personal connections; by those who are older and better known; by those who have managed to secure seats in the institutions through which culture's production is supposedly regulated. This sets up an opposition between producers of culture who feel themselves excluded from influence and those they see as blocking their path. Their opposition becomes a contest for larger allocations of the resources for cultural power. It is not, I stress, a contest simply between "intellectuals" and "the Party," or (*pace* Kagarlitsky [1988: 103]) between "government ideologists" and "dissidents"—although on the surface, the politicization of culture makes it *look* as if those who defend their cultural authority are doing so from a dissident position. The contest is, rather, between fractions of the cultural elite, differentially empowered within a system of domination that requires and supports the production of culture while allowing influence to only some of its producers.

The "space of legitimation," the "intellectual territory" referred to in the Introduction, has different positions in it, then. I define these by a mix of entitlements on two coordinates, modified from Bourdieu. Whereas Bourdieu defines the social space of cultural "distinction" in France as a two-dimensional one whose coordinates are economic and cultural capital, each of them matters of degree (fig. 1), I see the space of cultural politics in socialism as framed by the two coordinates of political status and cultural authority (see fig. 2).[27] The political dimension consists of holding formal bureaucratic office (Minister of Culture and Education, activist for culture and propaganda, head of a research institute, director of a publishing house, dean of a university) and/or titles having some political significance (president of the Writers' Union, head of the National Commission of Historians, president of the Academy, etc.). The "cultural" dimension consists of recognized cultural (or scientific or creative) authority—novelists and poets whose works have become well known, critics with a regular column in a cultural publication, members of the Academy (in Romania, most meaningful if elected between about 1955 and 1975), widely published scholars, university professors often appealed to for television or radio talks, and so forth. Position is more difficult to define on this coordinate than on the other because assessments of cultural authority are divided by the politicization of the cultural field, to which later chapters give witness. That is, people's factional allegiances influence whose cultural authority they will acknowledge. Even so, the authority of certain persons is recog-

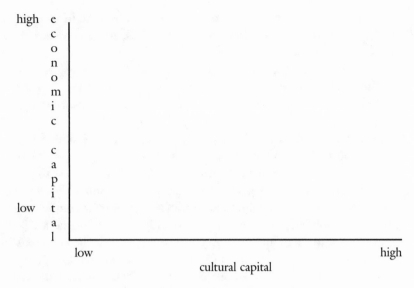

Figure 1 * *Coordinates of the Space of Culture in Capitalist Systems*

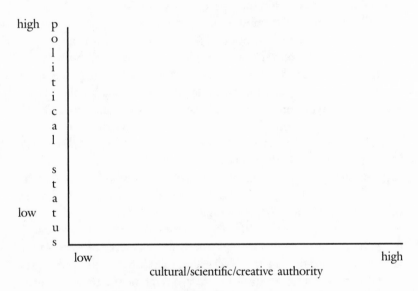

Figure 2 * *Coordinates of the Space of Cultural Politics in Socialism*

* Adapted from Bourdieu 1984: 128–129. Bourdieu's diagram extends its two axes to form four quadrants; it labels the vertical axis "capital volume" and the horizontal axis "+economic capital/−cultural capital" and "−economic capital/+cultural capital." My aim being simpler than his, I collapse this into the illustrative diagram shown in figs. 1 and 2, each axis representing volume of "capital" from low to high.

nized by all factions (for example, two who will be discussed in chapters 6 and 7, historian Prodan and philosopher Noica), as the competition to "capture" these scholars confirms.

The processes that take place within this field of positions are crucially framed by the mechanisms of bureaucratic allocation. This means two things. First, many participants strive continually to justify claims to resources, and in this process ideas about the Nation and "proper" representation of its values play a vital part. Second, there is a tendency for those pursuing greater cultural authority to seek some degree of upward mobility on the political dimension, so as to ensure access to the resources necessary for their activity. That is, the organization of the society presses cultural producers to convert some of their cultural authority into political status, which may then be used to augment cultural standing through increased access to resources. It is the rare intellectual, free of institutional pressures and laden with cultural authority—such as Prodan and Noica, just mentioned—who can continue to work at the lower righthand side of figure 2 without seeking to migrate northward within that space.

Because cultural and knowledge claims are intellectuals' only justification, however—that is, because they are constrained from directly exercising political power—the currency of the competition will be a defense of culture, of "authentic" values, of standards of professionalism and knowledge. (In the same way, Elias argues, German intellectuals in the eighteenth and nineteenth centuries, excluded from bourgeois activity, took their stand on the values of culture and the spirit [1978: 8–22].) Often these will be wrapped around definitions of national identity and national values. The stakes are who gets to write the school manuals that present a particular version of reality, or to produce an official history, or to define the literary "canon," or to render the lineage of philosophical knowledge; whose books will be published, and in what press runs; whose projects will receive investments that will facilitate still other investments later; whose works will receive prizes—valuable not because they increase sales and, therefore, incomes, as in the capitalist world, but because the mere receipt of the prize enhances one's claims to future allocations and promotes the values on which one has staked one's work (which may include, covertly, values of resistance to the totalizing effects of Party rule). Authors under socialism need mass publics to buy their works less than they need the attention of bureaucrats who will fund their projects.

I emphasize again, as I did in the Introduction, that I do not wish to reduce all intellectual activity to a quest for power. Some producers of culture are indeed opportunists looking for a route to power, but most are deeply committed to the notion of truth or value that they serve and for which they passionately argue. To prefer one over another value, however, one over another truth, *is political* in these systems, because these values and truths are reproduced only through claims made in their behalf and allocations made in their name. Such preferences and struggles also have political consequences, for as groups compete, those who win may do so by depriving their adversaries of what is necessary for cultural production. They may thereby also accomplish the center's work of disabling alternative foci of cultural activity.

As different kinds of intellectuals strive to support their values with bureaucratic outlays, or to win bureaucratic positions themselves, they must sometimes challenge the hierarchies already in place, attacking persons who already hold or seem to be gaining important titles and offices. There are several means for such an attack; I wish to mention three that relate to the above discussion. These three are invocations of market principles, concern with an audience, and alliance with the West.

I suggested above that uncontrolled markets are anathema to socialist systems because they move resources horizontally, rather than to and from the center—the movement proper to redistributive systems. The market as a distributive mechanism disrupts the constituted hierarchies of command. During periods of reform, when market mechanisms begin to affect the sphere of culture, talk about the market may reveal anxiety about its actual or potential effects in disrupting constituted hierarchies (see chapter 5). Even when culture is insulated from markets in fact, its real effects also make the market useful symbolically, for opposing whoever sits higher up on the ladder. To invoke the market in arguments about cultural production is to object to the constituted hierarchy, to seek to undermine it by invoking a rationality different from the one of centralized allocations. References to the market in cultural struggles often accompany more directly relevant questions about the values writers or scholars should be implementing—should novels treat only themes relevant to socialism, what place should ethnic identity have in a class analysis, can historians do pure intellectual history or must they also bring in the forces and relations of production, is Marxism the only form of philosophy, by what standards does one evaluate a piece of writing or a work of art, and so on. Questions of that kind and references to the market both have the same effect: they challenge an opponent's position and seek to deny it a higher place in the structure of cultural command.[28]

Second, I observed above that producers' attention goes more to the bureaucrats from whom they receive allocations than to the wider public; yet this is an oversimplification. Are there circumstances in which specialists in culture will want or be compelled to take their case to the public, to build or appeal to an audience? In general, they would have little reason to do so for purposes of marketability, which is of less importance than in capitalism: their revenues come more from the center than from sales. To the extent that market influences enter the cultural sphere and increase its commodification (as happened in Romania after 1978, for example), this will initially intensify the scramble for the few resources the center still allocates. Attention may also turn, however, to a mass audience, partly to win a readership and partly to convince the center to allocate more, on the grounds that one's activities are reaching a wide public and might have an effect on mass consciousness. Beyond this, producers of culture may appeal to an audience as part of forming a "cognizant public" (see Introduction; also chapter 4) who will recognize their claims to cultural authority. Some of these claims may support values alternative to those of the center; in such cases, appeals to an audience will challenge constituted hierarchies not by forming public "demand" (as would happen with mass appeals in a market system) but by setting up foci of meaning-production outside the control of the apparatus. We would expect the authorities to obstruct or disable appeals of this kind.

Third, in socialist cultural politics the challengers to existing hierarchies dispose of a potent weapon that is, in fact, constitutive of many of the arguments: invocation of "the West." Because the logic of socialist systems is opposed to the rationality of western political economies; because such western-linked notions as "market" and "competence" are antithetical to the bureaucratic principles of allocative command and patronage; because any refusal to accept the Party's rules and values automatically looks, to westerners, like dissidence; and because the societies of Eastern Europe are subaltern societies with subaltern cultures struggling for recognition in a world dominated by the more powerful West: for all these reasons, "the West" is a natural participant in cultural struggles. Within any contest among Eastern European intellectuals, a fraction that is trying to improve a disadvantageous situation may end by rhetorically allying itself with the West, whether by choice or by default. This alliance inserts into struggles over cultural values a representation of interests and identities that ties "the Nation" with the western heritage. The alliance has also itself constituted a re-source, for it has often brought external pressure to bear on leaderships that discovered, during the 1970s, how vulnerable their economies were to the noxious effects of western penetration.

I return to the matter of socialism's dynamic and its implications for culture. Contests of the above kind within the world of cultural produc-tion, contests that join intellectuals in struggle with one another and that link segments of them with the Party or in opposition to it, may ultimately serve to concentrate means of symbolic production within the apparatus of power. Claims and counterclaims directed at the bu-reaucracy for allocations that will sustain culture's producers are what animate the abstract tendency, whose systemic rationale I have dis-cussed earlier in the chapter, for the center to acquire "allocative capac-ity" even over the symbolic constitution of society. Such contests also animate the corollary tendency for central control to grow by disabling or destroying alternate foci of production and accumulation (discussed earlier in this chapter). Leaders trying to install a new symbolic order will aim to destroy or absorb into the political apparatus alternative orders and alternative meanings not yet bent to a new will. Wars are declared on cultural accumulations of an older era (intellectuals are purged, older authors are removed from bookshelves, school texts are rewritten), as new accumulations are slowly amassed to replace them.[29] The possibility of different claims and justifications, of a differ-ent construction of reality, that these older forms contain cannot be per-mitted to flourish. The extreme of this declared war is to be found in Pol Pot's Kampuchea or in Ceauşescu's Romania of the 1980s, with the razing of churches and buildings and entire villages that signify an "out-moded" social world.

These processes of the centralization of meanings and the attempted disablement of inconvenient older significances are illustrated in chap-ters 4 through 7. It remains only to set the stage for them by reducing the abstract arguments of this chapter to the concrete form they took in Romania between 1947 and 1989, and by describing how ideas about the Nation were effaced from Romanian politics and cultural life, only to reappear at their very center.

CHAPTER THREE

The Suppression and
Reassertion of National Values
in Socialist Romania

*No member of a verbal community can ever find words in
the language that are neutral, exempt from the aspirations
and evaluations of the other, uninhabited by the other's
voice. On the contrary, he receives the word by the other's
voice and it remains filled with that voice. He intervenes in
his own context from another context, already penetrated by
the other's intentions. His own intention finds a word
already lived in.*

—Mikhail Bakhtin

*A not very becoming practice has developed, comrades, to look
only at what is being done abroad, to resort for everything to
imports. This betrays also a certain concept of considering
everything that is foreign to be better, a certain prostration
before what is foreign, and especially before [the West]. Time
has come for [resorting first] to [our] own forces and only
afterwards to appeal to import. There are books printed in
tens of thousands of copies and which make an apology of the
bourgeois way of life, while good Romanian books cannot be
printed because of lack of paper.*

—Nicolae Ceauşescu[1]

The present chapter has a two-fold agenda in relation to those before it.[2] First, chapter 1 has shown the complex field of national symbols that intellectuals and politicians created prior to World War II. By what means did the Soviet-backed regime of Romania after 1947 seek to appropriate and displace that powerful discourse on the Nation? How did that discourse itself, partially autonomized in the institutional practices of scholars and the standards of effective political oratory, gradually reinsert itself into the new Marxist-Leninist context in which it was supposedly unwelcome? The present chapter addresses these questions, offering a quick history of the suppression and return of the national idea in Romanian politics after 1947. This history is essential to part of my argument in chapter 4, where I suggest that the national discourse was so powerfully instituted in Romanian cultural and political life that it at length subverted the discourse of Marxism, on which Party rule was based.

Second, chapter 2 described three modes of control (remunerative, coercive, and symbolic-ideological), as well as several elements of a model for analyzing real-socialist systems: their tendency to maximize the resources at the disposal of the political apparatus, their "economies of shortage," and the intrinsic structural weakness of socialist states. What did these general features look like in the Romania of the 1960s through 1980s? In answering this question, I show how the symbolic-ideological mode of control preferred by Party leader Nicolae Ceauşescu created a particularly strategic spot for producers of culture. I also suggest several reasons why the symbolic vehicles emphasized by the regime came to be *national* rather than something else, arguing in part that the very intensity and institutionalization of the language of national identity in earlier years contributed much to its later symbolic force. Had a national discourse not become so ideologically powerful prior to World War II, communist elites would not have been so compelled to capture this discourse for socialism's purposes.

Romania of the late 1970s and 1980s was a classic example of a breed that was becoming rarer during those years: a neo-Stalinist, highly centralized command economy conforming well to the bureaucratic-allocative model. Almost none of the expanded market forces, decentralized economic decision-making, or political pluralism emerging in Hungary, Poland, or the Soviet Union graced the Romanian landscape. The state persecuted independent entrepreneurship, increasingly raided peasants' "private" plots, militarized many enterprises so as to check sliding output, placed economic contracts under supervision by the General Prosecutor's Office, and chipped away at all enterprises' funds for paying workers (see Georgescu 1988: 75–76).

To call this a highly centralized system does not mean, however, that the center was omnipotent. Like all command economies, this one was host to vertical bargaining mechanisms and horizontal collusions with resultant hoarding, inflated investment requests, endemic shortage, and wholly unreliable information, all of which diminished the power of the center. When the severity of Poland's international debt aroused general consternation as of about 1980, the Romanian party leadership launched a campaign to repay Romania's debt ahead of schedule. This "debt crisis" exacerbated the weakness of the political center, which was at the mercy of its subordinate units for information and for the resources to pay off the debt. The repayment campaign diverted to export channels a significant share of production, which would ordinarily have entered internal redistributive circuits to keep the economy and the population in healthy condition, and this further aggravated internal shortages. During this decade, then, there was unusually high tension between top-level Party officials and managers, striving for maximal control over resources and reliable information, and units lower down the hierarchy of production and administration, scrambling to hoard the resources necessary to fulfill ever-tauter plans whose nonfulfillment drew ever more stringent sanctions. Amid the "overorganized chaos" (in economist Marvin Jackson's phrase) of Romania's political economy, its weak center appeared strong only through heavy resort to coercion, increasingly characteristic of Romania in the 1980s.

In addition to its unusually high centralization, Romania was unusual within the bloc for its mode of control. In its early days the Romanian regime, like most others, controlled its population chiefly by force, which was later relaxed and briefly supplemented in the 1960s with a few economic incentives (Jowitt 1971: 116–117). The 1970s ushered in a mode of control that was primarily symbolic-ideological, supplemented and then overtaken by coercive measures in the 1980s. Remunerative control strategies during those two decades were minimal. Expenditures on consumption suffered relative to accumulation, which received the unusually high ratio of about one-third of revenues.[3] (That is, Romania's leaders sought to overcome the stultifying effects of centralization on production not through reforms, but through forcing up the level of investment.) This means that symbolic appeals would not invoke living standards. Alongside references to Marxist-Leninist slogans, the most prevalent symbolic appeal in Romania, more than in other states of the bloc, was to values of the Nation (e.g., King 1980: 121).

A symbolic-ideological mode of control is discernible as early as 1967, with the establishment of a Commission on Ideology within the Central Committee, but its unequivocal signal was two speeches by Ceauşescu on July 6 and 9, 1971, referred to as the "July theses." Complaining that ideological activity had lagged behind other developments, the "theses" announced an intensified campaign to raise the people's consciousness towards forming the "new man." Ceauşescu explicitly rejected the use of wage differentials as incentives for performance (1972 [1971]: 203), insisting that consciousness instead of material incentives must motivate effort, and he criticized servile imitation of foreign, particularly western, habits. The emphases of these speeches gathered force relentlessly through the end of the next decade.

Part of the task of this chapter is to show why, within a symbolic mode of control, national ideology gained pride of place. The leadership did not restrict itself to this: speeches frequently invoked other notions, like the idea of progress, the importance of science, an ethic of work and productivity, and so forth. Occasionally one or another of these ideas, such as the notion of truth, was taken up more widely (see chapter 6). Had communist and socialist ideas been more robust prior to the Party's accession to power, these might have had more weight in its consolidation of rule. In their absence, however, the exhortations that evoked answer and disagreement—hence, I maintain, the most effective ones—were those concerning the Nation. The leadership's mode of control therefore settled upon the very discourse so richly developed in the interwar years. In consequence, a fierce struggle ensued to define and control the national idea.

The struggle became fierce for three reasons. First, appeals to national solidarity can potentially mobilize and thereby control labor; they were particularly important, then, to a leadership that continually refused to increase market forces or the standard of living to motivate labor. Second, the Party's competitors in the cultural intelligentsia were masters of a national discourse deeply embedded within precommunist institutions and practices, and those competitors could invoke national ideas in a more spacious and inclusive manner than the Party, which was compelled to tie national values rather narrowly to the Party's role in Romanian life. Third, the Party leadership's partiality to national values made these a ground for contests among different fractions of the cultural elite competing for resources from the state. Such contests became even more important under the socialist state than they had been in interwar Romania, for after 1947, intellectual activity lost most of its insulation from the political sphere. Political constraints on the market reduced the chances of independent livelihood for writers, for example; university professors received their salaries from the state and were prohibited from private tutoring; the state initially funded all institutions such as museums and research institutes, their employees living off salaries plus the occasional book published through censored channels. Under these circumstances, anyone with an idea to pursue had to get the attention of the bureaucracy, often accomplished through "defense of the Nation."

I should clarify two sets of terms I employ in my analysis. Although I repeatedly write of "the intellectuals" and "the Party leadership," the division between these groups is not easy to establish. Most of the "intellectuals" I discuss were also Party members; some were bureaucrats (directors of research institutes, for example); many would refuse the label "intellectual" to some persons I include in it, since the title to "real" intellectual status was itself a matter of dispute. At the same time, as chapter 2 made clear, these terms do not mean that the story told in the rest of this book is a story of "intellectuals" versus "the Party." On the contrary: most of the conflicts in the chapters to follow occurred not between "the Party" and "intellectuals" but between factions among the producers of culture. When I nonetheless use terms like "the Party" and "the intellectuals," I refer to a division between the very top political elite and members of the stratum of culture producers. The top Party leadership was relatively although not wholly unified, for under Ceauşescu differences of opinion at the top were routinely purged. I prefer to speak of a "leadership" rather than simply of Ceauşescu because I do not think he was the only significant actor at the apex of Romanian society: he headed a clique that held a great deal of power in a highly centralized but weak state.

General Developments in Romanian Politics After 1947

For Romanian society to acquire the characteristics I have outlined here—a neo-Stalinist centralized system based on a symbolic-ideological mode of control—required an evolution having four main components. First, during its initial two decades the regime embraced, with Soviet support, a Stalinist program of forced industrialization, which it then continued against Soviet wishes by asserting some independence in the early 1960s. Both the industrialization and the autonomy were essential to its future as a redistributive bureaucracy, maximizing the resources it could potentially command. Second, the eclipse of reformist impulses within the Party leadership precluded alternatives to a symbolic-ideological mode of control (such as the standard-of-living "social contract" that prevailed in Hungary at the time). This was the outcome of the process whereby Nicolae Ceauşescu consolidated his power as General Secretary between 1965 and 1974. Third, reliance on symbolic control necessitated creating an intelligentsia that might support the Party leadership's aims and reliably produce an ideological climate suited to its intentions. When it became clear that many intellectuals were nonetheless unwilling to play this game, the leadership set about destroying the bases of their power to oppose it. Fourth, the ascendancy of national symbols required displacing a rhetoric of communist internationalism with one of national values, evident in some quarters as early as the late 1950s and officially sanctioned in 1964–1966. The remainder of this chapter discusses each of these four processes, the first two summarily and the others at greater length.

FROM MINION TO MAVERICK: THE ROMANIAN PARTY DRAWS AWAY FROM SOVIET DOMINATION

When it began its ascent to power in 1944, the Romanian Communist Party was minuscule—proportionately the smallest in all of Eastern Europe (Shafir 1985: 27)—numbering a thousand by some estimates and at most a few thousand by others (King 1980: 18, 38). The reasons for its weakness are several, rooted in the social structure of interwar Romania: the low level of industrial development and consequently the small size of the industrial proletariat, the lack of interest of the peasantry (newly enfranchised and impropriated) in communist agitation, the banning of the Party in 1924 for promoting nationality struggles hazardous to the new Romanian state,[4] and the Party's consequent attractiveness for the national minorities, dissatisfied with their situation in interwar Romania. The last of these reasons greatly hampered communist recruitment of the majority population, since non-Romanians were so prominent in its ranks:[5] of the six First Secretaries of the Party from 1921 to 1944, only the first was an ethnic

Romanian. This fact helps explain later disputes as to whether the Party was a "national" or an "alien" institution. Recruitment was further hindered because the Party's illegal status impeded wartime partisan activities of the sort that helped to build a mass base in Yugoslavia and Bulgaria. The chief experience of its leaders was not practical politics but prison or temporary exile, its "cells" not organizational but the literal ones of the different prisons in which its members developed solidarity. These experiences shaped the units for factional rivalries among the leadership, particularly the division between the "muscovites," who had passed the years of illegality in Moscow, and those who had spent that time in Romanian jails. For all these reasons, it is indisputable that without Soviet support during the late 1940s, the Romanian Communist Party could not have attained power.

More or less firmly ensconced by 1948, the Party's factions continued their strife until the group led by Gheorghiu-Dej prevailed in the early 1950s. This group, dominated by ethnic Romanians and having purged its most powerful Jewish and Hungarian rivals, nonetheless submitted to Stalin's resolute internationalism and continued to accept, as had their opponents, Soviet directives concerning not only forced-draft industrialization but also the suppression of national values. A measure of the determination to industrialize is the 748 percent increase in resources devoted to Romanian industry between 1950 and 1965 (Crowther 1988: 63). Although the Party leadership could present industrialization as a patriotic necessity and in the Nation's interests (much as some interwar politicians had argued), in most other visible respects the leadership seemed prepared to renounce its nationality. Romanian history books suddenly gave the Slavs a preeminent role in forming the Romanian people and in many important past events; famous Romanian writers were shelved as unbefitting the consciousness of socialists; the Latin linguistic affiliations so carefully recreated by nineteenth-century linguists were obscured in 1953 by an orthographic change, which substituted the Russian-derived î for the latinate â—even in the name of the country, making "Romînia" out of once-Latin "România."

Along with these changes came a reorientation of Romania's formerly West European trade, two-thirds of which went in 1951 to the Soviet Union and other Warsaw Pact countries (Turnock 1986: 231).[6] A part of this "trade" took the form of war-reparation payments to the Soviet Union, mediated through joint companies (*sovroms*), which enabled extensive Soviet exploitation of Romanian raw and finished goods. Another part consisted of exports from both agriculture and the newly developing machine industry to the more advanced economies in the bloc, East Germany and Czechoslovakia. Complaints soon emerged from these countries that subsidizing uncompetitive Romanian heavy industry made no sense. As a result, the Soviets proposed restructuring intrabloc trade: Romania was to specialize in agricultural products and in consumer industry, leaving heavy industry to the Czechs and East Germans, who were better at it. By the late 1950s and into the 1960s, these proposals were being voiced ever more firmly, with demands that Romania modify its production plans.

This was the background to Romania's so-called "declaration of independence," a public statement issued in April 1964 that announced the Party's refusal to subordinate national needs to a supranational planning body in which others would dictate the form of the country's economy.[7] The declaration insisted that interaction among states within the socialist camp must be based on respect for the sovereignty and integrity of each. When two months later a Soviet geographer launched a regional integration plan for the lower Danube that would have divorced huge chunks of Romania's and Bulgaria's territory from the rest of their economies, Romanian economists responded with such outrage that the plan was retracted. From this point on, ideas were dropped for integrating Romania into anything but loose agreements with other bloc countries. Romania's trade within the bloc declined from two-thirds to under one-half by 1970 (Linden 1986: 356) while exchanges with the West and with other developing nations shot up. The country's reorientation to the West culminated in its entry into the General Agreement on Tariffs and Trade in 1971 and the International Monetary Fund and World Bank in 1972, trade preferences from the European Community in 1973, and U.S. Most-Favored-Nation status in 1975. By 1974 Romania's trade with the West exceeded that with the bloc (ibid., 360).

The "declaration of independence" had a number of far-reaching consequences, one of which is particularly important to the kind of analysis I employ for Romanian socialism. By refusing incorporation within a larger planning unit and by insisting on its right to develop heavy industry, the Romanian party apparatus assured itself the maximum possible accumulation of political and economic resources, including the autonomous capacity to produce means of production. This meant a larger, more complex, and potentially richer allocative bureaucracy, more capable of autarchically protecting the flows of value into and out of itself. Had heavy industry been reserved for other bloc states, this would have diminished the pool of resources available for the Romanian party to control. Neo-Stalinism and high centralization would have had a dubious future, rather than the bright one they were to enjoy. Another consequence of Romania's greater autonomy was its officially creating room for a form of communist rule that would be *national*. This possibility was underscored immediately following the "declaration of independence," with the publication of a volume of Marx's unpublished manuscripts entitled *Notes on the Romanians* (Marx 1964). In them Marx defended Romania's anti-Russian activities in the nineteenth century and its sovereignty rights—repeatedly breached by Russia (most recently in 1940)—over Bessarabia. This text made it possible to imagine a communist ideology compatible with the anti-Russian national feeling so widespread among Romanians (Shafir 1985: 50).

ELIMINATING REFORMISM

A second precondition of the Romanian political economy of the 1970s and 1980s was the prior elimination of what might be called reformist or technocratic forces. The significant moment for this came with the death of Gheorghiu-Dej in 1965, when a new leadership might have broadened existing initiatives toward decentralization. Although Ceauşescu emerged as the new General Secretary without apparent struggle, the policies that would come to characterize his reign were not clearly identifiable until the 1970s, suggesting that he required some time to expel those who disagreed with the policies he intended to follow (compare, for example, the accounts in Jowitt 1971 and Crowther 1988). Initially, it appeared that his leadership would make room for a technocratic elite—more broadly, for the "new middle class" of specialists, skilled workers, technicians, scientists, and low-level economic managers whom the industrialization process had spawned (see Jowitt 1971: 185)—at the expense of the high Party bureaucracy. Such a development would have furthered already-evident tendencies toward replacing a primarily coercive mode of control with more remuneration, including wage differentials and greater social benefits for the population (ibid., 187–189). Motivated in part by the imbalances and strains that accompanied years of overinvestment and stress upon the central planning mechanism (Jackson 1981: 266), Party planners and Ceauşescu himself aired proposals that would have increased the level of consumption, moderated accumulation and investment, introduced a degree of administrative decentralization and managerial autonomy, and ended the Central Committee's direct control over economic planning (see Crowther 1988: 82–83; Montias 1967: 79). Precisely these tendencies were at work in Hungary's Communist party at the same time and were to culminate in the 1968 New Economic Mechanism, which set Hungary on the path toward market socialism.[8]

In Romania, however, it appears that the bureaucratic opponents of these reforms, fearing a reconfiguration of power to the benefit of persons lower down the political hierarchy, succeeded in winning the General Secretary to their point of view (Crowther 1988: 83). Although some identify the definitive eclipse of reformism by the removal of Prime Minister Maurer in 1974 (Georgescu 1986: 50–51), well before that year it was apparent that a neo-Stalinist line was reemerging and that remunerative controls were being replaced by symbolic-ideological ones (see Fischer 1989: 109–119). In 1971, following a visit to North Korea, China, and North Vietnam, Ceauşescu's "July theses" inaugurated what has been called his "mini-cultural revolution," with renewed emphasis on socialist realism and attacks on intellectuals who failed to fall into line. In addition, the 1971–1975 Five-Year Plan recentralized the economy and renewed the massive levels of investment of earlier quinquennia (Shafir 1985: 107, 121).[9]

These developments were very significant for the subject of the present book. By abandoning a mode of control based on material incentives and shifting to symbolic-ideological ones, the Ceauşescu leadership saved itself from the decentralization of power inherent in many technocratic reforms. Moreover, it increased the relative weight of humanist and cultural intellectuals over technical ones. That is, because there was no reform of the Romanian political economy, engineers, economists, and enterprise managers lost some influence over the apparatus whereas historians, writers, and philosophers—the linchpins of ideological and symbolic creation—gained relative to them. This is not to say that the former were now inconsequential but only to insist that the policies Ceauşescu adopted implicitly created a privileged role for a cultural elite. From their capacity to produce persuasive images of the social world would come the symbols for his rule.

If we think of the field of politicking as a landscape on which different social forces rise up like hills and mountains, their height proportional to their influence in the field, then Ceauşescu's consolidation of power made the knoll of the cultural elite into a small mountain. This meant that the question of who would stand at its summit had suddenly greater moment than had been true a few years before. Together with the new General Secretary had arisen a new configuration of opportunity for the producers of culture.

Throughout the period of his leadership, however, they were increasingly to face three problems. The Party leadership would exert continuous pressure on the form of their cultural products. Their own ranks would be fragmented by competition for influence that only some of them could attain. Most importantly, the economic crisis of the 1970s and 1980s would bring the reintroduction of limited market forces. These consisted of laws that mandated "self-financing" (*auto-finanţare*), which meant that cultural enterprises—magazines, research institutes, museums, publishers, art galleries, and so forth—were now expected at least partly to sustain themselves. Although industrial production continued to be protected by "soft budget constraints," then, culture underwent a partial recommodification that subjected its producers (albeit differentially) to new economic pressures, in addition to the older political ones.

REGIME RELATIONS WITH INTELLECTUALS

Given the Party's resort to symbolic modes of control—given, that is, a Party that by 1971 had clearly announced its need to be supported by culture in one or another form rather than by standards of living—what relations arose between the top elite and the creators of culture? The problem of these relations was, of course, as old as the regime. Jowitt describes it as part of the process of "breaking through"— "the decisive alteration or destruction of values, structures, and behaviors which are perceived by a new elite as compromising or contributing to the actual or potential existence of alternative centers of power" (1971: 7). Shafir nuances this by speaking of how elites altered the prerevolutionary hegemony, not primarily by attending to the values of Romania's *masses* but by transforming those who *produce the instruments* of mass resocialization: writers, journalists, and so forth (Shafir 1983*b*: 395–396). He describes the early phases of Gheorghiu-Dej's Moscow-oriented regime as the "primitive accumulation of legitimacy" (see Meyer 1969: 192), meaning the effort to destroy the bases of hegemony potential counterelites could draw upon, and he inquires how Romanian intellectuals were then brought into the system of values championed by the Party leadership.

I employ a similar conceptualization in this section, using slightly different terms. With Shafir, I see the problem of altering prerevolutionary hegemonies as one that engages different fractions of the societal elite, first, and the masses only secondarily. Within the political and intellectual elite, a conflict emerges over symbolic values: what symbols are to be preferred, what accumulations of symbolic meanings are to be created, to what extent can they draw upon earlier accumulations of meaning, and in what conditions will symbolic values be produced. The conflict therefore concerns the *production* of symbolic and cultural values, their *evaluation* (a job usually done by critics and historians of culture), and their *appropriation* or even *expropriation*. If culture is seen as produced—like any human creation—within certain institutional relations and with certain material means, then how does a new political regime manipulate these so as to influence the kind of culture that is produced and to lay hands on symbolic values that will promote it? How can a regime protect the institutional and bureaucratic structures it creates for culture from being altered or subverted by persons who cling to an older definition of things? How does it open new sites for the production of symbolic discourses favorable to itself and close off old sites that might undermine it? The dilemma for those in power is to permit sufficient continuity with the preexisting hegemony so as to maintain socially effective cultural production, without permitting the continuities to overwhelm the new political project. The challenge for producers of culture, in turn, is to use their mastery of the symbolic repertoire and their cultural authority either to enter more fully into the halls of power or to build their own parallel empires.

An especially acute problem for all participants centers around how cultural authority is to be defined, what constitutes a monopoly of symbolic resources, and what *counts* as symbolic resources. This entails struggles to define what new cultural products will be recognized as having "quality"—that is, struggles to set standards of taste and of competence. It also includes a related struggle to define what prior cultural products are to be accepted into a newly forming canon, or perhaps better said, what *parts* of prior cultural products will be accepted: what earlier writers and thinkers, and which of their works, will form the authorized symbolic repertoire of Romanian socialism? Much of the conflict occurs through a process of symbolic reinterpretation, as some facets of prior writings and writers are singled out and blessed within a given system of evaluations, whereas other facets are suppressed, dismissed as nonessential, or condemned outright and the work rejected.

To give a quick example: literary critic Eugen Lovinescu was one of the first interwar figures to be restored to the patrimony of authors acceptable to a leftist regime, owing to his spirited opposition to interwar fascism and his adherence to liberal-democratic principles, yet in the 1980s these commendable items in his resumé were overlooked in order to revile his welcome of "alien" western standards. (The subtext of this was an attack on his daughter, one of the most active members of the emigré community in Paris and a pillar of Radio Free Europe's criticism of the Ceauşescu regime.)

The process whereby the Party leadership sought to reshape the instruments of cultural production is much longer and more intricate than can be told here. Specifics of it for the literary community can be found in Gabanyi's (1975) detailed analysis of regime-writer relations to 1974, to which the following discussion is much indebted;[10] Crowther (1988), Georgescu (1981), Gheorghiu (1987), and Shafir (1981, 1983a, 1985) offer further information. On the whole, told from the Party leadership's point of view, it is the story of a great disappointment, as the Party created a cultural intelligentsia after its own image, provided conditions it thought propitious for creative work, and saw many intellectuals reject its initiatives with demands for more freedom. The consequence of this disillusionment, which crested in 1968, was a long siege upon an already-laid infrastructure for cultural production. From the point of view of at least some writers and scholars, it is the story of a struggle to reconquer a space for the production of genuine cultural values and to create counterinstitutions to protect these, followed by a desperate defense of that space and those values from the Party leadership's relentless assault. The conflict of these two stories itself forms part of Romanian cultural politics.

The Party began the new relationship with culture by moves to destroy existing cultural accumulations and instruments. The Romanian Academy was abolished in 1948, for example, replaced by a new one whose members the Party selected; a law expelled from their posts all "bourgeois" university professors (e.g., 80 percent of those in the Bucharest philosophy faculty). All research institutes for history were merged into a single history institute, their several journals replaced with a new one under Party control (Georgescu 1983: 136, n.5). As mentioned above, the language itself, that most basic instrument of cultural production, was retooled with an orthography of Slavic inspiration, and certain words—such as "national"—were anathematized. Major works disappeared from schools and libraries, and writers and scholars were persecuted not just for "bourgeois" associations but simply for declining active collaboration with the new rulers. Control of education and the nationalization of the press and of publishing houses (not to mention all the financial supports for culture) put the most crucial means of cultural production in Party hands.

Additional moves aimed to create new instruments of culture to replace those destroyed. In 1947 the Party program announced that Romanian history would have to be written all over again, for its bourgeois form was unscientific and lacked the necessary materialist underpinnings (Georgescu 1981: 11). Textbooks were rewritten, and new treatises synthesizing historical and philosophical knowledge were commissioned that would emphasize materialism and the new cultural genealogies a socialist Romania should revere. A special school to train Party cadres was founded in 1948 and generously endowed. In 1950 the Party opened a school for writers, having already established a Literary Fund the year before. This Fund was intended to support writers in periods when they had no books in press, and it was used very shrewdly as an agent of resocialization: writers whose works the censor refused might nonetheless draw upon the Fund while reconsidering their attitude (Gabanyi 1975: 30–31). In the field of history, those few people who had already been working within a materialist framework were pushed into the universities and the Academy (alongside new historians trained overnight).

The initial period of restriction gave way to a small relaxation that lasted from 1953 to 1958. During these years, increasing numbers of intellectuals entered both the Party and the administration of culture; many of these persons were "liberals" whom it would later prove difficult to dislodge. At the same time there began the selective republishing of certain writers from before the war—the selective appropriation of earlier symbols now being redefined in socialist terms. It was doubly selective in that many works were still banned and even those that were not banned were abridged in publication, as they and their writers were repositioned in a new system of cultural evaluations. The relaxation also introduced an element that would prove important in later cultural politics. It was marked by speeches at the 1953 Party Congress, which, while they still insisted that art must be politically relevant, also encouraged a fight against dogmatism and against mechanical repetition of Marxist-Leninist doctrine (Gabanyi 1975: 43–44)—the same terms used by Gheorghiu-Dej in ousting the rival "muscovite" faction for their association with Stalinist orthodoxies. The campaign against them was instrumental in bringing into wider parlance the notion of "dog-matism" that would become a major weapon in cultural struggles throughout subsequent decades (see chapter 4). In the meaning that developed during this time, "dogmatism" meant the imposition of alien interpretations and values upon the national heritage, motivated by a dogmatic Stalinist view of what social transformation required. In later years, those intellectuals who had achieved positions in the cultural bu-reaucracy early on—including the liberals entering it in the relaxation of the mid-1950s—would be accused of "dogmatism" for having served a regime that had previously suppressed national values.

After several years of renewed restrictions at the turn of the decade, Romania's increasing "independence" from the Soviet Union brought another loosening of the conditions for cultural production as of the early 1960s. Artists and intellectuals once again entered the Party and the cultural bureaucracy, into which a measure of decentralization was introduced. Beginning in 1962, for example, the Writers' Union was allowed to award prizes, by which the Party leadership relinquished the right to set literary standards independently of the Union's member-ship[11] (Gabanyi 1975: 88). The publishing establishment was reorga-nized and decentralized, increasing the opportunities for writers to reach print and diminishing the Party's direct oversight of intellectual production. Interwar writings formerly considered taboo were readmit-ted to print—some works of poet Lucian Blaga, for instance. Elections to the Romanian Academy became freer, some of the older research institutes reopened, and earlier-suppressed journals reappeared (cf. Georgescu 1981: 34–35). With Ceauşescu's leadership in 1965 came even greater freedom and liberalization. The canon of acceptable cul-tural accumulations opened an even wider embrace back into the past, and the remaining intellectuals jailed earlier as counterrevolutionaries were released (among them philosopher Constantin Noica, discussed in chapter 7).

The seeming liberalization did not keep pace with the numbers of intellectuals who wanted more influence and opportunities, however; demands increased for still more cultural freedom. This was particularly apparent in the 1968 Writers' Conference, when younger writers sought to win top positions in the literary establishment and demanded dismantling censorship altogether, decentralizing and reorganizing all the institutions of literary production, and democratizing access to pub-lication (see Gabanyi 1975: 138–161). In fields other than literature, there were similar attacks on older "dogmatists" holding key posts in the cultural bureaucracy. These signaled an attempt by a newer group of intellectuals to take over cultural production and to separate it from politics (expressed, as in the interwar years, as a desire that aesthetic and cultural matters be autonomous of social concerns). This position, so clearly in conflict with the purposes of the Party leadership, made it obvious that the Party's policy of creating a broad educated stratum and trying to coopt it within the framework of Party membership[12] was not working as planned. Leaders were not prepared to enfranchise all those with title to cultural distinction. As a result, many intellectuals, whether they joined the Party or not, readily discerned a pattern of privilege— travel, ready translation of one's works, key positions in institutes and cultural organizations, professorships, regular columns in publications, acceptance of one's writings for publication—in which they too wanted a part. The pattern of privilege was nothing new in Romanian culture; it was merely aggravated by the increased number of aspirants to higher status.

The growing restiveness of intellectuals, evident especially in the Writers' Congress of 1968, did not meet with Party leaders' approval. Earlier in that year Ceauşescu, apparently realizing that cultural production had become too independent of Party guidance, had announced:

Man becomes free in the socialist system not because he is outside the action of social laws, but because by understanding their imperative need, [he] acts in their spirit for the conscious construction of society. Therefore the freedom of the individual is not in contradiction with the general demands and interests of society but, on the contrary, serves these interests. Therefore, when it happens that the general interests are disregarded, society is entitled to take the necessary measures so that these interests . . . should not be prejudiced (Ceauşescu 1969*b* [1968]: 621).

Thereafter, the Party began to place intellectuals under more constraint, intensifying the struggle both within them as a group and between them and the Party leadership. In 1970, the awards of literary prizes brought the leadership into open conflict with the Writers' Union (Gabanyi 1975: 177) and showed that the Party intended to recover the privilege of making such awards and of setting the standards of value they represented. Ceauşescu's "July theses" in 1971 launched an offensive against culture's autonomy, condemned the liberalization of 1965, reestablished an Index of prohibited books and authors, and reemphasized the necessary sociopolitical role of intellectual production.

For the remainder of this decade and the next, one measure after another assailed the independent status of the institutions of intellectual life: the Writers' Union, the Romanian Academy, whole fields of endeavor such as sociology[13] and psychology, the dispersed structure of historical research, certain cultural publications, and so on. The center gradually reestablished control over the publishing system and imposed rules that changed the criteria for membership in elective intellectual bodies. The numbers of students admitted into the nontechnical fields in universities were continually cut,[14] and vacant positions in research institutes remained unfilled. No one could pursue doctoral studies without approval from the local Party organization. In 1982, a scandal involving Transcendental Meditation served as the pretext for removing a substantial number of intellectuals from their posts.[15] Reduced press runs, mandated from the center, diminished both authors' earnings and the writers' Literary Fund, which derived from a percentage of all sales. The new rules for "self-financing" in 1978, mentioned above, worsened the already parlous state of many cultural organizations, for many of them found it exceedingly difficult in the environment of the 1980s to come up with their own means of support.[16] Following defeats at the hands of the Writers' Union during the late 1970s and early 1980s, the Party leadership simply blocked all further meetings of the Union after 1981. By not naming juries for literary prizes, it ended conflict over their award.

Prior to the annual Congress of Socialist Education of Culture in 1987, the first list of proposed delegates (consisting of university professors, high-school teachers, writers, and so forth) was rejected by top Party officials and replaced by a second list consisting of workers and security cops, indicating the leadership's definition of culture as a mass rather than an elite phenomenon.[17] The same point was made by widely institutionalizing the "Song of Romania" festival system, a mass phenomenon exalting popular culture over elite forms (see Kligman MS). Finally, the Party leadership laid siege to the Romanian Academy. First it successfully imposed Elena Ceauşescu as Academy member in 1974—completely destroying the institution's credibility in the eyes of the public. Second, it permitted no more elections of new members after 1977. Third, as the Academy's new head, Mrs. Ceauşescu expropriated its independent funds (consisting of donations by the members to support special prizes or programs) and diverted them into the central budget.[18]

This sketch of the changes in the organization of culture and the treatment of intellectuals makes clear the Party's shift, as of the early 1970s, from a politics of incipient reform to one of ideological control, in which the intelligentsia would be forced to play a major role and intellectual life would be organized to compel them to do so. The leadership envisioned propagating a variety of ideological norms—an ethic of hard work, principles of "socialist equity and ethics," notions of progress, and so forth. The role of humanist intellectuals would be to disseminate such notions through their novels, research, and philosophical speculation. For those who found this distasteful, suitable avenues for professional fulfillment would begin to disappear.

Party officials who reasoned in this way may have been surprised at the resistance their plans encountered. The Writers' Union proved exceedingly difficult to break apart. An intended reunification and recentralization of research in the field of history ran aground, reportedly, on the opposition of powerful heads of history institutes who did not want to lose their posts.[19] In some cases, the relaxations of the 1950s and 1960s had placed powerful persons in high positions—such as the editorships of certain magazines—where they maintained standards other than those intended by the Party leadership; getting rid of them was not always easy. More interesting, certain persons installed as apparatchiks caught the bug for "true" culture and came to the defense of authors and values one might not have expected them to uphold.[20] Some of these persons were in charge of powerful segments of the bureaucracy and had amassed large reserves of resources in the projects under their charge, making them veritable fortresses.[21] Other persons had managed to create publication channels that circumvented the normal path and brought out works that would otherwise have been stalled interminably in the political center.[22] While the Romanian Academy was, in 1989, literally dying on its feet, the Academy of Social and Political Sciences, founded in 1970 to oppose it and stacked with persons who were acceptable by the standards of that time, was becoming a potential locus of resistance to the complete takeover of culture by the Party leadership.[23]

One result of the Party's assaults upon the independence of cultural production was to divide the cultural field into warring camps.[24] The few positions of influence were now to be savagely competed for; so also was the power to define basic cultural values, for such definitions would determine the outcome of other contests. If enough writers were to insist that aesthetic and stylistic values should be judged autonomously of a work's social message—despite Ceauşescu's disagreement—then the positions of some literary critics would remain secure, whereas if these values were to fade, so would the voices of their champions. If philosophy were to be defined as popular wisdom (as some would have it) rather than as Marxism-Leninism or as the accumulated tradition of western philosophical thought, then certain people would become professors and researchers in philosophy institutes and others would not. If sociology as a separate field were to vanish, its ambitious practitioners—now ineligible for department chairs—would strive to impose new definitions of the sociological endeavor that would afford them the best vantage point for maneuver and influence.

The possible positions in this politicized cultural field differed for each domain of specialization. Certain disciplines were more central than others to the leadership's intentions. For example, history was crucial because of its treatment of the national past in which questions of origin and identity were embedded; this centrality placed potentially more resources at history's disposal (even if accompanied by more surveillance) along with a wider range of positions in this field than in nearly defunct psychology, for instance. Meanwhile, philosophy, once the central pillar of legitimation for a Marxist-Leninist regime, drifted comfortably into the shade. Literature was also privileged, owing to the central role of critics and writers in formulating and disseminating values to the public at large, but literary production was more deeply affected than history by self-financing. Writers' vulnerability not only to Party control but also to market forces may have contributed to their forming a more vocal opposition in the late 1980s than did historians. Within each of these fields, the specific issues dividing it into competing groups differed. Yet as the 1970s gave way to the 1980s, in each domain of cultural activity at least one group emerged that defended its position and its claims through a certain definition of national identity and a defense of the Nation. The next section shows how this new element entered the constitution of cultural politics.

THE REASSERTION OF NATIONAL IDEOLOGY IN ROMANIAN CULTURE AND POLITICS

The Romanian party's 1964 "declaration" marked Romania's public deviation from Soviet plans and affirmation of its rights as a sovereign state. A year later, at the Ninth Congress of the Romanian Communist Party, Gheorghiu-Dej's successor furthered this same process. Not only did Ceaușescu signal a restoration of old values by resurrecting the latinate spelling of the country's name (România), and not only did he assert Romania's equality with the Soviet Union by renaming the Romanian Workers' Party the Romanian *Communist* Party and the People's Republic of Romania the Romanian *Socialist* Republic, he also affirmed the continuing existence of nations under socialism. The crucial passage, the likes of which had not been heard in a public forum in Romania for nearly two decades, ran as follows:

For a long time to come, the nation and the State will continue to be the basis of the development of socialist society. The development of the nation, the consolidation of the socialist State comply with the objective requirements of social life; not only does this not run counter to the interests of socialist internationalism, but, on the contrary, it fully corresponds to these interests, to the international solidarity of the working people, to the cause of socialism and peace. The development and flourishing of each socialist nation, of each socialist state, equal in rights, sovereign and independent, is an essential requirement upon which depend the strengthening of the unity and cohesion of the socialist countries, the growth of their influence upon mankind's advance toward socialism and communism (Ceauşescu 1969*a* [1965]: 60).

In this and subsequent speeches Ceauşescu named and quoted famous Romanians from the national past, people who had not been invoked in official settings for years: turn-of-the-century historian Xenopol, for example, cited pointedly for his arguments in support of industrialization and against an agrarian Romania (ibid., 23). In addition, he made an explicit appeal for materialist research into the "real history" of Romanians (p. 85), reiterating this appeal in a later speech that clarified the relation among history, the Party, and the Nation:

We, Communists, consider it is a creditable mission to study, know and honor dutyfully [sic] all those who contributed to building up our nation, all those who laid down their lives for the Romanian people's national and social freedom. We, Communists, are the continuers of whatever is best in the Romanian people. The Communist Party did not appear in Romania in an accidental way. It is the result of a whole historical process of economic and social development, which led to the ripening of the working class, of the revolutionary struggle and to the formation of the Romanian Communist Party. How would it be possible for a Party which proposes to lead the people along the road of building a fairer system, the socialist system, not to know the past struggles? . . . How could a people feel without knowing its past, its history, without honoring and appreciating that history? Wouldn't it be like a child who does not know his parents and feels alien in the world? Comrades, it would undoubtedly be so (Ceauşescu 1969*a* [1966]: 435).

During the second year of his rule, mention of past Romanians became routine, including not just those whom a tradition of "democratic" struggle might willingly recognize but a much wider range from the pantheon of ancestral heroes. Such references were absent only from speeches honoring international occasions (such as the fiftieth anniversary of the Bolshevik Revolution).

To bring the Nation so boldly into the rhetoric of the Romanian party required not only a confident assessment of the Soviet response but also a skillful reworking of the past of the Romanian party itself. If the Party was now identified with national interests and if one were to trust its guidance, how was one to account for its having endorsed in the 1920s and 1930s the Comintern line that countenanced Romania's dismemberment? Ceaușescu addressed this ticklish problem in a 1966 speech celebrating the forty-fifth anniversary of the Party's founding. In it he censured the Comintern's earlier hostility to the interests of Romania, its stubborn blindness to Romanian realities, and the failure of early Romanian communists to make their own analysis of the country's history and development. He also pointedly observed that the Romanian party had been divided between those who accepted the Comintern's hostile line and those who continued to strive for the Nation's interests. The latter group finally prevailed, reaffirming the Party's role as a worthy guarantor of Romania's future. Ceaușescu repeated his view that only under socialism can the Nation come to full flower, stating that unlike capitalist nations, the Nation under socialism constitutes a progressive force, and averring that "the nation will continue to be for a long time to come the basis for the development of our society . . . " (Ceaușescu 1969a [1966]: 374).

With these speeches, Ceaușescu introduced major modifications into Marxist-Leninist theorizing about the Nation under socialism and the possible place of national values within Romanian socialist society. Far from withering away, the Nation—along with the State—would form a positive element in building socialism. Moreover, Ceaușescu accorded the socialist Nation, rather than the working class, the central role in furthering world progress (Schöpflin 1974: 93). His arguments also paved the way for identifying the Romanian Communist Party not just with the proletariat but with the entire Nation. This view subsequently became more and more explicit in Ceaușescu's speeches (and also in the organization of the discipline of history—see chapter 6), as evident in the following:

We must have a unitary history . . . in [which] the history of the Romanian people will also encompass the history of the revolutionary workers' movement, of the Social-Democratic Workers' Party, as well as of the Romanian Communist Party. There cannot be two histories, a history of the people and a history of the Party. Our people has a single history, and the activity of the Romanian Communist Party, along with other parties in different periods, constitutes an inseparable part of the history of the homeland (Ceauşescu 1983*b* [1982]: 67).

With these amendments to thinking about the Nation, the road was opened for reinserting the national past into the socialist present, for redefining the Nation in terms congruent with the tenets of Marxism-Leninism.

The leader's initiatives were picked up at once in publications of all sorts, some persons working on the theoretical analysis of the Nation in socialism (e.g., Gavrilă 1968; Colceriu-Leis 1968) and others turning—returning—to the problem of the Romanian national essence. In the same year as Ceauşescu's speech to the Ninth Congress there appeared an essay by philosopher and long-time communist Atanase Joja, entitled "The Spiritual Profile of the Romanian People." This article established a broad set of coordinates within which many subsequent writings on the topic were to locate themselves. Among the most important was an explicit rejection of the irrationality and mysticism that some in the interwar right had posited as fundamental to Romanian character. Insisting that all the greatest Romanians were rationalists rather than mystics, Joja pointedly observed that mysticism had entered Romanian philosophy only with the interwar fascists and should be seen as an imported, not a native, phenomenon (Joja 1965: 9). Basic to Romanian character, he held, are reason and *logos*, the predominance of Latin clarity over Dacian emotionality: "I consider characteristic of the Romanian psychology the apollonization of the dionisiac substrate, the disciplining and inflecting of violent pathos to the exigencies of form and measure. . . . Romanian culture is of apollonian type" (ibid., 8). These emphases on rationality and Latinity[25] were, of course, essential to a Party that prided itself on its own rationalist origins and was at the time moving away from its Soviet overlords. Predictably, Joja gave the national essence a materialist treatment, claiming that it is not inborn, fixed for all time, but changes under the influence of varying historical conditions: "Peoples do not purely and simply inherit their moral physiognomy, but they themselves forge it in the course of their history" (ibid., 6). Joja's essay was also interesting for its recuperation of some earlier giants of Romanian culture who had been accused of mysticism but whom he saw as exhibiting a spirit that was essentially "apollonian." Within these strictures—the rationality of the national essence, its Daco-*Latinity*, and its social and historical conditioning—Joja's list of Romanians' essential traits was broad enough to stimulate reconsideration of the essence from many different angles and disciplines.

The reconsiderations scarcely awaited this stimulus. In the years that followed Ceauşescu's speech on the Nation and Joja's reopening of discussions on the national essence, Romanian journals and books were once again filled with these two subjects.[26] As early as 1971, one author could write:

> In understanding and defining the concept of nation and its characteristic traits, the problem that is perhaps the most disputed and that arouses many debates and efforts at clarification in the philosophical, sociological, historical, and ethnographic literature concerns the spiritual physiognomy of the nation (Rebedeu 1971: 273).

Much of the impetus was theoretical refinement of the Marxist teachings that had so amply established the Nation's socioeconomic base. Some writers focused their attention on the national essence as a spiritual phenomenon. Others proposed that the idea of an integral national essence could actually make sense *only* in socialism, for in capitalism the social psychology of nations is divided by classes, whereas in socialism the national culture becomes fully integrated and can at last constitute a progressive force (ibid., 294, 297). Still others turned expressly to the interwar debates, inquiring which of those earlier contributions (the "progressive and democratic" ones) could be brought into a socialist view of the question and which (the "retrograde, chauvinistic, mystical, reactionary" ones of the fascists) must be rooted out (ibid., 277, 301–303). Literary critics immediately resuscitated the old question of the national essence in relation to art (Marino 1966; Simion 1966).

Accompanying the reintroduction of national values as an acceptable item of public discourse was the strengthening of a tendency already evident as early as the 1950s, with Gheorghiu-Dej's purging of the "muscovite" faction from the top Party leadership: a tendency to label one's opponents in a dispute "dogmatists." From the outset this label had a double meaning. It meant on the one hand those who subscribe (or are accused of subscribing) to "vulgar" Marxist-Leninist or Stalinist notions, such as proletarian internationalism or socialist realism in art, and on the other hand those who appear willing to sacrifice the values of the Nation, subordinating it to an outside power. Whereas that outside power was initially the Soviet Union, by the late 1980s people were being accused of dogmatism for advocating *western* values, for these too denied the worth of Romania's own cultural contribution and therefore stood in the lineage of "dogmatism."

The history of how "dogmatism" was constructed and wielded as an instrument of political struggle would make an intriguing sociological study, which I cannot offer here. I call attention to "dogmatism" in order to underscore the element of its history that is real, so that its subsequent social elaboration (see chapter 4) can be understood as such. The element that is real is that for over a decade the discourse on Romanian identity and all the practices associated with it had been driven underground in the name of a rigid interpretation of Marxism, an interpretation associated with Soviet dominance as well as with Romania's continued territorial vulnerability (owing to its large Hungarian population). Given the national passions so visible in writings from before the war, this experience was an exceedingly painful one for many Romanians, who felt themselves obligated to serve the interests of a power other than the one to which they felt allegiance. Against this background, the Party's success in reorienting the politics of the country and the language of Marxism during the 1960s, so that these were now seen as serving Romanian rather than Soviet interests, must be viewed as a major accomplishment,[27] which succeeded for a time in producing fair support for Party rule.

Why National Ideology?

Having signaled the post-1965 flood of writings on the Nation and its essence—a portion of which will be analyzed in subsequent chapters—I wish to take up one final question concerning the politics of the Ceauşescu era. Why did a Marxist-Leninist regime employing a symbolic-ideological mode of control give so much weight to an ideology that was *national*? This question has been handled at greater or lesser length by a number of political scientists, most of whom see the answer in the regime's need for public support, either in general or in its quarrel with the Soviet Union. Nationalism, it is argued, was the Ceauşescu leadership's main instrument for legitimating its rule with the populace and for keeping the intellectuals coopted or subservient (see, e.g., Croan 1989: 180; Crowther 1988: 79, 130; Gilberg 1990: 12–13, 248; Jowitt 1971: 275–279; King 1980: 125; Schöpflin 1974: 93, 101; Tismăneanu 1989: 330–331).

I do not adopt this line of argument. I see the national ideology that became a hallmark of Ceauşescu's Romania as having several sources, only one of which was its purposeful instrumentalization by the Party. To a considerable extent, I argue, the Party was *forced* onto the terrain of national values (not unwillingly) under pressure from others, especially intellectuals, whom it could fully engage in no other manner. These intellectuals were drawing upon personal concerns and traditions of inquiry that made the Nation a continuing and urgent reality for them despite its official interdiction. They were also engaged in conflicts among themselves for which, as before, the Nation provided a basic idiom. To use a different phrasing, Romanian intellectuals were utilizing something—the Nation—that we might call a *master symbol*, one having the capacity to dominate the field of symbols and discourses in which it was employed, pressing the meanings of other terms and symbols in its own direction. In addition, I see the national ideology as having an elective affinity, beyond any leadership's conscious manipulation, with certain inherent characteristics of Romanian socialism. Although I do not reject arguments such as Jowitt's, for instance, that Ceauşescu realized the necessity of fusing nationalism and socialism (1971: 279), I think the story is much more complicated than that.

The most obvious source of the restored national values was, of course, the quiet revolt of the high Party elite from Soviet supervision, as they insisted upon controlling Romanian society and not being dictated to by someone else. All social life, says Mikhail Bakhtin (who, as one of Stalin's victims, should know), is an ongoing struggle between the attempt of power to impose a uniform language and the attempt of those below to speak in their own dialects ("heteroglossia") (Bakhtin 1981). Soviet rule entailed the wholesale imposition of a language, Marxism-Leninism, that was native to almost none in Romania and congenial to few. From factional struggles and purges an ethnic Romanian leadership had emerged that, despite its genuine adherence to Marxist ideas, was also heir to two centuries of politics couched in a language of national identity—the dialect, as it were, natural to Romanian political life.

Romanians were not the only ones to reply to Soviet domination in a national dialect: it was evident in Hungary in 1956, in Poland then and even more so in 1968. But Romanian leaders replied to Soviet rule in that language more often than others, culminating in Ceauşescu's famous speech on the Soviet invasion of Czechoslovakia:

The penetration of the troops of the five socialist countries into Czechoslovakia constitutes a great mistake and a grave danger to peace in Europe, and to the fate of socialism in the world. It is inconceivable in today's world, when peoples are rising up in struggle to defend their national independence and their right to equality, that . . . socialist states should transgress the liberty and independence of another state.

. . . The problem of choosing the roads of socialist construction is a problem for each individual Party, each State, each people. No one can pose as an adviser, as a guide to the way in which socialism is to be built in another country. . . .

Among the measures that the [Romanian] Central Committee, the Council of Ministers and the State Council have decided to take are . . . the formation of armed patriotic detachments of workers, peasants, and intellectuals, defenders of the independence of our socialist homeland. We want our people to have its armed units in order to defend its revolutionary gains. . . . The entire Romanian people will not permit anyone to violate the territory of our homeland. . . .

Be sure, comrades, be sure, citizens of Romania, . . . that we [communist leaders] shall never betray our homeland, we shall never betray the interests of our people (Ceauşescu 1969c [1968]): 415–417, my translation).

It is true that after this speech thousands of Romanians flocked to join the Party who would never have conceived of such a thing the day before. At least one of Ceauşescu's motives, I nonetheless believe, was not this but a Romanian national reply to Soviet domination, a reply born of both interest and sentiment.

The forces underlying its national form, however, included both institutionally embedded traditions and the active pressure of national sentiment from below. Something like this informs Hugh Seton-Watson's observation that because both the Romanian and the Polish communist leaders of the 1950s enjoyed so little popular support relative to other East European Party leaderships, they were on the one hand more dependent on the Soviet Union for their position, but, on the other, more vulnerable to upward seepage of the universal anti-Russian sentiments of their own masses. The presence of a "solid layer of middle-level, devoted, indoctrinated cadres" would have impeded this seepage, but such a layer did not exist. In consequence, both of these Party leaderships ended by identifying more with the national sentiments of their populations than with their Soviet patrons (Seton-Watson 1964: 168).

Seton-Watson's insight is particularly apt for the relation between Party leaders and the educated stratum, with its privileged opportunity (compared with the "masses") to spread concepts and ideas. The university students, the cadres-in-training, or the youths who headed for the new Writers' School, were people deeply socialized into patriotic attachment. Many of them were fresh from a Transylvania recently dismembered, its northern part returned to Hungary in 1940 and rejoined to Romania in 1944 after much suffering; others were from a Moldavia whose Bessarabian portion the Soviet Union had just amputated. The national sentiments of such people were freshly aroused, and they entered an intellectual and political environment from which it had been impossible to extirpate all remnants of the "bourgeois nationalist" practices chapter 1 has described. These people did not share the vantage point of the top political circles, who perhaps believed (as some argue) that only by silencing national discourse, thus convincing Stalin that his former opponents on the battlefield were now his staunchest allies, could Romania be sure of retaining Transylvania with its large Romanian population and its crucial industrial resources.[28]

For persons less central to power, however, at least as they tell it in retrospect, an injunction to silence on the national values could scarcely be borne. Scholars spoke in the 1980s of the supreme effort with which they sought to take advantage, in the 1950s and early 1960s, of any opening to bring a "national" text into the emergent socialist cultural canon—the writings of patriot-historian Pârvan, for example, officially castigated as a fascist yet republished in a small and truncated edition as early as 1957. An ex-employee of a major publishing house described to me, perhaps with some politicization after the fact, how the very weight of the interdictions on what could be published inspired him and his colleagues to strategize the printing of "some Romanian culture," emboldened by the tacit support of their well-placed superior. A cleverly selected poem of the interdicted national poet Eminescu, inserted into school manuals; a novel by a particular writer following a staged preemptive attack that nonetheless mentioned the "democratic" social message of his books . . . By such means, the intellectual coarchitects of Romania's independent line were working desperately to expand the possibilities for their own generation's creative output, as well as satisfying anti-Soviet feelings and enlivening the grey landscape of socialist realism.

It is this sort of activity, this sort of pressure from below, that makes me agree with Jowitt when he says, "Ideologically, there has been a continuous and conscious attempt to incorporate, recognize and control the idea of the nation" (1971: 273). "Control" is precisely the word. Although Ceauşescu may have brought the national discourse back into public usage, he assuredly did not do so from a position of dominance over its meanings. Rather, he presided over the moment when the Marxist discourse was decisively disrupted by that of the Nation. From then on, the Party struggled to maintain the initiative in the use of this rhetoric. If national ideology struck outside observers as the most salient feature of Romanian politics, this was not because the Party emphasized nothing else but because the Nation was so well entrenched discursively in Romanian life. It was the one subject that was guaranteed to get Romanians' attention, because so many of them were using it themselves.

These underlying sources of prevalent nationalism were augmented by others during the 1970s and 1980s, when, as described in the section above, the leadership's assault on cultural institutions politicized the entire field of cultural production. As the Party's attempt to monopolize culture sharpened conflict among the producers of symbols and images, different groups began to compete by recourse to national values: chapter 5 will show how conflicting claims to represent national values permeated the field of literary criticism, for example. The older disputes among indigenist and pro-western definitions of the Nation reappeared, all sides claiming to represent the true national values. Implicit in any definition was (among other things) a program for the composition of the Romanian cultural patrimony. Should it include only those creations that place the Nation at their center, or the works of western or other cultures that have inspired Romanian creativity as well, tying it to world cultural circuits? For the former, schoolbooks must now omit the fairy tales of the Brothers Grimm and include only Romanian historical legends and myths; the portraits of Plato and Aristotle on the walls of philosophy departments must be removed and pictures of Blaga—or of Ceauşescu, that greatest of all Romanian theorists—put in their place.[29] Fights over the republication of earlier thinkers began to take special account of their attitude to national values. For indigenists, anathematized fascist Nae Ionescu was now acceptable but Lovinescu was definitely out. The different camps all strove to capture and subdue to their own readings certain especially great ancestors—Eminescu, Blaga, Eliade—for one simply could not afford to be accused of denigrating them, lest one be branded a traitor to the national cause.

Although it is true that some of the impetus for this manipulation of the Nation by intellectuals in the decades of the 1970s and 1980s was, precisely, the favor shown to national values by the Ceauşescu leadership (itself resuming this language, I have suggested, partly because of the intellectuals' ongoing attachment to it), I do not·think the role of identity questions under Ceauşescu is adequately explained by this "regime use of nationalism." These questions had already achieved their own autonomy; the Party could not simply appropriate them and wave them about at will. Intellectuals who engaged in arguments about national identity were not doing so because they were told to, or because they were allowed to (although that was of course a necessary ingredient): they were doing so because by these means they could give vent to passionately held resistance to Soviet and/or Marxist-Leninist rule and, at the same time, lay claim to a larger share of resources in a political world in which national values had only briefly ceased to carry weight. Their arguments filled the air with national talk that increased from barely audible in the 1950s to deafening in the 1980s. Even the Party sometimes had trouble being heard above the din. Perhaps it would not be too much to say that the Party's own national exaggerations reflect, precisely, the effort that was required to assert some authority over the national idea.

It is this utilization in argument, this discourse and counter-discourse, definition and counterdefinition, that made national ideology so salient in Romania. Few other ideas launched by the Party, no matter how incessantly repeated, managed to enter into such a dialogue. Contestation, not mere repetition, is the vehicle of ideology: a word or symbol is a means for forming consciousness only if it arouses a counterword, a reply. The words and symbols that did this in Ceauşescu's Romania—not because a Party leadership wanted legitimacy but because different kinds of human beings differently situated in the social world cared about those particular significances—were words about national identity. This is why Ceauşescu's regime found itself compelled, despite the Marxist-Leninist orthodoxy its leaders might have preferred, to base its symbolic-ideological mode of control on an ideology that was national. And because that regime participated in it, the national discourse was further invigorated for the politics of a post-Ceauşescu era.

Considerations such as these might be sufficient in themselves to account for the durability of national talk in Romania, but they were augmented as well by systemic tendencies within the Romanian form of socialist political economy: an economy of shortage, a system dynamic maximizing the apparatus's control over resources for redistribution, and a weak state trying to project the appearance of strength. Some of these tendencies increased after the early 1970s, reproducing national ideology through time well after its initial "causes" had been superseded.

The link between national ideology and an economy of shortage (to be illustrated further in chapter 5) can be provisionally summarized as follows. Within a system of shortage, consumers at all levels of the system—firms, households, hungry individuals—enter into competition to acquire the goods they need. Unlike capitalist "demand-constrained" economies, in which a premium is placed on mechanisms that facilitate *selling* goods, the premium in supply-constrained socialist systems is on mechanisms facilitating *acquisition.* Any device that expels potential competitors for goods plays a highly functional role in such a system, from the consumer's point of view. National ideology is such a device: it bounds the community, defining clearly who is in and who is out. Significantly, this use of national ideology does not emanate primarily from the top but flows throughout the ranks of disadvantaged purchasers lower down. It is in the interests of average folks, not the top elite, to reduce the pool of competing purchasers by keeping matters of identity firmly in mind. All socialist economies have exhibited endemic shortage to some degree, but this is particularly true of the most highly centralized ones—such as Romania's, which was also the most "nationalist." Although this does not explain why such ideologies arose in the first place, it may prove an important element in perpetuating them.

A related factor that *does* emanate from the top, or at least from the Party bureaucracy as it extends downward into society, is that national ideology serves well the systemic tendency of the political apparatus to maximize the resources under its control. In this way, its effects resemble those of the cultural "protectionism" of interwar writers who wanted a guaranteed space for their output, but under socialism such protectionist tendencies feed the process of accumulation of the political apparatus, not of individual producers. For these purposes it is not just any national ideology that serves, but a definition of national identity that is indigenist. Such a definition focuses on *local* production of values and their *local* appropriation: Romanian values for a Romanian apparatus. Indigenism creates a Romanian genealogy with no foreign cousins who might have claims on the output. As has been suggested above and as will be further illustrated in chapter 5, indigenism is precisely the definition the Romanian party leadership came increasingly to prefer.

A final set of points concerning the durability of Romanian nationalism, especially in the austerity-ridden 1980s (in which, of course, the validity of the two above points is enhanced), relates to the weakness of socialist states and their representation or symbolic projection of themselves as strong. I will sidle into this argument via Jowitt's fascinating discussion of "castle regimes" (Jowitt 1987). Jowitt speaks of two phases through which most Leninist regimes have passed, Consolidation and Inclusion, and he describes the sequence for the Soviet case, attending especially to how the Soviet leadership created and transformed a particular image of itself. Initially representing itself as the incarnation of the Great October Revolution, Stalin's Soviet Union was anxious

> to insulate its quasi-sacral identity from what were viewed as potentially "contaminating" domestic and international environments . . . The typical response of any organization *relatively secure about power and insecure about identity* is to adopt a dogmatically concrete definition of its essential features, to juxtapose that identity to its potentially contaminating environments, and to try to distance itself from and dominate those diffusely hostile environments. Organizations in the developmental stage of Consolidation typically adopt "castle profiles." Under Stalin the Soviet Union became a "Castle Regime" (Jowitt 1987: 306, original emphasis).

This meant the "sacralization" of the Soviet Party, set apart from the "contaminating" and "profane" realities of Russian society and of the larger world by ideological, political, and coercive "moats" (ibid., 307–308). The rise of new Leninist regimes in Eastern Europe aggravated Stalin's "contamination anxiety," Jowitt argues, and resulted in the creation of a bloc held together by mechanical rather than organic solidarity, each regime a replica and segment of the sacred center rather than a specialized piece of a wider ("organic") division of labor. These regimes too began as "castle regimes" separated from their contaminating societies by secret police "moats" (ibid., 309–311).

It was precisely these features, Jowitt says, that Khrushchev sought to alter as he moved the Soviet Union from Consolidation to Inclusion, reducing the ideological and political tension (the "moats") between Party and surrounding world and trying to bring the mechanically linked "replica regimes" into an organic division of labor. We have already seen what the Romanian leadership thought of this idea. For them, mechanical solidarity was preferable to organic: it gave their Party apparatus the hope of controlling more resources, and more significant ones, as I have argued above. To this elite, the Consolidation "phase" was more congenial than its successor. Here, I think, we see the difficulty inherent in conceptualizing the history of these regimes as one of secular trends or "phases." What the Romanian case seems to present us with, rather, is a regime that went from Consolidation (the late 1940s and 1950s) to Inclusion (the 1960s) and back to Consolidation (the 1970s and 1980s). I prefer the notion of modes of control, which in the Romanian case shifted from an initial period of coercive control to a brief experiment with remunerative/symbolic control, then to a mode at first symbolic-ideological and subsequently more and more coercive.

This modification of Jowitt's terms leaves intact his central insight, however, which is that Consolidation regimes with their "castle" mentality and images of contamination are obsessed with the problem of identity, a problem about which national ideologies have a lot to say. We can see how the Nation entered into the problem of regime identity for Romania by noting, in the third period even more clearly than before, a system of concentric circles—two tiers of sacrality and contamination. First was the continuing division between "sacred" Party and "contaminating" Romanian society, evident above all in the sovereign disdain with which the high priests of Romanian politics treated the pagans who were their unfortunate subjects; but in addition, the Party identified itself entirely with the Nation [30] and saw contamination as coming from *beyond* the national borders. This was apparent in many forms, including the determined construction of Romania as an island of truth in a sea of calumnies and falsehood—the image some historians projected after 1986 [31]—and in remarks such as these in Ceauşescu's speeches:

The migration of foreign tribes and populations . . . checked for hundreds of years the development of the Romanian people. . . . Another well-known truth is that first the more advanced Daco-Roman civilization, then that of the Romanian people, left their imprint on the existence of the migratory populations which settled in this land (1988: 2).

In other words, Romanians were superior to the contaminating nomadic tribes (Hungarians and Slavs) that surrounded and debased them.

This construction of a unitary Romanian Party-Nation as an extreme instance of symbolic control was taking place, I note, in the context of centrifugal tendencies perhaps worse than those of the interwar years, themselves so productive of national rhetoric. Some of these tendencies were induced by the leadership itself: seeking to transfer the advantages of blocwide mechanical solidarity to the next level down, it applied a policy of "self-provisioning" (*auto-gestionare*) at the level of each county and, insofar as possible, to commune units within them. Each unit was expected to be maximally self-sufficient in the foodstuffs and other materials it required—within the constraints of heavy central planning, of course: this was not part of a decentralizing reform. Counties and even cities bartered with one another in kind to make up shortfalls.[32] In 1980 a highly placed industrial bureaucrat told an American economist that the central ministries had lost control of investment flows and decisions, as the heads of large enterprises bypassed the ministries to go directly to Ceauşescu for things like permission to buy expensive foreign equipment.[33] In Jowitt's view, "self-provisioning" resulted in "socialist feudalism," the center increasingly powerless as it depended increasingly on the lower-level units whose products were essential to paying off the foreign debt.[34] Counties came to resemble independent fiefdoms, held together by the unending peregrinations of Ceauşescu much as Charlemagne unified his kingdom in medieval times. In a different vein, intellectuals in Transylvania spoke to me with intense passion of their projects to develop a "Transylvanian cultural politics," opposed to what was happening in the center. Others reported how the statue of Transylvanian philosopher-poet Lucian Blaga was moved—*without* the approval of Bucharest[35]—from an invisible corner of the Cluj city park to a place of honor before the National Theater. Alongside these centrifugal tendencies there remained the intractable problem of Romania's national minorities, particularly the Hungarians, whose mass, restiveness, and potential irredentism posed as many difficulties in the 1980s as they had in the Romania of the 1930s.

If these examples suggest an erosion of internal central control, the late 1980s eroded something else equally upsetting to the leadership: Romania's economic independence from the socialist bloc. While the 1960s and 1970s were the era of growing connections with the West, the 1980s saw the country's reincorporation into the East. The share of Romania's trade going to other bloc countries rose from 34 percent in 1980 to 53 percent in 1983 and to 57 percent in 1985; trade with the Soviet Union grew from 17 percent in 1982 to 22 percent in 1984 to 33 percent in 1986 (Georgescu 1988: 77). Without the Soviet market, less demanding than western ones, Romania's trade would have been in serious difficulty (ibid., 85).[36] These reversals accompanied battered relations with western states—the withdrawal of U.S. Most-Favored-Nation status and of some European ambassadors, for example—connected with western reassessments of Ceauşescu's human rights policies.

Here, then, are all the elements of a weak state presiding over a fragmented society and suffering a renewed Soviet dependency, yet speaking as loudly as possible of the unity and independence of the Nation.

To understand this speech as simply a manipulation of popular support impoverishes what was in fact a much more urgent and consequential project: to constitute, through discourse, wholeness for a reality that was in fragments and sovereignty for a vassal—to constitute a wholeness and a sovereignty that were imaginary. Years of trying to build up a state resting on a teleology of progressive change and an ideology of internationalism (with the acceptance of internal diversity) had ended in the realization that the state could adequately construct itself only in terms of what it had at first denied: a teleology of national continuity and an ideology of national values, premised on internal uniformity.[37] Through national ideology, the leadership represented its weak state and regime as the embodiment of a strong, autonomous, unified will (cf. Anagnost 1988; Lefort 1986). In December 1989, this imaginary construct was smashed, liberating the national discourse—now strengthened by its association with a monolithic power—for use in a new political environment.

An account of the prevalence of Romanian national ideology in the 1970s and 1980s must at the same time suggest, if only summarily, why national rhetoric penetrated Romania's "air space" so much more than that of other East European countries, as many external observers believe (see, e.g., King 1980: 121). First, any regime that opted for decentralization or for a mode of control other than the symbolic might not be expected to manifest much national rhetoric at the official level. Hungary presents the starkest contrast: the defeat of the 1956 uprising foreclosed any emphasis on national ideology and compelled a weakened Party to adopt a remunerative strategy, which it implemented via decentralization and reform. A similar argument could be made for Czechoslovakia after 1968, but in that case remunerative control came with higher centralization and coercion than in Hungary. Other regimes that retained a high degree of centralization, such as East Germany, did not face the Romanian regime's history of intense debate about the national identity: to the extent that such a thing had been part of German life in the 1930s, the entire raison d'être of Communist party rule in divided Germany was to oppose the forms and fascist consequences of German nationalism.

The evolution in Poland resembled that in Romania in several respects, but after experiments in the 1950s and 1968 with a nationalist legitimation comparable to Romania's, the Gierek leadership veered sharply into a remunerative mode of control, based in standard-of-living guarantees shored up not by decentralization, as in Hungary, but by imports. Bulgaria appeared in the 1980s to have entered upon an era of official ideologization not unlike Romania's, but this followed earlier modes of control in which remunerative strategies endured longer than in the Romanian case and accompanied a lower degree of centralization, with consequently less severe shortage. In addition, interwar Bulgaria—truncated rather than enlarged, and therefore losing rather than gaining national minorities—may have been less obsessed with defining the Nation than was Romania, for all the reasons mentioned in chapter 1; thus, Bulgarian communists perhaps inherited a less robustly institutionalized national ideology than did the Party in Romania.

I have tried to show here why I think one must see a national discourse in Romania as more than something used instrumentally by the Communist party but as, rather, inscribed in and emanating from many quarters of Romanian society. Because of its force in other quarters, because others used it in their own battles and sought to impose their own meanings on it, the Party had to strive as well to control the image of Romanian identity and to defend this image as adequately representing and protecting the Nation's interests. These efforts produced and reproduced Romanian national ideology, as a field of contention whose symbols were always open to other uses. In November 1987, for example, rioting workers in Braşov sang the hymn of the nineteenth-century national movement "Romanian, Awake!"; student demonstrators at Iaşi university the following spring gathered around the statue of national hero Alexandru Ioan Cuza, first sovereign of a united Romania. My discussion has not even mentioned some of the other important social actors with whom the Party contended—the Orthodox Church, for one.[38] Another exceedingly important participant, whom I leave out of this book only for lack of expertise and space, is the circle of Romanian emigrés, particularly in Paris and Munich, who shaped the broadcasts of Radio Free Europe and of several influential emigré publications. In offering their own images of Romania, they provoked counterimages from Romania's intellectuals and Party officials, who struggled to keep the emigré image from prevailing abroad.

To say that the Romanian Communist Party was merely one of several social actors who spoke a language of national identity in political struggle is not to say, however, that all these competitors enjoyed equal footing. They did not: the Party was institutionally more powerful than all the others, and it set the principal conditions of their speech. From the Party came the notions of Stalinism and dogmatism that would be so active in battles within culture in subsequent decades; from the Party came the initiative that brought a subterranean language of national values back above ground; from Party leaders came the restrictions on cultural activity that polarized the field of cultural production and amplified its language of conflict, a language that was national. And from the Party bureaucracy were disbursed the resources that sustained cultural life and that had to be competed for, ultimately, in the language the Party authorized.

That the Party authorized this language does not imply, nonetheless, control over its meanings or an end to symbolic battles toward this end, battles whose consequences should not be underestimated. The erosion of Romania's image as a civilized, *European* country contributed, in the late 1980s, to the difficulties and eventual overthrow of Ceauşescu's dictatorship. After years of western favor for the bloc's independent "maverick," westerners came to see Ceauşescu's Romania as an eastern despotism, unreliable in its adherence to European norms. Consequent suspension of Most-Favored-Nation status and normal diplomatic relations aggravated the misery and humiliation that led Romanians finally to rise up against the regime. The intimate tie between Romania's identity and the crumbling of Ceauşescu's dictatorship is nowhere better shown than in the letter six Communist party veterans addressed to Ceauşescu in March 1989, cited in my Introduction, which said,

Romania is and remains a European country, and as such it must move forward within the framework of the Helsinki process rather than turning against that process. You have begun to change the geography of the rural areas, but you cannot move Romania into Africa.

For the signers of this letter, Romania's European identity was a potent symbol both within the country and in the West, and Romania's threatened "move into Africa" a cause for rebellion.

This, then, was the environment for the cultural politics to be described in the chapters to follow. It was an environment of high centralization and tight control by a Party that nonetheless did not command its society; an environment of tremendous shortage in all spheres, with rampant competition for actual and symbolic resources. Its leadership's mode of control gave an implicit edge to producers of culture, while undermining their capacity to produce independently. Subsequent chapters illustrate the appropriation and reappropriation of national symbols, the definition and redefinition of cultural canons, the conflicting revalorizations of accumulated cultural values that resulted from this situation and that reproduced national ideology year after year, decade after decade, exasperating the attempts of the Party leadership to bring the national discourse within its exclusive control.

PART II

Cases

CHAPTER FOUR

The Means of Conflict: "Elitism," "Dogmatism," and Indigenizations of Marxism

---

Even if no other legal parties exist, other parties in fact always do exist and other tendencies which cannot be legally coerced; and, against these, polemics are unleashed and struggles are fought as in a game of blind man's buff. In any case it is certain that in such parties cultural functions predominate, which means that political language becomes jargon. In other words, political questions are disguised as cultural ones, and as such become insoluble.

—Antonio Gramsci

Chapters 5 through 7 describe three contests within three areas of Romanian culture—literary criticism, historiography, and philosophy. These are but three of the many contests and the many areas of Romanian culture in which the shift of emphasis within the Party leadership, its reassertion of control over cultural production, and the economic difficulties of the 1980s heightened the competition among intellectuals. Their competition took several forms that left no publicly written trace: quests for patronage and influence, gossip and backbiting, deals and compromises, and so on. In addition, it took the form most typical of combat among intellectuals: written words.

The words through which cultural producers fought were often specific to their disciplines, literati writing about aesthetics and literary values, for example, and historians about the "scientific" interpretation of specific events. A number of words and rhetorical devices, however, along with a number of tactics, regularly appeared in more than one context. In this chapter[1] I describe a few of the most frequent devices and tactics through which intellectuals tried to disqualify their opponents and to position themselves more favorably. The ones I illustrate here, some briefly and some in detail, were important elements of the struggles discussed in chapters 5 through 7; those chapters will be easier to follow if I describe the major rhetorical moves and their meanings in advance, even though the meanings were fully realized only in the context of particular disputes. I concentrate on (1) a series of concerns familiar from chapter 1—and therefore treated summarily here—about "foreign imports" and Romania's link to world culture; (2) accusations of "elitism," "fascism," "dogmatism," and "proletcultism"; and (3) the technique of bringing into one's intellectual lineage (or excluding from that of others) great figures of Romania's cultural past. This last technique, which I call "genealogical appropriation," may entail playing up (or down) suitable portions of a great man's opus so as to emphasize one's affinity with him, interpreting his work selectively, or, sometimes, creating an altogether new identity for him (for example, a poet is remade into a sociologist).

There was much more to the verbal conflict of Romanian cultural politics than merely random exchanges of barbed words: the environment itself gave certain verbal weapons added force. The reason was the nature of bureaucratic support for culture. As I suggested in chapter 2 and will argue further in chapter 5, much of the politicking in Romanian cultural life involved efforts to obtain support from the political center, whether in the form of funds, permission to publish, supplies of paper, perfunctory censorship, posts in universities and institutes, or other such things. To gain central backing required using arguments and idioms the center found persuasive. In this book I generally speak of these as arguments about *cultural representativeness*, with various contenders claiming to represent Romania's cultural interests best, in hopes that their program would persuade the center to support them. In Ceauşescu's Romania, there were two sets of idioms the center tended to find persuasive: initially there was only the language of Marxism-Leninism, on which the regime ostensibly rested, later joined by the language of national values, which coexisted with and increasingly displaced it. Appeals (or accusations against an opponent) that employed either of these two idioms were more likely to be efficacious than appeals or accusations couched in other terms.

Although these idioms were both privileged at the center, they did not enjoy equal favor among most members of society. Nearly all Romanians I have met, regardless of social position, are deeply attached to the values of the Nation, whereas the values of Marxism-Leninism have enjoyed the respect of almost none. Yet effective political action often involved using both idioms, often simultaneously. The conduct of intellectual politics therefore entailed what I call the "indigenization of Marxism": the incorporation of categories from Marxism-Leninism into arguments in which ethnic or national questions had priority. More precisely, it means the subordination of the imposed Marxist-Leninist discourse to the terms of the national discourse, resulting in the subversion of Marxism-Leninism's central terms.

My use of the word "Marxism" here is ambiguous. Strictly speaking, Marxism is merely a social theory that has inspired a variety of institutionalized regimes—Leninism, Stalinism, Gorbachev's perestroika, "Ceauşism"—in which the meanings of terms and concepts differ substantially from those in Marx's theoretical analyses. Although the institutionalized form is generally called "vulgar" or "orthodox" or "official" Marxism, to distinguish it from its nobler and more supple ancestor, for the most part I avoid this stylistically cumbersome qualifier. In what follows, it is the "vulgar," official meaning of Marxism that I intend, except in the few places where I explicitly state that someone is working with Marx's analytic tools.

To speak of the indigenization of Marxism is to draw attention to a major problem faced by Eastern Europe's Marxist-Leninist regimes: how could a language of politics that was imposed by force from outside become part of meaningful political action within a society? How did powerful preexisting discourses, such as the national one, domesticate the intruder, becoming in their turn part of its trajectory as the two bonded together toward forming a new hegemonic order? There is to my knowledge no literature on this topic, only some useful hints. Ernesto Laclau has written, for example, of the rhetorical form Marxism must take if it is to incorporate existing ideologies rather than running aground on them:

The validity of Marxism will thus depend on its capacity to interrupt other discourses, to constitute new objects and to produce a new field of understandings. Other discourses (the discourse of the nation, the discourse of democracy, the discourse of sexuality) are no longer superstructures, simply ideological reflections of an extra-discursive movement of things. They are material forces which constitute subjects, which produce effects and faced with which Marxism must prove its validity by the effects that it produces and not thanks to any kind of a priori ontological privilege (Laclau MS: 3).[2]

Regardless of what Party leaders might have hoped (and largely because of the imperious manner in which they employed Marxist terms), the rhetoric of Romanian cultural politics accomplished precisely the reverse. Instead of constructing Marxism as a separate and vital force, it indigenized Marxism, interrupted the Marxist discourse with a national one, and reproduced subjects for whom Marxism had little validity except, tenuously, in relation to the discourse on the Nation. Were it not that any competition for bureaucratic funds had to avail itself of concepts the bureaucracy had institutionalized, Marxism would not have entered cultural politics at all.

Contests for cultural representativeness in the language of national identity nonetheless had to entwine themselves with those Marxist terms. The present chapter illustrates how this took place, as specific vehicles of cultural struggle at the same time indigenized Marxism. Although the apparent outcome in socialist Romania was that national ideology flourished while Marxist categories withered, their awkward union may well bear fruit in the postsocialist era, in which such accusations as "elitist," "fascist," and especially "dogmatist" (all derived from the regime's official rhetoric) may well have an active life.

Foreign Imports, "Universality," and Representativeness

Chapter 1 has already shown that long before the communist takeover in Romania, one could accomplish heavy political work by accusing opponents of borrowing foreign models for Romania's cultural or economic development. Indigenists charged their "pro-western" enemies with betraying the national values in preference for things from abroad, which stunted the growth of values that might be nurtured at home. As I suggested earlier, arguments of this type effected a kind of cultural protectionism, insulating local cultural markets from the influx of foreign books and ideas (see Anderson 1983).

They also facilitated claims upon a political bureaucracy determined to consolidate the position of Romanian culture in a multinational state.

Exactly these same charges appeared in Romania of the 1970s and 1980s; all that differed was the context in which they were made and the systemic tendencies they served. With socialism, the relative significance of protected markets diminished, and claims upon the state became a much larger part of the sustenance for culture. Nevertheless, indigenists still accused their opponents of destroying Romanian culture by imitations unsuited to the national character. Their opponents sometimes counterattacked with the argument that if nothing but local values are produced and celebrated, Romanian creations will never enter the "circuit of universality," that is, gain world recognition as culturally valuable. Both sides insisted that theirs was the best defense of Romanian values, one group averring that it protects Romania from being overwhelmed by alien forms, the other that it guarantees the entry of Romanian culture onto the world stage, where the too-parochial products of an excessive indigenism will never appear.

Arguments about "foreignness" and "universality" were also, of course, arguments about identity, cultural representativeness, and another term linked with these two, "authenticity." Debates in many fields concerned how to define and represent a piece of Romanian culture to itself and to the world, some persons raising up any product regarded as local or "authentic" while accusing others of imperiling these with "foreign" values and standards. Appeals to "universality" were, in these people's view, merely a cover for cultural imperialism. The others pointed vigorously to great Romanian creations that had clearly been inspired by or "synchronized" with western developments. They invoked Romanians' European identity to argue why western influence was not necessarily so "foreign" and would generate cultural creations fully representative of the genius of Romanians. (Without such justification, one's translation of Baudrillard or Derrida might go unpublished.)

These arguments as to what was alien influence and what was genuinely representative crossed international borders to include Romanian opponents outside Romania as well as within it. One columnist for a cultural magazine sustained a long diatribe entitled "Short-wave Pseudo-culture," repeatedly questioning who is to define "true" culture and who is to represent it. The object of his attack was Radio Free Europe, run by a group he depicted as "traitors" (including the emigré daughter of "synchronist" Lovinescu [see chapter 1]) aiming "defamatory campaigns" at the culture of a Romania they had abandoned and now wished to destroy. Even this international attack, however, also targeted the pro-westernism of critics and literary historians inside Romania, calling their representativeness into question.

To a Romanian bureaucracy pursuing a policy of economic autarchy and dispensing support for culture during a fiscal crisis, the representation that probably seemed more suitable was one that reduced the cost of imports—a kind of "import-substitution" policy for cultural items (Romanian-made films, for example, rather than the American or West European serials common in the 1970s, and Romanian books rather than the western ones whose translation rights gobble up scarce foreign currency). For this and a variety of other reasons, the Romanian party leadership of the 1970s and 1980s opted for indigenist arguments over pro-western ones in the cultural sphere. This was evident in Ceauşescu's speech quoted at the head of chapter 3, as well as in many other pronouncements. It is unnecessary to dwell further on "foreign imports" as a weapon in cultural conflicts, other than to note that although such a charge usually criticized imitation of the *West*, it could refer as well to imitation of *Soviet* practices. This will be important in discussing "dogmatism," below.

"Elitism" and Cognizant Publics

One powerful way of undermining others' cultural representativeness was to accuse them of "elitism." To make such a charge was to select an instrument from the arsenal of Marxist understandings about class struggle and employ it to improve one's own situation, with respect to the authorities who dispensed funds and to the audiences at whom culture was directed. An accusation of elitism created two opposed categories: elitists, disdainful of the masses, and those ostensibly on the side of the masses, who write in a manner accessible to them and profess faith in their intelligence. Here are two examples:

The symptoms of elitist leanings are still frequent enough. We have heard insistent theorizing about the easy-going, lazy, dull, imbecile reader, incapable of deciphering the subtleties of modern literature. This comes from an elitist tendency that tries to belittle and inculpate the reader. The same tendency is illustrated also by the persistence of certain works that have no audience and are usually unreadable but are faithful to some elitist model. And we can detect an elitist direction in the excessive stake that some people place on specializing the act of criticism, by using an ostentatious terminology inaccessible to the uniniti-ated (Purcaru 1986: 67–68).

I am in the group of those who write contemporary Romanian literature . . . In fact, this group is the most numerous and powerful . . . The other so-called "grouplets," elitist and neo-elitist, are minor and peripheral, and only a certain (old) framework of activity helps them rise to the surface of the water, which they sometimes muddy so they can keep afloat without being seen for what they are: social residua . . . . (ibid., 156–157).

Clearly, neither masses nor Party leaders should trust such "elitist" writ-ers and critics to represent Romanian culture. Owing to their im-plied bourgeois origin (the "elitist grouplets" rest on *old* frameworks for action and are *social residua*), they hold the Romanian masses in contempt.

Another sin imputed to "elitists" was *cosmopolitanism*, a "non-Roma-nian" trait invoking the alleged foreign cultural preferences and/or ori-gins of certain Romanian elites of the past. Cosmopolitan elitists com-bine class sin with foreignness; such persons, this charge insinuates, cannot possibly represent the true spirit of the Romanian people. In contrast, it is understood that the accusing "patriots" can be counted upon to represent and defend Romanian culture properly, both to Ro-manian audiences and to the world. If to be culturally representative in Ceauşescu's Romania was to gain power and cultural resources from above, then a charge of elitism aimed to deprive opponents of access to those things.

Allegations of elitism not only influenced the positioning of groups in relation to power, however, but served more broadly to reconfigure places in the entire social pyramid that included persons of relatively lower and higher status. To make a successful claim to status as a bearer of cultural authority requires that this authority be acknowledged by others (Bourdieu 1985: 730–731), who recognize both that it is of value and that they themselves have less of it. Therefore, part of forming and reproducing elite groups is the formation of a unified field, which includes persons of "low" culture who will recognize the superior claims of those possessing "high" culture. Elites can successfully claim status as bearers of literacy, for example, only if there is a public that is sufficiently literate both to value this dimension and to acknowledge its own deficiency thereon. We might call this a "cognizant public," distin-guishing it from nonelite groups who are *non*cognizant—who do not participate in a unified field with those elites and thus do not recognize the significance of elite endowments and claims. A major means of forming a cognizant public is the "civilizing" mission some elites launch with their inner "primitives," whom they seek to illuminate with learning that will dispel the mists of darkness. Civilizing missions have been brought to colonial peoples by agents of imperial powers—the rhetoric of English imperialism is a fine example—and also by would-be national elites, civilizing the "backward" peasants of their own territories (as in chapter 1).

Seen in this light, charges of elitism attacked the allegiance of an opponent's cognizant public. This public consisted not only of bureaucrats, acknowledging the status of petitioners to favor, but of audiences for cultural products—audiences that took on new importance when Romanian culture was partially recommodified, as explained in chapter 3. To accuse a writer or poet of elitism could drive away potential consumers of his or her novels and poems. When directed at literary critics, it said to the audience, "Do not accept these people's judgment of my book; their interests are antidemocratic." The stakes behind such a charge were therefore threefold: it aimed to disqualify in political, social-status, and economic terms.

An accusation of elitism was a powerful weapon of exclusion, fashioned from a Marxist language and brought into the service of cultural-political battles. It took an idea saturated with the much-drilled notion of class struggle (which, I can affirm on the basis of twenty months' field research in Romanian villages, has not been without public effect) and employed it for competitive advantage. The tactic had a number of variants, such as the complaint that the actions of a certain group ignore "communal interests" or reek of a "proprietary attitude" to public goods or are characteristic of a "rentier mentality" (see Brăescu 1982*b* and *e*). All of them made an implicit appeal to Marxist notions so as to condemn something in the behavior of others. As will be seen in the examples of later chapters, the condemnation almost always implied a lack of patriotic attachment to the values of the Romanian Nation, which "anti-elitists" equated with the Romanian *masses*.

In counterattack some people appropriated Marxist terms of a different sort. They claimed, for example, to uphold "rationalism," a quality of the enlightened thought of which Marxism is the apogee, and to oppose "irrationalism and mysticism," cardinal sins in the official Marxist analysis of fascism and rightist currents in earlier times. A classic instance is one scholar's advocacy of interwar philosopher Rădulescu-Motru as greater than others of his time (such as Lucian Blaga), on the grounds that the former was a rationalist and the others strayed close to mysticism (see Ornea 1985*a*: 184–189). This implicitly accused Blaga's latter-day supporters of rightist associations unbefitting a communist. Other uses of official Marxist categories included conflicting claims as to who practiced "dialectical thinking" best and could, on these grounds, obtain preferment (see chapter 7). In many although not all such moves, the advocates of "rationalism" or "dialectics" were not defending notions to which they in fact adhered: they were making rhetorical use of instruments of inclusion and exclusion, a use that was parasitic upon the emphases of officialdom.

"Fascists," "Dogmatists," and "Proletcultists"

Central to many arguments in Romanian cultural politics under Ceauşescu were accusations and counteraccusations of dogmatism and proletcultism (or neoproletcultism), sometimes accompanied by insinuations of fascism. That is, persons on one or another side stated that their opponents were resuscitating the dogmatic Marxism of the early Stalinist period in Romanian socialism, with its vulgar attempt to intrude a "proletarian culture" ("proletcultism") into Romania's cultural life; or they claimed or insinuated that the opponents were latter-day bearers of the fascism of interwar Romanian politics. Although all sides had recourse to these terms, accusations of fascism tended to come more from one side and accusations of dogmatism more from their main adversaries. I will discuss "fascism" briefly first and "dogmatism" at greater length.

An accusation of fascism draws its force from one of the major legitimations of Romania's Communist party: the part it played in overthrowing the pro-Hitler dictator Antonescu in 1944 and in shifting Romania's wartime alliance from the Nazis to the Allies. In the late 1940s and 1950s, much of communist policy toward groups and individuals (deportations, purges, imprisonments) stemmed from their actual or alleged ties with the interwar fascist right. Early Romanian communism defined itself above all in opposition to fascism. Given this background, one sees how loaded were charges such as the following, which excoriated the writer of some religiously tinted poems appearing in a publication called *The Week* (see chapter 5):

The verses just quoted do not come from some week in the Middle Ages, nor from the weeks of "glory" of the Gîndirists. They saw the light of print just last week in number 599 of *The Week*, over the signature of Corneliu Vadim Tudor and under the stupefying title "Sincere Poems." . . . It is not the first time that this sincere poet drinks from the well of anachronistic conceptions and of the vocabulary of that spirit [*duh*], sad to recall, that proselytized in earlier days (L.B. 1982).

The wording of this attack openly links poet Tudor with the Gîndirists, the ultra-right-wing interwar group of N. Crainic (see chapter 1), which promoted a Romanian "spirit" (*duh*) based in Orthodoxy, anachronistic by Marxist standards.

Those who accused opponents of fascism rarely used the word "fascist" itself but, as in this example, contented themselves with evoking its associations—by mentioning "Orthodoxism," for instance, or the color green, worn by interwar fascists. Even more subtle was reference to current disputes as a resumption of interwar arguments between "traditionalists" and "modernists." Since everyone knows that most "traditionalists" were linked with the right, calling one's adversary a "traditionalist" was tantamount to a charge of fascism. Here is an example:

In the 1970s, the writers I have called traditionalists launched a very powerful offensive . . . . Using as polemical weapons—in a dishonest but effective way— a raised tone, insinuation, ungrounded accusation, and exasperating insistence, the traditionalists dominated the period in the sense that their human presence blurred the literary presence of others and even of themselves (A. Ştefănescu 1981: 2).

Behind this seemingly bland description, the author has conjoined his opponents with the fascist right, hoping thereby to disqualify them in the public eye.

Although it might seem that in a socialist regime claiming legitimacy from resistance to Hitler's allies, to be accused of fascism would be deadly, even worse was to be accused of proletcultism or dogmatism. The reason, as explained in chapter 3, is the sorry history of the suppression of national values under Stalin, experienced with pain by many Romanians attached to the traditions and values of their culture. For Romanian intellectuals of all kinds, "dogmatism" and "proletcultism" evoked the rigid political attitude that deviated all cultural production into channels entirely alien to most of culture's producers and also to its public. Over the period 1965 to 1989, this sorry history and its effects on politicizing national values were conjured up with references to "dogmatism" by persons having very different positions in the field of cultural production. Its meanings varied over that span as well.

At their root, "dogmatist" and "proletcultist" were euphemisms for foreign influence (Gheorghiu 1987: 60) whether this be Soviet or western, although the notions originally referred to the Soviet Union. These terms have two possible meanings: subservience to foreigners at the expense of one's own values (e.g., accepting Stalin's dictates even though they were injurious to Romanian culture), and contaminating cultural creation with political concerns (e.g., insisting on socialist realism even if the result was bad art). Although both were rooted in the political intrusion of Soviet values into Romanian culture, the "foreign" and "political" elements gradually became separated. Both meanings of the words must be kept in mind if one is to understand how people on opposite sides of an argument could utilize identical terms: on one side they meant "preferring international to national values" and on the other side "contaminating culture with politics." In the cultural contests to be discussed in chapters 5 through 7, the persons who most often accused others of "dogmatism" tended to be from the group for whom it meant preferring international over national values; as a result, my illustrations come from that group disproportionately. In the history of this rhetorical weapon, however, persons of all kinds had recourse to it, and in the 1980s the enemies of the above group increasingly returned their own accusations of "dogmatism" or "proletcultism," denouncing thereby their opponents' advocacy of an art contaminated by politics.

A few examples of these sorts of allegations will help to illustrate. A literary historian associated with the left since immediately after the war recalled the anti-westernism of those times, clearly implying their return: "Let us not forget that in the epoch of proletcultism all contact was forbidden with the 'decadent occident.' In those days it was very easy to throw around the term 'cosmopolitanism'" [a term that had recently reappeared—k.v.] (Crohmălniceanu, in Ungheanu 1985: 468). A philosopher described the cultural liberalization of the late 1960s, with implicit criticism of its reversal in the 1970s and 1980s, as follows:

[There occurred] a liberalization of thought, an acceptance of the fact that it is possible to think and to create culturally without holding to dogmas . . . . [E]xiting from the asphyxiation of dogmatism presupposed the rediscovery of the great sources of culture, an opening toward its universal and western values (Liiceanu 1983: 230).

A sociologist explained why he found literature an appealing object of analysis, lining himself up with the new indigenists and distancing himself from some of his "Marxist" colleagues in sociology: "In these conditions in which the social sciences have lagged behind the spirit of politics . . . and genuflect to dogmatism, literature has become the most faithful ideological expression of the [enlightened] new politics" (Mihu 1983: 215). In the context of an argument in which one literary historian objected to his adversary's having defined "class" in ethnic terms, the adversary rejoined:

I thought it was no longer reprehensible to speak about ethnicity, as it used to be . . . during the dogmatic epoch. Is it an "ethnic obsession" to talk about Romanian spirituality, about our origins and exemplary personalities . . . such as Eminescu, Hasdeu, Pârvan, Iorga, and Blaga . . . ? . . . Will we reach the point when we are ashamed to be their descendants and to be Romanian? (Sorescu 1982).

In a discussion of Radio Free Europe, a journalist hostile to it stated:

[Its tactics] belong to the adaptable dogmatic spirit . . . [and it] learned a great deal from the dogmatists of yesterday, with whom in many cases they collaborate. . . . And now, with the idea of establishing a "depoliticized" literature, now that the adepts of dogmatism have been wholly compromised, the Radio is seeking out what we might call dogmatism's "mute contemporaries." . . . [A] biographical study would prove that the "dignity" of many who claim they never had any connection to dogmatism rests on hot air (Silvestri, in Purcaru 1986: 369).[3]

This same journalist clarified the *opposite* of dogmatism thus: "In saying that [his own group] is anti-dogmatic, I wanted to emphasize that it proposes the idea of *fundamental values*, in contrast to the cultural direction of the 1950s [i.e., dogmatism—k.v.] that was so frigid (concerning the essence of the nation)" (Silvestri 1986). Finally, a literary critic disparaged the "leaders of aggressive proletcultism" for their attachment to a certain earlier critic, Călinescu, of dubious leftist credentials and a certain political opportunism:

After having sworn by [earlier leftist critics] Gherea or Ibrăileanu, our "up-to-date" critics have now put their faith in G. Călinescu, a feat not lacking in dexterity . . . . In the shelter of Călinescu's protean and secularized genius, the neo-dogmatists can breathe easily (Grigurcu 1981).

The persons who made the first, second, and seventh of these comments would be loosely grouped in one camp wholly opposed to those who made the fourth, fifth, and sixth (the third occupies an anomalous position). This variety shows how complex were the vehicles for mutual recriminations, which meant different things depending on the mouths from which they came.

Aside from the two different *meanings* of dogmatism and proletcultism given above (suppression of the national, and the intrusion of
politics), the terms had two somewhat different *uses*. The first was
against persons active in 1980s Romanian literary life who had been
instrumental in the earlier Stalinist suppression of national values. Most
of them were (and in some cases remained) of genuine leftist sentiment,
and some were not "ethnic Romanians" (i.e., they were of Jewish or
Hungarian origin). Given the evolution of Romanian politics, in the
1980s some of these "old Stalinists" were voices of liberalism and mod-
eration. Nonetheless, opponents could seize upon any opinion they
offered as recidivist, as resuscitating the antinationalism of those early
years. Such uses of "dogmatism" were addressed at specific persons
with specific pasts. Second was the use of "dogmatism" and "proletcultism" not *ad hominem* but in reference to a general climate in which
political influence from abroad overwhelms the development of national culture. Thus, in the late 1960s, some writers denounced as
"dogmatists" those early (Soviet-serving) Stalinists who stood in the
way of cultural liberalization, and in the 1980s these same writers were
themselves the objects of attack *together with* those early Stalinists, both
being accused of suppressing national values in preference to fashions
from the West.

The examples given above were mere sniper's shots fired at random
into the crowd, in comparison with the heavy artillery that was also
wheeled out. To exemplify, here is part of an article from a cultural
weekly, under the significant heading "Points of Reference for a Dialectical and Antidogmatic Consideration of Literature and Art."[4] The
author complains that dogmatism is once again making headlines in the
cultural press, despite numerous prior dismantlings of it; this necessi-
tates inquiry into what proletcultism and cultural dogmatism accomplish, in hopes of preventing yet another resurgence of them. First he
rejects the possibility that early proletcultist excesses may have resulted
from the unpreparedness and inexperience of the first generation of
leaders after 1947, and then he reveals their true objective:

The motor and justification of proletcultism were neither blindness nor inexperience nor lack of culture. The primordial objectives of cultural dogmatism
were insistently to compromise the national dimension of our literature and art
and methodically to heap blame upon them, and to undermine the foundations
of Romania's cultural essence. . . . Beyond any doubt, *the foreign model* always
lay close to the heart of true proletcultists, giving them courage and hope. . . .
The proletcultist adventure was in fact a plot against the Romanian spiritual
essence. Not by chance, the affirmation of proletcultism and cultural dog-

matism was possible precisely in an unfortunate moment when the national sentiment was purposely inhibited and in eclipse. . . . Once the Romanian people, under the leadership of its Communist party, regained its self-awareness, cultural dogmatism was compromised on the stage of history. . . . [D]ogmatists wore any clothing as long as it was foreign; they lined up obediently under any flag as long as it was not our own; their confessed aim was and is the liquidation of the historical roots of autochthonous culture. How else can one explain the fact that opposition to reediting the texts of Mihai Eminescu, N. Iorga, Vasile Pârvan, G. Călinescu and others comes exactly from them, prepared as they are to lie down in front of a train if necessary to keep *Romanian writings* from reappearing? (Pelin 1983: 4, original emphases).

One need go no further than this quotation to see that accusations of dogmatism and proletcultism were intimately involved with defining and defending national identity. Anyone claiming to defend the true values of Romanian culture might accuse enemies of *the* cardinal sin against the Nation: ties to Stalinist dogmatism, with its assault on national culture. (Chapter 5 will show more clearly the organization of the conflict from which the quotation emerged.)

Although this accusation is part of the contest over representativeness and cognizant publics, as with the example of "elitism" its terms involve an implicit relation to Marxism as well. The relation here, however, is not (as with elitism) to Marxist *conceptual* categories but to the actual institutionalization of Marxism in Romania via the Soviet army, a historical experience that gave "dogmatic" (foreign-imposed) Marxism a decidedly bad name. As a result, talk of "dogmatism" created *two* Marxisms, a bad one and a good one: the dogmatic, foreign one and an implied antidogmatic indigenous one, whose task was to denounce outside influence and serve Romania. The former is the Marxism of traitors and the latter that of patriots. Persons who deployed "dogmatism" in this way forged a bond linking proletcultism or dogmatic Marxism with foreignness and the *suppression* of national values. Others, their opponents, used this rhetorical weapon in a different way, forging a bond among (neo)proletcultism/dogmatism, the prostitution of genuine art before politics, and *disservice* to national values. Both groups were jointly accomplishing the same result: the construction of a link between definitions of national values and forms of Marxism. They were indigenizing Marxism by making some of the judgments relevant to its history inextricable from defense of the Nation. In a word, the link was that in Romania, good Marxists are patriots. This is a long way from Marx's observation that the proletariat has no country.

An additional extended example will show how "dogmatism" constructs this object—the Marxist patriot—alongside an indigenization of Marxism. The example shows Transylvanian sociologist Achim Mihu[5] launching an attack on the "dogmatists" who debilitated the career and scholarly output of Romania's most gifted twentieth-century thinker and philosopher-poet, Transylvanian Lucian Blaga (see chapter 1), thereby depriving Romanian culture of some of its most priceless values. Although Mihu's expressed object was the dogmatism of the 1940s and 1950s, his attack was also—given its badly outdated target—evidently on "dogmatists" of the 1980s, who were never specified. In an interview, Mihu defined dogmatism as any simplistic or sovietized reading of the works of major Romanian cultural figures, such as readings that dismiss Blaga as a "philosophical idealist," and he acknowledged outright that Blaga is for him a symbol of national values against dogmatic Marxism of this kind.

Mihu, who at the time had just become Party secretary in his university, defines thus the Marxism in whose name he attacks dogmatism and defends Blaga:

In our opinion, the [proper] militant spirit posits that in evaluating an event or creation we must situate ourselves openly on the side of the interests of our nation and of its consciousness—in which a decisive place is occupied by the values of unity, independence, and national sovereignty. Thus understood, this militant spirit is consonant with the militancy of the Party, which aspires to be the quintessential and condensed expression of the interests and necessities of our whole nation and all its citizens (Mihu 1988a: 70).[6]

In other words, Mihu is using his attack on dogmatism to construct a Marxism that is *national*. Although he expressed this privately as a move toward greater democratization and improvements in the real-socialist order, his brand of national Marxism could also be used to air claims we might perceive as both "politically correct" and culturally representative.

Mihu begins his discussion with Blaga's accepting the chair of philosophy at Cluj University in 1938 and his seeming reintegration into the normal round of things after 1945. Then, in 1948, Blaga was dismissed from his post without explanation. How, Mihu asks, was this possible, given Blaga's intellectual stature? He answers that the fault lies with "certain envies and professional ambitions," rather than with the wider political climate. Mihu's suspicions fall on one Pavel Apostol, who in 1945 was a fourth-year philosophy student at the university (under the name of Pavel Erdös, Mihu notes) and in 1948 was named professor of philosophy "in Blaga's place," having just completed his doctorate (1988*a*: 41). Initially a Blagan, Apostol now became a Marxist and rapidly achieved a powerful position in the political life of Cluj University. The rapidity of his conversion to Marxism leads Mihu to conclude that ambition drove him to campaign for the ouster of his former professor, Blaga, and his own installation in the latter's place. Mihu invites the reader to understand that Blaga had to abandon his great philosophical system owing to personal ambition on the part of a man bearing a Hungarian name (Apostol was a Jew).

Mihu goes to considerable lengths to disarm the alternative interpretation: that Blaga lost his teaching post because his philosophical system was too closely aligned with that of the interwar right, mortal enemies of the Communist party, and because he was not capable of shifting his intellectual allegiance to Marxist philosophy sufficiently to be entrusted with teaching it. According to Mihu, Blaga had established his distance from the far right, and if he was repeatedly accused of fascism by communist activists in Cluj, the reason must be sought elsewhere than in Blaga's actual loyalties.

Mihu finds the explanation in the gross distortions of Marxism that resulted from the charged nationality situation in Northern Transylvania, following the return of that region from Hungarian to Romanian control in 1944. In essence, he argues that Hungarian Marxists inside and outside Romania proposed a deceptive and treacherous "Marxist" solution to the nationalities problem in Transylvania: making the region autonomous. When students and Romanian intellectuals such as Blaga demonstrated in opposition, these "Marxists" accused them of being "anti-Marxist" and of obstructing harmony among the different nationalities. Because of Blaga's stature, says Mihu, he was an especially suitable target for these Hungarian chauvinist accusations in Marxist garb. Mihu claims that in fact, however, Blaga's philosophical construction, which promoted Romanian spirituality and the capacity of a reunited Romania to bring major creative contributions to the world, "was obviously opposed not to an original Marxism but to the revisionist and autonomist tendencies" that would deny Transylvania its rightful place in Romania (1988*a*: 48). From this Mihu concludes that Blaga's writing contained no reactionary content sufficient to justify his vilification as a fascist enemy of the new regime. Nor, Mihu asserts, did Blaga engage in activity counter to the new directions the communists promoted.[7] Therefore, we must seek to explain his exclusion from Romania's cultural life not by his thought or behavior but by something else in the politics of the time.

This something was a mistaken form of Marxism, namely the Stalinist-Zhdanovist distortion that equated acceptance of its own dogma with a positive Marxist attitude. Blaga could not be expected to fare well in an environment permeated by this "proletcultist" understanding of Marxism. The dogmatic Marxism of the 1940s and 1950s did not even fit the conception of Marx himself, who (in Mihu's view) recognized and respected true values:

Only in a reductionist form (as Stalinist-Zhdanovist dogma) could Marxism become the evaluative grid for negating all Blaga's merits in philosophical creation and branding him a reactionary. Moreover, only in an imperfect form could a politics originating in Marxism transform a theoretical and ideological difference into grounds for administrative measures [i.e., expulsion] (Mihu 1988a: 51).

This imperfect Marxism was then imposed upon Blaga under the "tutelage" of dogmatists, such as Apostol, in the newly constituted philosophy department. From his lessons in the new philosophy, it seems, Blaga decided against further philosophical writing, thus depriving Romania's cultural patrimony of the great achievements that would have resulted. Mihu's argument ends by observing that only the relaxed climate after 1965 [i.e., Ceauşescu's era] permitted Romanian culture to give Blaga his due, but this change does not mean that dogmatism has ceased to pose problems in cultural life. It must continue to be combatted.

Two things stand out in this account. Perhaps the more striking is the potent national sentiment at its base: the explanation that a famous Romanian intellectual was brought down by the personal envy and ambitions of a Hungarian Jew in concert with a simplified and dogmatized Marxism of Soviet origin, further distorted by the nationalist schemings of Hungarian irredentists. The second, less visible, is the use of "dogmatism" to construct two—indeed, three—Marxisms: (1) a dogmatic "Stalinist-Zhdanovist" one, imported under duress from the Soviet Union and wholly unsuited to Romanian conditions; (2) an allied Hungarian irredentist one,[8] equally dogmatic but with different goals, territorially revisionist and anti-Romanian; and (3) a tacit but clearly implied "good" Romanian one, whose very Romanianness kept it true to Marx's original intentions, unlike the other two. This last Marxism is evidently, Mihu seems to say, the one now pursued by the Party; far from standing in the way of Blaga's work, it would create all the necessary conditions for him to produce a brilliant philosophical synthesis that would bring world credit to Romanian culture. (This prognosis should be borne in mind in reading the fate of a comparable philosophical enterprise, covered in chapter 7.)

Mihu's argument gives us an excellent example of how accusations of "dogmatism" and its implications for national values also served to indigenize the foreign import that was Marxist ideology. The "good" Marxism Mihu has created respects authentic national values; it can be wrapped tightly around discussions of the Nation's character, interests, and culture. This "good" Marxism has little in common with the foreign Marxisms with which some might mistakenly identify it. It is a Romanian product, suited to Romanian conditions, and amply upheld by the Romanian Communist Party. It is Marxism rendered a political use-value for a Romanian political apparatus.

Mihu's attempt to "nationalize" Marxist ideology did not go unanswered, even though the answer was hidden. Although I encountered no published rebuttal of Mihu's argument, a typescript circulated underground that rejected its claims in very strong language.[9] The author, since deceased, was Blaga's son-in-law Tudor Bugnariu, an old communist who was active in the Party when it was illegal and who adhered until his death to an understanding of Marxism that preceded its institutionalization in Romania. Objecting to Mihu's use of his father-in-law Blaga as the vehicle for chauvinist personal denunciations of early communists, he also objects to Mihu's reducing everything to subjective motivations of individuals—a *safe* tactic, he says, especially where those in question are now dead and cannot defend themselves. A truly sociological account, in Bugnariu's view, must find the real causes of dogmatism, acknowledge the mistakes that were made, and ask what measures were necessary under the circumstances and what were abusive.

Bugnariu's explanation for Blaga's losing his post is simple: the society in which he lived had changed beyond his capacities to adapt, the Ministry of Education had passed a decree reorganizing the entire educational system and eliminating Blaga's department altogether—a decree applied across the board to many persons of Blaga's affiliations and not only to him—and Blaga's ideas were, objectively, utterly irreconcilable with the tenets of Marxism. Moreover, it is not true that he undertook no activities against the new order: he maintained contact with the clandestine rightist opposition, in hopes that American troops would overturn the communists and permit the restoration of the *status quo ante*. Given this, there was no way that Blaga could have continued to teach in a socialist Romania. Instead of discussing the climate in which Romanian communists might have found it necessary to dam up the philosophical creativity of a talented thinker, Bugnariu complains,

Mihu prefers to air thinly veiled antisemitic and anti-Hungarian sentiments and to anathematize individual persons. It is all too easy for
Mihu to cast aspersions on the patriotism of early communists: *he* had
nothing to suffer for his social origin, and *he* had smelled no whiff of
the gas chambers to make him view Stalin as a true savior. Bugnariu
concludes by musing over how angry Communist party Secretary Mihu
is that Blaga was forced to footnote his last writings with the names of
Marx, Engels, and major Romanian communist theoreticians.

Although Bugnariu's reply categorically rejected Mihu's analysis, it
nonetheless furthered Mihu's indigenization of Marxism: by offering a
rejoinder, it engaged him in an argument as to whether there really are
three Marxisms, two bad (the foreign ones) and one good (the Romanian one), and whether Marxism is or is not to be wrapped around national questions. Any subsequent discussion would debate how Marxism is related to patriotic sentiment or is affected by its national
provenance. Just as "dogmatists" had become, for some people, not
simply anyone who had participated in the original Stalinist version of
Marxist ideology and cultural policy but anyone who tried to discuss
any topic without explicitly introducing nationality, "Marxists" were
becoming defined by their adherence not simply (if at all) to the writings of Marxism-Leninism but to the "militant spirit" that places nationality first, as Mihu put it.

"Dogmatism" was an instrument fashioned over four decades and
visibly marked by its history. But whether the meaning was primarily
the contamination of culture by the dictates of politics or the suppression of national values in preference to international ones, what it
meant, in the end, was that some view was *unrepresentative of Romanian
values and interests* (cf. Gheorghiu 1987: 53). To accuse an opponent of
"dogmatism" was to seek his elimination from favor and from the competitive field. It was also to debilitate his access to older cultural values
seen as constituting the "national patrimony" or "heritage," notions liberally called up as part of restoring the Romanian past. As with charges
of "elitism," a charge of "dogmatism" signaled to the audience (non-
bureaucratic as well as official) that a producer of culture was not to be
trusted in his handling of national treasures nor to be permitted to augment his claim to cultural authority by appropriating them.

To the degree that "dogmatism" was an effective weapon, what made
it so was, of course, the double Marxism buried within it: a "bad" Soviet orthodoxy of Stalinist parentage, and an unarticulated "good"
Marxism that was Romanian and that sat in the halls of power dis-

pensing support for culture. Many of the invectives that employed dogmatism participated, then, in an indigenization of Marxism, constructing a Marxism cleansed of its foreign influences and presumably well-disposed toward native cultural products. Although for the great majority of Romanian intellectuals this Marxism was an object of scheming rather than of loyalty, it began to have unexpected supporters as the wave of chauvinism built to excessive proportions. (It is said, for example, that in the late 1970s some non-Party historians fended off an attempt to "dacianize" the newly commissioned *Treatise* on Romanian history [see chapter 6], by arguing that the work must be guided by the scientific principles of Marxism.)

Indigenization via "dogmatism" or "elitism" was crude, in that it did not engage the analytic categories of Marx's dialectical materialism in a sustained critique. There were, however, a few Romanian intellectuals who, with greater or lesser seriousness,[10] took on this more difficult task, criticizing Marxist theory for its failure to comprehend national phenomena and for its wholly inadequate treatment of them. Such scholars asked: How can one improve upon Marx's obviously defective analysis of national questions? What place ought ethnicity to have in a social analysis? Is it necessarily no more than a form of "false consciousness," or does it have an independent analytic status, and if so, what? To address this question was also a form of indigenizing Marxism, but it demanded much more intellectual work than most of those who invoked "dogmatism" were prepared to undertake.

Although I will not illustrate an argument of that sort in its own terms, I reveal parts of one indirectly in the following section, in which I consider another technique employed in contests among Romanian cultural producers. This is the technique of genealogical appropriation, whereby past heroes of Romanian culture were brought over onto one side in a contemporary argument by inscribing them within the lineage that side claimed as its own. Mihu's defense appropriated Blaga implicitly; the following example is much more overt.

Genealogical Appropriations:
Eminescu as Proto-Marxist

An excellent instance of genealogical appropriation as an element in cultural struggles is to be found in a remarkable and disturbing book published in 1984, sociologist Ilie Bădescu's *European Syn-*

chronism and Romanian Critical Culture. This is a very challenging work of ambitious scope and theoretical brilliance, based on a sophisticated knowledge of Marx and on a prodigious reading of western social science, both classical and contemporary. Reading it fills one with (among other sentiments) admiration for the author's ingenuity and the breadth of his thinking.[11] This complex book deserves a more extended and integral treatment than I can give it here.[12]

Bădescu's book has a triple agenda,[13] of which the third is the most important for my present purposes. First, he attempts to revise Marxist theory by inserting the concept of the Nation into the heart of a class analysis. Second, he offers a neo-Marxist interpretation of Romania's history of economic and political underdevelopment, and although he uses terms like "peripheralization" made fashionable by dependency theorists and by Immanuel Wallerstein's world-system theory, he gives his own original reading of these notions. Third, and most important for my objectives, his book is an explicit attempt to make famous Romanian poet and gazeteer Mihai Eminescu (1850–1889) the forerunner of this kind of radical social-historical theorizing. In this respect, Bădescu offers a form of argument that is indigenist:[14] it credits a Romanian thinker with having original ideas different from those of other early critics of metropolitan capitalism, such as Karl Marx and Friedrich List, and prior to comparable ideas that emerged later in Latin America and in western leftist sociology in the 1970s. Bădescu's work reprocesses someone clearly identified with the traditional right into a prescient spokesman of the left, and it does so in an overtly indigenist manner. Although Bădescu's indigenism links his work with parts of my discussion in chapters 1 and 5, I emphasize these ties less than his valiant attempt to make Eminescu a radical sociologist, fully worthy of inclusion among the precursors of Romanian Marxist thought—that is, his genealogical appropriation of Eminescu for Marxism and for sociology.

Bădescu's reinterpretation of Eminescu as radical theorist is not an easy accomplishment: both Romanians and outsiders have unequivocally viewed the poet as a stalwart of the Moldavian Conservative party, the party of a landed aristocracy not noted for its progressive ideas. Widely regarded by Romanians as their greatest poet, Eminescu has nonetheless been classed as xenophobic, chauvinist, antisemitic,[15] anti-Russian, and an exemplar of Romantic agrarian reaction, qualities that had caused most of his writings to be proscribed for a number of years.[16] When Eminescu's corpus was gradually allowed back in, it was by presenting him as the champion of the wretched—that is, by using a class analysis to describe the context of his work and then permitting him to raise his voice on behalf of the oppressed, as befits a socialist culture-hero. Shafir (1983a: 225–226) sees this as an *externally* grounded reintroduction of Eminescu: an exterior version of Marxism was the basis for reevaluating the poet's work, making it acceptable by bringing out his social concerns. The people who accomplished this retouching were old-style orthodox communists. Bădescu has set himself the more complicated task of legitimating Eminescu *internally*, within a genuine local socialist tradition seen as having its own priorities and analytic innovations.

My objective here is not to assess the plausibility of Bădescu's treatment of Eminescu but to describe what I see as the principal moves he makes in his argument. I am not, in any event, capable of assessing the argument's plausibility, since I have read little of Eminescu's poetry or political and economic writings, and one would have to have read them all in order to render judgment on this matter.[17] Moreover, I do not regard such judgment as essential to my purposes: Eminescu was a real and highly influential historical personage who emitted written products that have now entered into a process of readings and rereadings. The various readings and rebuttals form their own kind of social action and illuminate the nature of Romanian society regardless of their "correctness." Eminescu and his work have become a symbol, having a plurality of meanings and deployed in political struggles that have little to do with what he may "really" have meant. The point of the present discussion is to see what potential uses his multiple meanings are being put to, what kind of authority they are serving, and what processes of cultural struggle they illustrate—in a word, to discuss the cultural politics in which Eminescu became embroiled a century after his death.

Bădescu initiates his reinterpretation of Romanian history and his genealogical appropriation of Eminescu with several critiques of existing Marxist interpretations. These reduce to the following fundamental postulates: (1) Although in the West imperial strivings were checked by *bourgeois* revolutions, in Eastern Europe this was achieved by movements of *nationalities*. That is, nation takes precedence over class in analyses of East European history: "It was precisely the national revolutions in southeast Europe that provided the historical framework for the fall of empires in this zone, such that the true revolutionary forces in this case were nations" (Bădescu 1984b: 15). For Bădescu, the ethnic and national composition of the ruling classes provides the basis of Romanian history. (2) Peasants in this part of the world were a revolutionary and progressive force. Not for Romanians, Marx's famous "sacks-of-potatoes" argument about peasants in France! (3) Sociology should not place the history of dominant powers at the center of every analysis. To do so is to misapprehend the social forces that make history in the "peripheries," which are not adequately explained by "metropolitan" theories. Bădescu's conclusion from these postulates is that Marx may have given the best existing interpretation of metropolitan capitalism, but his analysis is inadequate for peripheral areas into which capital subsequently penetrated. To understand these processes, he claims, we must turn to Romanian thinkers, Eminescu first among them, who theorized the phenomenon of peripheral capitalism well before Latin American and other theorists after 1940. These Romanian thinkers admirably uphold Marx's historical materialist conception while avoiding "dogmatic" absolutization of his theory (ibid., 38–39).

In extracting from Eminescu's writings a coherent sociology for which he will claim materialist status, Bădescu is at pains to disable the widely held view that Eminescu's writings were xenophobic. Potential xenophobia is most evident in Eminescu's theory of "superimposed strata," which Bădescu calls "one of the most important contributions of Romanian sociological thought in modern times" (p. 254). This theory describes the activities of foreign elites that siphoned the surplus product from the country and sent it abroad in speculation and luxury purchases, as opposed to "fixing" it locally to develop local sources of wealth. Adopting Eminescu's terms, Bădescu refers to this stratum as a *xenocracy* (a regime that serves foreign interests [pp. 279–280]), which adopted an attitude of predation to the society they lived in and subjected it ruinously to western metropolitan centers. The idea of "xenocracy" in Eminescu's writings, Bădescu insists, is a wholly sociological and not, as has been charged, a xenophobic or chauvinist one (ibid.).

(It is never clarified in this argument how one is to know a "foreign" ruler from a "Romanian" one, given that some pure Romanian names are associated with some of the most predatory and devastating relations to Romanian society [any number of noble and ruling families of the past several centuries, not to mention the Ceaușescu family] and some "foreign" names [Rosetti, Cantacuzino, Xenopol] with acts of local benefit. The more one reads of Bădescu's Eminescu, the more it seems that everything evil—demagogy, tearing down of historical traditions, misery of the people—is the fault of immigrant foreigners whereas autochthones are associated with only what is good [see, e.g., pp. 258–259]. Whoever acted in the interests of the Romanian people was "Romanian" and whoever did not was "foreign," regardless of their actual national origin. That is, anyone not fixing capital locally is a foreigner by definition. Although Bădescu continues to insist that this theory is not ethnocentric, it is the murky swamp at the bottom of this slippery slope that fills one with misgivings as to where he is ultimately headed.)

In the remainder of his discussion, Bădescu catalogs the contribution of Romanian sociology, and above all of Eminescu, to understanding the effects of capitalist penetration into Eastern Europe. He calls Eminescu the first thinker of *any* nationality to distinguish between capital's manner of operation in the metropolis and in the periphery (p. 287). Eminescu's understanding of these problems enabled him to see that the "law of survival of the fittest" did not hold in the peripheries, where what survives is not the positive elements but the negative ones. Thus, the form of class struggle differs in the periphery from its form in the core: in peripheries this struggle takes the form of a struggle for the biological and cultural survival of a people exploited from without and from above (pp. 287–288). Bădescu views Eminescu's theory as not a Romantic return to an agrarian idyll but a demand for a nondependent development of capitalism, comparable to the path followed in the West, and he sees the poet's theories as offering an alternative ideology to that of bourgeois liberalism.

We can, therefore, consider that Eminescu is the adept of a sociology of materialist conception. . . . *The theory of the separation of a negative dialectic from a positive dialectic* in spatial-geographic frameworks is, to our knowledge, a world premiere. . . . Eminescu's conception of the historical becoming of peoples and cultures is incompatible with the flat and abstract vision of a unilinear evolutionism [i.e., with Stalinism—k.v.]. . . . As a sociologist of the forward movement toward civilization, his thought concerns, precisely, the paths of historical progress [and not a Romantic return to the past] (Bădescu 1984*b*: 311, original emphasis).

Let me recapitulate the claims Bădescu is making for his hero. Eminescu is the Romanian Marx, who offered the first theories of peripheral capitalism. He is the "father" of all subsequent materialist thought in Romania (p. 235). Although most of Marx's writings may have preceded his temporally, his are of equal value scientifically, if not indeed of superior value from a Romanian point of view. He is also the founder of Romanian sociology (p. 298). In fact, he is the father of *all* Romanian social thought of any kind, regardless of discipline: his sociology "*represents the moment from which depart all the lines, all the directions of modern Romanian thought, irrespective of their nuances and interpretations*" (pp. 235–236, original emphasis). Words like "founder" and "first" peppered throughout Bădescu's book make this a genealogical appropriation of a special kind: Eminescu has been made not just any old ancestor but the *apical* ancestor, *the* point of origin, *the* genitor. And as if this weren't enough, he is the formulator of a theory of underdevelopment that would later stand at the core of the western sociology of world accumulation (p. 242); he is "among the precursors of the new epistemological orientation in European sociology and culturology" (Bădescu 1984*a:* 2). His intellectual paternity thus flows beyond the bounds of Romania to fructify social thought around the world.

It is important to clarify what these claims accomplish. First, a man who has been regarded as important chiefly for his Romantic poetry has been made the first Romanian exponent of radical critical theory. This is far more than simply touting Eminescu as a champion of the wretched and, therefore, as compatible with socialism. He has been expropriated from nineteenth-century Romantic literature and revalorized, in the most literal sense, into a source of symbolic accumulations of an ideological sort proper to a specifically Romanian Marxism. Together with Bădescu's insistence on the fundamental significance of the role of nationality in sociological explanation and his other conceptual innovations, this argument revises Marxism substantially. It entails reading Marx closely and suggesting necessary modifications of his work, modifications that Romanian thinkers of Marx's day—Eminescu—were offering, Bădescu affirms, without due recognition. It also serves, however, the creation of a "good" Marxism, a Romanian one, to oppose the "bad" one of dogmatists, proletcultists, Stalinists, and irredentists. Once again, then, we see a form of argument that accumulates intellectual use-values for the political apparatus, by specifically combining an interpretation of Marxist and neo-Marxist concepts with a focus on national problems.

Alongside this rehabilitation of Eminescu and creation of a localized Marxism, a second noteworthy process is taking place. It is significant that Bădescu makes Eminescu not just a Marxist but also a *sociologist*, for the environment of Bădescu's effort was one in which sociology itself had been almost wholly suppressed. As one of the most bourgeois of the bourgeois sciences, sociology had an uneven career in socialist Romania. It was initially banned outright, along with all philosophies but dialectical materialism. During the 1960s sociology was resurrected, its practitioners emerging from the shadows of philosophy institutes and departments and told to find out what was really going on in Romania's "multilaterally developing society," through research into agricultural collectivization, social mobility, the formation of attitudes among youth, the operation of the mass media, and so on. As of the late 1970s, the discipline was once again cast into the shade, departments undone and doctorates denied, as the results of its research had shown all too well what was happening in the "multilaterally developing society." Sociologists responded to this re-peripheralization of sociology by consciously or unconsciously defending their discipline and trying to ally it with other powerful currents or fields, such as literature[18] or history.[19]

Bădescu's response to the peripheralization of his discipline was both to join it to history and to adapt a new indigenism, with all its benefits (see next chapter), from literature into sociological theorizing. He also placed himself within the line of leftist thinkers, from Marx on down; but his Eminescu-first indigenism demonstrates clearly that in Ceauşescu's Romania, it was no longer sufficient for sociology to justify itself by offering Marxist analyses.[20] To claim the attention of Romania's leadership and of those who allocated its goods, sociology had to be not merely Marxist but national, tied to indisputable national values. Bădescu's genealogical appropriation of Eminescu was thus directly tied to the fate of sociology: it shows us how an indigenization of Marxism could become joined to questions of cultural representativeness, justifying a sociology that treated problems of *the Nation* in a Marxist manner and did so in the lineage of the greatest of all national figures, poet Mihai Eminescu.

This discussion of Bădescu is, I must emphasize, highly selective. I have underscored the part of his argument that shows the technique of genealogical appropriation, at the expense of the history of Romanian underdevelopment that would seem the book's chief burden. I would nonetheless defend this selection, however, on the basis of reviews of the book. Although a few commentators admired his "anti-dogmatic materialism" and "exemplary use of dialectics" (*Luceafărul* 1984: 4; Mihu 1988*b*: 225, 227), what caught the attention of his admirers (see *Luceafărul* 1984; Riza 1985), his detractors (Cătineanu 1985; Manolescu 1984), and those with mixed feelings (Mihu 1988*b*) was his genealogical tour-de-force with Eminescu, which all of them saw as the heart of the book.

The two most important reviews, indeed, refused the genealogy Bădescu had created. Literary critic Manolescu—by no means an orthodox Marxist—savaged the book and ridiculed its pretensions:

No one else has claimed equivalence for the historical roles played by Marxism . . . and eminescianism . . . and it seems to me from all points of view exorbitant. Without wanting to diminish somehow the importance of the poet's sociology, to put it on the same ideational level with Marxism is unsustainable by rational argument. . . . Affirmations such as these seem to me out of keeping with the elementary truth that Eminescu was not a historical-materialist sociologist, which does not mean that his sociology has no merits or lacks theoretical validity. But I ask to what use his change in status is being put (Manolescu 1984).

Regarding as political pamphlets much of what Bădescu viewed as scientific sociology, Manolescu denied Eminescu a coherent sociological system and found there only the pen of a gifted journalist; he crisply refused Eminescu the label of "historical materialist," preferring him in the more familiar role of political conservative. Manolescu's genealogy for Romanian sociology and Romanian materialism differs from Bădescu's: it runs through the socialist Gherea, as well as various interwar Marxist sociologists and the interwar liberals Zeletin and Lovinescu, whom Bădescu attacks. In suggesting this countergenealogy, literary critic Manolescu was aiming not for his own position in a different lineage of materialism or sociology but, rather, to refuse Bădescu the right to claim himself jointly a materialist sociologist *and* heir to the greatest hero of Romanian letters. Should such a claim be accepted, it would make Bădescu and his associates absolutely invincible competitors in the struggle for attention from a Romanian bureaucracy.

Evidence that Bădescu too saw as crucial his combined claims for materialism and sociology as eminescian is the first sentence of his rebuttal to Manolescu's review: "Was Nicolae Manolescu listening to the voice of his vocation when he entered upon a terrain totally foreign to him: sociology and Marxism?" (Bădescu 1984*a*). Loudly claiming both sociology and Marxism for himself, he accused Manolescu of theoretical confusion and of moving the discussion from sociology to political ideology. Bădescu's reply made it plain that aside from the proper place of Eminescu in the lineages of Romanian thought, a major issue was who can speak for Marxism, and how sociology's contribution to it and to Romanian culture is to be assessed.

A different contestation of Bădescu's genealogy for Eminescu came from sociologist Mihu, in a review written two years before the articles on Blaga discussed above. Mihu was somewhat readier than Manolescu to accept the idea that there is a touch of materialism in Eminescu's writings, and ready indeed to accept Eminescu as a sociologist—which would give a big lift to Mihu's discipline (just as this revisionist genealogy would orphan Manolescu's line of literati). Mihu's opening paragraph applauded Bădescu for doing "a service to the affirmation of today's Romanian sociology," and he later stated outright, "Without hesitation, we can agree with the idea . . . that there is a close and not at all peripheral link between M. Eminescu's social-political thought and sociology" (Mihu 1988*b*: 225, 236). Additionally, he congratulated Bădescu for having the courage to break out of "dogmatic" Marxist categories. But Mihu was not prepared to acknowledge the paternity of Eminescu unreservedly, seeming to prefer a more collateral relation. He was reluctant to accept Bădescu's transfiguration of Eminescu from conservative to radical (Mihu 1988*b*: 238, 247) and was skeptical of Bădescu's view that Eminescu was not xenophobic (p. 237).

Most of all, Mihu was put off by Bădescu's claims that Eminescu was the *first* sociologist for Romanians, the apical ancestor, the founder. Good Transylvanian that he is, Mihu saw his own sociological ancestry as longer and as rooted not in Romania but in France: Tocqueville, Comte, and so forth (pp. 236–242). He sought to insert Eminescu into that more European line, a line that would include Marx without making Eminescu his superior (pp. 233–234). In short, Mihu refused Bădescu's indigenist claims for Eminescu and the indigenization of Marxism for which Bădescu was using him. Mihu argued this by saying that since sociology is older than Eminescu, if Eminescu is a sociologist then he cannot be the first one; we can speak only of his place in "an accumulation (a temporal succession) along the course of its development" (p. 242).

This may seem a minor cavil on Mihu's part, but in my view it is crucial. What Mihu was denying Bădescu was the right to appropriate *all* the gains of Romanian social thought towards his own ends, all too closely linked with the aims of the Ceaușescu regime. By making Eminescu not an apical ancestor of a local (if major) clan but merely a member of the larger "tribe" of European sociology, Mihu was insisting that sociology has its own symbolic accumulations independent of the Nation, accumulations rooted in a disciplinary past that cannot be expropriated at will.[21] Although Mihu was soon to throw in his lot with the politically ambitious, as of 1984 (when he wrote his review) he had not abandoned his aspiration to intellectual recognition resting on cultural and disciplinary authority, independent of politics.

The technique of genealogical appropriation was widely practiced in Romanian cultural politics (and will doubtless continue to be, as it is in other countries), as persons from one or another "camp" sought to incorporate various past figures into the line in which they included themselves. Sometimes these appropriations were combined, as in Bădescu's case, with indigenizations of Marxism, the insertion of Marxist language and theoretical claims into a discourse in which the Nation had priority. An excellent example from a political position diametrically opposed to his is a book by one-time Stalinist Ileana Vrancea (1975), who made a case for including literary critic Lovinescu in the line of Romanian Marxist thought. Other instances laid no claim to a Marxist heritage but merely constructed lineages convenient for the sorts of claims a scholar or writer wanted to air. Philosopher Blaga, for example, whom no one would try to inscribe in a Marxist lineage, was the object of attempted appropriations from opposing sides, as some claimed him for indigenism and others for Europeanism, so as to present themselves as his defenders and, through him, as defenders of Romanian cultural values.

All who engaged in such actions, across the whole spectrum of intellectual politics, shared a single tactic: they made available to themselves the penumbra of meanings associated with past figures of major cultural significance. To the extent that accomplishing this involved moves that also indigenized Marxism, they participated jointly in making notions derived from official Marxism new cover terms for *national* issues, terms that entered into the expulsions and the struggles for cultural accumulations that will be discussed in subsequent chapters. Through this, Marxist categories continued to play an ideological role alongside national ones, both of them undergoing alterations in the process. Their efficacy depended not on people's belief in them but on their use in social struggle.

Whether or not the long-term result would have been to *constitute* belief in the (properly indigenized) categories of Marxism is a question that time will no longer tell. As the politics following Ceauşescu's ouster made clear, his dictatorship engendered a public revulsion that has ruined "communism"'s reputation in Romania. From the outset, however, the discourse of Marxism-Leninism had been an unwelcome guest for most Romanians. It had refused for many years to take seriously the categories that counted, in their experience: the categories of national values. Marxist ideas were important to cultural producers largely as a means of smuggling into cultural contests the national ideas that mattered most. Those latter ideas soon took over, interrupting the discourse of Marxism and redefining its purposes. The principal contribution of indigenized Marxism was to reproduce a national ideology that now had increased efficacy before a political apparatus operating awkwardly on Marxist credentials.

The indigenization of Marxism—the domestication of an imposed language and the subversion of its categories—occurred through the rhetoric employed in contests, such as those within the sphere of cultural production. What I have suggested in this chapter and the one before, however, is that in this process the discourse of Marxism was not just indigenized: it was overthrown. Its social agenda was forced to capitulate to the agenda of a different system of ideas. Intellectuals on both sides of cultural debates contributed to this outcome, but particularly those who most insisted on inserting national values into their talk. This was—paradoxically, as will be seen in chapter 5—the same group who most noisily placed culture at the Party's service. Chapter 5 will show how the various participants were arrayed and where the advantage lay among them.

CHAPTER FIVE

Romanian Protochronism

It has suddenly become clear, that the validity of an aesthetic judgement depends on the "site" from which it has been made and the authority ascribed to that site; that the authority in question is not an inalienable, "natural" property of the site, but something fluctuating with the changing location of the site within a wider structure; and that the authority of the site traditionally reserved for the aestheticians . . . is not any more to be taken for granted.

—Zygmunt Bauman

In times of crisis, literature in Eastern Europe invariably becomes politics in disguise.

—Ivan Sanders

During the 1970s and 1980s, increasing numbers of Romanian writers and literary critics were drawn into an argument over an idea called "protochronism."[1] This idea encouraged critics and literary historians to look for developments in Romanian culture that had anticipated events in the better-publicized cultures of western Europe (thus, "proto-chronos": first in time). From literature, protochronism spread into other fields: chapter 4, for instance, showed an excellent example without the protochronist label—Bădescu's argument that poet Eminescu was Europe's first radical sociologist of peripheral capitalism. Clearly symptomatizing the plight of subaltern cultures dominated by metropolitan centers, protochronism soon attracted the attention of a Romanian party leadership that also wished to raise Romania's image in the esteem of the world. Romanians and outside observers alike have considered protochronism among the strongest manifestations of national ideology under Ceauşescu—even, perhaps, that leadership's basic ideology.

Protochronism was an intensified resuscitation of interwar indigenist arguments about the national essence; yet its context distinguished them from it. The labels "traditionalist" and "modernist" now often covered accusations of fascism and dogmatism; to protect internal markets was less of an issue, in socialism, than before; and the logic driving Ceauşescu's personality cult—into which the very term "national essence" entered[2]—differed from the logic behind similar cults around interwar leaders such as Codreanu. Nevertheless, the impression of continuity that emerges from anthologies on the national essence, drawing their contributors equally from before and after 1945 (e.g., Marcea 1975; F. Mihăilescu 1981), is not misleading. As before, the parties to the argument used it to express their views on foreign imperialism, foreign alliances, and the problems of Romania's political and economic development. Literature was once again in the forefront of the arguments; and as before, many other disciplines found the Nation and its values a handy rhetorical arena for waging competitive struggles. Indeed, the resumption of these debates after 1970 confirms my argument in chapter 1, that "the Nation" had become deeply embedded in intellectual life. In Ceauşescu's Romania as before (but more so), producers of culture sought to persuade state bureaucrats of their *cultural representativeness*, the aptness of their vision of Romanian culture for Romania's true character. The field of participants was as diverse and complex as before but could be grossly dichotomized into two camps, using many of the labels and accusations of their predecessors forty and fifty years earlier.

In this chapter I explore the debate around protochronism and show how it appropriated not only the terms but many of the great figures of interwar (and earlier) Romanian culture. I describe the protochronist idea, interpret the conflict as in part a struggle over forms of cultural authority, and suggest how the protochronist variant of national ideology worked in a socialist "economy of shortage." In brief, I argue that protochronism's characteristics follow from the context in which it arose, as Romania's leadership renounced a moderate reformism and returned to a more centralized Stalinist political economy with an unusual emphasis on ideological control strategies. As Romania's economic crisis deepened and new policies of "self-financing" made cultural producers more dependent on the market—however crippled it was by political considerations—the struggle among producers of culture intensified. This struggle took especially acute forms in literature and the arts (as opposed to history, for example), because these areas of culture were made especially vulnerable to the market and were deprived of state subsidies more than were "academic" specialties, where salaries from teaching and research posts continued to provide reliable sources of support that many writers and artists lacked. These "market" factors were responsible, I believe, for creating within literature more overt opposition than existed in other fields. The opposition manifested itself in the reaction to protochronism.

Those writers, artists, critics, and others who, in response to straitened circumstances for cultural creation invented and spread the protochronist idea, had great impact: they contributed to centralizing Romanian society, to expanding the political apparatus, and to eliminating other sorts of values (and other national groups) from the competition for resources in resource-strapped Romanian society. So also, to some extent, did those who opposed them, expending their energies in a joint defense of intellectual authority rather than in a more substantial critique of power. That is, protochronism in culture did not simply *reflect* but *was part of*—literally, constituted—the construction of a centralized Romanian system very different from that of Hungary, for example, or Poland.

Clarifications

My analysis in this chapter requires some preliminary clarifications. First, I follow Bourdieu (1975) in seeing theoretical discussion among Romanian intellectuals as a form of practical competition. This is by no means to suggest that the combatants simply manipulated national identity to pursue power: they were intensely committed to the values in terms of which they waged their arguments, as I have discovered time and again in my encounters with Romanian intellectuals of all kinds. I do wish to suggest, however, that this very commitment itself contributed to giving a particular form to arguments that have additional stakes, less clearly seen. Second, strengthening that form was the censorship under which the debates were waged, a censorship both internalized and institutionally imposed; this made it sometimes impossible to pursue certain kinds of struggles except by adopting the terms of earlier arguments, whether or not their vocabulary accurately captured the current issues. Third, the adoption of those earlier terms tended to divert the discussion into already established channels, turning an argument about the grounds for establishing, circulating, and accumulating literary values into one about fascism, patriotism, betrayal, and antisemitism. These double constraints on the form of discourse require one to look not only at the issues expressed on the surface but also at those discernible in images and metaphors the participants employed.

An additional point of clarification concerns whom I include as parties to the debate and what labels one should apply to them. Actual or potential participants in the debates about protochronism occupied a wide spectrum of positions, some more exaggerated than others. Moreover, the distance between the opposite poles increased as of about 1980; hence, statements taken from the decade of the 1980s are likely to be more extreme than those that initiated the argument. In this analysis I cannot do justice to nuances. I simplify both my discussion and the image of reality it projects by illustrating with relatively more polarized positions. I use these more often than moderate ones because I believe that exaggerations and departures from the norm are usually more revealing for social analysis than the norm itself. The politicization of the field of literary criticism in the 1980s was such that it was difficult not to be drawn into one camp or the other (Condurache 1981: 3). It is nevertheless true that between the opposed camps lay an intermediate zone in which people equivocated, partially disagreed, or said nothing publicly while revealing their sentiments through the company they kept.[3]

I simplify additionally by using only those statements made by persons within Romania, even though some major contributors to the debate were Romanians living abroad. Exaggerations on the protochronist side were associated especially with emigré Iosif Constantin Drăgan in Italy and, on the opposite side, with Radio Free Europe in Munich and its contributors in Paris. Opposition from Radio Free Europe was probably instrumental in pushing certain protochronists within Romania toward more uncompromising stands. Because I believe the stakes (indeed, the entire game) differed greatly for emigrés as opposed to persons inside Romania, I exclude emigré statements except for occasional reference to their effects on persons in Romania. Nevertheless, they were crucial in setting the terms of internal argument, for protochronism was in part a struggle over how to represent Romania and its values, both internally and abroad. Radio Free Europe amplified and broadcast back into Romania one set of representations (largely the opponents to protochronism) that otherwise might have been stifled by censorship. For this reason, protochronists reacted vigorously to these broadcasts.[4]

Up to now, I have spoken of "protochronists" and "their opponents." Labels for the opposing sides proliferated, making it difficult to decide how best to characterize them for descriptive purposes. Opponents of protochronism referred to themselves variously as "democrats," "modernists," "upholders of the critical spirit," and so forth, and to the others as "protochronists," "nationalists," "traditionalists," the "Barbu Group" (after one of the most powerful and visible members), the "neoproletcultists" (the designation Radio Free Europe often used), and the "nationalist Stalinists" (i.e., heirs to "dogmatism") (see Shafir 1983a). Protochronists, for their part, tended to call themselves *patriots*, and they often (but not always) rejected the label of traditionalism; they categorically refused that of Stalinism, instead accusing the *other* side of "dogmatism" and "proletcultist" leanings. They acknowledged the term "protochronism" and associated themselves with it enthusiastically, sometimes using it in self-reference. Sometimes they called their opponents "europeanizers," "modernists" (meant pejoratively), or "synchronists" (after their reading of Lovinescu's theory [see chapter 1]); more often they simply wrote "certain people" or "certain critics." That both sides called themselves true patriots and accused the other side of dogmatism and proletcultism is a sure sign that those labels were doing more than simply describing.

On occasion, one or the other side used the terms "right" and "left" to characterize the argument. Opponents might link protochronists with the far right of the interwar years, on the grounds that their nationalist extremes were similar; yet this labeling rarely entailed referring to themselves as the "left" (a label most were loath to claim). More than one protochronist argued to me, however, that *protochronists* were the left; and an opponent of them called herself[5] part of the *right*. Romanian intellectuals listed the same sets of publications as sharing positions on one or other side of the debate (*Literary Romania, Romanian*

Life, and *Twentieth Century* as opposing protochronism, for instance; *The Week, The Morning Star*, and *The Flame*[6] as favoring it), but differed on which of these groupings should be called "right" or "left." These labels are further complicated by the involvement of the emigré community at Radio Free Europe. A number of them had had ties to the interwar right (as protochronists gleefully observed), yet they often backed protochronism's opponents, whose history rarely included such ties. When the Radio took a positive attitude to someone whom protochronists admired, however, and who *did* have past associations with the right, such as Constantin Noica (see chapter 7), the possible referents for "right" and "left" became even more confused. These confusions confirm what we might suspect, namely, that the terms "left" and "right" acquired such complex meanings in socialist Romania that for me to use them would obscure more than it would illuminate. They served as weapons of exclusion, not reliable descriptions.

Amid the proliferating insults and insinuations, I find the label "protochronists" the most neutral and will employ it in this chapter. (I underscore, however, that in avoiding a term such as "nationalists" in preference to "protochronists," which refers to something more specific than the general conflict of which protochronism was but one sign, I use this label as an umbrella for a collection of phenomena that not everyone would see as fully interlinked in Romanian cultural life.) A label for the opponents of protochronism is harder to come by, since the opposition did not form a unified camp. For want of a better solution, I give it the somewhat whimsical designation "antiprotochronists," also used by the protochronists. This term captures the fact that these persons were united, if at all, chiefly in their opposition to protochronism. To speak of "antiprotochronists" underlines where the initiative in the debate lay: with the protochronists, who set the agenda and placed others on the defensive. This resulted from the connection between protochronism, on the one hand, and, on the other, power and the central imperatives of the socialist system, as I will explain below.

It is difficult to suggest the relative sizes of the protochronist and antiprotochronist forces. Several of the latter insisted to me that the weight of the former within the community of writers and critics should not be overemphasized, and they arrived independently at maximal estimates of about 15 to 20 percent. Protochronists would probably have disputed this figure, but I do not have one from them to offer in its place. The question is complicated by the large number of persons who did not take public positions on the debate and whom one could count only by assessing the values implicit in their work—for example, an author who made no public rejoinder to protochronism yet translated western writers was probably antiprotochronist. People of this sort, claimed my antiprotochronist associates, were the norm among culture-producers. The one clear sign that antiprotochronists numerically dominated the Writers' Union (a subset of the full set of writers), was that they were able to exclude all protochronists from positions of leadership within that body in elections in 1977 and 1981. More precise indications than this are impossible.

I draw my data for this analysis chiefly from published statements, for the protochronists, and chiefly from interviews, for their opponents. In particular, my illustrative quotations come disproportionately from protochronists, owing to their differential appearance in print. (Most of my interviews, by contrast, were with their opponents.) As of about 1980, the opposition to protochronism became largely *oral*: those whom I interviewed said this was because as of that time, censors generally blocked the replies they would have liked to make to protochronist attacks on them. Those few who voiced opposition publicly (e.g., Manea 1981) risked being subjected to campaigns of vilification that made speaking out scarcely worth the cost. A rare exception was an antiprotochronist article published by one of the very top Party officials (Rădulescu 1986), to which—for once—protochronists could not respond.[7] Aside from this and a few other overt statements, the opposition tended to signal its existence primarily through veiled statements in commentary on other topics, through references to the contemporary resurgence of interwar debates between "modernists and traditionalists"—a way of calling their opponents fascists, as I explained in chapter 4—or through essays in praise of Europe (e.g., Paleologu 1983), rather than through overt rejoinder to protochronist challenges.

In addition to having been silenced actively, many of protochronism's adversaries were silent by choice. They saw this as a form of critical eloquence that condemned without appeal a work or idea others had supported enthusiastically. As one participant put it,

Sometimes silence is necessary for a critic; . . . by entering into a dialogue, you make at least partly plausible the flatterers' absurd position; refusing them a dialogue covers them gradually with ridicule, like a light rain (Manolescu, in Purcaru 1986: 144–145).

Another argued, in an essay entitled "The Significance of a Critic's Silences," that measuring a critic's silences enables one to weigh his morality: what books does he refuse to comment upon, and when is this morally good or reprehensible (Dobrescu 1984: 255–256).[8] Whether chosen or imposed, the relative silence of this group makes its version of the dispute harder to exemplify. In asking what was at issue in the argument over protochronism, then, the evidence I offer is mostly what protochronists complained about in public, supplemented with my interviews. This reflects to some extent the actual field of talk within which protochronism unfolded, as well as the relative coalescence of the groups and their situations within the political field of force.

I wish to add a final clarification of a different sort. The position I take by the end of this chapter may lead some readers (particularly those of East European origin) to conclude that I think attachment to national values is blamable and inevitably serves the centralization of power. I disavow such a conclusion. Attachment to the existence and the well-being of one's nation has nourished much human nobility, creativity, and enhancement of spirit. This can be said of many of the persons who figure in the present and later chapters. My own concern, however, is with the forms assumed by domination and particularly with the role of national ideology in deepening it. To examine how those who use the Nation—even if it be to create more room for their Nation in a system of global power—construct dominations of their own leaves me little room to pursue the benefits that issue from national values. This does not mean that I dismiss such benefits as inconsequential.

The Birth of Protochronism

In 1974 there appeared in the Romanian cultural publication *Twentieth Century* an article by the literary critic Edgar Papu, a scholar in his seventies. Papu had begun his career as the university assistant of a famous interwar aesthetician, literary historian, and philosopher of culture; had spent a few years in prison after the change of regime; and following a decade or so of miscellaneous employment, had been rehabilitated and retired with a pension. His article, "Romanian Protochronism," argued that contrary to views widespread in Romania, the national literary tradition was not largely inspired by western forms but was highly original. Moreover, he said, Romanian literary creations had often *anticipated* creative developments in the West (such as surrealism, dadaism, and so forth), even though these anticipations had often not been acknowledged as such because they were little known abroad. In arguing that "Thus, . . . one of the dominant defining traits of our literature in the world context is protochronism" (Papu 1974: 9), he meant to signal Romanian developments that temporally preceded similar developments elsewhere. His complaint was less that foreigners did not recognize Romanian achievements than that Romanians themselves were inadequately appreciative of their own capacities, being obsessed with imitating western forms—what he called synchronism, in a biased reading of the key term in interwar critic Lovinescu's main work (which treated not just imitation but also cultural differentiation [see chapter 1]).

Three years later, Papu fleshed out his idea with a book illustrating it extensively. His essays showed that one or another Romanian writer had anticipated the Baroque, Romanticism, the revolutionary values of 1848, the styles or themes of such European writers as Flaubert and Ibsen, and so forth.[9] He did not claim that Romanian creations had *influenced* western art forms, only that they had been prophetic. As his aim, he continually stressed the need "to stimulate knowledge of ourselves in our own consciousness" (1977: 19), to counteract Romanians' tendency to see themselves as *backward*, to overturn their image of their position in the world. In short, he was concerned with Romanians' self-image and their recognition of their own values. People should not think of Romania as part of a periphery, he said, but as lying on the central crossroads of the world's great civilizations (1977: 11), receptive to all currents and therefore capable of creatively synthesizing this diverse set of influences in innovative ways (Papu 1976).

Before entering into the remarkable reception accorded Papu's idea, I should note two things about the context in which it arose. First, the idea of temporal priority, which appears often in national ideologies, had circulated in the Soviet Union during Stalin's time—sometimes carried to ludicrous extremes—when Soviet scholars found their people first in every invention of any importance (see Kagarlitsky 1988: 131–133). Thus, even though Papu's Romanian priorities concerned only the West, his idea of Romanian protochronism consciously or unconsciously belittled (while also imitating) Soviet pretentions to grandeur. I believe this way of tweaking Soviet noses furthered the lengths to which Romanians—who have generally been anti-Russian—sometimes took protochronism, as the country grew ever more economically dependent on the Soviet Union after 1980. Second, Papu's article appeared in the aftermath of Ceauşescu's "July theses," described in chapter 3. (Indeed, *Twentieth Century* actively commissioned the article in the wake of the "theses," Papu's protochronist views being already known.[10]) Ceauşescu's speech had included exhortations such as the following:

A not very becoming practice has developed, comrades, to look only at what is being done elsewhere, abroad, to resort for everything to imports. This betrays also a certain concept of considering everything that is foreign to be better, a certain—let us say—prostration before what is foreign, and especially before Western makes . . . . You well know that in the past Eminescu criticised and made fun of such mentalities in his poems. The more so we have to do it to-day. . . . We are against bowing down before everything that is foreign. . . . Time has come for [emphasizing] the need to resort to [our] own forces in the first place, . . . and only afterwards to appeal to import (Ceauşescu 1972: 205–207).

There are books printed in tens of thousands of copies and which make an apology of the bourgeois way of life . . . while good Romanian books cannot be printed because of lack of paper (ibid., 219).

Given such emphases, protochronism was assured a brilliant career.[11]

Following the publication of Papu's article, other writings appeared that carried a similar argument, usually also employing the term "protochronism" (e.g., I. Constantinescu 1977; Zamfirescu 1975, 1979). The argument heated up once the influential critic Nicolae Manolescu (1977) gave Papu's book a mixed review, calling attention to the excesses that might flow from its otherwise interesting analyses. This review provoked an indignant reply (Anghel 1977) and a series of more extensive discussions. The cultural weekly *The Morning Star* organized long exchanges on Papu's work in 1977 and 1978 (see Ungheanu 1985), and again in 1985 (*Luceafărul* 1985), and made it the subject of numerous interviews, as did *The Flame*, *The Week*, and other publications (e.g., Purcaru 1986; Ungheanu 1982). Increasing numbers of books analyzed the idea or based themselves wholly or in part upon its premises (e.g., Bădescu 1984*b*; Popescu 1987; Rachieru 1985), while articles set out to show that even those unsympathetic to the idea sometimes implemented it unwittingly (e.g., Sorescu 1983). President Ceauşescu himself weighed in with protochronist claims—announcing, for example, that well before Gorbachev, he had had ideas about factory self-management and other reforms of perestroika (Deletant 1988: 88).

This, then, was what protochronism meant—in its advocates' own terms—when it first appeared: a concern with Romanians' self-image and with the relation of Romanian values to the rest of the world. Let us begin the task of understanding protochronism's significance by following these surface terms a bit further. The defense of Romania's self-image, in the form of a reaction against cultural contempt and cultural domination from the West, was vividly expressed in protochronist interviews and other publications. Protochronists were indignant at Romanians' practically inborn inferiority complex that makes them see their own culture as inferior; at the wrongheaded idea that Romanian culture consists of leftovers from others' cultural feasts and that its natural role should be "spiritual vassalage"; at the image of Romanians as "a species of troglodyte, whose 'barbarism' must be 'civilized' according to laws that are not [ours]"; and at the "defeatist doctrine that divides the world into major and minor cultures" (Purcaru 1986: 85, 190, 366, 374). Authors decried "the sick complex of our inferiority" and complained that

[Synchronists] do not become alarmed when negative things are said about our literature. It is no mistake, they say, to assign our literature a subordinate status, . . . for this is always the case with literatures of small, minor, or peripheral cultures dependent on larger centers. . . . But we should not expropriate Romanian literature of merits it objectively possesses (Ungheanu 1985: 389, 401–402).

[Our literature] cannot keep limping along behind European civilization, subject only to the law of synchronism, fixated on a peripheral identity. . . . [Our culture] is not a subaltern culture and the road to our values does not pass through the West (Rachieru 1985: 37, 40).

Romanian artists are less popularized in their own country than are foreign artists of lesser stature. This phenomenon unfortunately takes place in the consciousness of those who control the programming of art, persons who treat a national value in one way and a foreign personality in another (Brăescu 1982a).

The "backward" consciousness hasn't much faith in its own powers to create, and even if it does acknowledge them, it considers that the validation of these values is in the exclusive competence of foreign cultural centers (Ungheanu 1985: 464).

Finally, some observers lamented that such disdain for Romanian culture comes not only from foreigners but also from "the secret contempt that Romania's previous ruling classes held for the national culture and their kow-towing to all things foreign" (Zamfirescu 1975: 48).

The chorus of protochronist outrage over West European cultural dominance and its local effects was not wholly unison. Some reviled Lovinescu's notion of "synchronism" and its latter-day adherents, imitators of the West, as disdaining local cultural values; they viewed as anti-Romanian any advocacy of a European identity, which perpetuates the "theory of cultural centers and peripheries" and is a form of "cultural terrorism" (Purcaru 1986: 370). Others merely regretted that Romanians have spent so much energy in their obsession with "synchronizing" themselves with the West, when their destiny ties them to the orbit of Byzantium (Zamfirescu 1975: 64). Some insisted that protochronism and synchronism should work together (see Purcaru 1986: 63, 87, 330–331; Rachieru 1985: 36–48), such that a culture develops its specificity through encountering other cultures relative to which it is ahead in some respects and behind in others. But regardless of the specific mix of westernization and local values postulated, most protochronists agreed that there must be a weakening of the absolute western reference that produces subaltern or "child" cultures (Rachieru 1985: 26), and they called for greater cultural policentrism and the diversification of cultural voices (*Luceafărul* 1985). All of them insisted on the need to develop cultural dignity.

To readers acquainted with Ceauşescu's foreign policy and its attempt to carve out for Romania a position of relative independence in the world, these emphases of protochronism will sound familiar. Indeed, they characterize many anticolonial groups and movements, whether in socialist or other contexts; they are ideas that deserve to be taken seriously, as part of the emancipation of oppressed peoples. Declarations of independence abounded in protochronist talk. "[Papu] affirms the creative independence of Romanian literature" (Ungheanu 1985: 387). "We ought not to explain a culture only through the influences exercised upon it, for then we do not explain its originality; we should not make the evolution of a culture contingent upon the permanent implanting of such influences, but should judge cultures for what they are . . . " (ibid., 394). "Winning aesthetic sovereignty is . . . essential for the future of our nation, whose principal terrain for affirming itself is that of the spirit, of cultural values" (Zamfirescu 1983: 376). "Protochronism seeks the annulment of norms that place a literature in excessive creative dependence and subordination to the values of other literatures" (Purcaru 1986: 62). "If a country aspires to its independence, why shouldn't a culture also aspire to independence, to standing on its own?" (ibid., 331). "Can one speak of real independence if a nation is prevented . . . from exercising its right to culture?" (Tudor 1986: 230).

At issue was not only political but economic independence, just as it was in the Ceauşescu leadership's (unsuccessful) striving toward economic autarchy. Protochronist writing was rife with imagery of the *production*, *consumption*, and *circulation* of value, the relation of the internal and external markets, and the matter of symbolic accumulation. "[Lovinescu saw] the basis of Romanian cultural activity in an undifferentiated borrowing, *synchronism* automatically presupposing *imitation*—thus a role of consumer and almost not at all of creator. . . . [He believed] that we have created nothing and have imported everything" (Ungheanu 1985: 387, 397). "[The example of writer X] is a protochrony that, having not been treated as such, lost its right to European circulation" (ibid., 441). "[We decry the] neglect of [our classic cultural] fund, together with the importing . . . of certain values from elsewhere, which do not enrich us" (Purcaru 1986: 102).[12] Both the direction pursued by the Romanian leadership and the implications of protochronism shared a kind of protectionism, an emphasis on restricting the influence of the West on the Romanian market. Both implied an initial autarchy that would later reverse itself—a sort of primitive accumulation that would become self-sustaining, that can generate development *without* infusions of foreign materials and capital (be this cultural or economic).

One particularly clear way in which both protochronists and their opponents posed the relation of Romanian cultural production to international circulation was in terms of the relationship between "national" and "global" [*universal*], a theme that provided a principal arena of more or less direct debate between the different groups. Both sides asserted that the relationship of Romanian culture to the worldwide circulation of cultural values is of great importance, but the direction of the envisioned relationship differs for the two camps. Antiprotochronist writings tend towards an implicit capital-import model that generates development and subsequent export: they advocate bringing in the cultural values of the West so as to improve native literary products, which might then enter into international circulation on their own merits, gaining world stature for their creators and for the Nation.[13] Protochronist writings, on the other hand, advocate staunching literary "imports" and the currency drain they imply,[14] protecting the local market, promoting recognition for the contributions Romanians have made to world culture, and perhaps (although this is not certain) even *reversing* the flow of values within literature.[15] This contrast appeared in Papu's initial formulation of protochronism, which affirmed that Romanian creations are *original*, not *copies* or *imitations* but genuine *creations*. It was almost as if he were seeking to secure the patent on certain ideas that have circulated profitably in the West, to make Romania a major world center for the production of value.

That the matter of circulation is seen as directly linked with accumulation—indeed, with *capital* accumulation—is apparent from the following:

In our times, when peoples and scholars everywhere have become increasingly preoccupied with inventorying the accumulated human goods [*bunuri*] and the intellectual potential of humanity, a people and a culture owe it to humanity to acknowledge their riches [*avutul*] . . . . If we are preoccupied with speaking about our place and our role in the continent's past, then, this is not arrogance but a stocktaking of the capital that we can deposit in the common treasury of world values (Zamfirescu 1975: 8).

Note the emphasis on indigenous accumulation and "export" into the world stock of cultural capital. And one moderate protochronist expressed very directly the consequences of these considerations for the national treasury:

If our journals in international languages were [better], we would greatly increase their capacity for exchange, transforming them into a veritable hard currency [*valuta*]. We ought also to stimulate the possibilities for international scientific contracts, organize international doctoral courses in our country with foreign students, etc., so that at least some of the hard currency revenues gained thereby might be used to improve our own scientific information. . . . Having up-to-date knowledge and a healthy, intense metabolism with other cultures is a necessary condition for . . . entering into international cultural competition (Marcus, in Purcaru 1986: 247–248).

This last commentator's reference to "cultural competition" and its link with the circulation of cultural products brings us to one of the most significant issues in the protochronism debates: the nature of competition and market success and the values that generate this success. It is very clear from statements of both protochronists and their adversaries that this was a serious problem. Among the former, considerable attention went to asking what determines the recognition of contemporary works and whether circulation is or is not an indication of it. For example, Papu distinguished between a work's world-class *value* and its world *circulation*, the former being intrinsic to the work and not depending upon the latter (Purcaru 1986: 89). Another protochronist proclaimed, "A value remains a value whether or not it is recognized" (ibid., 373), adding that the process of entering into world circuits can be distorted by imperialist expansionism and dogmatism, whereas the assessment of value itself is not subject to these influences. There were recurrent complaints about the unfairness of world-market competition: for example, "Let me say parenthetically that synchronism inculcates the idea of competition, yet in practice European or more broadly occidental cultural life . . . raises competition to a level that precludes real communication and the natural osmosis [of values]" (Ungheanu 1985: 438). Their musings on this problem led protochronists to propose their own criterion for determining value: the notion of *priority*. For them, being first ought to guarantee recognition.

Antiprotochronists, for their part, took issue with that idea.

The protochronist complaint is . . . often enough legitimate, to the extent that values from other national cultures—equivalent with the values of Romanian culture—have entered into the European or world circuit while ours have not. But this defect is not going to be remedied by overblown gestures such as the 600-page manuscript (rightly rejected by the publisher) proving that Eminescu discovered relativity theory before Einstein (Cătineanu 1985: 46).

It is not so important, I think, to hold—sometimes exaggerating to the point of the ridiculous—that we were the first, even if we were ignored . . . as that we were truly creative. What use would we have of all these protochronist initiatives . . . if we could not show the world that we had created true monuments? From this point of view, I consider it . . . [unimportant] if a Romanian should have written before Milton, Tasso, and others a work that was comparable but naive and rudimentary . . . . Our pride should not consist in being first but in being great (Manolescu, in Purcaru 1986: 147).

To determine that something came first in the formulation of a certain idea or in the use of a certain procedure represents a real gain in knowledge if we can also prove that, through diffusion, the idea or procedure fertilized national and European literature. . . . But in the situations invoked by our "protochronists," the question of diffusion is not posed. . . . [I]t is not the modern reading that seems to me contestable, the effort to "discover" in past writings the confirmation of our present ideas, but the tendency to transform this into an argument about priority. Which is, may I be forgiven the word, pure sophistry. The literary memory . . . retain[s] only those priorities which had some influence (Dobrescu 1979: 165).

All three of these critics were insisting that the guarantor of success is not priority but something else—originality, quality.

The same point was made even more revealingly by an antiprotochronist art critic (Pleşu 1981). He asserted that the successful entry of Romanian values onto the world circuit is not something that can be strategized, nor is their failure to be recognized simply a "slip-up in diplomatic relations governing the circulation of our values on the international market and of international values on our market" (p. 191). World status for Romanian culture will not be attained by "a nationalism that makes exaltation profitable,"[16] nor by simple assertion: "Some say that to succeed in the competition for world status, the surest method is not to *do our work* elbow to elbow with the others but to *tell* everyone how competitive we are" (p. 195). The statement points to fundamentally different means of participating in the world cultural market: by producing comparable products whose high quality will make them competitive, or, rather, by a dictatorial strategy—one might call it *illocutionary*—unconcerned with whether the products are competitive. The latter all too often characterized the participation of command economies on world markets.[17]

Given Romania's political and economic colonial status and the relatively little notice its culture has received on the world stage, the protochronists' anxieties about independence and self-image can for the moment be taken at face value. But why, we may wonder, were all these writers in the epitomal command economy talking so much about circulation and the market? I believe that we see here the effects of the partial recommodification of culture in the sphere of literature and the arts, discussed in chapter 3. The Party leadership's response to the economic crisis that began in the 1970s included cutting state support for culture and requiring institutions such as theatres, museums, publishing houses, and cinemas to be at least partly "self-financing." Whereas in the 1950s and 1960s all of these had enjoyed full state support—accompanied, of course, by political interference in their activities—suddenly in the late 1970s they were ordered to fend for themselves. This was not easy, for many of them, because reduced state subsidy did not mean reduced interference: thus, theatres and cinemas were expected to attract a public while playing to the satisfaction of the bureaucracy. Unusual survival strategies emerged: theatres that made and profitably sold coffins from their props department, or cinemas that advertised in huge letters the name of a politically acceptable film that no one would want to see, while actually running a film people would want to see, its name to be found on a tiny notice near the door.

For writers the consequences were felt especially through their publishing houses. The regime of self-financing put publishers in a bind, for (like western university presses) most of their publications were unprofitable. Only in literature was this not the case; yet literature was ringed with interdictions. Despite an official dismantling of censorship, the resistance of many writers to Party control made censorship procedures in many cases more time-consuming and stringent than ever. Restrictions on the use of paper and the size of printings made it difficult for presses to operate in the black, since what passed censorship might not have buyers, and what would have buyers might be permitted no more than a modest press run. Because of self-financing, however, when a press did get something through censorship without a restricted circulation, it would print large quantities so as to make money, knowing that the book would be sold out overnight solely from the rumor that it had been held up in censorship.[18] Indeed, one critic (A. Ştefănescu 1981) noted that the politicization of literature had had the effect of enlarging its audience!

It would be misleading to suggest that market forces prevailed, in literature, for not only did political constraints and subsidies continue to operate but personalistic ties could influence the size of a press run, as they could influence virtually anything in Romania. Nevertheless, the problem of sales ceased to be the negligible concern it had once been. Writers whose works sold unusually well could expect presses to work hard to get their books, which would ensure a press's budget for the year, and to ignore the works of unknown or esoteric writers. Under the new quasi-market conditions, many writers—especially young ones—had more difficulty publishing than before. They were by no means enthusiastic about being thrown onto the market from the safe womb of state subsidies, preferring, as one writer acknowledged to me, a state-supported art that assured writers a central place in society and insulated them from the market (cf. J. and C. Garrard 1990: 185–186; Haraszti 1987; Konrád and Szelényi 1979: 70).

These circumstances created problems for writers on both sides of the debate. Because some novels and poetry of the protochronists sold unusually well, antiprotochronist critics harped on the question of "standards" according to which, they said, other writings ought to be preferred. At the same time, protochronists—indeed, all artists—had reason to advocate protectionism of the internal literary and artistic market, given that sociological research found consumers of culture to favor western products overwhelmingly. (One national survey showed that among Romanians' most-loved authors was Alexandre Dumas, and that American and European films drew by far the largest television audiences.[19]) From this it could be assumed that the institutions mediating cultural production—presses, cinemas, TV, and so forth—might prefer something other than Romanian products, especially under the rules of self-financing, and that without some form of cultural protectionism this preference would give Romanian authors and artists fewer outlets for their works. Considerations such as these clarify one protochronist's complaint that "some books about 'structuralism' and 'semiotics' rot on the shelves while others that could sell hundreds of thousands of copies circulate in runs of confidential size. We ought to do better 'marketing' and not nourish people with questionable studies on Bachelard" (Brăescu 1982*b*). I suspect that the inherent protectionism of the protochronist idea was not, as some might think, opportunistically modeled upon the protectionism of official economic policy: both expressed a particular response to the problems inherent in their particular situations.

Although my discussion so far has emphasized the problems of political and cultural independence and writers' new vulnerability to market forces, the arguments that brought these problems to the surface were saturated as well with an obsession with literary *values*: how these are to be recognized, how they are tied to circulation and to quality, who determines them and changes them. The question of value and struggles over it lay at the heart of the protochronism debate, the stakes being who would establish criteria of value within the Romanian literary community. The consequences of winning the right to establish such criteria included the power to make and unmake literary careers and institutions, to promote particular aesthetic or political standards, and to influence the politics of culture set by the Party leadership. Exploring these implications of protochronism requires, first, some knowledge of the social world of Romanian literature and of the forces supporting the rise of protochronism within it.

Writers and Party in Socialist Romania[20]

The history of writers in Ceauşescu's Romania offers an excellent example of how institutions created for one set of purposes— to harness literary production to the will of the Communist party—became instruments toward a different end—preserving certain literary values that a subsequent Party leadership was intent on destroying. The most important of these institutions was the Romanian Writers Union,[21] formed in 1949. In each of the two liberalizations of Romanian cultural life—the small one following Stalin's death, and the much larger one of the 1960s, encouraged by Ceauşescu as he attempted to consolidate power—one particular group (which I will call faction A[22]) gained and expanded control over the Union, increasing, as well, its presence in the Communist party and in key positions related to publishing (see Gabanyi 1975: 67, 161). Many of these literary leaders had experienced years of frustration and "socialist-realist" constraints on publishing their work and were thus reluctant to loosen their grip on leading roles. Their double entrenchment at the top of the literary establishment constricted the channels of upward mobility, resources, and access to privilege for other writers (ibid., 164), who would form "faction B." The blockage was only slightly eased by admitting a few new faces into the literary leadership at the 1968 Writers Congress (ibid., 141, 161; Shafir 1983b: 414), but manuscripts remained backlogged and authors grew increasingly impatient.

During the late 1960s, the community of writers and critics was in ferment, as younger members sought even further liberalization, pressing for the abolition of censorship, the end of the rule of "Party hacks" and "dogmatists" over literary products, and so forth. Much of the energy for the ferment came from the Party's reintroduction of national values into what could be written. This rediscovery of "the Nation" had a marked effect on all those who had been socialized during the internationalist 1950s; many of them were soon to appear on *both* sides of the protochronism debates. The enthusiasm for liberalization would probably have driven writers even further afoul of the Party had not Warsaw pact troops invaded Prague in August of 1968. In response to this, Ceauşescu gave his famous speech condemning the invasion; it was a gesture that won him more goodwill than could have been imagined a short time before, bringing into the Party innumerable intellectuals who had recently regarded themselves as apolitical or even oppositionist.

The liberalizing ferment had had its casualties. The most significant was Eugen Barbu, an important writer and editor of a major cultural publication, later a member of the Central Committee; he had a sizable following among a subset of the younger writers, soon to swell the ranks of faction B against those who had been responsible for Barbu's downfall. (Barbu's connections saw to it that within two years he received the editorship of another cultural magazine, *The Week*, which was to host protochronism's most egregious excesses.) This polarization of the literary community with Barbu as rallying point was aggravated in 1979, when an accusation of plagiarism mobilized his supporters and sharpened still further the conflict between them and his accusers.

Pitted in opposition, then, were the powerful faction A and people like Barbu who had suffered from its strength. Faction A was unwilling to relinquish privileged positions or share hard-won perquisites; having finally made it to relatively easy publication, good incomes, translations, trips abroad, and so on, they were now reproducing for new cohorts of writers and critics the same pattern of blocked self-realization they themselves had suffered in the 1950s. Both Romanian and foreign analysts of this period agree in seeing the fierce literary battles of the late 1960s and early 1970s as only superficially about artistic conceptions, the deeper causes lying in struggles for access to privilege (see Gabanyi 1975: 141; Gheorghiu 1987: 58). From the "disenfranchised" new generations of writers came many of the recruits for faction B, adding their complaints to those of that faction's senior generation that felt itself to be excluded by the entrenched Union leadership of faction A.

The events of the late 1960s had firmly seated one wing of the literary community in positions of governance within it; the "July theses" of 1971 and the three years following them provided the fulcrum upon which the systemic balance of power would slowly shift to the other faction during the 1970s[23]—the years of the rise of protochronism. The "July theses" had two important implications for the structure of opportunity within the literary world. They made the leadership of the Writers' Union even more anxious to hold onto its privileges, lest infusions of new blood bring the wrong people into high positions, and they showed writers eager for greater influence a new channel through which this might be achieved: specializing in the production of ideology (for a new symbolic mode of control) within the literary field.[24] The latter possibility was soon manifest, as within two to three years the editorships of the largest-circulation cultural weeklies passed into the hands of faction B, whose brand of "reformism" differed significantly from that of those in faction A who had initiated the reform movement of the late 1960s.[25] Thus, the field of forces contained three major players: the Party leadership, faction A of the literary community, dominating the organizations of literary production (the Union, universities), and faction B, the protochronists, allied with the Party leadership and increasing its hold over publications and censorship—the organs of dissemination and broad cultural influence.

During the 1970s and subsequently, Party leadership and Union were locked in battle over how much independence the latter, with its autonomous funds and its carefully honed democratic statutes, would be permitted. At the Writers' Conferences of 1977 and 1981, the

Union succeeded in outmaneuvering at least some of what the Party leadership intended for it, rejecting the Party's first choice for president and installing its own governing council in 1977. Similarly independent moves almost succeeded in 1981 as well, but the Party leadership managed to replace the president elected in 1977, who had become inconvenient by insisting that the Party respect its own legal statutes on the Union.[26] Protochronism was implicated in these battles, for by imposing a rule of secret elections for delegates to the 1981 conference, the Union membership managed to exclude from it *all* the major figures associated with that movement. In retaliation, the protochronists launched a campaign to have the Union dismantled altogether (see below).

Subsequent attacks upon the Union rendered it almost impotent. Parts of the Union's funds were frozen and thus made unavailable for the very important purposes they had served until then (support of writers who, for any of a number of reasons, did not have works in print, or publication of books and journals through the Union's publishing house). The available funds tended to go to persons favored by those administering them—increasingly, friends of the protochronists. After 1981, no more Conferences were allowed despite a concerted effort by the Union's governing council. The Party imposed—over fierce opposition from the members—new membership requirements, including approval by one's local Party organization and occupancy of a salaried post; these undermined the status of writer *as a profession* and reduced writers' independence. Questions of membership became moot, in any event, for the Party leadership almost wholly obstructed the admission of new members after 1981, lest the membership become even more vigorously oppositional. Meetings of the Union's sections (by geographical location and by specialty—poetry, prose, and so forth) and of its governing council were forbidden, since such meetings could produce new schemes to outsmart the Party. These interdictions effectively paralyzed the workings of the organization, including the award of literary prizes that would set standards and form the literary canon.

Here, then, is the context in which protochronism appeared and spread: a crisis in possibilities for upward movement and greater influence within the existing literary establishment, resulting in factional struggles within the older generation and subsequent cohorts of writers; a major shift in the Party leadership's strategy of governance in 1971/1974, away from liberalization, reform, and democratization and toward greater emphasis on ideology, force, and centralization; and an economic crisis that paradoxically increased market forces for literary products within ongoing central control. The spread of protochronism was the sign of the struggle for power within the literary establishment. Within this context, attention focused on how to establish the values for judging literary products and what relation they should have to the political sphere. This made room for a reordering of the hierarchy of writers according to newly ascendant criteria. To put it differently, the determination of value, and of the symbolic and cultural authority that rests upon accepting certain criteria of value, were suddenly up for grabs. Writers who enjoyed reputations from cultural authority accumulated according to aesthetic criteria were now vulnerable to challenge from those who, by setting culture to work for the Party's symbolic-ideological control mechanisms, could mix cultural authority with politics toward greater influence over cultural production. The protochronism debates were the form taken by this new conjuncture between politics and culture.

Protochronism and Politics

THE DETERMINATION OF VALUE

The word "values" appeared countless times in the utterances of people in all positions in the protochronism debate. Persons on all sides agreed on the basic premise that cultural products *have* value, the only question being to assess it properly.[27] There was talk of "fundamental Romanian values," "reference points for national values," "the defense of our values," "the patrimony of national values." One participant summarized the basic issue behind protochronism as "what is the mechanism for promoting and recognizing values? What is the mechanism for bringing them into the cultural consciousness of humankind?" (Marcus, in Ungheanu 1985: 444). To some extent, protochronists saw this problem (like that of international circulation) as involving *importation*—the importing not just of foreign writings, but of foreign standards of value: "We easily accept any foreign deprecation, or acclaim just as easily any positive foreign appreciation, as holding immediate authority. But what is in question is *our* values, which we ourselves have to know how to appreciate. . . ." "It is interesting that, avoiding all the gains of Romanian criticism . . . appeal is made to foreign critics—excellent for their literatures but not always appropriate for us" (Ungheanu 1985: 415, 126). But I believe there was more to it than just another facet of protectionism, for the quotations make it clear that *some people* are recognizing and advocating those foreign standards, and it was those people and their values that protochronists intended to overthrow.

Participants saw the question of values as related intimately to the question of criticism. Everyone, it seems, agreed that the role of literary criticism is to sustain values, and that this role was not being properly served. For example, an antiprotochronist defined criticism as "that which must maintain a vigil over the preservation of the dignity of value" and "imped[e] ambiguity about values" but which has "lightly consented to the installation of a state of confusion and, what is more, has contributed to consolidating it" (Dobrescu 1981: 3). And from the other side, "Far from being a minor quarrel about words, the proportions of [this] critical dialogue obligate us to rethink the entire history of our culture. . . . Thus, it is not a matter just of sentimental attachment but of the very stakes of criticism and, implicitly, of critics" (Rachieru 1985: 37). This echoes Papu's insistence that protochronism had less to do with *creating* literary values than with their *recognition* or *reception* (ibid., 453). That is, the problem was not in the sphere of production but in who sits in judgment over the product.

Why were values and criticism so central to these debates? Because virtually every major stake in literary life revolved around how its "values" are to be defined, a highly conflictual process. Critics have a fundamental role in this process, for critics are the persons who hold a social mandate to produce legitimate classifications of artistic value (Bourdieu 1984: 28). Given that the role of critic is well institutionalized in literature above all, that field comes to serve as a kind of "epistemological police" for cultural production in general (Gheorghiu 1987: 75),[28] defining and protecting values by promoting certain works into the category of "values" and excluding others. Criticism and the values it sets, moreover, form the basis for the recognition and further accumulation of cultural authority. Therefore, any contest involving values inherently poses alternative grounds for such accumulation, challenging the basis upon which other accumulations have been built. In so doing, it affects not just individual literary careers but the possibilities for acquiring public resources. This is because in a system of scarce and centrally allocated resources, any group seeking to acquire the wherewithal for an activity must persuasively argue that its version of that activity is more representative of certain values than is the activity of others, claiming the same resources on comparable grounds.

Protochronism reveals, then, a struggle to control the definition of literary values—for stakes that were enormous: the very foundations of literary life. The issues through which these stakes come to light can be separated into several parts: sales and prizes and press runs, determining the literary "canon" for the present and future, influence within the organizations (such as the Writers' Union) that mediated artistic production, influence over the bureaucracy that determined culture's existence, and access to numerous important sources for augmenting cultural authority, whether this be combined with or independent of political status. Relevant to this last point are questions of how cognizant publics are formed who recognize the cultural authority to which a writer or critic might lay claim.

PRESS RUNS, LITERARY CANONS, AND INFLUENCE WITHIN THE WRITERS' UNION

Some of the best evidence as to the stakes in this power struggle comes from the concerns protochronists expressed in their writings and interviews. Particularly eloquent are those edited by Purcaru, who provoked his interlocutors with leading questions about how "certain critics" had attacked their work, and a set of interviews during 1982–1983 in the Literary-Artistic Supplement of the young people's edition of the Romanian Party daily (*Scînteia tineretului*), which was the launching pad for the assault on the Writers' Union, mentioned above.

A major set of concerns was access to print. Although this problem loomed particularly large in protochronist writings, it was not just theirs but was also expressed to me by writers across the full spectrum of positions. Protochronists complained about the distribution of space for literary criticism in journals, inadequate for expressing the full range of opinions, and they called for a new journal solely for criticism (Piru, in *România literară* 1977: 9). "The absence of a larger framework for activity, the lack of a sufficient number of columns for literary criticism and of critical debates prevents the full intellectual potential of our literary history and criticism from being realized" (Ungheanu, in *România literară* 1977: 9). Persons of all kinds objected to the difficulty of getting long-written books published while "certain writers" clog up editorial plans with manuscripts not even begun (see, e.g., Brăescu 1982a). "Books about structuralism and semiotics rot on the shelves while others that could sell hundreds of thousands of copies circulate in confidential runs" (Brăescu 1982b). Asked why all his books had appeared with difficulty, after five- and six-year delays, one writer replied that "ideological" referees had complained that his works lacked aesthetic value or were politically irresponsible[29] (Brăescu 1982d). Although the complaints just cited were all from protochronists, many could have come from the mouths of their opponents as well, equally concerned about delays, the size of press runs, and the number of journals (see, e.g., Manolescu, in Purcaru 1986: 148). They reflect real and understandable frustration at the reduced number of publications and the stiff competition to get one's works into print, a process in which it was insinuated that "certain critics" or writers had undue influence (even though the real cause lay in the Party's cultural policy).

Another source of irritation in protochronists' writings was the matter of prizes, reviews, and privileges. They spoke often of persons whose work ought to have received a literary prize but to whom critics had responded with a "surprising silence." Several commentators aired the suspicion that not deserving *works* but particular *persons* receive (or are denied) the prize (e.g., Purcaru 1986: 178, 328)—that is, biased juries give prizes to their friends—and another complained that prizes always seem to go to the "modernists" rather than to people like himself (Zamfirescu 1982a: 7).[30] Allusions to the "conspiracy of silence" by "certain critics" and their "literary quarantine" of various (protochronist) writers accompanied complaints that the review sections of "certain" journals are held in a monopoly grip. When it was not silence that rankled, it was negative reviews, or positive reviews of writers seen as deservedly obscure (ibid.). There were objections that "certain critics" like to legislate what subjects are unsuited, on aesthetic grounds, to literary creations: history, everyday social issues, and so forth. All these comments mentioned particular critical values that were hindering broad public recognition of and acceptance of protochronists' work and obstructing their access to the privileges that would come with prizes and awards.[31] Some mentioned overtly the medals and material advantages of the old-guard "dogmatists" of faction A (Purcaru 1986: 322).

A third stake in the power struggle was control over the literary histories, compendia, dictionaries, anthologies, and especially the school manuals—in a word, over determining the literary "canon." Several protochronists were distressed that "major literary values" were being excluded from the consciousness of schoolchildren, who would spend lifetimes with a "distorted" image of Romania's true literary canon. To prevent this, they declared, the writers of school texts must be *objective* and *nonpartisan* (e.g., Purcaru 1986: 258). One participant suggested that the best people to write such manuals are not necessarily university professors but, preferably, literary historians or critics (ibid., 263); this protochronist complaint reflects the continued preponderance of their opponents—1960s "liberals" and "old dogmatists"—in the major university chairs. Protochronists worried not just over the authors of school manuals and whom they have included or left out but also over the persons chosen as manuscript referees: "You will sometimes find that they are the same names, the small and 'large dictators' dictating, unfortunately, in this domain as well" (ibid., 159).

A sustained assault on the problem of the literary canon appeared in an article in *The Week*, entitled "Who Educates the Teachers" (Tudor 1981). This article begins by saying that everyone is entitled to an opinion about books, but personal opinions should not enter into official manuals used in instructing pupils. Singling out (antiprotochronist) critic and university professor Nicolae Manolescu as the guiding light of a particular manual, Tudor goes on to denounce the inclusions in this manual as having "rewritten a new order for Romanian literature, that accords long-standing values a lesser importance than others that the passage of time has not yet consecrated definitively in either national or larger terms." He lists contemporary writers the manual leaves out and others undeservedly given much coverage—people like synchronist Eugen Lovinescu, for example—and he deplores the limited coverage of writers like Eminescu in contrast with the extensive treatment of certain contemporary authors. Expressing his alarm that Manolescu is on the editorial board of the school manuals for more than one high-school grade, he says, "[The problem is] the *permanent* teaching of these year after year, in successive grades . . . . When the pupil sees that year after year, throughout the final years of high school, the same people and biographies recur, he will naturally conclude that the old classics are outdated and are not really all that classic." He ends his broadside by accusing the manual of "rendering old errors permanent and serving them up to the younger generation in new packaging as the proper set of values for understanding Romanian civilization. By what criteria are the authors of school manuals designated?" (Tudor 1981). That Tudor was challenging the process whereby Romania's literary canon is fixed could scarcely be clearer.

This problem was perceived from the other side as well. For over a decade, a team of writers and critics under university professor Mircea Zaciu, in Cluj, labored over a Dictionary of Romanian Literature. Work on it stalled in the mid-1980s owing to endless fights, instigated from outside the work collective, as to who should be included and who omitted from the dictionary. By report of some involved in the project, a major issue was whether to include "certain political figures." The collective balked, saying it was concerned only with literary values, not politics. According to my interviewees, persons well-placed politically, at the instigation (it was suspected) of leading protochronists, objected to the publication of a work with "all these names, all these consecrated values." The book's publisher defended it to the hilt until convinced by "high circles" that it would never fly, and even though the entire huge manuscript had been typeset and was in galleys, the fonts were melted and the volume dropped. Zaciu's team saw this as the decisive defeat of the antiprotochronist canon.

Making allowances for the subjectivism of both this account[32] and the published ones referred to above, it is nevertheless clear that the "consecration of literary values" had become a great privilege in Ceauşescu's Romania, one over which there was a fight to the death. Authors complained of constant diminution in the number of books of literary criticism that were included in publication plans, and they described to me the subterfuges through which they might get a book of criticism published by insisting that it belonged in some category other than criticism. What was at issue in this dispute—a dispute involving more than just various kinds of writers and critics but high functionaries as well—was the institutionalization of ideas of value. These would shape the definition of cultural authority and the sources of past cultural production upon which a person's literary reputation might build. They would shape, as well, the terms in which people could appeal successfully for support of their activities—how to argue with a press editor, with a censor, with a government minister, and how to appeal to the public. Phrasing the struggle in this way enables us to see why it engaged such intense and genuine passions on both sides of the debate, for people's entire life-work, their self-image as professionals, and their notion of their contribution to human creativity, were all at stake.

Value is institutionalized not only through determining an artistic canon but also through the organizations that mediate the production of culture—in Romania, the Writers' Union, the Union of Plastic Arts, the Composers' and Musicians' Unions. Of these the Writers' Union was by far the most important, despite the serious erosion of its authority and resources during the 1980s. To have a position in this organization, with its own press and its Literary Fund, meant the chance to influence the kinds and amounts of things to be published, the formation of committees that would write school manuals and give out literary prizes, the disposition of the several magazines published under the Union's aegis, and so forth. A struggle to control the Writers' Union was one of the most important issues expressed through protochronism.

The struggle was evident in concerted attacks by protochronists upon the Union's very structure. One finds numerous criticisms of its leadership, obliquely accused of obstructing within the Union the "large process of democratization taking place elsewhere in Romanian society," of having made itself into a "council of the wise," a "self-constituted mandarinate." Protochronists called for rotation of offices and for decentralizing both the Union and its material means, so that these do not rest in just a few hands "which are not even the most hard-working" (Purcaru 1986: 72, 115, 156). One critic objected to the Union's failure to make a formal and public rejoinder to the defamatory campaigns led from abroad against certain books and certain writers (a reference to Radio Free Europe's campaign against protochronism). The critic viewed this as urgently requiring a collective defense, because of its implications for the all-important entry of Romanian writings into the international circuit of cultural values (ibid., 72). There were also complaints about how to achieve Union membership. These not only reflected the protochronists' resentment at their voting minority but also, I suspect, aimed at recruiting young writers frustrated by the long and difficult process that membership had become (owing, of course, not to Union leaders but to restrictions imposed from the Party center, but this fact went unmentioned).

The attack was even more direct in the 1982 interviews in the Party's Youth daily, mentioned above. Nearly every week there appeared some negative comment about the Union, whose leaders "treat it as their personal fief" (Brăescu 1982*b*), and whose meetings are allegedly preceded by corrupt backroom buying and selling of votes in which "so-called intellectuals behave like electoral traffickers" (Brăescu 1982*d*). The unions were accused of elitism:

The structures of the unions for artistic and creative life have not changed in thirty years. Monopoly of power, abuse of power in the area of creation, monopoly on opinions and abuse of opinions, all perpetuated via long terms of office—these are the realities, the effects of these encysted, dogmatic structures, and the causes of dogmatic and elitist phenomena. And above all, this encystment is firmly maintained in parallel with the suspect and questionable efforts at "modernization," at "synchronism" and "avant-gardism." We must decentralize this excessively centralized organizational structure, valid only when it was formed thirty years ago. We must "synchronize" it with the true state of contemporary Romanian socialist democracy (Brăescu 1982*c*).

Another interviewee went on at even greater length about how the Union offers sinecures to people who create nothing and are a species of *rentiers*, parasitic on the work of others who contribute consciously to building up the revolutionary ideological artistic heritage. This writer also objected that the Literary Fund of the Writers' Union is swelled by receipts from a small number of people whose books sell exceedingly well and who thereby support a large fauna of "stipendiaries" and uncreative parasites. That an organized campaign had been taking place was nicely signaled by the last interview in the series, in which protochronist Zamfirescu announced his lack of solidarity with "those who led the campaign against the Union and the Literary Fund," likening them to peasants who seek to rid the barn of mice by burning it down (Brăescu 1982*g*).

The terms of this campaign—talk of the need for "democratization" and "decentralization"—show how complex the battle had become. Reading these texts, one might think that perestroika had made an unexpected and premonitory (protochronous!) appearance in Romanian literary life of the early 1980s. Yet the objective of protochronist reproaches was not a societal restructuring but an attempt to break down, through an "indigenized Marxist" rhetoric, an organization dominated by a different faction actively maintaining reputations and standards of value that the challengers wished to overturn. What prevailed in the broader political context was wholly the opposite of democratization and decentralization. The judgment one places on this talk of decentralization will depend on how one assesses the systemic tendencies being promoted by the work of the different factions, a point to be taken up again below.

Concerning the terms of argument more broadly, those relevant to making the points discussed so far—about press runs, setting the literary canon, and influence within the Writers' Union—involved not only notions about the market but some of the weapons of struggle discussed in chapter 4. Protochronists made frequent use of notions from the Marxist critique of capitalism, turned to the service of their own goals—reference to "rentiers" and "literary profiteers," for example, to describe the "elitists" at the head of the Union: "The Union has gone from being the property of the community to being that of a group of actionaries who invest very little and in exchange exploit to the maximum . . . . [It must return to] dedicating itself to the ideological and professional effort according to absolutely collective criteria" (Brăescu 1982*f*). The suggestion that opponents are "dogmatists" and xenophiles lurks within references to their being "well oiled with vodka before their meetings" (Brăescu 1982*b*)—"vodka" (rather than Romanian țuica [plum brandy] or French cognac) signalling stalinophilia. Many of these texts also have overt accusations of "dogmatism" and "proletcultism," and of antiprotochronist "Europeanism" as denying the values of the national character.

Antiprotochronists, for their part, also called their opponents "dogmatists" and "neoproletcultists" (see, e.g., Grigurcu 1981: 2), in reference not to the Stalinist suppression of national values but to the contemporary contamination of aesthetic criteria by politics—characteristic, they said, of protochronism. More common, however, was antiprotochronist representation of their opponents as fascists. This was accomplished above all by labeling the contemporary debate over protochronism a resuscitation of the interwar struggles between "traditionalists" and "modernists," corresponding respectively to protochronists and their opponents (e.g., Condurache 1981; Dobrescu 1981; A. Ştefănescu 1981). The effect was sometimes sharpened by referring to latter-day "autochthonism." Since most of the interwar "traditionalists" had been execrated or imprisoned as fascists, the message behind these labels was unmistakable. (The association was rendered explicit in Rădulescu [1986: 13], the only antiprotochronist with sufficient political clout to make such an accusation out loud.) Its hoped-for effect was to disqualify the "new traditionalists" in the eyes of both public and bureaucracy, for the rhetoric (if not also the sentiment) of opposition to fascism remained strong in Ceauşescu's Romania.

Beyond the stakes concerning literary value, pursued chiefly through accusations of dogmatism and fascism, there were additional stakes concerning the grounds upon which cultural authority should be recognized and accumulated. Although the same rhetorical weapons served those battles as well, this set of issues shows especially clearly how charges of "elitism" and the technique of genealogical appropriation were used to build one's own claims to cultural authority and to undermine one's opponents.

CULTURAL AUTHORITY, "ELITISM," AND GENEALOGICAL APPROPRIATIONS

I have suggested at several points that how literary values are determined is closely tied with establishing a writer's or critic's authority in the world of culture. To establish cultural or creative authority was one means of gaining entry into and advantage within Romania's cultural politics; the other was political title or influence, whose holders also attempted to convert even that into a claim to recognition in cultural terms. Recognized cultural authority was essential to claiming cultural representativeness, or to discourses about "authenticity," which were important weapons in the horizontal competition for central resources. In other words, one of the relevant publics for a claim to cultural authority was the bureaucrats who implemented the state's cultural policy. Another possible public was the readership to which novels, poetry, and criticism had to appeal under the conditions of "self-financing." With the debate over protochronism, both of these publics became objects of competition: their tastes had to be formed such that they would recognize one rather than another set of claims. To use the term proposed in chapter 4, they had to be rendered *cognizant* publics.

A "cognizant public" is one that recognizes and acknowledges the bases upon which an elite makes a claim to superior status. Their recognition depends upon accepting the values that underlie such a claim—values of strict adherence to professional standards, for example, or values of patriotism as prior to purely aesthetic criteria. When these values are contested, the formation of cognizant publics oriented to them can become a contest also. This may be a function of struggles within an elite relating to its immediate environment or may result from changes in the social order in which a given elite's position is embedded; in Ceauşescu's Romania, both of these obtained. Members of Romania's cultural elite therefore had two reasons (their opposition to each other, and the revolutionary goals of the Romanian Party) for competing to form their own cognizant publics, receptive to them as alternative bearers of cultural authority based in different values. In this contest the antiprotochronists were in much the weaker position, owing to the others' superior access to mass media.

The communists' vast extension of education since 1944 contributed much to a potential reconfiguring of social recognition. Some acknowledgment of this appears in the following protochronist statement:

After 1944, when the working class took power, the possibility of a major politics of Romanian culture appeared for the first time. "The worker spirit" meant, concretely, the possibility for any speaker of Romanian to be able to *read* his writers, through eradicating illiteracy, . . . through calling the entire people to cultural life (Zamfirescu 1975: 49).

Communist rule also contributed the notion that cultural "elitism" is a bad thing and should disqualify those guilty of it from social recognition. When protochronists accused their opponents of elitism, as they so often did, they were partly addressing one or both of the cognizant publics whose tastes they wished to form. To affirm their own allegiance to the masses and their respect for the intelligence of common people, while accusing others of elitism, aimed to reeducate those in the audience who might be partial to the European values others were espousing. Protochronists decried the elitism that resisted patriotic poetry, political poetry, and literature with rural themes (recall the peasantism favored by interwar traditionalists). "Literary elitism . . . detests 'pasturism' and, naturally, dislikes the direction formerly taken by [a populist interwar newspaper], whose aim was our obligation to the people" (Purcaru 1986: 66–67). The message to a cognizant public is that it should reject the sorts of readings offered by these "elitists," who allegedly hold the intelligence of common readers and the values of rural folk in contempt.

Forming a cognizant public includes not only "civilizing" the public into one's preferred values and sustaining its attachment to them but also, sometimes, *re*civilizing it: forming new cognizances for a public already cognizant within a given distribution of values. That is, forming cognizant publics in literature may entail not only teaching people to read but teaching them *re*readings, in relation to which one's own reading will acquire greater authority than the readings of other specialists. This point was recognized in an early statement about protochronism: "Protochronism proposes a 'correction' of method and an exercise of elementary aesthetic (re)education. 'The professor must return to the classroom' . . . " (I. Constantinescu 1977: 4).

Such rereadings occupied a central place in the protochronist agenda. An excellent example is the one treated in the preceding chapter, Ilie Bădescu's recasting of Conservative-party stalwart and Romantic poet Eminescu into a radical sociologist. Bădescu was not alone in rereading the poet in ways that mitigated one or another problematic aspect of his work: aside from Papu's (1977) rereading of Eminescu as a precocious existential philosopher, absurdist, and writer of free verse, other scholars worked to cleanse him of the taint of xenophobia and antisemitism (e.g., Popescu 1987). This effort was not restricted to protochronists, for their opponents too had to create an acceptable Eminescu to include in their own alternative lineages. Since no one could afford to be considered a denigrator of Romania's best poet, *all* had to reread Eminescu and to socialize their publics into new values for assessing him. It was an integral part of sustaining their own reputations and, through this, of fighting for the literary values they believed in.

The same process occurred not just through rereadings but through reediting works of earlier Romanian writers and thinkers—and this proved to be yet another arena for protochronism's challenge to the values of its opponents. During the 1970s and 1980s, reeditions from the interwar period in particular became so common that works from those earlier years occupied a large percentage of the shelf space in bookstores. Protochronist writings made it clear that these reeditions were far from neutral activities: several people complained that "someone" was blocking projects to republish the works of one or another important writer of the past (e.g., Diţă 1988; Pelin 1983; Purcaru 1986: 117–118, 122–124, 188, 325).[33] Such a charge was one way of insinuating that one's opponents did not share "fundamental Romanian values" and must therefore be dogmatists, aliens, traitors, or otherwise culturally unrepresentative.

The republishing of older great works began, in fact, before World War II under state sponsorship but was interrupted by the imposition of Soviet-style socialism. For the initial years of Communist party rule, many intellectual figures from the Romanian past were castigated and their writings suppressed as reactionary, bourgeois, racist, chauvinist, and worse. Persons who in their writings or their political activities had been associated with conservative currents suffered particularly under this regime. Some of them, such as the poet and philosopher Lucian Blaga, were still alive and saw their futures, once assuredly brilliant, crash about their ears. (Blaga went from being a famed and admired professor of philosophy at Cluj University to working as a minor functionary in the library, his old books banned and his new ones unpublished.) The only past figures whom one could invoke in support of present ideas were the prewar socialists, of whom there were inconveniently few.

Even before Stalin's death, however, and more so after it, Romanian intellectuals both inside and outside the Party—especially some leaders of the Writers' Union—began to push for relaxation of these strictures and for selective restoration of past national values. For example, in 1953 the president of the Writers' Union (a communist active in the new regime since its inception) wrote an article calling on the Party to republish more Romanian classics and criticizing proletcultist excesses that had suppressed them (Vrancea 1975: 225–226). Between 1953 and 1956 the works of certain interwar writers began to appear (although many of the most important products and thinkers of that period remained under interdiction [Gabanyi 1975: 55, 59–60]), and the 1956 Writers' Conference actually formalized the idea of "selective continuity" with respect to the intellectual heritage (Rachieru 1985: 16). Following a hiatus from 1958 to 1963 or so, ever more works and writers reentered the public realm.

Amidst the rush to reedit earlier works, however, ticklish problems were encountered that delayed certain reeditions. Perhaps the most delicate of all concerned Romanians' greatest poet, Eminescu, already mentioned above and in chapter 4. Among the reasons why republication of his corpus posed serious difficulties were not only his Conservative-party associations and hints of antisemitism but his violently anti-Russian sentiments. Many writers resisted discreet suppression of parts of his work, for finally freed of the harshest censorship, they could not countenance its imposition under any pretext. Thus, even those unenthusiastic about Eminescu's journalistic writings found themselves supporting the publication of his entire corpus, leaving it to high Party authorities to pick their way through the resultant thicket. In the context of delicate decisions such as those concerning Eminescu and other great figures with a history of rightist associations, protochronists liked to insinuate that delays in republishing those works could only be explained as obstruction from the left—meaning, as any Romanian reader would know, residual "dogmatists" of the late 1940s and early 1950s, the contemporary euphemism for antiprotochronists.[34] This left had included a disproportionate number of Jews and other national minorities; its contemporary familiars were thereby cast as *un-Romanian*, unpatriotic, quite evident in their alleged suppression of the works of great patriotic writers.

How are the reeditions related to protochronism and to the matter of cultural authority? In an oblique reference to protochronism, Gheorghiu suggests (1987: 80) that it nationalized cultural capital by reestablishing internal genealogies: any protochronist claim for priority of one or another Romanian author would incorporate both the author and the intellectual current he preceded (the Baroque, Romanticism, cybernetics, and so forth) into the lineage of Romanian producers of culture, founders of local branches of cultural capital accumulation. The question of reeditions, however, suggests that matters were more complex than this. To be sure, a protochronist demonstration did nationalize cultural capital, and it did so by an extended *invocation of a name*, linked in this way with a particular intellectual lineage. Such invocations are a common device whereby scholars and writers in all fields and countries bring famous predecessors into their intellectual genealogies. But to reedit a work is more than merely to invoke a name: it is to bind oneself textually *in extenso* to the words and intentions of another author—a procedure by which one recuperates a great deal of the cultural authority those words contain. Reeditings involved, then, genealogical appropriations that also appropriated cultural authority, thereby augmenting the accumulated authority of the self-appointed "heir" and of the lineage of persons and values he claimed as his own.[35]

To clarify my meaning, I make perhaps unorthodox use of Bakhtin's notion of *double-voiced discourse*. A double-voiced discourse is defined as an utterance that has an internal relationship to someone else's discourse (1984: 186). Bakhtin suggests that any utterance having its own intention may be made the object of another utterance, being incorporated into the second utterance in the service of a different set of intentions. Sometimes the intentions of the second speaker do not penetrate the first utterance; its intentions are left intact. But, he continues,

[T]he author may also make use of someone else's discourse for his own purposes, by inserting a new semantic intention into a discourse which already has, and which retains, an intention of its own. Such a discourse, in keeping with its task [i.e., if it is to achieve its effect—k.v.], must be perceived as belonging to someone else. In one discourse, two semantic intentions appear, two voices. . . . Two equally weighted discourses on one and the same theme, once having come together, must inevitably orient themselves to one another. Two embodied meanings cannot lie side by side like two objects—they must come into inner contact; that is, they must enter into a semantic bond (Bakhtin 1984: 188–189).[36]

The work of reediting Romania's great cultural figures accomplished precisely this. A reedition amounts to a massive utterance made under one set of circumstances with one set of intentions, and now infiltrated with the intentions of the new framing utterance to which it is subjected. At the same time, the editor of a "classic" succeeds in making a statement without having to accept responsibility for it, and he accumulates its cultural authority. His name and his work of editing form a semantic bond with the authority enjoyed by the classic author whose words he frames with an introduction and exegesis—often extensive, and definitely influencing how the work will then be read.[37] A scholar wishing to promote certain values that his political environment makes it awkward if not impossible to state might do so partially, augmenting his own accumulations through them, by forming a semantic bond with another whose intentions he recasts to suit his own. To all but the most sophisticated reader, his own intent will remain hidden behind the words of the original producer.

The reeditions gain significance in conjunction with protochronism, for protochronists were claiming to protect—and therefore were taking over—the cultural authority embedded in some of the greatest works of Romanian culture. The past literary values protochronism defended were in no way bogus ones. Protochronists, in effect, sought to *expropriate* cultural authority accumulated under the previous social order and put it to work within the new one, by inserting the giants of the past into their own genealogies. In response, antiprotochronists too made genealogical appropriations, defining themselves as the true continuers of one or another grand Romanian tradition and proper heirs to the cultural authority those contain. Both groups sought to capture the major figures of the distant and more recent past, sometimes struggling to control the very same persons (Eminescu, Blaga, novelist Marin Preda[38]). While many of these struggles occurred simply in written polemics, the most durable genealogical appropriations were made through reeditions. Reeditions of works by the major figures of Romanian cultural life show us, then, how these figures became not merely symbols to be fought over, not merely ancestors in competing intellectual genealogies, but servants of competing grounds for accumulating cultural authority.

COMPETING VALUES AND THE CONCENTRATION OF CULTURE IN THE APPARATUS

These competing grounds for authority reduce, ultimately, to authority resting on distance from the political versus authority resting on proximity to it. Both positions can present themselves as "patriotic" and as defending national values. Although protochronists tended to rely heavily on these notions, their opponents took their patriotic stand on values such as "the critical spirit," "lucidity," and the "autonomy of the aesthetic." For example: "The truest devotion to Romanian literature manifests itself through judging it with maximal lucidity" (A. Ştefănescu 1981: 2). Authors such as this would say that any other stance is suspect, smacking not of true cultural values but of those of the "bureaucrat's briefcase" (Grigurcu 1981: 2). As one antiprotochronist explained the struggle to me, the real stake in the opposition to protochronism was to protect the critical spirit. Whereas for protochronists everything that is Romanian is by definition good, he said, in fact *not* everything Romanian is good; one opposes protochronism so as to be able to continue emitting judgments selectively—so as to be able to say, occasionally, against the chorus of voices insisting that everything is fine simply because this is Romania, "Everything is *not* fine." Such judgments require keeping the realm of the aesthetic independent of politics—the sole condition, in this critic's view, for a criticism worthy of the name and a Romanian culture worthy of attention. People holding similar opinions saw the danger to national values as coming from the incursion of politics into the sphere of culture and argued that they were defending the national interest on these grounds.

Protochronists saw things differently. For them, "Romanian culture is inconceivable outside the idea of the homeland [*patria*]" (Brăescu 1982*e*: 3). Protochronist Bădescu was more specific: asking what should regulate the circulation of cultural values, he wrote that Ibrăileanu had replied "the critical spirit," but we say, rather, "the national idea," the only thing that is not corruptible by passing events (*Luceafărul* 1985 [6]: 4). Protochronists readily accused their opponents of lack of patriotism and of making the Nation vulnerable to foreign influences. This criticism was so treacherous that antiprotochronists had to go out of their way to combat it. For example, critic Manolescu concluded his interview with Ilie Purcaru (1986: 148), "My homeland [*patria*] is Romanian literature. As a critic, I am a citizen of literature and will serve it as long as I live. My profession is patriotism." [39] More generally, protochronists viewed strictly aesthetic judgments as only one of several bases of evaluation, alongside political and social criteria, and saw all focus on aesthetic matters as a dodge. That the aesthetic was a bone of contention is evident in two illustrative quotations from protochronists:

Our literary criticism has acted to stimulate a literature with social and political courage, at least in theory. But doesn't it seem unnatural to you that . . . discussions of the socio-political texture of various books are *lacking* in courage? However great one's phobia for the excessively simplified and ideologizing criticism of the 1950s, not to give critical discussion to the ideological content of a novel seems to me to shortchange it. . . . To take refuge behind modalities, construction, writing style, semiotics, etc. [i.e., aesthetic questions—k.v.] means so many desertions from achieving an integral critical assessment and has de-ideologizing effects (Purcaru 1986: 64–65).

The magazine *Morning Star* hosted not long ago a roundtable about false standards of critical exactingness and false literary hierarchies; in fact, about criteria that—waving the banner of the autonomy of the aesthetic—promote uncertain values and contest incontestable authors (ibid., 270).

Chief among the sociopolitical criteria protochronists favored was nationality, as is evident, for example, in one critic's proud observation that *The Week* was fiercely defending the concept of ethnicity in art (Sorescu 1982).

Cognate arguments raged in literary criticism earlier in the twentieth century: whether evaluation of a work should rest on aesthetic judgments alone or must also satisfy ethnic criteria, and the closely related matter of whether art is considered autonomous of social processes or is determined by them. In Alexandrescu's interpretation of these arguments (1983), those favoring the autonomy of the aesthetic fostered the development of a symbolic market that was more or less autonomous of other factors. Conditions of self-financing make plausible a similar interpretation of the arguments of the 1980s, even though the literary "market" was heavily subject to political control. In the context of the 1980s, to argue for the autonomy of the aesthetic or to insist that aesthetic judgments be primary was to insulate cultural production from politics, from having values set outside the literary community, in the Central Committee. It was a position that promoted the formation of a "pure" cultural authority, immune to the twists and turns of political life, and that situated the legitimation of cultural products squarely within the community of professionals, rather than in the Party.

For analysts external to the situation, there is no reason, on the face of it, to prefer a "pure" cultural authority to one that explicitly integrates its political commitments into its defense of cultural values. If the political commitments were those of pluralism and democracy, most westerners would applaud; politics in culture takes on a smutty connotation only when the context is "totalitarian." To assess the significance of the antiprotochronists' insistently apolitical identity and of the protochronists' indigenism requires that we look more closely at how these two positions intersected with the tendencies of socialist systems. This means looking not at whether one or other faction espoused principles explicitly *of socialism*, as understood by Marx, Lenin, Gramsci, and others, but at their relation to the central dynamic of real-socialist societies: maximization of control by the political apparatus over all resources, within conditions of endemic shortage.

The debate around protochronism affords outstanding illustration of how politics *within* culture became the politicization *of* culture, the drawing of cultural production into the sphere of use-values controlled by the apparatus. What began as a debate on a single terrain, for stakes that were par excellence cultural, became a contest over different grounds for accumulating cultural authority; some of these grounds entailed conversions from the political sphere. It seems beyond doubt that Edgar Papu intended nothing more than to reorient the readings given to classic texts. His aims were those of the average professor who has a good idea and hopes to shift the evaluations of competence and excellence in his own favor. Some of those who picked up the notion of protochronism did so in the interests of getting around the obstacles to their advancement in a literary profession dominated by others reluctant to make room for them. Even these opportunistic uses of protochronism amounted to playing essentially the same game, for the same stakes: seeking to build cultural authority on the basis of an innovation that potentially undercut the authority of others, through its insistence that only those accumulations based on indigenous values were legitimate. By indigenizing their cultural genealogies and seeking to create "qualitative leaps in spiritual activity . . . [on the basis of] the quantitative accumulations of [our] predecessors" (Ungheanu 1985: 419), protochronists followed the protectionist strategy of earlier cultural movements analyzed so insightfully by Gheorghiu (1985a, 1987, 1990).

But at a certain point protochronism, a plausible idea invented within the cultural sphere, came to be perceived as useful to the Party leadership and to people with political ambitions.[40] It became a valuable political instrument, wielded by persons whose genuine passion for the theme was itself doubly useful to a political leadership needing forms of legitimation that were genuine and not imposed. As the leadership's mode of control became more resolutely symbolic-ideological, with increasing reliance on national ideology in particular, the incorporation of national cultural values became an even more important adjunct to political goals than before. The emphases of protochronism intersected neatly with these goals, making it available for political uses that were sometimes extreme. Its insistence on "original creation" echoed the Party's productionist bias. Protochronist writings supported the personality cult of Ceauşescu, the relative autarchy attempted in the Ceauşescu era, the interweaving of Party history with the millennial history of Romanians,[41] the call for socially/politically relevant art, the aggressive emphasis on territorial borders that might in fact be even bigger than the ones now on world maps,[42] and the resistance to Soviet imperialism in all quarters.

Within a social order whose dynamic was to maximize the control of the apparatus over resources, protochronism promised a literature that was *Romanian*, values that were *Romanian*—that is, literature and values of scant use to any but a *Romanian* state. Protochronism argued for a literature that was Romanian first, expressed openly its intention of being useful to the state, and created lineages of Romanian cultural heroes through whom the broad reading public might be linked to the past and bright future of the Nation. Theirs was a literature that both lent cultural authority to the political sphere, giving the Party leadership the appearance of being supported by learning and culture, and gained its producers (writers) and its policemen (critics) great political influence. It pushed cultural production into the service of a new political order and enabled the executors of that order to penetrate a field of activity that had resisted such penetration.[43] And it helped to construct a fictive monoethnic cultural heritage from the political reality of a multi-national state. These effects constitute the "use-value" of protochronism to the political apparatus.[44]

I believe it would be a mistake, however, to see this advance of socialism's maximization principle as happening entirely at the Party's behest.[45] Protochronism was not brought about by the Party leadership's eagerness to shore up its legitimacy with nationalism (indeed, some protochronists appear to have exceeded what the leaders might intend[46]). Although its emphasis on national values indeed appealed to the leadership, this is far from revealing the processes through which it emerged. For these we must look to how the Party leadership's retreat from political and economic reforms and its increased politicization of culture established a new environment, within which commitments, passions, calculations, hopes, principles, and irrational traits of personality might drive individual writers and critics into new courses of action. Persons with ambitions for advancement that were being frustrated, with talents insufficiently recognized, now saw their chance. In attaching themselves to protochronism as part of their bid for cultural power, writers and critics were taking advantage of new opportunities, not reluctantly implementing dictates from above. Some of them were motivated by feelings of dislocation, marginalization, and other sources of personal pain.[47] Others were simply young writers and critics for whom ever-more-reduced publications and printing runs were destroying their chances to publish. For the price of their adherence to certain values, many found a place in protochronist publications.[48] On both sides were people working out their life trajectories within the confines of a particular organization of their world, who spoke a language of national identity as part of promoting themselves and their values. Nearly all of them had a deep commitment to their notion of what Romanian culture should be. Most of them carried that same commitment into the new structure of opportunities of the 1990s.

What protochronism shows us, then, is not how the Party directed culture but how the organization of Romanian society engendered specific kinds of contests between fractions of a cultural elite, struggling for greater influence within their own sphere of competence and interest and striving to secure the cultural authority essential to maintaining their positions as producers of culture. The motivations of those involved in this contest were less a conscious intention to build their cultural authority in (or against) the service of a political regime than their desire to realize their professional hopes and give voice to the values important to them. Their social order facilitated this for some of them, by enabling them to convert cultural into political authority; protochronism was one means. Within their social space, defined by the two dimensions of political status and cultural authority, protochronism moved persons from zone 1 to zone 2 (see fig. 3). By championing the indigenist values so useful to the political leadership, protochronists hoped to gain greater control over the resources that would accrue to whoever most persuasively "represented" Romanian culture. This control might even include entering the apparatus itself, becoming members of the Central Committee, serving as watchdogs over opportunities and publications, and in this way enhancing the reception of their own works, which would build their reputations as producers of culture.

Protochronism and the opposition to it also show us more than simply a conflict about nationalizing cultural production or about the

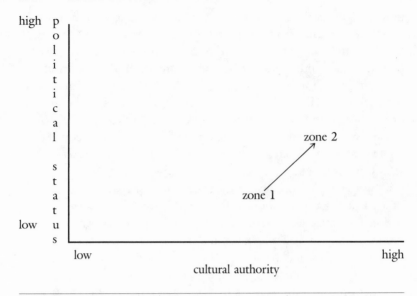

Figure 3 *Protochronism in the Space of Cultural Politics*

problems of being a subaltern culture, as some of the terms used might suggest. They show the possibilities and constraints within which literary production unfolded in this social system. The form of this system, which gave absolute predominance to the political sector and sought to incorporate all other values under its umbrella, pressed action ultimately toward the political. It undermined the basis for the independent formation of cultural authority along autonomously professional lines; it facilitated mobility within political terms over mobility within professional organizations. The latter was the kind of mobility preferred by persons wishing to resist the transformation of their society into what they perceived to be an overcentralized tyranny.

One must also note, nevertheless, that not merely protochronists but their adversaries as well contributed to this politicization of culture. Some of those who sided against protochronism had in an earlier day enjoyed the benefits of an alliance with politics. It was in part their political situation that had enabled them to displace Barbu, catalyzing the formation of his faction—a faction that would take advantage of the newly opened space close to power after 1971/1974. The succession of groups allied with the Party meant that whoever was displaced had no claim to status *other* than the defense of cultural authority. By struggling, as a result, to constitute and define cultural authority in their own terms, by giving protochronists an answer, by contending with them for cultural representativeness, these adversaries helped to refine the instrument protochronism delivered into the hands of the Party. Even more important, because the two groups exhausted their energies in striving to preserve elite status as they variously defined it, neither ameliorated the repressive conditions that made their conflict so sharp.

Protochronism and Shortage

The analysis in this chapter has aimed at showing certain characteristics of Romanian socialist society that the protochronism debates reveal. I have described how the language of argument was linked with the partial recommodification of culture and, more broadly, with a struggle for opportunities within the cultural sphere. I have pointed to the way in which accusations and counteraccusations about cultural representativeness, including alleged betrayals, "elitism," and implications of incompetence, were part of the competition among groups for centrally distributed recognition and cultural resources. In addition, I have suggested that the debate in general, but protochronism in particular, tended to deliver cultural values to the political apparatus. In this final section I wish to suggest how protochronism functioned within the "economy of shortage" that was endemic to socialist political economies of command type, such as that of Ceauşescu's Romania.

My argument will be clearer with the help of an extended example. It consists of a piece entitled "Ideals," written by protochronist Corneliu Vadim Tudor but not signed by him.[49] The article appeared in *The Week* in 1980 (not long after the unfavorable disposition of editor Barbu's plagiarism case) and provoked outrage from Jewish circles inside and outside Romania, as well as from the United States:

In all times and in all provinces during their temporary separations from each other, Romanians had, alongside a unitary essence and an acute sense of their common history, also a national ideal. We can even say that as life's cruelties grew more terrible, so much the more ardently did we wrap our heart in the flag of this ideal, so much the more vividly did the cathedral of our heart embody the solemn mass [*missa solemna* (*sic*)] of our faith in victory. Our illustrious scholars, as well as the anonymous geniuses who created our folklore, left unsettlingly deep evidence to this effect. And the hour is not far when their work will all see again the heavenly light of print. We argue here . . . for putting back into circulation the sacred texts of our civilization, gathered into a collection that might be called the **"National Library"**: the political writings of Eminescu, the speeches of [a long list], the entire works of Nicolae Iorga, . . . the *Trilogy of Values* of Lucian Blaga, and many many more. They are the unsurpassable treasury of our patrimony, and even if the authors of one or another of them participated in some mistakes and excesses, their fundamental works remain and are goods that have been gained, springs of the spirit ever awake for the consciousness of Romanity everywhere. We have the fortune to live today closely united under the sceptre of an exceptional political doctrine. . . . It obliges us to be equal to the ancestral ideals that it carries on, . . . to defend and raise to superior heights all that has been won [lit. conquered] to now with such sacrifice. This is the Romanian line, and we will never abjure it. Naturally, we owe no one an accounting of what we do, we are free, we are the majority, and masters in our own country; the historical choice for a Romanian kind of communism was made and taken to heart by millions of loyal sons of this country. And to those who accuse us of all sorts of nonsense, we will say that if to love your *patria* above all else means nationalism, then we are nationalists. . . . We, people of culture of the Romania of these heroic years, love the Communist party not only for the new vision and fresh spirit it has enthroned in the whole evolution of Romanian society, . . . but also in equal measure owing to its truly revolutionary courage in understanding that a nation can build itself only through the people of its localities who have been born here for hundreds and thousands of years and who do not abandon the front of work when things get tough. The Party knows . . . that the highest honors should go to those who accomplish patriotic deeds, . . . not to visitors eager for gain, . . . clad in foul-smelling tartans,[50] Herods foreign to the interests of this nation who . . . make people dizzy with their speculator patriotism. We have no need for lazy prophets, for Judases who lack the dimension of Romanian self-sacrifice in their blood, so easily purchased. As Eminescu rightly said, "A floating population cannot represent the stability of institutions, cannot represent the deep-rooted sentiment of the idea of the state, of harmony and national solidarity" (*Săptămîna* 1980).

The only thing this article lacks is the paean to Ceauşescu that closes most comparable texts.[51]

Many features of this article deserve comment, such as its plea for unexpurgated reeditions of great works (howsoever imperfect their creators),[52] its conception of culture as wealth (a "treasury"), its startling religious language,[53] its assertions of national independence, its patriarchy and military flavor ("loyal sons," "conquered," "heroic"), its express alliance of "culture" with the Party, and so on. I will neglect these so as to concentrate on its xenophobia. That the article is patently anti-semitic is beyond doubt. It forms part of more than one set of attacks on Jews by protochronist authors.[54] At the same time, Tudor's piece is more broadly xenophobic: it is, especially, anti-German and anti-Hungarian, as is evident from the references to people abandoning "the front of work when things get tough" and to being "born here for hundreds of thousands of years," which sneer at German emigration and the arrival of both groups a mere millennium or less ago.

This text, like many other protochronist writings, is an act of exclusion and policing. It excludes from the Romanian "feast" anyone not having a pure Romanian pedigree, and it polices the borders of "the Romanian people" against pollution by other bloods, races, creeds, and histories. Its techniques are similar to those of other protochronist policemen of the cultural elite (notably Purcaru, Silvestri, and C. Sorescu),[55] whose writings display a strong penchant for dividing up the cultural world into armed camps, exiling members of the opposing camp, and anathematizing writers whose personal characteristics are not to their taste. They denounce the elitists, dogmatists, and other traitors who sell out the Romanian people to foreigners peddling false values.

Among the most widespread of the techniques used in these police actions—a technique they share with European rightist and fascist movements earlier in this century (see Rogger and Weber 1965; Linke 1986)—is recourse to organic imagery and to metaphors of kinship. Organic images grow wild in their texts, for everything from Ceauşescu's relation to the people on through the people's tie to the land, but particularly for the link between Romanians and their culture. Early Romanian writers are seen as "fathers" [*strămoşi, părinţi*] of contemporary culture, related to it through lineal genealogical ties (see e.g., Zamfirescu 1975: 46–47; an entire section is called "Spiritual Ancestors"): "[T]he unity of contemporary Romanian literature is indestructible, for it was and is tied organically to the interests and hopes of the people" (Purcaru 1986: 156). Not only this, but culture itself is seen as an organism, a being with a soul that has both organicity and vitality, linked to generations (a solidly biological concept) of creative geniuses perpetuating the line of their spiritual forebears (Zamfirescu 1975: 46). For example, one author writes of the "personality" of Romanian literature (Ciopraga 1981), describing culture as an organic phenomenon with blood ties to sister cultures (such as those of Romania with France). This is a very different image of culture from one that represents it as a marketable commodity, for instance, or as a set of traditions embedded in a community *not* seen as an organism.[56]

What this organic imagery accomplishes, of course, is a decisive bounding of a community seen as "natural" and as separate from all those persons and communities whose metabolic processes spring from different roots. Boundaries conceived as organic and genetic are nearly always more rigid and exclusive than those conceived as "cultural": one can learn a new language and new customs, and one can change one's religion, but one's bloodline is a given, manipulable (if at all) only by a lengthy process of genealogical revision.[57] Whereas persons on the wrong side of a cultural boundary may try (or be forced) to cross it by cultural assimilation, the ultimate fate of those on the wrong side of the bloodlines is not voluntary action but expulsion or death.

It is the categorical nature of the ostracism effected by organic imagery that suggests the link of protochronism to Romania's "economy of shortage." In socialism's "supply-constrained" political economies, the nature and the results of competition were very different from the nature and the results of competition within market-based, "demand-constrained" systems. Competition in the latter eliminates the unsuccessful from further participation and accumulates the profits and economic capital of the successful. This is because capitalist firms are usually subject to what Kornai (1980) calls "hard budget constraints," meaning that (certain major exceptions notwithstanding) they are not bailed out if they cannot turn a sufficient profit: they go bankrupt. Competition within socialist systems proceeded otherwise. Because their budget constraints were "soft," with firms receiving state subsidies regardless of their market success, the unsuccessful were never quite eliminated. This was the more true of socialist systems such as Romania's—as opposed to that of market-reforming Hungary—in which the highly centralized command structure perpetuated a shortage economy minimally alleviated by market forces. I would venture the generalization that competition in such systems always involved *positioning on a scale* rather than elimination from the field. In Romania, then, regardless of whether competition occurred in the production campaigns within factories, in the bargaining relations between firms or ministries and the central planning apparatus, or in the cultural competitions of the "Song of Romania" folk festivals,[58] the result was less a *reduction* of the field of competitors than their *hierarchization*.

If in formal terms soft budget constraints mean that competitors are never wholly eliminated but merely fall farther down the ladder, in actual terms a system of extreme shortage *must* eliminate competitors, for even those far down the ladder can still claim some resources from those higher up, whose chances are jeopardized. Shortage levels in austerity-ridden Romania of the 1980s were unparalleled in any other East-bloc country; only *labor* was in less than short supply, for there were not enough materials to employ it. To a situation of such extreme shortage the excesses of protochronist rhetoric offered a solution, one that expelled competitors who were not of Romanian blood or did not act as if they were.[59] The organic imagery and lineal emphases within protochronist language provided strong means for excluding, rather than merely hierarchizing, competitors; these means were far stronger and more rigid than the emphases of the opposing side on "aesthetics," "standards," or "quality." The effects of this climate of expulsion were felt in events as diverse as Romanians losing their jobs for having relatives abroad and the disproportionate exodus of Hungarians and Germans from Romania as the 1980s wore on.

That the talk of the protochronists became progressively more extreme as shortage and crisis in Romania deepened would appear to confirm the hypothesis of their interconnection. An idea with much to recommend it at the outset, protochronism was initially discussed in a relatively calm manner on both sides. By 1980, however, the tone had changed, as can readily be seen by comparing the fairly measured language of the initial discussions published in 1977 and 1978 (see Ungheanu 1985) with that of Tudor's article (above) or of Purcaru in many of his interviews. During the 1980s protochronist writings achieved a level of linguistic violence suited only to a full-scale societal crisis. The crisis was real.

For excluding competitors, there are no other means—especially not within the ideas of Marx and Lenin—as effective as racist nationalism. Thus, radical exclusions and their potential to alleviate shortage are best achieved through exaggerating certain forms of national ideology. It was not just the presence of a national discourse in the speech of Romanian intellectuals, but the particular *form* of it in the mouths of protochronists, that enjoyed these elective affinities with an economy of severe shortage. And because soft budget constraints favored firms over households, which were the final units in a chain of upward deliveries and the point at which shortage ultimately came to rest (see Kornai 1982: 24–27), the effects of the protochronist rhetoric of expulsion were not confined to intellectual exchanges. Sown widely throughout Romania by the large-circulation cultural weeklies the protochronists monopolized, protochronism's effects had fertile soil within the population at large. This fact, and the shortage certain to continue for some time after Ceauşescu's fall, virtually guarantee a place for national ideology in the politics of the post-Ceauşescu era.

The goal of this chapter has been to assess the significance and to account for the spread of an idea that arose in a small corner of the academy, literary criticism. Its modest origins would not have led one to imagine that it would be picked up by historians, sociologists, ethnographers, philosophers, mathematicians, and the General Secretary of the Communist party. Certainly Edgar Papu did not anticipate this reception, for he had been peddling the idea unheeded for several years before it suddenly took off. Its take-off, I have suggested, was part of a recentralization and ideologization of the Romanian political economy. This produced a new configuration of opportunities, in which protochronism proved useful to persons competing within the sphere of cultural activity so as to redistribute power and values within their fields. With its emphasis on *national* values and on symbolic accumulations from *local* production, protochronism served to generate new symbolic or cultural authority within different academic and journalistic disciplines.

Just as occurred in the first half of the present century, however, embedded at the heart of these new symbolic accumulations was the *national* idea. Much as protochronists and their opponents resisted one another's point of view, both shared a common ground: the Nation and its proper values. The debates therefore reinforced the tendency for intellectual activity to revolve around definitions of these, rather than around something else. Despite socialism's radical transformation of the environment for cultural production, then, the conjuncture of the 1970s and 1980s once again reproduced "the Nation" at the root of academic and creative endeavor. Through debates like those concerning protochronism, national ideology was perpetuated—at the expense of Marxism—as a potent force in Romania's ideological field.

CHAPTER SIX

Historiography in a Party Mode: Horea's Revolt and the Production of History

The only absolutely certain thing is the future, since the past is constantly changing.

—Yugoslav aphorism

Historians are dangerous people. They are capable of upsetting everything. They must be directed.

—Nikita Khrushchev[1]

Literature and literary criticism, discussed in chapter 5, were not the only areas in which the Party's attempt to recentralize culture and yoke it to a symbolic-ideological mode of control sharpened competition among producers of culture. Similar processes also occurred in the discipline of history, a field even more central to the Romanian leadership's painstaking efforts to construct a new hegemony.[2] While literature and art, for Marxist-Leninist leaders, are merely means for expressing new social values to raise the consciousness of the "masses," history, for them, undergirds the very foundations of rule.[3] Marxism-Leninism everywhere has justified itself with a theory of history—dialectical or historical materialism—for which it claims the status of a science. For Marxist-Leninists, a correct understanding of the past is essential to correctly foreseeing the direction of historical development and to determining policies for the future. The laws of history that Marxism-Leninism reveals and institutionalizes in the Communist party have been the cornerstone, then, of these regimes' legitimation, as are ideas of public participation and consent, for parliamentary democracies (Eidlin 1987).

Added to the general significance of history for Communist parties is a specific link between historiography and the construction of national identity. Notions of the past reinforce identities in social orders of all kinds but became institutionalized toward this end during the formation of Western European nation-states, a pattern with overwhelming influence upon their step-siblings in Eastern Europe. For those nations-in-formation, as I suggested in chapter 1, history-writing was intimately connected with forming national consciousness; historians were among the main inspirations for movements of national independence in the region (R. Seton-Watson 1922: 28–32). Historiography became, therefore, inevitably political. This was doubly true given that history defines in time and space the boundaries a political formation will occupy—a function especially vital in areas such as Eastern Europe, where territorial boundaries have been constantly challenged and revised. In consequence, it was not only in the communist period that the line separating patriotism from scholarship in Eastern Europe was sometimes difficult to draw. Nor was it only in that period that a historical idiom lay at the center of political language: for three centuries or more, East Europeans have used history and its interpretation to speak about relations with their neighbors and about their national identity, the Ceauşescu era doing no more than to enlarge this linguistic repertoire with hidden references to socialist internationalism or points of Marxist theory. In sum, as Robert King put it (1980: 171), in Eastern Europe "the past is not a subject for harmless small talk."

These statements of what is broadly true about historiography, national identity, and politics in Eastern Europe apply with full force to Romania. In the words of Romanian historian Al. Zub, "From the beginning, a harsh necessity compelled our men of letters toward study of the past, transformed into a means of struggle to preserve our ethnic being . . . " (1983: 36). Romanian scholar/politician Nicolae Bălcescu (among countless others), writing in the mid-nineteenth century, exemplified this well when he explained why he was doing a history of Prince Michael the Brave: "I wanted to complete a work about Michael the

Brave and to lay the foundation stone of national unity" (Bălcescu 1974: 8). There is an unbroken line from this historian-militant to the army officer in the Center for Military History who said to me in 1988, his hands trembling with emotion, "These [questions of Romanian origins] are not just academic questions! What is at stake is the very existence of a nation!" The contexts in which these two men spoke differed greatly, as did the implications of their work for the course of social development, but the thorough-going commitment to a *politics* of history-writing was the same. In socialist Romania, one found this commitment at all points in the field of historical production, from those attached to the central organs of Party rule to those most divorced from them, and in virtually all themes on which research was carried out.

For these reasons, the discipline of history has been a field especially rich in contests and conflicting claims and an especially appropriate site for examining the politics of culture and identity in socialist Romania. One must nonetheless bear in mind that historiography has an important relation to power in systems of other types as well. From ethnographic accounts of how tribal peoples revise their genealogies on up to German revisions of the Nazi past,[4] we see history serving an important ideological role in societies of all kinds, including our own, and forming an element of culture that is interwoven with politics everywhere.[5] Acknowledging this requires that we ask not (*pace* Ranke) how history "really happened" in a given society and how it has been politically "distorted" but, rather, how visions of the past are made. How, in other words, is history produced? How was its politicization shaped by socialism's peculiarities, and in what relation to matters of national identity?[6]

The present chapter addresses these questions of how "the past" was produced in Ceaușescu's Romania and how its production was intertwined with national ideology. Taken at face value, such questions pose the agenda not for a single chapter but for an entire book.[7] To address them in a brief compass requires taking a specific example, rather than trying to survey the whole field. A number of topics in Romanian historiography might serve this purpose, such as the "dacomania" of the 1970s (an exaggerated concern with the Dacians in the origin myth), or 1980s revisions in the history of World War II.[8] The example I select is relatively arcane and invisible, compared to those just mentioned, and it engaged nowhere near as many intellectual energies as those, or as the arguments described in chapter 5. My example is a debate concerning the status of an event—variously describable as an uprising, a revolution, a revolt, or a rebellion—that occurred in 1784 and whose bicentennial was celebrated in 1984 (when I happened to be in Romania for research). I choose this case because I participated in it to some extent and thereby saw something of how it was produced—which changed my interpretation—and because despite its relative invisibility, it illustrates many of the production processes within Romanian historiography under Ceauşescu.

Parameters of the Production of History in Socialist Romania

Romanian history, like literature, was produced through individual and institutional rivalries for the resources that supported historical research, and through arguments about the values that research should pursue. Such rivalries were at least as politicized as those in literature, owing to the unusually central role assigned to history under Ceauşescu's reign—unusual even by the standards of Marxist-Leninist regimes. There were several reasons for this. Some of them were of a quirky, personal nature and others resulted from the regime's internal consolidation and its international relations. The most eccentric reason was that the brother of the Romanian president, General Ilie Ceauşescu, had a true avocational passion for the study of history; he promoted it and influenced its direction from his very powerful vantage point. President Ceauşescu himself exhibited tremendous interest in history also, but in his case it was not clear how much was enthusiasm and how much was strategy. There was room for strategy because of historiography's place both in the conduct of Romania's international relations and in this leadership's mode of control. I will discuss the first of these points briefly and the second at greater length.

At the most general level, historical references often indicated actual or intended relations with the powers to which a small country like Romania is subject. I illustrated this in chapter 1, and I would add only that even in the 1970s and 1980s, official statements about Romanian origins (were Romanians Daco-Roman or purely Dacians) revealed the Romanian leadership's feelings about its problematic indebtedness to the West and its tensions with the East. More important, for my purposes, were the country's international relations with immediate neighbors. Because the study of history inevitably entails reference to a country's territorial borders, historiography is part of the relations between neighboring states. In Romania's case, this has been aggravated by the instability of Romania's boundaries throughout the twentieth century. Thus, what is or is not mentioned in the national history, the way certain events are treated, which events are mentioned and which left out, the kinds of maps that accompany an analysis—all these become signals about neighborly relations. Romania has had grave territorial disputes with Hungary and the Soviet Union: Hungary claims parts of Transylvania held by Romania since 1918,[9] and Romania claims most of the Soviets' Moldavian Socialist Republic (which Romanians call Bessarabia), a region disputed between Romanians and Russians for almost two centuries and taken from Romania in 1940. One can often detect important changes in the political winds blowing between Romania and the Soviet Union in veiled Romanian references to Bessarabia (see King 1973: 220–241).

More overt diplomatic conflicts on the terrain of historiography have occurred between Romania and Hungary. Hungarians lay claim to Transylvania on the grounds that when Hungarians first settled there, in the tenth and eleventh centuries, the area was (they say) empty of inhabitants; this entitles Hungarians to the land by right of conquest. Romanians, in contrast, maintain that they were not absent but were there all along, perhaps not visible in the most open spaces but near the foothills, which offered better protection from the endless waves of nomadic invaders from the East. Each side represents the other as nomadic and itself as settled during the crucial tenth through twelfth centuries. As a result of this dispute, Romanian historians have long been obsessed with proving continuity of Romanian settlement from at least Roman times to the present. This preoccupation has been apparent across the entire range of social locations, from the "most political" historians to those most divorced from power.

Although Hungarian-Romanian disagreements on the terrain of historiography have been routine for years, they flared into the worst relations in postwar times with the 1986 publication of a handsomely produced three-volume *History of Transylvania*, issued in Budapest under the aegis of the Hungarian Academy of Sciences and bearing all the marks of serious scholarship.[10] The part on the Middle Ages predictably gave the Hungarian view that there were no Romanian inhabitants in Transylvania when the first Hungarians arrived. The Romanian reaction to the publication was extreme.[11] Ceauşescu gave a violent speech denouncing these lies and calumnies (see *Scînteia*, February 28,

1987), Romanian historians were mobilized to produce a quick translation (for restricted use) and a scathing rebuttal,[12] workplaces all over the
country were besieged with Party activists holding emergency meetings
that denounced the "lies and calumnies" and reaffirmed the "scientifically correct" version, the media overflowed with articles in which
historians deplored the falsehoods perpetrated by their Hungarian colleagues, and a full-page ad was taken out in the London *Times* (April 7,
1987, p. 8) entitled "A Conscious Forgery of History under the Aegis
of the Hungarian Academy of Sciences." In this near-hysterical atmo-
sphere, many in the general public began to worry that Romania was
about to be invaded by its neighbor and that Transylvania would be lost
again, as it had been from 1940 to 1944 at the cost of much suffering.
It seemed that official circles in Romania were fanning this fear, perhaps
to keep the army whipped up and at the ready (Shafir 1989*a*: 4–5).[13]
Diatribes against Hungary became frequent in the press during the late
1980s, increasingly linking accusations of *territorial* revisionism with
the *ideological* "revisionism" that so distinguished Hungary's approach
to solving the crisis of socialism from the approach of the Romanian
Party (Shafir 1989*b*: 3). Thus, in relations between Romania and Hungary, questions of territory and of political and economic reform became thoroughly knotted together with questions of history. Historiography was in effect the basic ground upon which those international relations were reproduced.

Beyond its importance in the international sphere, history was crucial to the symbolic element in the Romanian leadership's symbolic-
cum-coercive mode of control. History was a major source of new symbolic resources for the apparatus to deploy and a fundamental site for
reappropriating older ones. Ceauşescu referred to the historical profession as "the historians' front," in the military sense, vital to shaping
both the national and the materialist facets of his regime's ideology and
to socializing the public into a particular set of values. To consolidate
this "front" had required new institutional arrangements that drew the
production of historiography more and more tightly under central control.[14] Institutes of historical research, together with their journals, were
completely reorganized in 1948; university professorships were emp-
tied and filled; first a preliminary (1947) and then a major new synthesis of Romanian history were commissioned (four volumes of the
latter appeared during the early 1960s). No sooner was this structure in
place than it was modified again, reflecting the new relations with the
Soviet Union and the reinsertion of national values into official politics.

Historians and historical figures who had been suppressed were rehabilitated and new themes were approved that had recently been anathema.

The most unequivocal sign of history's apotheosis was the 1974 Program of the Romanian Communist Party, issued for the Eleventh Party Congress, which began with an eighteen-page summary of Romanian history. This summary traced events from Dacian and Roman times through successive foreign overlords and local uprisings, the development of capitalism and the proletariat, the creation of the Party, and its rise to power in the war against fascism (see Romanian Communist Party 1975: 618–635). Four years prior to this Congress, there had been a full-scale reorganization of the Romanian Academy. It was shorn of responsibility for the various institutes of history, which were brought more fully under the control of the Party's Central Committee. Subsequent measures allowed Ph.D.s to be given only to persons acceptable to their municipal Party organization, prescribed the precise content of courses to be taught in history, and even fixed by fiat the dates of major events to be celebrated, in an ever-intensifying obsession with festive commemorations (see below). In 1976 Ceauşescu called for a veritable fleet of new works of historical synthesis, including a multivolume treatise on the military history of the Romanian people and yet another new synthesis of the national history. The latter, to occupy ten volumes, was to be guided by ideas in a fat brochure drawn up by a handful of Party historians and circulated to all the institutes participating in the project (Georgescu 1981: 75).

The central place of history-writing for the leadership created an environment of both opportunities for and constraints on historical production. On the one hand, the more Ceauşescu insisted on collaboration from the "historians' front," the more difficult it became for historians to work on subjects other than those listed in the program of the Romanian Communist Party or to offer interpretations other than those favored higher up. People taking a different line would find their works inexplicably delayed at the publishing house; in any case, all historians found their writings more closely scrutinized than were the works of scholars in less strategic fields. On the other hand, as one energetic historian confided to me, it was wonderful to be a historian because so many more resources were potentially available to that profession than to most others. One had only to know how to get them. Historiography's ideological importance meant that it could win relatively more of the center's resources and was relatively less exposed to the "market" forces I discussed in connection with literature. Therefore, competition within history was, I believe, less market-based and more bureaucratic in nature. Perhaps for this reason (on the argument suggested in chapter 5), there was somewhat less overt opposition to the regime among historians than among literati. This is not to say that all historians followed the "Party line"—far from it, as the present chapter will show—but their opposition was different in form from that of writers and critics.

One final and crucial point about Romanian historiography is that nearly all Romanian historians were producing a product that was by definition "indigenist," even though some of them did so by canons derived from the West. Most of them wrote the history of their own land, not American or Asian or world history, and it was of interest chiefly to Romanians and of maximum use to a Romanian state. Because of this, Romanian historians automatically produced something of potential value to the political apparatus, something whose details were readily appropriable no matter how resistant an individual author might be to instructions, enticements, or fads. In this, historians differed somewhat from those writers and artists for whom a major aim was to create products that would have both local *and "universal"* significance—Romanian values that would conjugate with the dilemmas of humankind more generally and therefore would bring Romanian realities to international attention. Although I would not want to make too much of this difference between literature and history, both of which might employ western techniques even for a work on indigenist themes, I believe that the difference made the political apparatus somewhat less anxious to "disable" production in history-writing (see chapter 2) than in other fields until very late in the 1980s. It isolated and silenced historians somewhat less than writers or philosophers, whose products more easily slid out into that intolerable zone independent of the center. I will return to this point at the end of the chapter.

The moves to bring history ever more fully into the control of the Party apparatus nevertheless occurred in counterpoint with some centrifugal tendencies within the discipline. There was tension between Bucharest and the provincial capitals of Cluj and Iaşi, where many scholars resisted Bucharest's repeated breaches of the regional division of labor, as historians in the capital sought to impose interpretations of phenomena (such as regional histories) that regional centers feel better equipped to handle.[15] To these centrifugal impulses should be added the effects of the 1978 law for greater self-financing by cultural enterprises (see chapter 3). This enabled certain entrepreneurially minded groups (particularly in the provinces) to slip sometimes through the net of control, thereby arousing envy and backbiting from others.

Beyond these centrifugal tendencies, the institutional structure of historical research was itself somewhat fragmented. The 1978 *Encyclopedia of Romanian Historiography* required a full thirty-four pages to describe all the institutions associated with history, including universities, research institutes, museums, archives, and so forth. These institutions were administratively subordinate to various superior bodies, which ranged from the Ministry of Defense through the Council for Culture and Socialist Education, the Party's Central Committee and its subordinate Academy of Social and Political Sciences, and the Ministries of Education and Interior. While this did not mean real pluralism in the production of history, it did leave room for competition among parts of the bureaucracy that sustained historical research. For example, a rumor circulated in 1984 concerning a central plan to unite all history-producing establishments within a single centrally controlled Institute of National History. As of 1989, however, this had not occurred— owing, it was said, to fierce opposition by the directors of various institutes whose positions would have been lost in such a merger.[16]

There did appear to be a major clash between the institutes doing the history of the Party and military, on the one hand, and those doing Romanian history more broadly, on the other. Behind it lay a wholesale redefinition of the object of historical study, as Party/military historians strove to integrate the history of the Party into the whole history of Romanians instead of keeping these as two separate spheres. The new object of study was called "the entire people" (*întregul popor*); each moment of Romanian history was now to be presented as leading inexorably toward the fulfillment of Romanians' destiny in the formation and guidance of the Party. In this potential merger of two institutionally separate histories, the question was, who would engulf whom? Would the Party/military institutes swallow up the others or be swallowed themselves? This competition quite probably stood behind a number of innovations and debates in the profession during the 1980s.[17]

This is the context, then, for my exploration of the debate over a rebellion led in 1784 by the Transylvanian peasant Horea. It was a context in which the political center strove to dominate the production of history, in which historical questions had inevitably international effects, in which institutes struggled for control over the history of Romanians, and in which idiosyncratic avocations joined with strategic manipulation of history and with deep patriotic feelings of all Romanian historians to form a highly politicized environment for history-writing. In the remainder of this chapter, I show how a specific argument within historiography was in part an argument over national identity, linked with international disputes. I argue that the example illustrates processes through which the production of history entered more firmly into the control of the political apparatus and reinforced both an ideology of the Nation and an ideology of knowledge. That is, I argue that debates such as the one over Horea helped to strengthen Party rule, despite the intentions of those who thought they were opposing power; yet at the same time, I suggest, oppositional activity among historians nonetheless had pluralizing effects.

The Debate Over Horea's Revolt [18]

THE EVENTS

In the late 1970s, the opening salvo was fired in what was to become a battle over the Transylvanian peasant Horea.[19] This opening salvo consisted of the publication of a massive two-volume scholarly work entitled *Horea's Uprising*. Twenty years in the making, it was published when its author, Academician David Prodan from Transylvania, deemed it ready, which proved to be a few years before the event's bicentennial. The book was widely praised as definitive by scholars all over Romania. Within two years, however, certain other historians began to herald the coming bicentennial with articles or chapters stating that what Horea had led was not merely an uprising but a revolution. This point of view received its fullest treatment in a volume that hit bookstores just before the bicentennial week, its title proclaiming *The Popular Revolution under Horea's Leadership*. The author, Academician Ştefan Pascu (also from Transylvania), in whose institute I was then doing research, invited me to attend the event that would "launch" his innovation to the public: a historians' conference being held in Brad, a town near the village where the revolt had broken out exactly two hundred years before.

A bus took the participants—about thirty-five scholars from research institutes, museums, and universities all across Romania, plus some county-level political officials—to the conference site. There, the mayor of Brad greeted them with, "Welcome to the conference on the peasant uprising, uh, revolution." Two sessions of scholarly papers followed, read to audiences totaling about three hundred people and reportedly consisting of teachers, some engineers, and various functionaries.[20] What they heard was a series of specialist arguments in elaborate Academese. Many of the papers, according to one participant (a professional historian well-versed in the history of the revolt), implicitly but not overtly contradicted points that would later emerge as crucial to the debate. Many had no doubt been written without knowing that the context would make their once-uncontroversial positions suddenly contentious. All but one paper title had the word "uprising" in the printed program, but in their delivery two more speakers shifted their usage from that term to the other.

Following these sessions, the visitors went by bus to several villages in the area, important sites in the revolt, to be met by small crowds of flower-bearing, uniformed children and their peasant or miner parents. Horea and his revolt became the occasion of prestations between the visitors and each of these groups: the children offered songs or poems on revolt themes, answered by speeches from the scholars and from functionaries of the county and the locality. The persons entrusted with these speeches spoke of the event—*ex tempore*, and in simple terms accessible to ordinary folk—as a revolution, the first in the series of Romanians' social and national struggles that led to socialism. The audiences varied in size from about twenty to about a hundred persons, most of them being teachers or peasant/worker parents of the children who greeted us. At each place, homemade cakes and brandy marked the event as a festive occasion across social boundaries; in some, performances of folk music heightened the festive spirit. In nearly all, the greeters, audience, and hospitality committee had been kept waiting for as much as two hours in the late October chill for the ever-more-delayed arrival of the scholarly entourage.

The festivities resumed on the second day with a "scientific plenary session," held in a large auditorium for an audience of five hundred to six hundred persons. The great majority of them almost certainly had some advanced education, except for a number of high-school students (perhaps 20 percent of the crowd).[21] On the stage, a long table was decked out with a giant banner announcing, "200 Years Since the Popular Uprising Led by Horea" (the printed program called it the "Uprising of the Peasants under Horea"). Seated at this table were a number of dignitaries: the mayor of the town; an army officer from the

Military Press, which had issued Pascu's book; an army general specializing in history; three university professors from Romania's major intellectual centers; Professor Pascu; the first party secretary and the secretary for propaganda for the county (its two most powerful political officials); the head of the county Committee for Culture; a researcher from Bucharest's prestigious Iorga History Institute; and the director of the county history museum, organizer of the affair.[22]

The party secretary for propaganda opened the session, welcoming us to the bicentennial celebration of the peasant uprising (*sic*—see note 18). After her came the officer from the Military Press, who was to "launch" Pascu's book to the public. Invoking the two-hundredth anniversary of Horea's revolution, he explained that the army had a custom of supporting reference works of patriotic character and had approached Pascu to do something worthy of this event. He emphasized the patriotic sentiments stirred by the book; its arousing one's love for the regions where the revolution had taken place and for the national borders there; its proof that Horea's revolution had inaugurated the chain of social and national revolutions that had become permanent features of Romanian history, culminating in the completion of this struggle in our day, under the Communist party. After him came Pascu with the first of two long speeches. Its major themes were his book's patriotic character, in no way conflicting with its scientific value; its being based upon newly collected documents [this meant that even though Prodan's "definitive" work was recent, advances in understanding the revolt could be expected as part of the progress of science]; its being inspired by a speech of Romanian President Ceauşescu, wherein the event was termed a revolution; and Horea's having sacrificed himself for the social-national cause, prefiguring later struggles that led to the Communist victory forty years ago.

The microphone was now taken by the first party secretary. Citing a different speech of Ceauşescu that used the word "uprising" [this quote appeared on the printed program as well] and employing that word throughout, he nonetheless set forth many points of the argument for "revolution": that the movement was not just a class action but also a national movement and contributed to the political cause of the Nation; that it covered a huge territory, not just a small area; that it had the most radical program of its day, which demanded overthrowing the nobility, taxing them, distributing their lands, and so forth. Like several others, he invoked an intimate connection between the present and

Horea's uprising, seen as the start of the modern era and as preparation for forming the unitary Romanian state. He noted that the uprising showed the peasantry's progressive character, since it anticipated by five years major principles of the French Revolution. Weaving his tapestry of talk seamlessly into the present, the first party secretary emphasized throughout it the problem of *national* rights and that problem's solution under the guidance of the Communist party.

At the end of this speech came a moment of patriotic exaltation, as children in Pioneer uniforms brought the public gratefully to its feet with recitations of poetry and beating of drums. Professor Pascu then began his next speech, equating the defense of country with the defense of the [ethnic] people and crediting the peasantry with much sacrifice in this struggle. He reminded his hearers that in Transylvania, oppression had been both social (class) and national, for peasants were mostly of one national group and nobles of another. Thus, because any peasant struggle in Transylvania was also a national struggle, Horea's movement was national in character; it became a revolution the moment it delivered its radical ultimatum. These people were not just a ragged peasant band, he insisted, but had true military organization. [Pascu continued on, drawing parallels between the rebels' organization and that of the socialist state.] The revolution covered a broad territory; it envisioned not a restoration of an old order but creation of a new one within a single ethnically unified country, bringing together a people that had been divided under different ruling nations. This revolution was of such amplitude that it became a European problem. It voiced the concerns of the French Revolution five years ahead of that great event. And when Horea was executed, he cried "I die for the nation," confirming his role as a national martyr.

After this came two speeches by university professors, who did not state their disagreement with Pascu overtly but contradicted his arguments point by point, albeit in a covered, monotonous Academese. Both called the event an uprising; both emphasized that the peasant rebels were fighting only the class, not the national, struggle, the latter having been purely an intellectuals' and clerics' concern. Any other view misreads the historical evidence, they claimed, insisting that the uprising's undeniable *consequences* for the Romanian national movement nonetheless imply nothing about the peasants' *intentions*. They could find no evidence at all that the rebels aimed to create an ethnically unified country—a mistaken view, they said, repudiated in Prodan's magisterial work. They agreed that the uprising was indeed noted in Europe but objected that it was in no way comparable with the French Revolution, for the social structures of the two cases were completely different. The second of these speeches invoked a spirit of scientific responsibility toward the peasant masses who had sacrificed themselves two hundred years before.

Following a short break, the session resumed with papers that continued to air the same argument, usually in an understated way, as some called the event an uprising and others a revolution. The same points emerged repeatedly: the event's significance in European history and particularly in relation to the French Revolution, its territorial scope, the importance to be accorded its radical ultimatum, whether it was a ragged peasant action or a disciplined military one, its place as medieval versus modern in the periodization of Romanian history, and its class versus national character, with implications for the people's revolutionary resources.[23] Concluding five hours of this plenary session, the head of the Committee for Culture read a long cable addressed to President Ceaușescu from those assembled, thanking him for giving such importance to Romanian history and to the study of the peasant uprising.

This conference opened the floodgates to a veritable deluge of celebrations of Horea, which filled the national media for the entire succeeding month and then abated somewhat, only to overflow into the media again a bit later with the anniversary of Horea's capture and execution. Many of the retrospectives served as battlegrounds for the ideas of uprising and revolution, and in these the same themes surfaced time and again: Horea's role in the national struggle, his preceding the French Revolution, the radical ultimatum, the military organization, and so forth. In all these events, the "uprising" position was upheld by people (often Prodan's former students) other than Prodan himself, who maintained a complete public boycott of the whole affair.[24] A small sample of events honoring the rebellion included: speeches to open the university year; two long television films (covering two evenings each) and a series of radio programs; exhibits in schools and libraries all over the country; sessions of student essays about the event; discussions held by university personnel for high schools, military officers' groups, factory workers; a full-length film, an opera, a play, and at least two novels, all produced for the bicentennial; a theatrical production mounted by the ethnographic museum; and a symposium at the annual meeting of the Romanian Academy's Transylvanian branch (at which someone was overheard to mutter, "I'm sick to death of Horea").[25]

MEANINGS OF THE DEBATE

What did the battle over Horea mean, and what does it say about identity and the politics of Romanian historiography? How were the performances summarized above produced? What purpose was a long-dead Transylvanian peasant serving for his historian-descendants? I begin answering these questions by asking about the social situation of those involved and then looking at what the terms of the debate imply about national identity. From this I turn to what this struggle over meanings suggests about Romanian socialism. Although the festivities of 1984 were not the first time that Horea had become politically useful after his death (in the interwar period he had "become" not a revolutionary but an emperor[26]), the socialist context of this more recent debate very much affected its production and its systemic implications.

The Actors. Any assessment of the significance of this debate requires understanding who its participants were and what institutional and societal positions they held. Its most vigorous protagonists, Professors Prodan and Pascu (born in 1902 and 1914), were both professional historians trained by the same professor prior to World War II. Although similar in being members of the Romanian Academy and in their prolific output, they differed from one another in several respects, of which the following are the most important. Prodan, unlike Pascu, had long participated in a leftist intellectual tradition and was a social democrat before the communists came to power. Although never a Party member, he was for decades the premier dialectical materialist in his profession. He retired early (in a political dispute) from the university position he had received in 1948, and he worked independently thereafter. Pascu not only was a (postwar) Party member but was politically very active, much more so than the reclusive Prodan. As the head of a number of professional organizations and institutions, he could hardly avoid politics, owing to the system's great emphasis on history.[27] He was for several years a candidate member of the Party's Central Committee, and he exerted much influence upon the historical thinking of President Ceauşescu's brother Ilie, whose principal counselor he was rumored to be.[28] More interdisciplinary in orientation than Prodan, Pascu's work usually aimed at comprehensive synthesis of existing scholarship, with somewhat less archival documentation than one found in Prodan's exhaustively documented and highly specialist works.

In a word, Prodan's reputation rested solely on his scientific authority, whereas Pascu's contained a large admixture of political status.[29]

Although I cannot say who instigated Horea's "revolution" after a half-century of scholarly and popular reference to the event as an uprising, I can show that it was unambiguously associated with circles close to the center of power, rather than more strictly academic ones. My basis for this is an extensive though not exhaustive check of the institutional affiliations of persons publicly using one or the other of the labels "uprising" or "revolution." Counting only those to whom I could assign a professional affiliation with history—that is, excluding journalists as well as politicians reading ghost-written speeches—I classified their performances in the two symposia I attended and in their publications (books, news articles, and papers in a number of journals, ranging from that of the History Association to that of the Central Committee's History Institute).[30] I placed institutions into two groups: (1) those administratively attached to the Communist party and the Ministries of Defense and Interior (which included the police), and (2) those under the Ministry of Education, Council for Culture, and Romanian Academy. This grouping reflects my view that the strategic core of rule in Romania consisted, by that time, of concentrations of force, together with the Party; the other institutions were relatively more distant from orthodoxy, control, and international politics. The grouping also conforms to figure 2 in chapter 2, political status being associated with "strategic core" institutions and scientific authority with the others. Figure 4 shows my view of where a few persons in the debate were situated in the field thus defined.

My sampling turned up forty-five professional historians who had written or pronounced on the subject of Horea since the appearance of Prodan's book and whose institutional affiliations I knew. Of the forty-five, 31 percent used the term "revolution," and 71 percent of them fell in the "strategic core" institutions. These people included the head of the History Institute of the Central Committee and the editors of that institute's specialist journal; the two historians from that institute who were widely reputed to be virtual counselors to the Party leadership on matters historical, as well as watchdogs over all history books published (their textbook cited parts of Pascu's argument on Horea verbatim);[31] another army-general historian; and two of the three historian-members of the Central Committee (the third waffled). Of the almost two-thirds of the forty-five who opted for "uprising," 96 percent were in

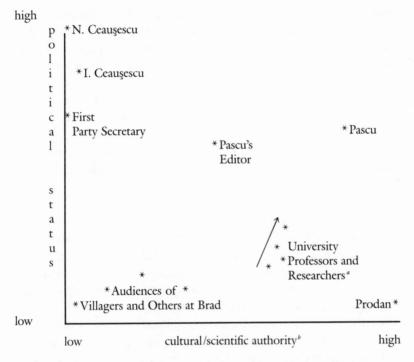

[a]The arrow marks the direction aspired to by people switching to "revolution."
[b]See note 29 for this modification of the label on the horizontal axis.

Figure 4   *The Space of Political Status and Cultural Authority in History–
Writing. Approximate Locations of Selected Participants in the Debate
over Horea. (Author's estimations, not necessarily reflecting views of participants themselves.)*

institutions distant from the core—universities, research institutes, regional museums.[32]

   It therefore does not seem inappropriate to see "revolution" as an
idea having currency in, if not actually introduced from, the highest ruling circles, whether at their pet historians' own initiative or through
guided suggestion.[33] The obvious question then is, why did top political circles—or some segments of them—wish to sponsor this innovation? What ideological and political work was it doing for them? What
sorts of divergent claims, and about what areas of Romanian life, were
buried in the points being disputed? These questions have several possible answers, largely speculative, since we cannot directly explore the
innovators' conscious intentions[34]—nor would an answer reduce to

these, in any case. For purposes of this chapter, the most important answers are those relating to definitions of Romanian national identity and the defense of professional standards. Other important links to questions of Marxist-Leninist theory are covered in Simmonds-Duke (1987: 199–201). The significance of "revolution" for a Party founded on Marxism is crucial to understanding the debate over Horea in its entirety, but my aim here being somewhat less comprehensive, I refer readers to Simmonds-Duke for that discussion. I note only that the merger of Party history with Romanian history entailed constructing a series of "revolutions" prefiguring the communist one; Horea's "revolution" was clearly to be one step in this series.[35]

The "Revolution" and National Identity. Professor Prodan's book on Horea did not intend to make any statements about Romanian national identity. Notwithstanding his passionate and deeply rooted national sentiments, his aim in the book was to illuminate part of the history of *class* struggle, which would later be joined with the national struggle led by intellectuals (see Prodan 1971, 1984). Professor Pascu's reply, however, transformed the discussion by bringing it into the lineage of the decades-long arguments on Romanian identity and the national essence, summarized in chapter 1. This was clearest in the argument that Horea's revolution preceded that of France and thereby brought Romania into the modern era—a claim that made eighteenth-century Transylvanian peasant society the most progressive in the world, after America. Such a claim was at one and the same time an implicit statement of decolonization with respect to the Soviet Union and a refusal to acknowledge Western Europe's leading influence. It insisted that Romanians can achieve major social progress on their own, even ahead of other areas considered to be more powerful or progressive. This claim was all the more striking, of course, for being made just prior to the bicentennial celebrations in France. One might even see Pascu's argument as not simply an "aberration" based in Party circumstances but a necessary reaction against the hegemony of France in Europe's self-understanding (cf. Trouillot 1989).

Asserting that Romanian peasants anticipated the French Revolution was a variant of indigenism: to use the appropriate contemporary term, it was openly protochronist. Its central proposition was "Romania first," or "We do not stand with any of you Easterners or Westerners." This is what it meant to say Romanian peasants anticipated (i.e., were not influenced by, achieved on their own) such major western developments as the principles of the French Revolution. A similar assertion of priority—this time over the Soviet Union—was implicit in the point about Romania's "entering the modern era," departing earlier than neighboring Russia from a state of backwardness.[36] This protochronist position on Horea was a clear signal, then, to the West as well as to the East, that despite overwhelming debts to the West and increased trade and credits with the Soviets, Romania intended to be vassal to no one.[37]

Besides making a protochronist statement to East and West, Pascu's "revolution" constituted a direct provocation to neighboring Hungary. This is most evident in two points from the conference above: assertions of the rebellion's wide territorial extent and of its having not solely class objectives but also explicit national ones. The borders Pascu proposed went right to the present national border with Hungary and even somewhat beyond, including the entire area of Transylvania that is still contested by Hungarian irredentists. Therefore, the argument for "revolution" aired indisputably international claims of an aggressive sort. Calling the event a revolution that was not only class but national in character made the claims especially strong (in the interpretation of some scholars with whom I spoke), for this was a tougher statement against Hungarians, who were then ruling the area and who still dispute the borders. Inherent in the idea of revolution is a degree of class-consciousness and premeditated intent that uprisers may lack; this stronger consciousness is a stronger indictment of the injustices experienced under oppressive Hungarian rule. The argument for revolution contained an anti-Hungarian statement of another sort as well: if Horea's movement is presented as a *national* movement, then one can no longer argue that all members of the exploited groups joined to resist oppression in "brotherly" struggle, without regard for national differences, as had been argued in earlier socialist texts.[38] Thus, Hungarians had ceased to be revolutionary "brothers."

The audience intended for this argument would appear to be a large one. It included not just the peasants and miners in Brad, and not just those groups in Romania who regarded the defense of the Nation as their moral task (a major part of the self-definition of East European intelligentsias past and present), but an international audience as well. Evidence for the last is that pamphlets publicizing the "revolutionary" view were distributed at an international conference held in Bucharest that summer, attended by a number of western scholars. The "revolution" was thus not merely a candidate for acceptance into the public's beliefs about their past, a legitimation of their Party, or an appeal for support from others in the elite; it was also a veiled act of territorial aggression.[39]

The "Uprising," Science, and Europe. For intellectuals whose scientific authority was less mixed with politics, these issues of international relations were either of no interest or unacceptably phrased. What mattered to them were, on the one hand, a defense of "scholarly methods" and "scientific integrity," guaranteed by separating science from politics, and on the other hand, their relationship to Europe. The relation of science to politics was the issue most often stated by the partisans of "uprising" with whom I discussed the debate. (Compare the importance of the "autonomy of the aesthetic" for antiprotochronists, in chapter 5.) They were concerned, first, to defend proper use of scientific terminology, arguing that Pascu's position violated standard Marxist usage. Indeed, this was Prodan's main complaint: he found laughable the attempt to apply the term "revolution" to an event that so clearly defied the chief theoretical characteristics of one (it failed to bring in a new social order, had no class leadership prepared to effect the transition to such an order, and consisted overwhelmingly of peasants—whom Marx saw as a nonrevolutionary class). Second, the "uprising" group was concerned with assessing events properly in context and interpreting evidence in a scholarly manner. They refused to see the revolt as part of the national (rather than class) struggle, because they were convinced that this simply did not fit the social context of the times and involved the worst sort of presentism. Most proponents of "uprising" accepted as definitive Prodan's weighing and rejection of the evidence for nationalist goals among the peasant rebels; they considered his scientific judgment impeccable. As for Horea's anticipating the French Revolution, this offended not only their idea of proper context but also their sense of proportion: there was simply no apt comparison between the social structures of, and the consequences issuing from, the two cases. In the opinion of the uprising group, then, the revolutionaries' perversion of these scientific axioms was a politically motivated corruption of science—a judgment the revolutionaries of course rejected. In Pascu's first speech (above), he openly avowed the harmonious coexistence of science and patriotism; moreover, he often criticized Prodan for withdrawing from public life, saying this was an abdication of the civic responsibility any intellectual must fulfill.

In the eyes of the uprising group, it was not just science that had to be defended but the group's sense of its intellectual heritage, insulted by the indigenism of the argument concerning the French Revolution. For many Romanian intellectuals in both past and present, cultural ties with Europe have been a major value. The West has provided them with literatures and techniques fundamental both as professional tools and as statements of identity against the barbarians in the East. The Romania-first protochronism of Horea's "revolution" undermined values that people in the "uprising" group held dear for themselves and their country. In a sense, the entire debate over Horea boiled down to the steadfast adherence of that group to values they associated with the idea of Europe and Enlightenment science, ideas whose vigor among many East European intellectuals has often struck western observers with tremendous and poignant force (see Kundera 1984). The "science" whose eclipse they feared was simply one of many pan-European values to which they were deeply attached.

What emerges from the struggle over Horea, then, perhaps unexpectedly, is a debate over disciplinary practices and, alongside it, an argument about Romania's identity in the world. Some participants emphasized ties and values rooted in Western European civilization, considering the others' disregard for these values as barbarism. They were defending a notion of Romania and of intellectual practice rooted in scientific authority untainted with politics. Others, preoccupied perhaps with Romania's delicate international situation between eastern and western creditors, spoke for a Romania independent of all allegiances and a scientific authority based in political considerations.

THE PRODUCTION OF THE DEBATE: INDIVIDUAL AND INSTITUTIONAL COMPETITION

I have described above a struggle between two groups of historians, using largely the terms that appeared in their arguments and referring to their overt behavior. I would now like to speculate about the competitive processes from which, I believe, Horea's celebration emerged. My speculations rest on those old ethnographic standbys: intuition, overheard gossip, and rumor. The two competitive forms I discuss are individual mobility strivings (similar to those discussed in chapter 5) and competition among the institutions that produced history-writing. My objective in these remarks is to show that notwithstanding Romania's high degree of central control, the system was also permeated with anarchy and competition, aspects of socialism's "weak state" (see chapter 2).

For some readers, this argument may come as a surprise. How, given Horea's ubiquity, could it be said that the center was weak? It is in dealing with questions such as this that no scrutiny of the *products* of Romanian culture—the sort of material used in many political analyses of these systems—can substitute for understanding how the products are produced. Horea was ubiquitous precisely *because* the regime was relatively weak. Its main contribution to his excessive commemoration resided in (1) its insistence that cadres of all sorts give ever-increasing evidence of massive activity; (2) its provision of at least some funds for such activity; and (3) the well-known official fondness for rituals celebrating secular heroes and dates, especially an obsession with certain kinds of round numbers (10, 25, 50, 100, 200, etc.) (see Binns 1979–1980). Once these general directives and supports became part of the definition of the world for the average Romanian, in a societal context of shrinking resources and much-intensified competition for them—the situation after the mid 1970s—then most of the resulting behavior came from society's members and not from the directives of a power concentrated at the top.

Horea's bicentennial was a great example of how to fleece the state, part of various people's efforts to build and feather their own nests or pursue their own individual and institutional objectives at state expense. Each of the events celebrating Horea had to be organized by someone: a party activist from a school or factory, the editor of a press, the director of a museum or library, the head of an institute or film studio, the features editors of the many newspapers and magazines, the leader of a student history circle. Sometimes these people had received a directive from their superiors—also driven by an activity plan. This was common for holidays that were mandatory fields of political activity, such as the dates of Romanian independence or of liberation from fascism, but Horea's revolt did not appear to be a mandatory field of this kind. Nevertheless, any museum director, institute head, factory-level Party activist, or features editor constructing an activity plan for the year knew that such a significant date in national history would be a sure-fire winner in the competition for funds and for "brownie points" with those higher up.[40] One would have to have been a fool *not* to celebrate Horea, when all the system's tendencies were putting more and more pressure on directors of cultural institutions and activists and intellectuals to puff up their dossiers, raise their productivity, or lose their jobs.[41]

That the Horea extravaganza came in part from just such careerist motives was brought home to me in a casual conversation with one organizer of a "Horea spectacular," who described his tenacious fight to get approval and funds for it and the efforts that were required of him to justify why his particular enterprise should have a claim to Horea. He told me quite bluntly his motives for doing so: since the public had relatively high interest in Horea, his special event would bring him a "profit" in ticket sales, essential to mitigating his museum's desperate economic straits. Given how unnecessary this gentleman's revelations were—it would have been easier for him to insist, as most Romanians did (especially to foreigners), that the government was coercing this performance from him—I am inclined to believe his story. The example shows to what extent Horea's heroism and martyrdom had become a resource for advancing individual and institutional careers by preying on the state, given the environment the leadership had provided.

In this instance, the persons most anxious to colonize Horea were bureaucrats and intellectuals (including Party activists in institutions), the groups in Romania most likely to turn nationalism and national history to their own uses.[42] The fate of Horea's rebellion in Ceauşescu's Romania reveals for us that society's very peculiar character, in which excessive centralization was yoked with extreme anarchy. In Horea's case, the anarchy came from multiple uncoordinated colonizations of his rebellion, including those by writers, activists, administrators, army and Party historians, and petty bureaucrats who staged the five months of celebration. The centralization, on the other hand, reveals itself in the way each of these groups saw its funds, permissions, mobility, recognition, and so forth as coming *from the top*. Centralization of the resources necessary to survival encouraged precisely the sorts of performances Horea evoked. Yet this was a very far cry from a totalitarian regime's imposing its will on intellectuals and using them to legitimate its rule.[43] And the picture that emerges—of rampant conflict as groups competed for the resources necessary to survive and move forward—is a much less orderly picture than one showing society on the run before a powerful Party, even though in some contexts some of the time some groups in the Party undeniably had the upper hand.

Some of the competitiveness I have just described reflected individuals' anxiety to improve their own positions; sometimes it was also combined with their ambitions for the institutions that supported them. The information available to me enables me to do little more than guess about the latter. Such guesses are nonetheless worth making, if I am right to suggest that the special position of historiography in cultural production made it subject more to bureaucratic and institutional competitive processes than to the quasi-market ones discussed in chapter 5. This would make the processes I am about to suggest proportionately more significant in shaping cultural politics in historiography than in other domains.

Behind Horea's extravaganza, I believe, lay the struggle among institutes of history, mentioned earlier in this chapter. With the incorporation of the history of the Party into the history of the "entire people," there ensued a major battle between the Party History Institute (and what I believe were its allies in Military History) and the other institutes of history, to control research into this new object. The "revolutionary" innovation served an offensive by Party-based historians, by emphasizing the role of military organization in the peasant revolt[44] and by making Horea a precursor of the Party's revolutionary struggle. These historians could then link Horea's revolution with their interpretation of other events in which they invoked a "tradition" of the "struggle of the entire people," constructing a unitary, organic entity made up of the army and Party and entire people (see, e.g., I. Ceaușescu et al., 1985: 43, 101, 132).[45] Through the "revolution," these historians appropriated Horea into their own genealogy. That the innovation was launched by someone not in a Party or Military History Institute (albeit someone with intimate ties to General Ilie Ceaușescu) does not disprove my hypothesis, for once the "revolution" was out, it still had to collect supporters. Those it collected had their own agendas.

It is even possible that the Party and Military History Institutes actually commissioned Pascu's book on Horea's revolution. Such, at least, was the claim of the book's editor, as already mentioned. This suggests the additional possibility that institutional struggles were tied with wars among different publishing houses. The publishing industry was no more unified than was historical research: different presses had different relations to censorship, were subordinated to different segments of the bureaucracy, and could expect varying levels of subvention. Energetic action by a publishing house could increase its power relative to other houses and its standing in the bureaucracy at large. Therefore, directors and editors strove not especially (or not only) for more resources *from the center* but for prestigious acquisitions that might enable them to secure other prestigious titles; they amassed resources, from any quarter, that could be transformed into bigger projects and more activity. In a word, they acted like segments of the allocative bureaucracy described in chapter 2. The impetus for such acquisitions would be only in part to help a press stay in the black under the rules of "self-financing." More important, such acquisitions would enlarge that publisher's allocative capacity.

I base this proposal on an overheard conversation in which the director of a major publishing house discussed at length with one of his historian authors the significance of his having acquired for his press (and this was how he phrased it) the rights to reediting the enormous output of interwar historian Nicolae Iorga. When I observed that it sounded like a huge headache because of all the work, he replied triumphantly that far more important was the prestige this would bring his publishing house and the additional authors he could hope to attract thereby. In short, it would augment his power as a bureaucrat. By analogy, the Military Press that published Pascu's book had acquired for itself a major "name," an author appreciated by many in the broader public and in the history profession. This press enjoyed special status: its books did not pass through the usual censorship channels, and it was in a strong position to bring out daring works, but it suffered somewhat from the army's generally negative image in the intellectual world. Acquiring Pascu's book may have been part of an institutional strategy to brighten up its list. This might also facilitate its access to more resources: the editor of Pascu's book himself complained to me that third-rate novels could command paper to publish 80,000 to 100,000 copies, whereas he had to wage veritable war to get a press run of 50,000 for a history book. Having heard awe-inspiring tales of another editor's vigilante efforts to secure the paper for a large press run of a fat book, I find it easy to believe that editors and directors of publishing houses would hatch plots for such ends as increasing their claims to paper.

Readers skeptical of this picture of institutional scheming and resource-mongering have perhaps not drunk enough brandy in the company of Romanians employed in producing culture. One need not believe all the details to see useful patterns in how they spoke about their work: directors who pulled strings to commandeer an entire railway car and went with it in person to the paper factory, so as to transport and store the paper a typesetter required; scholars who worked out special research contracts ("self-financing") that generated independent monies with which they put out special publications, using a trick of enumeration to exceed five-fold the plan originally approved; authors who picked up their manuscript from the censor's office and, en route to the typesetter, substituted uncensored pages marked identically to others that they pulled out. The work of cultural production was full of similar stories, institutional and individual. When I asked two such culture-bandits what was at stake for them, they replied, "It's a struggle within history!" "To obtain influence?" I asked. "No: a struggle to determine the future course that Romanian historiography will take." One would have gotten this same answer, and just as passionately felt, from persons on either side of the Horea debate. Behind the reply were stakes such as who would write the school manuals (labeling Horea's event a revolution?) and who would form the historical consciousness of the next generation, or the disciplinary practices and areas of concern of young researchers.

The Centralization of Historiography under Political Control

In chapter 2 I presented a model of real socialism as driven by a tendency for resources to concentrate under the control of the political apparatus. Both there and in chapter 5 I sought to show that one of the chief mechanisms for this outcome was competition *within the intellectual "space,"* rather than between "scholars" and "Party." The present example, I believe, illustrates this same point. From an argument rooted ultimately (I can state with some assurance) in a simple personal vendetta between two historians, one of whom was always trying to outdo the other, who disdained him, there emerged two camps of partisans arrayed against one another, with auxiliaries scurrying back and forth between them. The argument between Pascu and Prodan mapped out a field of discursive possibility. Upon it, persons and institutions rounded up followers and fortified positions, annexing the debate to their own projects. The positions represented, on the one hand, protochronism and a defense of truth as political, and, on the other, Europeanism and a defense of truth as scientific. The underlying issue was, should the scientific authority of intellectuals be auxiliary to political status? Where is the center of gravity in the field of forces whose coordinates are "culture" and "politics"? The answers were, inevitably, cast in the idiom of national identity.

How did this argument serve to concentrate resources further under the control of the political apparatus? I believe this occurred in at least two important ways: the debate reinforced certain ideological premises useful to power, and it afforded the political center a display of power that projected an image of regime strength while undermining the perception of possible alternatives. In other words, I suggest that the *staging* of the debate had significant effects on its audience, quite independently of its specific content. I do not regard these outcomes as the actors' conscious intention. Rather, I suggest that relations of power—understood in something closer to Foucault's sense than to Weber's—act most significantly in ways that are nonobvious and, for this very reason, are especially important to identify.

A fundamental systemic consequence of the "revolutionary" innovation, in my view, was that it constituted, or built up, political power. To redefine the past is to display mastery in the present: whether the redefinition is accepted is perhaps less important than the fact of its having been paraded. Control has flexed its muscles, demanded attention, announced itself. Its vehicle has been something familiar to all—a personage from the past that nearly anyone with a fourth-grade education has heard of[46]—and now something is being done with him: he is being changed. Better said, as any Transylvanian peasant would, "*They* are changing him." Over the long run, this change would enhance power by subjecting the opposed intellectuals to defeat, if the new label were to stick. I am less interested in that possibility, however, than in another, concerning the average Romanian rather than the elite. Changing Horea would be significant for power not through altering uneducated TV-watchers' view of Horea's achievement but in a more subtle way, involving the effects of a limited set of techniques on a fairly narrow audience: the inclusion of villagers in the spectacles and in the parade of academics at the conference described above.[47]

The afternoon visits of learned "gentlemen" from around the country, making speeches about Horea's revolution to local groups of peasants and miners, could not fail to impress upon their village hosts the importance of the occasion. The visits were impressive in more than one respect. First, they were unmistakably framed as political-ceremonial events: no villager who had ever watched television could fail to realize that the form of our reception was identical with that given the country's most important people, especially the Ceauşescus. The children lining the walkways, the flowers handed to persons in the procession, the speeches and applause, the mixing of these with the basic rituals of village hospitality (brandy and cakes), all this together with the awe in which villagers hold people of higher learning: the whole configuration made for a profoundly marked display of power and knowledge, brought into the schoolhouses and village halls of simple folk. The manner of the display left no doubt as to who was important and who was there merely to serve.

Within this frame, and second, the ceremonies communicated to these folk the significance of their history, a history important enough to bring a group of distinguished scientists from all over the country into their villages. The message was communicated in the most visceral way, by bringing people's bodies into the forums in which the message was being delivered in live public events (rather than in the more personal and mediated space before the television, at home). Some of these bodies—the children's—did not just spectate but in fact recreated Horea's life and deeds, in the (much rehearsed) poems and skits they enacted for the visiting scholars. The commemorative festivities engraved into people's neurons both the power of the state that subjected them and the historical notion of identity that was the occasion for it.

A third vital element of the festivities was that they showed the state's control over Time, not only through displaying its power to control the past (and therefore the present) by parading a redefinition of history, but also through proving its capacity to expropriate the time and effort of others. The occasion was a magnificent display of the state's ability to gather up Time from living persons and redistribute it to the dead. By mobilizing the bodies of so many children and parents, who waited for hours in the cold, by compelling people to procure rationed flour and sugar and to provide the time and labor necessary for making the cakes, together with the hours of drill implied by the impressive synchrony of the children's recitations: by all this, people's bodies were informed of their subservience to a defining power. The celebration quite literally em-bodied history and subordination as aspects of people's daily existence. With all this, Horea and his connection to power, state, and Nation became lodged in these villagers and schoolchildren at a level more profound than the one touched by their television shows or memorized textbooks: he and all he implies were lodged in their very bones.

In all these respects, Horea's celebration both displayed and further constituted power, by dramatizing subjection. Horea was a godsend to Romania's weak state: he provided an excellent pretext for projecting an image of strength, offering the populace a visceral experience of their subordination and building up their belief in the regime's power— which, of course, strengthened it in fact. Through commemorations like Horea's, Romanians gradually came to believe they had no alternative. This, by the definition offered in the introductory chapter, constitutes a legitimating moment.

It was a moment ironically confirmed by those very intellectuals who believed that they were opposing power and yet contributed to legitimating it. Their contribution was partly an effect of how the event was staged. First, the division between stage and audience, between Savant Dignitaries in procession and humble villagers immobilized by waiting, was a division defined in terms of relative amounts of knowledge: between those fit to speak and others fit only to spectate. It reinforced the notion that authority was the preserve of *experts*, not of lay persons, which excluded all but the educated from a meaningful political role. Second, uninformed observers by no means realized that those up on the platform were arguing with each other; all they saw was the gap between experts and themselves. This blurred the public perception of distinctions among categories of expert—divisions within the elite— and reduced the chance of crosscutting alliances from the stage to the audience.[48] It separated those who most possessed the means for organizing to change the existing system from those who might be a constituency for such change. If subjection is, in part, the undermining of alternatives, then the practices that commemorated Horea deepened people's experience of subjection: to authorities "in the know."

The simple staging of these events was but one of the ways—an indirect one—in which all participants, regardless of their position, were constituting authority for the regime. All of Horea's partisans, revolutionary or not, were locked in a single endeavor despite their disagreements: giving greater force to the premise of expertise/knowledge and to two other fundamental premises of Romania's political ideology, the premises of the importance of history and the Nation. It was precisely in debating about Horea that "uprisers" and "revolutionaries" combined to create ideological performances by which the Romanian population became further subjected to those "in the know," as well as to perpetuate Romanians' historical and national consciousness—cornerstones of both the Romanian state and all others in Eastern Europe. The premise of the importance of history was, of course, the terrain on which the entire debate took place. By the very fact of debating, all sides acknowledged that the past was a vital concern. Since none of these clearly important people was saying "So what?" to any of the historical questions, innocent observers could only conclude that these questions were crucial. Similarly with the Nation: by proposing different concep-

tions of national identity and the national struggle, the antagonists reinforced the long-held notion, basic to public and scholarly discourse
for two centuries, that Romanians' national identity and its political defense are of fundamental significance. To argue that Horea was or was
not struggling for the Nation suppressed asking whether the national
struggle was worth all this fuss: the fuss itself said that it *must* be. Regardless of whether one was saying "Romania first" or "Romania with
Europe," then, one was insisting that the question of national identity
remain on the agenda.

That these two ideological premises (Nation and past) were being
reproduced seems clear enough. The premise about knowledge, however, warrants further comment. In discussing the implications of the
various views on Horea, I pointed to the "uprising" group's defense of
the notions of truth and science; yet it was not only they who had such
concerns. Indeed, the argument between uprisers and revolutionaries
was important in part because between them, the disputants gave added
ideological force to the notion of "truth"—which served, of course,
both the premises of Marxism-Leninism and the position of the intellectuals who guard truth's portals. Unlike literature or philosophy, historiography is a major site for constructing notions about truth, since
Marxism claims history as a science (a claim so empowering for Romanian historians that I never heard one dispute it, unlike their colleagues
in the West). Socialism's historians do not waste their time with mere
historical interpretations: they head straight for the chambers of true
knowledge.

The defense of truth ran through the speeches of both sets of participants in the public debate on Horea, as my summary above made clear.
Professor Pascu, for example, affirmed clearly that his patriotic version
of Horea's revolt was in no way incompatible with the historical truth,
an opinion with which his editor concurred. The concern with truth
was even more evident in later writings by some of these same people,
particularly in the wake of Hungary's *History of Transylvania*. That work
elicited from Pascu and another historian a book called *The Dangerous
Game of Falsifying History*. Its various papers were entitled "Misrepre-
senting and Falsifying History," "The Past Must Be Revealed," "Incontestable Truths and Contestations of the Truth," "Readjusting History
or Readjusting Frontiers?," "Who Benefits by Distorting Historical
Truth," "A Firm Position against the Falsifiers and Denigrators of Our
National History," and so on (Pascu and Ştefănescu 1987). One reads
in these papers, as well as throughout the popular press and other

professional writings, especially by Party-based historians (e.g., I. Ceauşescu et al., 1985; Popescu-Puţuri 1983), a virtual obsession with the ideas of truth and falsehood. Texts announce as their aim, for example, "serving historical truth" and giving a "true image" of "what really happened" (I. Ceauşescu et al. 1985: vii, x). History is defended as the "science of truth," in which "the truth will always out" (Pascu and Ştefănescu 1987: 73). "True science," it is claimed, will combat the errors propagated by those who fail to do an objective analysis of social realities (Popescu-Puţuri 1983: 41).

In some texts this interest slides into an association of *Romania* with truth and *foreigners* with falsehood. For example, two historians attack a colleague as follows, addressing their question to those overseeing the journal in which he published:

How was it possible that nobody realized the fact that [X] is known in the Romanian historical front as an element of discord who falsifies our national history, promoting non-scientific theses which can frequently be found in the works of foreign historians concerned with slandering the history of the Romanian people . . . ? (in Pascu and Ştefănescu 1987: 227).

Ilie Ceauşescu writes darkly of views asserted "without any foundation [by] certain foreign historians led by interests external to science and the objective truth" (I. Ceauşescu 1984: 15). Another historian urges his colleagues to combat "falsifications of historical truth, manifestations of cosmopolitanism and national nihilism" (Ş. Ştefănescu 1978: 37),[49] and yet another objects to the denatured theories and interpretations through which dominant powers propose that their damaging rule was actually progressive (Popescu-Puţuri 1983: 41).

Although it is clear that most of these comments were addressed to "falsifiers" and "denigrators" in neighboring Hungary (or the Soviet Union, but this was less often implied outright), reading a number of such texts gives an overall impression of Romania as an island of pure truth surrounded by a sea of polluting foreign calumnies. It is the task of historians to propagate the truth, to bring light to the world's ignorant and misled. Those in another camp, the Prodans and others of Romanian historiography who thought of themselves as opposing the intrusion of power into their field, represented truth and its protection differently: their image was not of *Romania* surrounded by *foreign* pollutions of the truth but of contaminations of truth *internal* to the country. This is not to suggest that such scholars saw no falsehoods propagated from abroad about the Romanian past but only to emphasize their alarm at the pollution of scientific authority by political intentions.

Truth, says Michel Foucault, is a system of procedures for producing, regulating, and circulating statements; it is linked with the power that sustains it and has power-effects that extend it. In the struggle to define and control "truth" in Romanian historiography we see a clash between different proposed systems for producing and circulating statements. One of these systems was heavily associated with rule by the Communist party and expressed grave doubts about the veracity of statements coming from beyond Romania's borders. It calls to mind Jowitt's image, introduced in chapter 3, of the pristine "castle regime" that conceives of itself as surrounded by a polluting environment. Proponents of this approach piled up science and truths about the Nation in the service of their castle regime's representation of itself to the world. The second system, associated with Prodan and his like, made its appeal to standards of competence and professional integrity as these are defined in the West. Pollution, for it, came from the contaminating effects of politics upon the purity of science. Both groups used ideas about truth to defend their corner of the intellectual terrain, one group defining its corner by proximity to politics and the other by distance from it (see fig. 4). Members of each group roped off their corner from that of their colleagues by claiming the right to define "truth" by their own criteria.

These images of pollution and purity make it clear that beyond simply versions of the truth, what was at stake was also *morality*, scientific responsibility as a kind of crusade. This applies to historians on all sides of any dispute. Some decried "methods alien to the spirit of science and *the ethics of research*" (Pascu and Ştefănescu 1987: 66, emphasis added). In a letter that solicited historians' aid in producing new books about Bessarabia, the author appealed to "a name and a *conscience*." Others invoked a "spirit of scientific responsibility toward the peasant masses who sacrificed themselves two hundred years ago" (as mentioned earlier in this chapter). Admirers of Romania's next-most intransigent historian after Prodan, Al. Zub of Iaşi, often referred to him as a "high priest" of historiography.

The emphasis on moral superiority as integral to cultural and scientific authority was shared by all pretenders to intellectual status, even those close to the political axis. It rests in part on East European intellectuals' historical sense of "mission," and it appears to have served as a basic entry qualification for occupancy of *any* corner of the "intellectual space." Through their passionate defense not only of truth but of its morality, historians showed that building scientific authority entailed affective investment, rather than the cultivation of distance and disinterest generally associated with the defense of Reason. The sense of moral righteousness about truth gave arguments in historiography the messianic quality that arguments in literature drew from notions of *value* (literary, aesthetic, social, etc.).

I have been arguing in this section that scholars and Party officials participated jointly in the business of creating, strengthening, and utilizing cultural symbols that have ideological force. It was not the specific content of their statements but the constitution of the discourse as a whole that made it ideological: by not making explicit the premises on which a debate was occurring, participants reinforced those premises as grounds for disputes and claims. Through their invocation alone—even if in argument—notions such as knowledge, Nation, and history, so crucial in the Romanian context, acquired and gained force in the social practices of this society, since none of them was dismissed as a basis for contention. Because both sides to the argument accepted that it was about knowledge, the Nation, and the past, no one questioned whether these things ought to have paramount significance. It is through such unwitting suppressions that ideology is constituted, and, with it, certain grounds for legitimacy: through suppressing the questions that would bring alternative possibilities to the fore.

I have also been suggesting that although we usually think of "ideology" as residing in the content of a message, most of the ideological consequences in Horea's celebration resulted, rather, from the practices that implemented it. Horea was passed through specific practices, which occurred in public contexts across a divide between speakers and hearers. From this staging, the public understood that something significant was being said, even if they did not grasp all its implications, and that power was being exhibited. These two things—the form of the discourse (the debate) itself, and the practices through which it was made public—show how historiography helped to serve the center's legitimacy in ways not usually remarked upon.

I would not want to conclude, however, that opposition had only system-enhancing effects. If nothing more, the reproduction of ideological premises such as Nation, past, and science made those available not only for the regime but also for use *against* it, by persons who might defend the Nation against its corrupters in the seat of power (an argument with much historical precedent). At the end of the next section I return to this question, asking what other consequences for power lay in historians' attempts to resist it.

Historiography in a Party Mode

I have suggested above some important ways in which the debate about Horea created or reproduced symbolic resources that could be usefully incorporated by the apparatus of power. In this final section I move beyond the specifics of the debate over Horea to consider briefly a few elements of historiography as a property of the Romanian political apparatus. What direction might history-writing have taken, had the system's centralizing tendencies been allowed to play themselves out?

One important aspect of the history to which the political apparatus aspired was the new subject being constructed: the *entire* Romanian people. Class struggle was gradually fading out, along with the separation between the Party and Romanians' other history. Peasants were becoming a revolutionary class, their "vanguard" provided by self-made rural intellectuals like Horea. Whenever a past Romanian seemed to have done something contrary to the national interest, it was claimed that either he had no choice, or he was serving a *longer*-term national interest; or he was made out to be an alien of some sort who was not even really *in* "the people." For example, some historians were maintaining that fascism in Romania was a marginal phenomenon until the ascent of the Reich imposed it on Romanians, who were either powerless to resist or were "aping foreign ways" unsuited to the national character (I. Ceauşescu et al., 1985: 12; see also C. Sorescu 1982). In short, Romanians who were not victims were traitors, which is to say not really Romanians. As the history of the people was stretched back ever more distantly into the mists of time, it was ever clearer that the "people" important to Romania were the ethnic Romanians, not the Hungarian, German, or Gypsy minorities who entered the area after the ninth century. As with protochronism, then, we see the creation of a history that would expel aliens from the community of the valued. This kind of history aptly fits not only an economy of shortage (see discussions in chapters 2 and 5) but also Lefort's definition of a "totalitarian ideology" (Lefort 1986: 284–286); it represented the weak state of Ceauşescu's Romania as the powerful, unitary embodiment of "the entire people."

The kind of history being produced by people close to the Party shows exceptionally well how fully the national discourse had superseded the characteristic emphases of Marxism.

Second, the new history rested on a very novel kind of time, being newly defined. I observed above that in Horea's celebration, people experienced an appropriation of their time, seized and put to other uses by an external force. But the recasting of time went well beyond this, and historiography was the sphere *par excellence* in which it took place. Through various means time was flattened, rendered motionless—despite all the Marxism-inspired slogans about progress and the forward march of history. These means included decontextualizing events, an express denial of the principle that events differ according to the context in which they occur. Thus, a notion like "revolution" would mean the same thing for an event in prehistory and one in the present, for the Party was timelessly embedded in both. New dispositions to historians and publishing houses prohibited the use of any but Romanian place-names in a publication, regardless of the time period being discussed;[50] therefore, ancient and medieval historians were to use totally anachronistic labels for the places about which they wrote—tantamount to calling the zone at the mouth of the Potomac River "Washington" in a discussion of the year 3000 B.C. The economic autarchy Ceauşescu advocated was retrospectively found to have been a goal of many past leaders; the centralized Dacian state of 70 B.C. was the same kind of state as in the ninth or twentieth centuries A.D. Romanians had been Romanians since time immemorial. Ilie Ceauşescu's book, for instance, held that the people had always been one and the same; it was not transformed each time a new migratory people (Romans, Slavs, Mongols) entered the area: "[I]t is well known that the Romanian people remained always the same, consolidated, unitary and homogeneous in the hearth it had always occupied," at most borrowing a little of Roman civilization or a few words from the Slavs (I. Ceauşescu 1984: 16).

A time was being constructed that was timeless, that did not pass, and in which the Party was ever-immanent. Campeanu expresses this admirably: "Becoming is replaced by unending repetition. Eviscerated of its substance, history itself becomes atemporal. Perpetual movement gives way to perpetual immobility. . . . [H]istory . . . loses the quality of duration" (1986: 22). This curiously flat time was teleological, but in a manner different from the progressive teleology of Marxism: substituted for this was a teleology of continuity and immanence, the Party held in time's womb from the first moment. The combination of this teleology with the loss of the durative element in time was wonderfully captured in a Romanian joke: "What do we celebrate on May 8, 1821? One hundred years until the founding of the Romanian Communist Party."[51] It was also a time obedient to administrative fiat. This emerges clearly from the decision of the Party's Central Committee to fix the date upon which King Burebista had formed the first Dacian state on the soil of what is now Romania (Georgescu 1981: 65). A problem that archeologists and historians had been unable to resolve through de- cades of research was thus settled by the stroke of Ceauşescu's pen. The time being created, then, was a time responsive to the Party's will, a time of which the Party was master. It was a time very different from the "homogeneous empty time" that Anderson sees as characteristic of the nations constructed by capitalism, better resembling the time proper to precapitalist sacred and imperial worlds (1983: 28–40).

The same point appears differently in Nicolae Ceauşescu's *The [sic] History of Romania* (Ceauşescu 1983a), a collection of texts from speeches in which he mentioned historical events. The book is orga- nized in five sections, the first containing observations about the neces- sary relation of historiography to politics and the remaining four cover- ing Antiquity and the Middle Ages, the fourteenth to nineteenth centuries, 1821–1918, and 1919–1948. Crosscutting this ritual bow in the direction of real time is the organization of texts within each sec- tion: they are strictly in the chronological order *of their enunciation as speeches*. That is, an event of 1300 A.D. mentioned in a speech from 1968 will precede an event of 350 B.C. mentioned in a speech of 1969. What better evidence of the Party's desire for mastery over time, its ca- pacity to redefine the entire dimension of temporality in human affairs? And rightly so: time, like language, is among the ultimate means of pro- duction in social life. The definition of time can affect, for instance, such time-bound social realities as labor's productivity and surplus value.

The appropriation of how history is produced appears in other fea- tures of Ceauşescu's *History* as well. The volume was put together by the director of the Institute for Party History, whose preface states that the book is intended to guide professional historians, brimming as it is with insights and theoretical formulations that will enhance their work on all the problems of Romanian history. Ceauşescu is presented as having restored to Romanians their heroic ancestors and glorious past, whose *true significance* he has revealed. Through him "we have become able to know our parents, our forebears, to become ourselves" (Popescu-Puţuri 1983: 8), that is, without the Party's knowledge of the past we would be ignorant, without the First Father we would have no access to our genealogy. Ceauşescu urges us to seek our history *at home* (ibid., 9), that is, not to go looking for Romanians in relation to Europe or elsewhere, as some historians do. The work is explicitly presented as a means of subsequent historical production: Ceauşescu's precious theoretical and methodological insights provide firm ground for producing monumental treatises to synthesize Romanian history and for properly understanding the raw material provided by historians' research (p. 47). The volume's concluding scientific apparatus, it is said (p. 50), aims to guide those wishing further knowledge of Romanians' multimillenary history. The bibliography of this 534-page text is 10 pages long and lists only one author: Nicolae Ceauşescu, *the* authority, *the* standard of historical competence.

This, then, is the ultimate in historiography in a Party mode. Some of its creators were apparatchiks, like Popescu-Puţuri (above), but others were more than this: professional historians, people like Ştefan Pascu, whose colleagues once regarded his work as of high quality by professional standards and whose writings turned to creating revolutions for the apparatus. Pascu was not the only professional historian to involve himself in debates like this, taking a side that had clear implications for power. Among others who did so were many deeply convinced that their form of professional practice was a patriotic duty and a service to their Nation. Some of them were, surely, "opportunists" (just as some of their more timid opponents were "cowards"—no side here held the moral high ground), but some were also passionately dedicated to what they saw as the most important values: a shoring-up of Romanians' self-confidence, for example, or an opposition to perceived denigration from abroad. These people were attached to institutions whose cause they furthered by scheming to outdo rival institutions, less supportive of the "right" values for the Nation, and to deprive those of the resources for history-writing. From their competition proceeded the centralization of control.

What was the attitude of Party-mode historiography to those historians who resisted its blandishments?—to the Prodans and Zubs and others who pursued their own agendas, setting what *they* defined as a standard of both morality and scientific authority? Were these foci of "independent production" disabled? Historians who achieved a certain degree of eminence were difficult to disable, in part for the very reason that they produced things of value to "Romania." Travel visas might be denied, as a gentle hint; manuscripts might be stalled interminably, but most would at length see print, unlike the columns of a literary critic or the volumes of a poet who offended the authorities.[52] More common than silencing would be persistent efforts to coopt these persons, with their accumulations of moral and professional standing, into the projects of the center. Protochronists, for example, repeatedly approached the eminent and outspokenly anticentrist Prodan and Zub with proposals that would create the appearance of their adhesion to protochronism—such as awarding them prizes for their work and soliciting their aid for protochronist initiatives. Although this attempt at cooptation did not come from the Party center proper, one can point to many others that did, such as well-known historian Dinu Giurescu's report that high officials had coerced his signature for an anti-Hungarian diatribe in 1984, thus associating his charismatic name with their designs.[53]

What, if any, resources were available to those historians who nonetheless wished to resist cooptation? Besides the moral standing and scientific authority that made them targets of it in the first place, not much. The political center knew how to find the chinks in a scholar's armor that would make him consider such an offer seriously—his daughter's entry into university, his wife's keeping her present job, his invitation to spend a few months in France. From this point of view, what enabled Academician Prodan to insist on his professional autonomy was precisely his lack of such encumbrances (no children, himself and his wife retired, minimal ambitions for travel). The only thing that might give leverage to this sort of historian and those who associated their name with his was independent recognition of his scientific reputation: most especially, recognition from the West. Intellectuals recognized and supported in the West had a bit more freedom of maneuver than others, because the authorities were more reluctant to silence them. Thus, Academician Prodan's election to honorary membership in the American Historical Association in 1986 was greeted with jubilation particularly by those historians who thought of themselves as seeking to emulate his example.[54]

How, given my conclusions in the previous section, could their opposition to the center have any efficacy? I argued there that "uprisers" who saw their debate with "revolutionaries" as opposing the incursion of power into historiography nonetheless helped to reproduce the national ideology and the enthronement of knowledge, both of which potentially served the political apparatus by providing it with legitimating moments. How, then, could those historians who wished to keep alive a different definition for their discipline do so without in some way serving power, howsoever inadvertently? To what extent was anything accomplished by those historians who saw their life's work as to perpetuate values and definitions of the past different from those the Party privileged and amplified?

Besides reinforcing ideologies about the Nation and knowledge, which might help to legitimate other regimes than Ceauşescu's, I believe they did. Their effectiveness was less in the content of their arguments than in their professional practices. Even though to defend knowledge and expertise might strengthen those grounds for the Party's legitimation, to insist on other standards for professional competence necessarily pluralized the environment, thus defying the attempted totalization of all productive means. To insist, as did Prodan, that history is written by consulting documents year after year, decade after decade, and by specializing in a period and learning its idioms, its rhythms, its eccentricities, was to offer a professional model different from one that footnoted only secondary sources and speeches of Ceauşescu or that "specialized" in the entire run of Romanian history from the Paleolithic to modern times. A history book that upheld the specificities of the contexts it described, or that refused to see a modern state or a Romanian people in 150 A.D., was a history book difficult to appropriate within the time-flattening, decontextualizing definitions of historiography in a Party mode. A historian who refused to answer the attempted recastings of his argument, so as not to be drawn into the terms set by his opponent, like those marginalized academics who refused to join the Party even in exchange for a university post, were demonstrating for all to see that there was not just one option for producing history, even though the alternatives were perilous and disheartening.

It is for this reason that Prodan became, in his own lifetime, a symbol, and a symbol far less ambiguous in his properties than the peasant rebel who was his hero.[55] For those historians who hoped to maintain a space within the intellectual terrain that did not require political validation, he unequivocally represented the longevity and strength of disciplinary practices antedating the present regime. Romanian historians have spent over two centuries arguing fiercely and publicly about the past, producing a body of discourse and professional practices that achieved a certain autonomy. Earlier forms of them continued to live and breathe in people like Prodan, who learned them in a previous era and transmitted them by inculcating norms of what a research discipline should consist of. Like all academic disciplines, historiography is a collection of practices, very material in their unfolding and recalcitrant to change. Such practices made intellectual activity within a field of disciplinary endeavor not just a Party-serving instrument but an independent force in the world. Its traditions and their revivification made historical interpretations difficult for the center to change without a struggle.

These practices impeded the concentration of resources and means of cultural production in the political apparatus in a variety of ways, but one particular example will make the point. When Ceauşescu appealed to the "historians' front" in the mid-1970s to produce a new ten-volume synthesis of Romanian history, he was appealing to a profession recently fortified by the rehabilitation of persons sidelined during the Stalinist era. The discipline was peopled then by a variety of practitioners, more and less malleable, more and less ambitious. But just as with the Writers' Union in the same period, the leaders of the profession tended to be "reformers" and nonapparatchik professionals installed in strong positions during the late 1960s and early 1970s. These people, entrusted with producing the new *Treatise of Romanian History*, busily set about doing so according to their idea of proper professional norms.

By the time the first volume—the one that treated Romanian origins—was ready, however, dacomania had become the rage in Bucharest. Directors of institutes were instructed to change their subordinates' contributions to the *Treatise*, reflecting more Dacian and less Roman influence. Those responsible for the first volume refused to do so. In consequence, the typeset fonts for that volume were melted down and neither it nor any of the others—long since completed in the drawers of their compilers—appeared.[56] The reason was partly professional intransigence and partly, it is rumored, the opposition of the ambitious centers specializing in military history; having not been written into the initial publication plan, they proceeded to block it henceforth. If this rumor is true, it shows institutional rivalries (rather than central *diktat*) disabling foci of production that resist the center's embrace. And if it is not, we are left with a great silence, defiantly produced by certain historians insisting on pluralistic standards and plural interpretations. As this example makes plain, we must draw conclusions about the forces that produced culture in Ceauşescu's Romania not just from what was written but also from what people refused to say.

This chapter has shown, on the basis of an insignificant argument about a long-dead Transylvanian peasant, how debates that seemed to be about labels were also debates about Romanian identity; how what looked like an opposition to values promoted by the center helped to strengthen some of the regime's supports; how competition between individuals and institutions within the framework of a bureaucratic-allocative system tended to bring the production of history further within the control of the political center; and finally, how at the level of professional practice, there was nevertheless a certain friction against these centralizing tendencies. In the final chapter, I describe a case that scrambled some of these outcomes and that offered friction against centralizing tendencies not only at the level of practices but at that of explicit content, as well.

CHAPTER SEVEN

The "School" of Philosopher Constantin Noica

I dream of a school in which what will be taught is, quite frankly, nothing: where people will live peacefully and modestly, in a corner of some town, and a few young people will come there to free themselves of the tyranny of professors. . . . Don't you see that they too have something to say, to affirm? And that we do not always have anything to tell them? We are merely mediators between them and themselves. . . . States of spirit, that's what must be given to others; not contents, not advice, not teachings.

—Constantin Noica

C'est une trahison de pactiser avec le siècle.

—Julien Benda

Țara piere și filozofii se pieptănă.
(The country is dying and the philosophers are fixing their hair.)

—Romanian proverb

During the decade of the 1980s, Romanian intellectual life was much enlivened by the publication of two books, *Jurnalul de la*

Păltiniș (Journal from Păltiniș) and *Epistolar (Letters)*, one written and the other edited by Gabriel Liiceanu, a philosopher in his mid-forties.[1] I call the persons involved in these books and the events around them the "School" of Constantin Noica, Liiceanu's mentor and the explicit or implicit focus of much of the discussion. For many intellectuals, the two books were the event of the decade, despite the fact that the strictly philosophical issues raised were accessible to almost no one. The books harvested a bumper crop of reviews, commentary, denunciations, and other public notice, and they brought to the surface with nearly unprecedented clarity a number of issues in the politics of culture. Indeed, despite their origin in a community of philosophers and their arguments for the place of philosophy in Romanian culture, I see their significance as lying chiefly outside the domain of philosophy proper, in the sphere of cultural politics. It is from this angle that I discuss Noica's "School."[2]

The people in Noica's innermost circle were among the most marginal, and their form of cultural production (metaphysics) the most arcane and generally impenetrable, of any of the events, persons, or arguments discussed in this book. Yet because these philosophers' arguments intersected with literary criticism and with protochronism, they achieved much greater visibility than did the debate covered in chapter 6, concerning the much more central and accessible domain of history. My discussion of them includes ever-widening circles: first Noica himself; then his closest disciples and other persons with whom they interacted intensely (I refer to these as the "Noicans" or "Noica School," even though several of them clearly stated their difference from Noica and from each other on fundamental points); and finally a larger circle of persons more or less sympathetic and more or less hostile to Noica and/or his closest disciples.[3]

The Noica School forms a fitting conclusion to my treatment of cultural politics in Ceaușescu's Romania. Even more clearly than the phenomena discussed in previous chapters, Noica was directly continuous with the interwar arguments on the national essence, for he was a central figure in the cultural battles of the 1930s, and (with the posthumous publication of some writings of his last years) he pursued his work on the national essence even beyond his death, in 1987. We see in the "Noica phenomenon" a number of issues treated in previous chapters, as well as some additional ones that have not yet emerged. The issues include the struggle between protochronism and its opposition or between indigenists and westernizers, divisions between intellectuals and the larger public, rival claims to cultural representativeness in the name of national values, competition among various disciplines to lay hold of cultural authority, and—albeit peripherally—claims about the place of Marxism within legitimate culture (thus, about variants of a Marxist tradition within Romanian cultural life). The issue of culture's relation to power is also central to this set of events; but to a degree not overtly encountered in other instances discussed in this book, so also is an opposition between centralization and pluralism, an argument about how to resist totalization in the production of values and how to protect them against political usurpation.

This last issue crosscuts and blurs the relatively clear demarcations of alliance and opposition that emerged in previous chapters, for Noica was an unusually complicated character. If certain figures in earlier chapters had, from the western point of view, a fairly consistent relation to power, in the present case it was precisely the ethics of a relation to power that became tricky. Noica was by no means the intransigent hero of an opposition to totalizing Party rule that one might see in the major antiprotochronists or historian David Prodan. Similarly, Noica had a more complex relation to interwar culture than someone like Prodan, who was also producing in those years. Although Prodan spent the 1930s as a largely unnoticed leftist buried in a provincial archive, whence he was catapulted into a university professorship after 1945, Noica (together with Mircea Eliade and Emil Cioran[4]) formed the center of a group of cosmopolitan Bucharest intellectuals in the orbit of right-wing philosopher Nae Ionescu,[5] an association for which he later paid dearly. Noica's past and recent history made very ambiguous his relation to the Communist party and the entire field it defined; this quality gave him a special symbolic value. Much of the discussion to follow is about a contest among different groups to capture Noica as a symbol, a contest that reveals major questions about philosophy, cultural production, the role of national identity in it, and the relation of culture to power.

In brief, this chapter offers the following interpretation. Whereas factional rivalry in historiography, literature, and literary criticism tended to emerge as questions about which faction or institution best represented Romanian cultural or scientific values, in philosophy questions of representativeness intersected with questions about the very nature of the discipline and its place in culture and national life. This is because of all academic disciplines, philosophy was the one earliest annexed by Communist party rule, which institutionalized Marxism-

Leninism and materialist philosophy and suppressed all other forms of philosophical thought. The subsequent "crisis" of Marxist legitimation in Romania partially liberated philosophy from its servitude to power, but it had then to reconstitute its fullness and respectability. This created, I believe, an environment in which despite the comfortable dominance of a certain group of philosophers in the institutions of philosophy, there was perhaps more room there than in other fields for marginal tendencies to seek and receive a hearing. Noica's followers give us a revealing instance of how activity at the margins could draw attention to itself and potentially shift the discipline's center of gravity. In other words, this chapter shows how a group even more marginalized than the early protochronists of chapter 5 gained visibility, by a very different strategy. Inherent in their marginality, however, was a sense of urgency that caused Noica's followers to emphasize culture's saving (soteriological) value, its capacity to prevent Romanians' extinction. This "saving" emphasis positioned them close to religion and, hence, at odds with power, as did the kind of cultural accumulation they advocated, as well. Compared with the practices and arguments treated elsewhere in this book, those of the Noica School came closest to articulating both the confrontation of culture with power and the possibility of an alternative vision—the foundation of a diversified ideological field and, through this, of transforming society from within.

It is important to emphasize what my treatment of Noica is not. First, it is not a comprehensive discussion of Romanian philosophy, which contained much greater diversity than I can encompass. More than chapters 5 and 6, the material of this chapter describes tendencies far from the center of the discipline it treats, even if what it describes was very much the center of interest for a substantial number of Romanian intellectuals. Second, owing to my minimal knowledge of philosophy, I make no pretense of explicating the particulars of Noica's work, which I leave to others (see, e.g., Karnoouh 1987, 1990). My summary of his thought rests on discussions with or published treatments by Romanian philosophers. Yet because Noica became a figure of symbolic importance well beyond the tiny world of philosophy, a figure liberally invoked by literati, journalists, Party activists, and others just as unqualified as I am to assess his contribution, I feel justified in adding my amateur reading to theirs so as to explore the sociology of his fame. Noica, like all symbols, had more than a univocal specialist "meaning." It is defensible to ask how he was variously understood and manipulated, with tactics that sometimes included wrapping him in a professional discourse impenetrable to the uninitiated, as different groups tried to fix his significance in ways favorable to their own enterprise and inimical to that of others.

Who Was Constantin Noica?

That Noica was an ambiguous character can be easily established with a few opinions:

Constantin Noica has an anachronistic and picturesque air, and like Don Quixote, he makes us both laugh and cry. We will never be able to decide if what is crazy is his madness or our seriousness (A. Ştefănescu 1984).

Even a passing glance shows the *rarity* of a cultural product [like Noica]. . . . In political economy, rarity is not the principal criterion for establishing the value of products, although in certain special cases such as gold, diamonds, and radioactive metals, rarity does play a part. . . . This rarity can be real or be maintained by various strategies of supply and demand. . . . One might add that gold has been used both for wedding bands and also for not-so-honest transactions. What good is Noica? . . . Without malice, I would say that . . . he is useful for everything (Antonesei 1987).

Noica . . . is a hermit who wants to bring order to the world and to culture, without realizing what a dreadful sophism he has fallen into (Simion 1983).

Many questions will be asked as to whether Noica was a believer. . . . And all sorts of things will be said, each of them with some basis in fact. As for me: he asked me a number of times to bury him in this hermitage. He could have asked for something else, for he was not lacking in ideas nor indifferent to death. But here was where he wanted to be. I have no further comment (Noica's friend Transylvanian archbishop Antonie Plămădeală, at Noica's funeral).

Noica was not a religious man (Noica's friend N. Steinhardt, monk).

Noica and his followers constitute without doubt the most significant intellectual event of this decade; what they are trying to do is of vital importance.
    Noica and his group are not very significant, really; there are other far more important books, such as [one proving Romanian continuity in Transylvania]. It's true fewer people will read them than Liiceanu's, but they will *last*. Noica's stuff is just froth: for most people, it will have no impact. (Two opinions overheard at the Institute of History, Iaşi.)

Noica contributed much to creating his own mystique and "multivocality" in his lifetime. For instance:

If anyone should interest himself in my scholarly activity, I ask that he *not* take account of the following: 1) my biography, which has no content, in good part from my own intention. . . . I lived my life in an idea, *and in nothing else*, in contrast to those who have something else and therefore have cause to mourn. I am in what I have published (1988: 10, original emphases).

The basic outlines of this nonbiography include his birth in 1909 to a well-placed landowning family; he received his B. A. in philosophy in 1931, did advanced studies in France and Germany, and received his doctorate in 1940, having already won a prize for his first book (1934). His list of subsequent publications is immense, including at least twenty-six books, many of them translations or exegeses of Plato, Kant, Hegel, and Descartes. He received a special prize from the Writers' Union (of which he was a member and from which he received a gener-ous pension), as well as posthumous award of Austria's Herder Prize for significant cultural achievements within the East bloc.

Upon this spare scaffolding Noica hung a few alluring ornaments. In 1974 he settled himself at the top of a mountain—a truly rarefied atmo-sphere for philosophical speculation. His abode lay near the border sep-arating Transylvania from Romania's southern region, a zone in which two other major and controversial interwar philosophers also resided (Cioran, Blaga); hence, he picked a location both marginal *and* central within Romania and within philosophy. Except for the hordes of visi-tors who invaded his peace in his latter years, he led an ascetic, almost hermit-like existence in a single chilly room, furnished with rented ob-jects, in a cabin that reminds philosophical cognoscenti of Heidegger's. A celebrated photo shows him and Liiceanu walking up a mountain path, their backs to the camera. His express rejection of all but the most occasional contacts with Bucharest, Paris, and other cosmopolitan cen-ters dramatized the marginality that was both imposed upon and em-braced by him.

This marginality was crucial to the biography Noica denied having. Although his refusal of established positions antedated the communist regime (he declined a post as university lecturer in 1934, retreating to the mountains to translate detective stories), the biography he would suppress contained his brief period of adherence to the fascist Legion of the Archangel Michael. This and his class origin made him *persona non grata* once the communists came to power. They placed him in forced domicile for several years and then imprisoned him for "counterrevolu-tionary" activities.[6] For ten years after his release in 1964 he held the only regular post of his life, as researcher at the Center for Logic, whence he retired with a small pension. It was after this that he settled in a room in the mountaintop cabin at Păltiniş and began in earnest to tutor a few disciples he had acquired along the way. He never served as professor in a formal sense; he translated this necessity into a virtue, claiming that being marginal was the best guarantee of undistracted pursuit of the Idea.

Noica's refusal to speak openly about the determinants of his marginality, to clarify the degree of his commitment to fascism and perhaps his regrets, contributed to his protean quality and to the ambivalence with which a wide variety of people regarded him. For Noica, however, this silence made possible an inversion of symbolic values: he turned his exclusion into the sign of election by cultural destiny, his handicaps into spiritual qualifications, and his distance from officially promulgated "culture" into a title to represent a form of culture that was deep and genuine (Gheorghiu 1985b: 76–77). This increased his appeal to young people disgusted by the flatness of what passed for culture as created and transmitted in formal institutions.

To see why Constantin Noica became so important in contemporary Romania requires a sketch of his philosophical thought, most especially of that part of it which dealt with Romanian identity—what I will refer to as his "Romanian writings" (see, e.g., his *Rostirea filosofică românească*, [*Romanian Ways of Speaking Philosophically*], 1970, or his *Sentimentul românesc al fiinţei* [*The Romanian Sentiment of Being*], 1978). My summary of Noica's philosophy comes from a comprehensive sketch of it by Andrei Marga,[7] who identifies Noica's fundamental goal as a critique of reason and modern rationality and an attempt to redefine them away from their scientific, positivist-technocratic senses toward meanings more suited to spiritual creation. On this reading, Noica was a critic of modern society whose program for transforming it was not a political but a spiritual revolution, and who consequently explored not the sociopolitical but the philosophical conditions of such a change (Marga 1988: 45).

Noica's critique of modernity led in two directions, Marga suggests. The first was a reexamination of the solutions offered by earlier philosophers, particularly Plato, in whom he saw an exemplification of how to live so as to promote growth and fulfillment.[8] The second was to challenge techno-scientific rationality by exploring alternative ways of apprehending the world. Here his vehicle was a detailed analysis of traditional Romanian forms of thought as embedded in linguistic usages. The result, Noica believed, was a model of the world very different from the excessively mechanistic and dichotomizing world view of the modern West. On this work rests Noica's subsequent notoriety. Not only did he unlock a specifically Romanian worldview that offered greater hope than the western one, but he also effectively created his own special means of production for philosophy in a Romanian mode: he gave a series of Romanian words (*întru, petrecere, sinele*, and others) such an intense and rich reading as to saturate them philosophically (and make them almost untranslatable).

Noica himself situated this endeavor in Hegel's concepts of universality, particularity, and singularity (see Noica 1987*a*). In taking up these questions he was reopening a major concern of Romanian interwar thought—how the particular relates to the general ("universal"), or how small cultures can participate meaningfully in a global order dominated by others. Noica hoped to give this problem, rooted in European thought and Romanian realities, an answer of European (general) dimensions based in Romanian (particular) material:

[M]y obsession is to rehabilitate the individual, but not as an isolated individual, rather as the individual invested with the power of the general. On this account I abandon the skies (the general) so as to see them mirrored in our own waters (quoted in Liiceanu 1983: 149).

His solution to how the particular should be related to the general was to emphasize the simultaneous participation of the particular in its own particularity and in the general as well, thus to recenter attention on the particularized, or "idiomatic," value. Noica wrote,

[I] object to the practice of both traditional and modern logic, which subsumes the individual under the general; both Aristotle and modern set theory integrate the part into the whole and the member into the set. To such a logic of subordination, of hierarchy in the military sense, . . . [I] oppose a logic . . . in which the part is not placed *in* the whole, but the whole together with the laws on which it rests is placed within the part (Noica 1987*a*).

Marga (1988: 47) observes that the concept appropriate to this understanding is the *hologram*, in which the individual is loaded with all the senses of the general and holds within itself all the latter's logical forms and relations.

In a word, Noica's objective was to construct for both Romania and the world a harmonic theory of the ontological relation between tradition and modernity.[9] The very nature of his project made him interesting and useful both to defenders of "tradition"—protochronists and their allies—and to the "modern" partisans of a Romanian link with the West—the Noica School and those associated with it. Very few of those interested in Noica understood the subtlety of the problem he was posing or the solution he attempted; more important was to appropriate him so as to legitimate the goals of one or another faction within Romanian culture. Protochronists—for example, critic Silvestri (1985)— interpreted his aim as the definition and rehabilitation of Romanian identity and his analysis of language as an effort to achieve a spiritual morphology of Romanian thought that might reveal the "ethnic subconscious." For such readers, Noica was preoccupied with questions not of reason but of Romanianness: "the meaning of Noica's work is to offer the world a Romanian solution," as do the creations of Romanian sculptor Brâncuşi (Silvestri 1985: 8).

Noica was not entirely disingenuous in his reaction to this sort of reading, a fact for which antiprotochronists criticized him severely.[10] It is true that he wrote often about the positive values of European civilization as a model for Romanians ("we Europeans") and that following an attack for exposing himself too readily to use by power (Tudoran 1982), he ceased his journalistic writings for a time; when he resumed, it was largely in antiprotochronist journals.[11] Nonetheless, he refused to take a more categorical stand against "patriotard" uses of his work. One "eye-witness account" reported Noica's publicly claiming to be a protochronist himself (Coja 1984). He permitted republication of earlier "Romanian writings," which some commentators have found to be rife with Herderianism, Romantic nationalism, and arguments close to the hearts of protochronists (see, e.g., Karnoouh 1987).

Noica's hesitation in setting himself off from protochronism was understandable, for it was the resurgence of national values that enabled his return to Romanian cultural life. As Liiceanu put it:

Noica burst into Romanian culture beginning in 1968, thus at the time when two distinct and parallel phenomena had taken place in Romania: on the one hand, a liberalization of thought, an acceptance of the fact that it is possible to think and to create culturally beyond dogmas; on the other, a preference on the part of official politics for upholding national differences rather than supranational integrating theses. Noica's entire thought . . . was a response to a twofold objective need: the need to regain originality of thought, after years of mental monotony brought on by a dialectical and historical materialism reduced to the level of schoolbooks; and the need for self-definition, for regaining a national consciousness (Liiceanu 1983: 230).

The opening to national values was Noica's opportunity. His early embrace by protochronists secured it, for among the enthusiastic recipients of his 1970 book *Romanian Ways of Speaking Philosophically* were future protochronist standard-bearers Paul Anghel (1970) and Mihai Ungheanu (1970).

As Liiceanu's summary makes clear, the restoration of national values was only one side of a coin whose other side was equally crucial to Noica's return: the diminution of philosophy's role as principal legitimator of Romanian communism.[12] This diminution was relative, for in a formal sense Marxism and materialist philosophy remained central, in a rigidified and sloganized form; yet far more of the weight of legitimation came to be borne by nationalism and by disciplines such as history. With the dethronement of materialist philosophy, Noica's kind of metaphysics became possible again—as one philosopher told me, "Now that philosophy is no longer king, it is actually possible to do something interesting in it." Moreover, students began having access to texts that could not have been used before, particularly the writings of philosophers from the West, and possibilities increased for talented philosophy students to travel to the West for study. Among those who benefited from these opportunities were two of Noica's chief disciples, Andrei Pleşu and Gabriel Liiceanu.

The dethronement of materialist philosophy has two implications for this discussion. First, it restored to philosophy debate over the definition and proper lineage of the discipline and over what constitutes philosophical competence. This meant that in philosophy as in other fields, conflict arose as to whose version best represented the discipline and what prior accumulations should be reintegrated into it as the necessary means for philosophical production. But second, such possible redefinition always contained an implicit threat to the still-official legitimating ideology, Marxism. To change the definition of philosophy was much more fundamentally *political* than were debates over values in literature, history, sociology, ethnography, or most other fields. In a word, mentioning Plato in a system that viewed itself as ideal was not an innocent gesture.

This second reason and the ambiguity at the core of Noica's endeavor help to explain why his thought and teachings became so heavily politicized, why it became so important that those aspiring to political influence "capture" him by emphasizing the nationalist aspects of his philosophy, and why political authorities kept their distance from him despite this. Because philosophy was *not* just any old discipline, a movement some saw as "cultural dissidence without politics" cut very close to dissidence of a more broadly based kind, for which reason the secret police soon learned to keep the central Noicans under constant watch.

Noica wanted to do "nothing more" than open up thought, after an era in which thought had been firmly closed. But in some fields of intellectual activity, "open thought" was far from harmless.

The Battle Over Noica as a Contest for Representativeness

It is clear from this preliminary sketch that Noica was rich in ambiguities, making him an excellent prospect for symbolic manipulation and competing genealogical appropriations. How did he vault from the sphere of mere thinkers into the sphere of contested symbols? The means for this was the two books published by his follower Gabriel Liiceanu, in 1983 and 1987.[13]

Liiceanu presents his *Journal from Păltiniș* as the diary he kept between March 1977 and July 1981, recording his encounters with Noica on the mountaintop at Păltiniș. The journal describes his trips from Bucharest to visit Noica, sometimes accompanied by other "disciples"; their discussions on topics both elevated and mundane; and colorful anecdotes concerning Noica and his views on culture, philosophy, and the proper action for a cultured person in a politicized world. Some of these views are nothing short of outrageous, but for over half the book Liiceanu merely notes them without protest. Only belatedly does he present himself as differing with his master. This gradual emergence into disagreement constitutes the book's expressed aim: to illustrate a "paideic model" in culture, the model provided by Noica, who knew not only how to instill cultural values in the absence of any institutional base or formal resources but also how to enable his followers to liberate themselves from his tutelage. The theme of "separating" from one's mentor is basic to the book's structure and its content. Liiceanu ends with a magnificent characterization of the teacher from whom he has learned even how to criticize one who taught him so much.

The *Journal* was followed four years later by *Letters*, consisting of correspondence that the *Journal*'s publication had provoked among Noica, his immediate disciples, several of their close associates, and a few other persons. This book to some extent repeats but also further develops issues raised by the *Journal*, and it opens new issues as well. Both the *Journal* and *Letters* work some important effects upon the reader. For one thing, both but especially the *Journal* create a strong

sense of Liiceanu as *authoritative* in speaking for and about his mentor—the affection and intellectual intimacy radiating from these pages
give him a fair claim to monopoly over Noica. Second, both make philosophizing very *accessible*, by presenting it through ordinary conversation. Even though the ultimate philosophical stakes of the issues under
discussion are often invisible to the general reader, as conversations
they not only are accessible but convey the impression that deep philosophical matters can be discussed like the health of one's friends or a
quarrel with one's neighbor. Thus, the books reveal a philosophical
world that is important and within reach. Third, despite this impression
of accessibility, there is nonetheless a great deal of talk about *exclusions*:
what is and what is not a worthwhile activity, who is or is not a good
philosopher or cultured person, and so forth. Finally, the books present
the Noicans' world as one that institutes *disagreement* as the norm and
as the most nourishing environment for thought and growth. This
premise enabled *Letters*, in particular, to embrace the contradictory re-
actions it provoked.

THE DEFINITION OF PHILOSOPHY AND THE
CLAIMS OF INTELLECTUALS

The *Journal* and *Letters* were greeted with a chorus of
dissonance.[14] Some reviewers hailed one or the other as "a spiritual adventure unlike nearly any other in Romanian culture" (Pecie 1984),
"exemplary, . . . a journal of ideas, showing the meeting of two persons
of high consciousness engaged in a relation of love and self-realization"
(Doinaş 1984), "courageous" (Papahagi 1987), and "one of the most
significant texts . . . of recent times" (Marino 1987). Others, resentfully
seizing upon the exclusionary maneuvers and contesting Liiceanu's
claims to authority over Noica, spoke of the "fortified stronghold of ex-
clusivist arrogance" revealed in the books (Steinhardt 1983), decried
"Noicism, this sickness of Carpathian provenance" (Dinescu 1986),
accused Liiceanu of an "egotistical" presentation of Noica filtered
through "dogmatism" (Mihu 1984*a*), or found the works "unworthy
of philosophy" (Barbu 1988 [April 8]: 2). Through their reviews, reviewers took potshots at one another, accusing others of "cheap readings" of the book (Enescu 1987) or supporting the attack of those
writing in other publications (Buduca 1987; *Luceafărul* 1987). Most
reviews took one of two basic strategies: either they praised the books
and their author (and implicitly the other disciples), while expressing

reservations about Noica (e.g., Ciachir 1983; Doinaş 1984), or they reviled the disciples and praised Noica, whom they sought to defend from his scheming usurpers (e.g., Geană 1986; Macoviciuc 1986; V. Mihăilescu 1985; Stroe 1984). These repeated efforts to sever Noica from his disciples betrayed an intense rivalry to define Noica and to pass final judgment on his "paideic" example and his Romanian philosophy. Readily apparent in most of the negative reviews, this contest was also acknowledged by the main Noicans as among their primary motives for publishing the books.

Although criticism came from more than one corner of the cultural field, it was particularly virulent from the protochronists. It is not difficult to see why Liiceanu aroused such a reaction, for he had written:

Bucharest continues to lie under an offensive by "protochronism," a cultural symptom that in departing from an inferiority complex, always ends in "the refusal of Europe" and the exaltation of eastern and autochthonous values. Seen thus, protochronism . . . achieves excesses that remove culture from the condition of minimal purity the spirit requires in order to develop itself undisturbed. And here something odd is happening. [He describes how Noica's "Romanian philosophy" contradicts his having urged his followers toward western culture and the quest for universal spiritual values, and how they feel betrayed by him.] [H]e has allowed himself to be invoked by all those babblers who play a tune that is well received. That Noica is claimed from two different directions has given birth to a confused situation he himself nourished and in which, for God knows what reason, he indulged himself with irresponsible grace. For those who will come after us, for those now coming of age in cultural terms, this confused situation cannot help having unfortunate effects. How many will rediscover the vein of authentic culture, in this small battle in which some invoke him from culturalist positions, others from autochthonist positions, and still others, exasperated by both of these, combat and detest him from still other positions? (1983: 137–138).

Several negative reviews singled out this passage for comment. A direct reply to Liiceanu's question came in one of the most critical of all, by Ion Stroe, a professor at the academy in which Party cadres were trained:

In the first place, the vein of authentic culture was opened by the orientation of the historic Ninth Congress of the Romanian Communist Party.[15] Let us recall that the revolutionary and dialectical spirit of this Congress puts into an authentic dialectical perspective the problem of rethinking the national values. . . . Noica himself was able to produce his most numerous and significant works by integrating himself in this process of creation and innovation. Noica is inscribed as a dialectician in the history of our philosophy above all through his postwar contributions . . . . The qualitative leap in Noica's thought is marked by his works written from the Romanian perspective (Stroe 1984).

The exchange raises two separate questions: the relation of Noica and the Noicans to Marxism, and their relation to national values. Both, however, reduce to the question, how is philosophy in Romania to be defined? Are ethnic questions an obstacle to it, an aid, a *sine qua non*? Is proper treatment of the concepts of Marxism necessary? Different answers to these questions would ramify into several other issues: which past writings—past accumulations of culture and values—should be incorporated into Romanian philosophy and which are irrelevant? What behaviors, what mechanisms of transmission, are appropriate for the devotee of philosophy in Romania? In what institutions is philosophy best created and protected? As with the protochronist debate in chapter 5, these questions received a variety of answers, and the answers expressed different notions of value underlying different claims that one or another program best represented both Romanian philosophy and Romanian culture more broadly.

Because the competing answers were more numerous than can be covered here, I will touch on only three: materialist philosophy, which I will consider but briefly, "Noican" philosophy, and what I will call "ethnophilosophy"—the latter two laying claim both to a decisive definition of philosophy and to Noica himself.[16] These latter two were much smaller than either the former or the large group doing what we might call "normal" philosophy (in a Kuhnian sense), which consisted of history of philosophy, analytic philosophy, epistemology, and so forth, usually having minimal "materialist" content and a heavy western emphasis.[17] Its practitioners distinguished themselves from the Noicans chiefly by doing more "curatorship" and transmission than philosophical creation and by avoiding metaphysics, Noica's specialty. This group and the older materialists occupied most of the university positions and institutes of philosophy.

One cannot discuss a contest over the definition of philosophy and its place in Romanian culture without at least a ritual bow in the direction of what held center stage for two decades: Marxist philosophy. My bow will be only ritual, because Marxist philosophy in Romania did not reproduce itself into a second generation: in the 1980s, scarcely anyone was carrying on serious philosophical inquiries of a materialist sort, nearly all having moved in other directions. Yet the *rhetoric* of institutionalized Marxism continued to permeate philosophy and to set a particular agenda for philosophical thought. I will use a magazine interview with the director of the Institute of Philosophy in Bucharest, Gh. Cazan (see Brătescu 1988), to provide a summary of this agenda, distinguishing it parenthetically from Noicism. (I used this interview because it happened to be at hand; its emphases do not depart visibly from those of countless comparable articles in diverse publications.)

In this interview, philosophy is defined as a *social science* (rather than, as Noica would say, a form of cultural creation), whose role is to pursue scientifically rigorous research aiming at *explanation* (Noica would speak of speculation or interpretation) so as to enrich and develop the revolutionary ideology of the working class. This kind of philosophy exists in continual confrontation with idealist philosophies (such as Noica's). Among the persons Cazan names as having published the "most representative Romanian contributions" to contemporary philosophical thought, he makes no mention of either Noica or ethnophilosophers. The problems philosophers treat include "fundamental processes of socio-economic and spiritual reality proper to the construction of socialist society in our country, philosophical implications of the technological revolution, processes of forming and transforming socialist consciousness," and so forth. The objectives of such work are to solve social problems in the present, not simply to speculate (as Noica does). From Cazan's list of those who represent the tradition of philosophical research in Romania, it is clear that even materialist philosophy benefited from the resuscitation of national values after 1960, for the list includes what one could call both "progressive" and "irrationalist" or "mystical" thinkers from the Romanian past. The accumulated philosophical learning that a contemporary philosopher should master, therefore, includes not just the texts of Marxism-Leninism (unmentioned, but understood) but also Romanian philosophers of stature, nearly all of whom had been trained in Europe. Cazan's interview clearly implies that philosophy is to be judged by combined standards of political utility and professional competence, the latter defined in relation to a written and specialist rather than popular tradition (emphases Noica would accept).

The relations between materialist philosophy and the Noican or ethnophilosophical variants were complicated, as the latter two set themselves off from each other partly by use of terms privileged within the former. This is most easily seen in various uses of the word "dialectic," as in Stroe's reply to Liiceanu, above. Here is Stroe again, this time claiming proper use of dialectics not just against Noica's followers but also against "dogmatic" materialism:

Liiceanu rejects not just Noica but Romanian dialectical thought, Romanian philosophy in all that makes it most specific. . . . We do not intend to give him lessons in dialectical materialism, . . . nor to remind him of the Romanian contributions to philosophy over the past two decades [a clear reference to Ceaușescu's thought—k.v.]. He could have found out, had he been animated by an objective spirit, that there is another dialectic besides that of the bad textbooks from which he was taught. Noica and Liiceanu are at opposite poles . . . One [Noica] is a dialectician . . . [but] Liiceanu missed the lesson that he could have learned from Noica: the lesson of dialectics (Stroe 1984).

Stroe thereby places Noica *within a Marxist tradition* (which Noica would abjure) and excludes both his followers and "dogmatic" Marxists of an earlier era, who ostensibly corrupted Liiceanu's (and many others') philosophical thinking. Here we see a contest over correct treatment of dialectics, while charges of "dogmatism"[18] are used to lay waste other claims within philosophy.

In this environment, Liiceanu too found it necessary to claim skill in dialectics. He did so in a peculiar way, in the Preface to *Letters*, where he announced his hope that the book would transcend its spatial and temporal particulars to become a lasting cultural value: to enter the realm of *logos*.

An organized quest (even if it is by chance) within the space of *logos* is called dialectics. Dialectics—a word that has been much abused lately and whose sense has been lost—gains back its original purity: the confrontation of consciences that seek clarification in the region of a truth that may or may not be found. Dialectics is, for this reason, the very *performance* of philosophy . . . (1987: 7, original emphasis).

Letters therefore claims the status of a philosophical work *by virtue of* its method, which is the "very performance of philosophy" and which recovers the original meaning of "dialectics," abused by materialists and others.

These uses of "dialectics" show that although both the Noicans and their critics felt compelled to draw upon a language established by Marxist philosophy, they did so not primarily to displace materialist philosophy (which neither could manage to do) but to strike at one another. It is this battle that I wish to concentrate on, chiefly for what it reveals about the issues at stake, both implicit and explicit, for the Noicans.

One might object at this point that in setting up "Noican" philosophy and "ethnophilosophy" I am not only giving unwarranted stature to two pygmies but also improperly pairing a truly *philosophical* movement with a bunch of amateurs having no such status. Indeed, several Romanian readers of this chapter complained of precisely this. Because the objection shares the value position of the Noicans by privileging professional philosophy, with its particular stake in professionalism, I refuse the challenge. Who is "truly professional," "a real philosopher," a "serious intellectual," and so forth, is less important for my purposes than that the Noicans and the ethnophilosophers were engaged in a hostile dialogue about the definition of philosophy and culture. Inspecting their dialogue helps us to understand what each of them stood for and, from this, the larger field of culture in its relation to politics. I will proceed, then, to outline their different answers to questions about what sorts of accumulated capital are the "stock" upon which philosophy should draw and where this stock resides (in print, in souls), what raw materials are needed for good philosophical production, and what are the grounds for competence.

The philosophy advocated by Noica's followers—and, as they presented him, by Noica himself—emphasized imported (western) values that provide raw material for speculation, the remaining raw material coming from one's individual talents ("genius"), with competence defined through professional or expert claims. Noica's pronouncements as reported in the *Journal* and his actual philosophic output made it clear that for him, the foundation of philosophy could not be built on any "inheritance" but that of Ancient Greek and more recent European philosophical thought. For Noica and his followers, the "means of philosophical production" were the stocks of cultural capital professional philosophers have accumulated over centuries, indeed millennia, of thought, largely in a written tradition: an immense stock of cultural values. This immense stock must in some sense be *reappropriated anew* by any individual claiming title to the discipline: one does not draw upon it automatically through membership in a community. Although it is true that Noica—unlike his followers—also found philosophically relevant "raw materials" in Romanian traditions, he most certainly would not regard this as sufficient basis for philosophical creation, which can occur only within a philosophical *discipline* of speculative thought established above all by the Greeks and the Germans.

Noicans defined "true" philosophy not just by placing it in a genealogy of written professional texts but also by delimiting it from science, the arts, or literary criticism (see below)—that is, by positioning it in a larger field of academic and expert specializations, rather than by its relation to national matters. They also insisted on stringent and specialist standards of professional competence—"the exigencies of something well done." This point was made in an article in which two Noicans compared their translation of fragments from Heidegger's

Being and Time with two other versions, one of them used in the philosophy department of Bucharest University. They concluded that the other two translations were far from accurate and gave a false image of the original, owing to the fact that the other translators *did not understand well enough the philosophical content* of the passages in question (Kleininger and Liiceanu 1987: 96). This was a blatant claim to superior professional status on grounds of competence in the European (rather than some other) philosophical tradition—that is, a blatant apology for professional expert status as understood in the West.

In contrast to the Noican view of philosophy was that of the ethnophilosophers, which was that contrary to the Noicans' denials, a major philosophy *can* be built up using the "raw material" of the national language and spirit. Far from being irrelevant or an obstacle to philosophy, these can produce model philosophical works (Stroe 1984; Macoviciuc 1986; Coja 1984). A perhaps extreme example of this view was the interest in *Geto-Dacian* philosophy (that is, the presumed philosophical precepts of one of the peoples seen as ancestral to present-day Romanians) and more generally in the *unwritten* philosophical wisdom of the Romanian people. These interests appeared in articles such as two on "Proverbs, the First Philosophy of the Romanians" (*Calendar* 1988) and "Elements of Unwritten Philosophy in Romanian Culture" (Iancu 1988), and a series of essays on the philosophy of the Geto-Dacians, by a low-ranking researcher at the Philosophy Institute (Vetişanu 1982i-iii). These articles carefully explained what characteristics a philosophy ought to have: a logical structure, a generalizing character, an ontological universe and a theoretical content, the emission of judgments, and the objective of finding general truth. That is, the articles displayed an explicit intention of defining what philosophy is. They also emphasized an *unwritten* accumulation of *popular* (rather than learned) philosophical wisdom, acquired simply by being *born into* the Romanian people (or so one gathers—the matter was not spelled out). This requires much less individualized acquisition through patient study than is implied in Noica's view. Here is an illustrative passage:

The archaic form of Romanian philosophy . . . is to be identified with *unwritten philosophy*. . . . It is an *implicit philosophy*, unsystematic, a state of the spirit, a spiritual attitude, a protophilosophy, on the basis of which there will develop an *explicit philosophy* as an exercise of the spirit, as doctrinaire thought . . . affirmed particularly through the means of individualized thinkers [as opposed to the collective mentality—k.v.]. Constantin Noica . . . refers to this wisdom as the beginning of knowledge, as the prehistory of philosophy. . . . Elements of unwritten philosophy have existed in Romanian culture ever since the Romanian people and its spirituality were formed . . . [and owe much to] the autochthonous vein of Geto-Dacian spirituality. . . . [Thus,] Romanian philosophy did not spring up belatedly . . . [but has been] a perennial value of Romanian spirituality (Iancu 1988, original emphases).

In this ethnophilosophical definition of philosophy, the prior accumulations upon which philosophy should draw are not other writings in philosophy but the reservoirs of Romanian spirituality. One article specified that what is accumulated—literally, amassed as treasure [*tezaurizat*]—in popular philosophy is *life experience* (rather than other people's writings or thoughts) (*Calendar* 1988). Insofar as written philosophy is important, it will be exclusively the Romanian philosophies of people like Lucian Blaga, "denigrated" by the "importers of European values"—that is, by the Noicans (Macoviciuc 1986). Thus, Romanian philosophy would be built not on the cultural accumulations embodied in other (western) philosophies but on some alternative kind of symbolic accumulation: perhaps one might call it racial.

None of this seems outrageous from a certain anthropological point of view, to which the notion of an "ethnophilosophy" resting on oral and experiential foundations is quite congenial. Parallel ideas are found even in some writing in social theory—one thinks of Gramsci's emphasis on "common sense" as the philosophy of the masses oppressed by the hegemonic ideologies professional philosophers have created. What makes these examples significant for my purposes is their express claims for a certain kind of philosophy, carefully defined as such, and resting on certain kinds of accumulation. Precisely by virtue of their invoking someone like Noica, these claims reveal a contest to define the field. Ethnophilosophers and their allies joined this contest for representativeness not merely by offering competing images of philosophy but by seeking to disqualify their opponents. They accused the Noicans (unlike Noica, they would say) of being *elitists* (Macoviciuc 1986), dogmatists and xenophiles (Stroe 1984), persons seeking to usurp a fame they otherwise could not earn (*Contemporanul* 1987), and generally hostile to the values of "the people" in both social and ethnic senses.

The opponents these writers perceived were not limited to Noicans, however, but included other philosophies as well, whose definition of the discipline they also contested. This is evident especially in complaints against persons who "anathematize Blaga and Pârvan so as to publish interviews with Heidegger and Lukács" (Vetişanu 1982iii). Thus Noicans (Heideggerians) and Marxist philosophers (Lukácsians) alike were accused of importing foreign values and dismissing the greats of indigenous philosophy.

In spite of [the admiration of Plato and Ovid for it], Geto-Dacian philosophy has been neither recognized nor included—even in its most general lines—in our dictionaries and encyclopedias. It was not even in the *History of Romanian Philosophy* . . . . What was the reasoning of our researchers, specializing in every philosophy except that of our country? "We have no texts"; "those are only statements *about* the philosophy of [Geto-Dacian priest] Zamolxe . . . " . . . The spiritual infirmity of these would-be specialists is apparent from their very negations. After all, from Socrates we have no texts either, only Plato's statements about him, yet his philosophy is in the encyclopedias (Vetişanu 1982ii).[19]

These ethnophilosophers waged war against all the persons entrenched in university departments and institutes, who monopolized the writing of dictionaries and encyclopedias (recall the protochronists' distress at the authors of school manuals and anthologies) and who defended symbolic accumulations that are *written*, failing to recognize the important sphere of *orality*. The targets of this sniping were not the Noicans, who had no institutional clout, but old "dogmatists" and others who manned the central fortresses of the discipline. For ethnophilosophers, these people clearly lacked elementary philosophical competence, which ethnophilosophy would define as above all a *spiritual* qualification (rather than an expert one).

This last observation reminds us that each of the parties we have been discussing—Noica himself, his followers, and ethnophilosophers—spoke from a marginal place in the institutions of culture, and the form of their marginality appears in the claims they made for philosophy. Noica's many decades of near-complete removal from normal employment in state institutions of culture and his lack of success in obtaining official resources for most of his projects accords well with his representing culture as absolutely autonomous, as a selection *by virtue of* exclusion; the only thing "institutionalized" about him that was relevant to claiming cultural preeminence was his *name* (Gheorghiu 1985b: 76–80). His main disciples were only somewhat less marginal to the formal institutions of philosophy and culture: Liiceanu was thrown out of his initial post in the Institute of Philosophy for refusing Communist party membership, and from there he went to a research post in the Institute of Plastic Arts—not exactly the center of philosophical production. There he joined fellow Noican Pleşu, who had lost his teaching post during the Transcendental Meditation scandal (see chapter 3). For both of these people, the publication and other professional channels

normal for philosophers were sharply restricted; except for their integration into the Writers' Union and their ties with important figures in
literature, their marginality would have been even greater. Equally marginal to the philosophy establishment were the ideas peddled by ethnophilosophers; their situation was comparable to that of the early protochronists (who joined them in attacking the followers of Noica),
denied professional visibility by an entrenched group in both philosophy and literature. This is amply attested by their complaints against
"dogmatists" of not only Noican but also materialist breed.

Each of these came to the contest for representativeness with a proposed strategy that would privilege certain values and therefore shift
the center of gravity within philosophy or culture itself (and perhaps
some resources as well) somewhat in the direction of the particular mar-
gin they occupied. The nature of the strategies proposed helps to reveal
more fully the field of values within which Romanian culture was being
produced, for any *credible* strategy must promote values that resonate to
at least some extent with values championed by groups closer to the
center; otherwise the claims would have no credibility at all. It was precisely the furor raised by Noica's School that suggests *credible* activity at
the margins of central values, activity that evoked opposition from
others who were also marginal and upwardly mobile.

One way to gain insight into people's view of the social world is by
looking for images of purity and pollution in their discourse, as I did
with the "truth-morality" of historians in chapter 6 (cf. Handler 1988:
47–50). How did Noicans and others envision pollution in the cultural
world, and what does this imply by way of purifying activity? For both
Noica and his followers, "The territory of culture must be protected
only from unwarranted ambitions, from the ignorance of the ignorant,
and from imposture" (Kleininger and Liiceanu 1987:85). That is, the
chief source of pollution is *ignorance*, *incompetence*, and *cultural imposture*, which means that purification comes from cultivating professional competence and disseminating its results.[20] For their opponents,
pollution comes from *external borrowing and imitation*, the introduction
of foreign cultural matter. Thus, the purifiers will be "[t]hose who do
not chase after imported universalist models, those who use their *own*
heads to think" (Stroe 1984). The two positions legitimate, respectively, an intellectual strategy in which accumulation of *knowledge* and
expertise takes pride of place, permitting a defense of *truth*, and a protectionist strategy aimed at *reducing foreign competition* for an internal
symbolic market and at defending cultural *self-sufficiency*. Each strategy

entailed a clear attitude toward the standard preferred by the others. The Noicans rejected cultural autarchy outright, regarding imports as integral to professional competence and local production; their opponents viewed claims to professional competence with skepticism, especially when borrowing underlay them, and supported a competence that is innate in the ethnic collectivity.

Each of these alternatives played upon values supported by one or another group more centrally situated in either the political apparatus or cultural institutions. Given my discussion of protochronism, I need not expand at length upon the values being supported by ethnophilosophy: these show once again how persons lacking control over professional institutions (the Writers' Union, the institutes and university departments of literature and philosophy) compensated by seeking an accommodation with the nationalism of the Party leadership. For none of these people was "professional competence" a significant value, and for at least some of them, national identity was a veritable obsession. Noica and his followers, by contrast, had no grounds for claiming a place in Romanian culture *other* than expertise and creation based upon it. These remained credible values *only* because of the appeal to reason, knowledge, and expert status that lies at the heart of dialectical materialism as a science of society. In appeals to competence, Noica and materialism had common ground: for example, Noica willingly recommended publication of a treatise written by a materialist philosopher, which he found truly excellent and original. The "official" philosophy shared more with Noicans than with ethnophilosophers, who therefore became alarmed at the credible threat Noicism posed despite its marginality. After all, Marxist philosophy and Noica shared a genealogy from the Greeks up through Kant and Hegel, a genealogy the others wanted to make philosophically irrelevant.

It is important to be clear, however, just how explicit a claim the Noicans, with their references to competence and expert status, were laying to a *specific* kind of social space. Like antiprotochronists with their emphasis on aesthetic values independent of politics and like those historians who insisted on scientific standards of research, Noica and his followers were resisting the invasion of the intellectual "space" by the values of the Party. Theirs was a poignant attempt to reconstruct and defend an eroding authority for specialization that was professionally rather than politically defined. It was the strategy of an intelligentsia excluded from power and anxious to maintain elite status through claims to expertise and cultural authority.

SALVATION THROUGH CULTURE AND THE
PRODUCTION OF URGENCY

This claim to expert status was not made strictly in its own name, however, but in the name of creating durable cultural values. It was a plea voiced by Noica, above all, for whom cultural creation informed by competence was not only the proper aim for intellectuals but the very basis of Romania's *salvation*. For Noica, cultural action was vital for the fate of the people:

[T]he destiny of peoples, according to Noica, passes through culture, and peoples who have not created great culture—like the Hittites or the Etruscans—have disappeared from history. Cultural capital [*sic*] and cultural production, and not its degree of participation in world events, are what assure a people's survival. The history of a people is therefore the history of its *culture*. Noica made of this an existential proposition; and he took it upon himself to such a degree that he gave testimony to it in both the interior and the exterior order of his life. He chose to serve Romanian culture with a passion which proved that not just culture pure and simple was at stake . . . but the very being of a community, to which only culture could give the depth and degree of certainty essential to it. Otherwise we cannot understand the persistent hint of missionarism in the principal moments of his life and in his works themselves (Liiceanu 1983: 234, original emphasis).

As Noica expressed the same idea to me, "The fate of Romanians as a people is to disappear if they do not create something truly remarkable." This cultural missionarism, pursued within images of salvation and with an overriding sense of urgency and desperation, were exhibited to some extent by others discussed in this book (D. Prodan, the antiprotochronists, some protochronists as well), but its unusually strong presence in the work of Noica and his followers has led me to postpone discussion of it until now.

The missionarism behind Noica's advocacy of culture as the only means by which peoples could continue to exist—could be saved from extinction[21]—was noted by many commentators. As one reviewer summarized it, for Noica culture was not *a* form, but *the only* form, of salvation (Ungureanu 1983). Noica's salvational idea was sometimes limited to the notion of *survival* (culture is the people's only chance to survive [Doinaş 1984]), but it was also colored by the religious associations Noica occasionally invited—his constant reference, for example, to the biblical parable of the prodigal son. Of all the areas of culture, he said, only theology offered a direct route into philosophy. He encouraged or permitted himself to be linked with religion's meanings, most strikingly in his request to be buried in the hermitage near Păltiniş (where, following Orthodox monastic custom, his grave is marked with nothing but his first name). In the eulogy delivered at his funeral, the Transylvanian archbishop (Plămădeală 1987) emphasized the religious dimension visible in some of Noica's early writings: parallels of himself with the Apostle Paul, quotations from the Bible, repeated use of the words "savior," "spirituality," "humbleness," and so forth.[22] Many others also wrote of Noica in monastic or religious imagery (Simion 1983; Teodorescu 1987), sometimes in extended form (Steinhardt 1988), and both Noicans and others spoke of his style of teaching as an "initiation into a mystery" (Liiceanu 1983: 161, 227; Ciocârlie 1988: 23).

Noica's followers (especially Liiceanu) often used a similar language of salvation, of spiritual refreshment and purification. For example:

Noica sent us to the great texts and instruments of European culture, . . . as wellsprings for a spirit that is not closed up in provincial frustrations and vanities. For our generation, he represents a guarantee of the spirit in its cultural variant, as a spiritual purification that must be maintained and propagated through ongoing access to the verified sources of this purification. Perhaps never before in Romania has culture achieved such a value as the instrument of salvation. To master Greek, Latin and German, to translate and edit—in a world wounded unto death by twenty years of dogmatism—Plato and Plotinus, Kant, Kierkegaard, Nietzsche, Freud, or Heidegger, to write erudite and refined books—all these were moments in a ritual of liberation of the spirit. . . . This discreet and unspectacular liberation . . . was and still is the form in which certain great values of today's Romanian spirituality will survive (Liiceanu 1983: 232–233, 236–237).

Similarly, "[T]he endpoint of Noica's teaching was cultural creation as a strange form of modern sacrality" (Liiceanu 1983: 235). Such imagery expressed not just Noica's aims but the mission of his followers also. Liiceanu has said that he published his *Journal* so as to communicate a cultural experience that was "salvational," a word he has used repeatedly in connection with culture.

By constructing his cultural mission as one of salvation and equating a people's culture with its life, Noica brought the penumbra of religious meanings associated with such saving missions into the service of his own project. This project amounted to gaining attention for his kind of intellectual activity by tying it directly to the Nation's fate—by what I called in chapter 1 the "defense of the Nation." For such a project, religious imagery was apt not only because it might win attention from persons for whom religion was still a value—one opposed to Marxism-Leninism—but also because the church too provided centuries of "defending the Nation" through a comparable strategy of assuming its values would outlast those of secular regimes.

The form of salvational enterprise Noica (and his followers, especially) adopted was not, however, a leisurely one: among its salient features was an urgent, almost apocalyptic, sense, which the imagery of salvation played an important role in sustaining. Like many other Romanian intellectuals, Noica's followers sought to mobilize public attention by continually invoking the *urgency* of the task at hand. From the preface to Pleşu's book on ethics:

The reader will note a certain disproportion between the scope of the problems attacked and their laconic, if not indeed brisk, treatment. Written with a constant sense of *urgency*, the text continually indulges in suggestion and sketchiness . . . (Pleşu 1988: 9, original emphases).

In another passage he again referred to "the *urgency* of a preoccupation with ethics" (p. 30). Liiceanu often spoke of the present moment as a "moment of spiritual urgency" (e.g., 1987: 150). Others noted the sense of urgency also:

Noica proposes virtually that his disciples behave as if the world were about to end, or is in any case irremediably condemned, thus all that counts is to preserve wisdom (along with the wise) (Antohi and Petrescu n.d.: 14).

From the opposing side, a protochronist jeered at the "alarmist tone" in which Liiceanu wrote about protochronism "as if he were talking about an invasion of locusts" (Sorescu 1984: 4). The themes of culture as salvation and urgency come together nicely in a passage from another Noican:

As I understand it, if the *Journal* succeeded in troubling people's spirits, this was not because through it they finally had the revelation of Culture but only to the extent that, in a moment critical for Life, they had the revelation of culture *as life*, or, perhaps more exactly, of a life that can be saved through culture lived with authenticity and desperation (Kleininger in Liiceanu 1987: 120).

The question of urgency appeared frequently enough in print but even more often in direct encounters. In innumerable conversations Romanian intellectuals of very diverse persuasions pressed upon me and others present the urgency of their mission to support "true" culture or to resist the incursions of power into the cultural sphere. They spoke of the "desperation" with which small countries seek to define a place for themselves in the world; of the sense of having no time to waste, no place or situation in which they felt secure; of their existence as an "experience at the limit," needing wild attachment to the last values worth struggling for; of the dread that they would fail to develop fast enough the cultural values to which they adhered so passionately. Their intensity of expression and depth of feeling were remarkable. Some intellectuals even commented upon this urgency as something peculiar: one Noican asked me whether I knew of movements of similar "cultural desperation" (his words) elsewhere in Eastern Europe or whether it was peculiar to Romania.

We might see this sense of urgency, in the manner of Bourdieu and similar analysts, as a strategy by which a certain group of intellectuals enhances its claims to public attention and status. Promoting a sense of urgency would speed up the process of redefining a marginal situation within one's field or of repositioning one's marginal field itself, closer to the center. Zygmunt Bauman offers an interpretation of this sort. He identifies intellectuals as a structural element in societies whose individual members suffer from a socially produced "incapacity" to conduct their life business on their own. This makes people dependent on the advice or assistance of others—intellectuals, experts, and so forth—who thereby dominate them:

[T]he intensity and scope of their domination depends on how acute is the sense of uncertainty or deprivation caused by the absence of knowledge in an area serviced by a given group of sages, teachers or experts. More importantly still, it depends on the latter's ability to create or intensify such a sense of uncertainty or deprivation; to produce, in other words, the social indispensability of the kind of knowledge they control (Bauman 1987*b*: 20).

On this interpretation, the urgency expressed by Noica's followers and other intellectuals would enable them to intensify their claims to domination, based on their particular expertise and competence: notions about salvation and urgency were vehicles for promoting their own indispensability. The religious overtones of the idea of salvation, Bauman might argue, give these philosophers something close to Foucault's "pastoral power"—that is, claims to elite status based on qualities exercised "for the benefit" of the dominated (Bauman 1987*b*: 19).

Although these interpretations doubtless contain much truth, anyone who has ever had a strong feeling is going to find them insufficient. Any analysis that aims to "unmask" surface manifestations (feelings, ideological expressions, defense mechanisms) by exploring the motive forces underlying them should also attempt to tie those underlying motive forces to the particulars of the surface forms. From a sociological point of view, one ought at least to specify how these "strategies," *qua* properties of the cultural field, become translated into passionate conviction. I will argue here that unlike cultural producers in the West, who often present an image of *disinterest* from the political and economic supports of their cultural prestige (Bourdieu 1980: 262) and whom Bourdieu sees as *misrecognizing* the link between these, Romanian intellectuals cultivating urgency were rendering in fully recognized form a fundamental characteristic of their situation in contemporary Romania.[23]

In general terms, a cluster of linked emotions, including a sense of urgency and a related sense of anxiety, was constituted by the workings of Romania's command economy. The intensity of shortage, endemic to Romania's highly centralized form of socialism and aggravated by 1980s austerity policies, produced continual uncertainty as to whether and where the basic necessities of daily life could be obtained. Augmenting this were the countless ways in which the political center expropriated the populace of its initiative and control over the requirements for existence. Further anxiety and uncertainty came from the actual or presumed workings of the repressive apparatus, above all the secret police, which was believed omnipresent. Here we see power as a "productive" force, in Foucault's sense, the products being a certain kind of emotion and the experience of incapacity and dependency Bauman speaks of. In a daily experience shot through with externally induced uncertainty and anxiety, subjective feelings of desperation and urgency were not surprising. To communicate a sense of urgency about one's project for saving Romanian culture was, under these circumstances, simply the intellectuals' way of transposing into the sphere of their work the tensions that permeated their entire quotidian existence.[24] It made heightened claims for the one area in which they felt efficacious.

More specifically, certain properties of the field of cultural production meshed with these general tendencies. Bauman, defining intellectuals as a "spot" or "territory" "inhabited by a shifting population, and open to invasions, conquests and legal claims as all ordinary territories are" (1987*b*: 19), argues that a characteristic of the modern world is the invasion of this territory and the erosion of intellectuals' claims to expert status. As the market increasingly becomes the main site for judgments, for authority, and for forming tastes, polities no longer require the "legislating" functions of intellectuals (ibid., 159, 168). In Romania of the 1980s, the "spot" of intellectuals was also under siege—not because the market had made intellectual production irrelevant, as Bauman argues for the West, but because a portion of expertise had been institutionalized in the form of Party rule, which assimilated other intellectual platforms. By reducing the spheres of uncertainty that a cultural intelligentsia could plausibly claim to "manage"—even while increasing the sphere of uncertainty itself—and by making Party-controlled experts and planners the only people with any hope of managing uncertainty effectively, the Party produced a crisis for intellectuals. The leadership's vogue for national ideology enabled those of protochronist persuasion (whose success was also, for them, an urgent matter) to invade and secure territories formerly in other hands, increasing the sense of desperation of people threatened with "eviction" from their space.

In a word, the terrain of intellectuals was gradually being brought under the disposition and control of the political apparatus and into the "corporate property" that contained all the society's means of production. Within this corporate property there was little room for *individual* creation, *individual* symbolic accumulation, such as those the Noicans favored. Their desperation and sense of urgency were suited to a fight that was, and was perceived as, unequal. Its stakes were not just one or another cerebral specialty but people's sources of livelihood, and it struck at that point so underestimated in analyses of objectively located strategies, tactics, and interests:[25] people's "interest" in a meaningful life. Perhaps the Noicans expressed this urgency more intensely than others because their definition of philosophy and their cultural project were relatively more marginal than others within the intellectual "spot"—more institutionally marginal than writers, for instance, and more symbolically and theoretically marginal than history. But all fields shared in the same reorganization of territory that threatened to render certain forms of intellectual activity meaningless or nonexistent and their proponents superfluous.

These comments on salvation and urgency are meant to fill out the otherwise-scrawny notions of "interest" and "strategy" which would reduce all intellectual activity to a form of scheming. In my view, one must include in the "strategies" proper to the cultural field some mention of the textures of experience within it—textures that should be analyzed in relation to the kind of society in which action is occurring, rather than simply elided within a model of "markets for symbolic goods."[26] This criticism is not to deny, however, that the Noicans' messages of salvation and urgency were also part of a larger struggle for

power, being waged through arguments about the nature of philosophy and the suitability of various pretenders to its throne. It was a
struggle to bring a greater share of central resources into the service of a
particular set of intellectual values. In the case of Noica's School, the
values so urgently defended were both a particular kind of expertise—a
specific definition of philosophy—and also the more general terrain of a
cultural production relatively free of *partinost* and indigenist content,
and openly oriented to Europe.

REPRESENTATIVENESS AND THE PROCESS
OF CULTURAL REPRODUCTION

One final element of the struggle for representativeness,
the claims made for Noica's "paideic model," will lead us into the more
conventionally political implications of Noica's School.[27] Both in its
subtitle (*A Paideic Model in Humanist Culture*) and in its preface, Liiceanu's *Journal* announced that it intended to offer a model of cultural
training that was "*exemplary*." Such wording makes this claim the heavy
artillery of a battle as to whose definition best represents culture. The
stakes behind such an assertion, however, were somewhat different
from those covered so far, or from the ones discussed in chapter 5 (a
struggle to set the criteria for evaluating and disseminating literary
works). To speak of a "paideic model" was to launch the very touchy
subject of cultural reproduction: who would control the processes by
which culture is transmitted to the next generation, and in what institutions would this occur. The Noican claim to define "culture" now entailed a program not just for producing and distributing it but for mo-
nopolizing or directing its reproduction through time. Thus, what was
chiefly a matter of *contested valorification* of culture in the case of literary
criticism becomes a matter of *contested reproduction* of culture in Noica's
case: would reproduction take place within or outside the instances that
were officially authorized?

Tied to this was a major element of Noica's cultural campaign, not
yet mentioned: his search for twenty-two geniuses. He described it to
Liiceanu as follows:

I have often been asked to convince Eliade to return for a visit. The idea then
came to me to tell those who made this request that we don't need to bring
Eliade back, because in fact we have him here already, and not just one of him
but twenty-two times over. If there are 22 million Romanians today, then one
young person in a million probably has genius. But for these twenty-two geniuses we must have trainers (Liiceanu 1983: 172).

Proposing himself as trainer, Noica proceeded to knock on the doors of local authorities, asking that gifted young people be employed for a time in fictive jobs the way top athletes were, so as to perfect their capacity for cultural performance. This quest constituted Noica's most direct assault on the formal channels of cultural transmission.

The "paideic model" was the only aspect of Noica's program to which his external admirers took exception. They strove to pin it on his followers by saying that Noica had intended to make culture accessible to a wider audience but the disciples had perverted this into a paideia that was "elitist." Challenges to Noica's paideic example asked what, if anything, in the disciples' experience could be considered exemplary (e.g, Geană 1986: 96) or repudiated the idea that anything "paideic" had in fact occurred:

[Noica] meditates and behaves like a philosopher (*I refer to his writings*), but [Liiceanu behaves] unphilosophically. . . . Liiceanu missed the lesson that he could have learned from Noica . . . : the lesson of dialectics. The relation of teacher and disciple would then have justified itself. *Such a relation is not present here*" (Stroe 1984, emphases added).

The first sentence of this comment reveals one of the most frequent devices for challenging the "paideic model": a rhetorical separation of Noica's *person/life* from his *work/writings*. Liiceanu and Pleşu in particular, among Noica's followers, insisted that Noica's existence, his person and his biography, were more important than the content of his work. Reminding readers, for example, that Noica had denied the importance of his biography, which was reducible to his books, Pleşu comments:

[T]hose who believe this—and Noica in the first place—are mistaken. . . . Circumstances in today's Romania are such that what counts is not Noica's *opus* but more importantly his *simple existence*. His "role" is more significant than his "philosophy." It might eventually emerge that his whole speculative apparatus, with his Romanian etymologies . . . will prove of secondary or strictly "historical" importance, compared with the memory of his *presence*, salutary for several generations of Romanian intellectuals trapped by the consequences of a tragic formative void. . . . What is exemplary is precisely Noica's *biography*. His opus is merely important in a certain academic sense (1985: 5, original emphases).

What Pleşu underscores is the experience of cultural transmission that Noica offered his followers, an experience they play up by purposely downgrading his work, with its "Romanian etymologies." The emphases of their opponents were, of course, precisely the reverse:

The path toward Noica's thought does not go to Păltiniş [the location of the paideic experience—k.v.] but through his *writings*. To go to Păltiniş is only to become mired in the anecdotal and the accidental. The true path is rather the path of the concept in its dialectical purity. . . . This *Journal* has not convinced us that there occurred in Păltiniș an encounter between teacher and disciple (Stroe 1984).

Here Stroe questions the personalized model for transmitting culture, so unlike the forms of public education. By putting Noica's biography in parentheses, he also suppresses Noica's fascist past, embarrassing to the position critics like him had staked out on the ideological terrain. For these people, it was the national content of Noica's writings that counted most.

Such reservations concerning Noica's paideia encourage our suspicion that these critics were speaking from a position close to the political apparatus and in defense of its means. Despite Noica's refusal to distance himself verbally from power, at the level of practices his paideia was utterly opposed to the regime of practices implemented by the authorities. The antithesis was not just in the obvious fact of his promoting cultural values and grounds of cultural accumulation at odds with official definitions (western "imports" and so forth). Nor was it just in his effort to foster *thinking* and the capacity for independent thought, instead of rote memorization and mechanical repetition, or a "standard of living" defined in spiritual rather than material terms. Noica's "School"—his way of transmitting cultural values—instituted a wholly different relation of authority: an antihierarchical distribution of speaking and listening roles, individualized rather than mass processing of students, a subjection to authority that was voluntary rather than enforced.[28] One reviewer observed that among the most striking features of *Letters* was its plea for *love* as part of authority (Breban 1988: 62).

This "school" contained none of the panoply of power-serving disciplinary procedures that Foucault has revealed in the conventional medium of education. Instead of the discipline of a small classroom arranged in a grid, in which the body of the pupil accustoms itself to hours of obedient and docile immobility, the practices of Noica's "school" were open and peripatetic. Mentor and disciple moved freely between the undifferentiated space of Noica's room and the hills outside; climbing the slopes was the body's accompaniment to the mind's ascent into thought. Noica promoted a "return to culture" that was to "the culture of Adam, preceding the fall into the sin of a culture that has been officialized and institutionalized. But to achieve this . . . he had to reinvent Socratism and make it live again" (Liiceanu 1983: 235). These very characteristics of his paideia bore fruit in the careers of those who were "subjected" to it, as the following section will show.

From Cultural Creation to Political Action

During yesterday's walk, Gabi asked me two inappropriate questions. The first: in what does philosophy's efficacy consist? The philosopher puts the world in order, he says, . . . but the world pays no attention. The second, perhaps more inappropriate: given the transience of this world, to what end all our strivings? . . . "How does philosophy enter into the world," is what Gabi is asking me (Noica, in Liiceanu 1983: 188).

The contest over representativeness between the Noica School and other kinds of philosophy or cultural values was only one form of the politics in which Noica and his followers engaged. Other forms involved heated and more or less explicit arguments among themselves, about the relation culture ought to have to power: about their own activities as intellectuals in relation to the state. These arguments divided participants who would otherwise find themselves on a single side of cultural arguments—that is, they complicate the lines of force that emerged in chapter 5. Antiprotochronists were by no means squarely lined up behind Liiceanu (see, e.g., reviews by Dinescu 1986; Doinaş 1984; Iorgulescu 1987; Marino 1987; Papahagi 1987; Simion 1983), nor were all Noica's followers of one mind. Their disagreements centered upon two themes that were linked to one another: what intellectual disciplines best promote Romanian culture (the claims of philosophy and literary criticism are weighed against one another), and how should claims to cultural representativeness be tied to considerations of ethics or morality. The questions were linked because positions on the second one became significant in adjudicating the first, and because both were a cover under which the participants developed a strategy for an intellectual opposition to power.

UNIFYING THE FIELD OF OPPOSITION: PHILOSOPHY, LITERARY CRITICISM, AND ETHICS

Among the debatable views Noica expressed in the *Journal* was his insistence that philosophy is the only true guardian of cultural creation and that all other areas of intellectual life should acknowledge its preeminence. He addressed this view particularly to writers and literary critics. Although nearly all of Noica's close associates and most reviewers of the *Journal* took strong exception to his "philosophical impe-

rialism" and intolerance, Liiceanu continued to defend it until late in
the exchanges of *Letters*, for which discussion of this problem formed
the intellectual backbone.[29]

From Marga's summary of Noica's work, it appears likely that
Noica's motives for placing philosophy above literary criticism were
much more complicated than most participants realized. In subordinating "judgments" (the sphere of criticism) to "reason" and "concepts"
(the sphere of philosophy), he was preparing his more general criticism
of modern rationality. Noica understood, with Kant, that any system of
judgments emanates from a particular model of reason; if one aims to
redress the problems of modernity by revising the model of reason
underlying those problems, this implies a consequent revision in the
system of judgments as well.[30] Philosophy is therefore the most fundamental endeavor because it is the only one addressing fundamental
questions about the very nature of man in the world. On this reading,
Noica hoped to move entirely outside the constraints of the protochronism debate, for example—concerning who is empowered to define values—by calling into question the entire ground on which such a
debate was premised. This, in my view (see chapter 6), is the only move
that promises to transform ideological discourse.

The discussion never attained such lofty heights, for most reviewers
turned it into a sort of turf war in a low-level struggle for cultural representativeness and for "modeling the souls of the young" (Liiceanu
1987: 150), as people argued over which kind of endeavor, philosophy
or literary criticism and artistic creation, had contributed more to Romanian culture and offered the *preconditions* for the other. (For example,
one reviewer contended that without the reeditions of earlier philosophy *literary critics* had pioneered in the 1950s, philosophy would have
had no place to work: not philosophy but literature cleared the cultural
arena of dogmatism and socialist realism, enabling real cultural creation
to recommence in all fields [Papahagi 1987]). People demanded how
Liiceanu and Noica could envision a culture that excluded the arts
(Doinaş 1984), accused Noica of "imperialism" and "cultural hooliganism" (see Liiceanu 1987: 196, 198),[31] and declared outright that it
was precisely Noica's intolerant rejection of the validity of fields other
than philosophy that had driven them out of his immediate orbit (Paleologu 1980, and in Liiceanu 1987: 89).

The discussion may have begun as one of representativeness, but as it
was refined in the course of *Letters*, it came to be also about what institutional framework is more suited to protecting cultural values. This

is especially apparent in an exchange between Liiceanu and Sorin Vieru (Liiceanu 1987: 138–181), where Liiceanu makes it clear that the question is not chiefly an abstract one concerning "rights" to represent culture (what he called supremacy *in principle*) but the actual, concrete situation of different kinds of cultural activity within Romanian political life (*historical* supremacy). Because the postwar suppression of all but materialist philosophy left literati no interlocutors in the world of theory, he says, the empty space was filled by theoretically uninformed criticism. Critics who simply do not know what they are doing comment on books indiscriminately, regardless of their qualifications, and total ignoramuses feel entitled to assess works like Noica's, for which they have nothing approaching the proper competence (a reference to protochronist commentators) (1987: 147–148, 170–172).[32] Liiceanu implies, furthermore, that owing to its politicization, criticism no longer actually assesses *value*, having been reduced to "delight in power. Here is born the tyranny of the administrative in the modern world" (1987: 174).

What Liiceanu appears to be saying is that to grant literary criticism equal status with philosophy *in the present moment* would be to court disaster. Although allies of the Noica School may still weigh heavily within the Writers' Union, the offensive of its enemies into the very corridors of power means that this cannot be presumed to last: the entire domain of literary production may well become the playing field of protochronism. One must not, under these circumstances, make an argument *in principle* for the equivalence of philosophy and literary criticism in determining what cultural values should be promoted and what should be killed. It is almost as if Liiceanu is arguing that only a decentering, a marginalization, of cultural production can preserve "true" values intact. A strongly institutionalized field like literature may be (in the wrong hands) a more dangerous site for determining cultural values than a marginal field such as the "dethroned" philosophy of the 1980s, and particularly Noica's marginalized version of cultural transmission and standards for value. (We might note that such an argument accords with Liiceanu's not having, himself, a strong institutional position to defend.)

All the evidence in the structure of *Letters*, however, suggests that Liiceanu was alone in upholding this strategy for protecting the values he espoused—values that our analysis must continue to regard as subjective judgments among a larger range of possible judgments, none of which should be analytically considered "true." As their discussion of a cultural-political strategy proceeded, what prevailed instead was a plea for *pluralism*, voiced by several of the most eloquent letter-writers in Liiceanu's collection. They argued that hierarchizations like Noica's, together with all disciplinary divisions, should be dropped and the validity of *all* "genuine" cultural values recognized and defended—in other words, that the political assault upon "genuine" values required all persons supporting them to close ranks by acknowledging and accepting diverse specializations. This in turn would mean consciously refusing provocations over representativeness within and between disciplines, so as to focus on the larger struggle to defend the worthiest values for culture as a whole. To overdo a metaphor, these producers argued to pool their capitals so as to respond more effectively to the concentrated power that defined their productive environment.

My discussion states the issues too baldly, perhaps, and does not render them in quite the terms used by the participants. In addition, the pluralist strategy emerged as much through the structure of *Letters* and the sequence of its exchanges as through outright statement.[33] Nonetheless, conversations with other intellectuals inside and outside philosophy, on topics unrelated to the Noica School, convince me that any argument for pluralism was consciously intended as a political means for opposing centralization. To advocate pluralism, whether in a highly obscure theory of the nature of the Absolute or in a reminiscence between a philosopher and a poet, was to unify the field of opposition to power.

Arguments for pluralism were one way in which this field was unified. A second was to insist that cultural action be ethically or morally mediated. What brought the disputatious *Letter*-writers together was their common agreement—and common opposition to Noica—on the principle that cultural creations are valid only in the light of moral scrutiny. All insisted, that is, that "creation in and of itself is not a moral act," that "culture is not beyond good and evil" (Enescu 1987): that supremacy should be accorded not just to whoever possesses universally recognized cultural authority but to whoever offers a model of public conduct (Gheorghiu 1988*a*:5). Noica's public conduct was to *withdraw* from public life. He chided his followers for their urge to defy Benda's dictum against forming a pact with the times, for wanting to "climb down into the arena" to struggle with earthly powers rather than keeping their sights on the "Idea" (see Liiceanu 1983: 201–207). Here is the significance of the "separations" so central to Liiceanu's two books, for it was precisely with Noica's model of public conduct that all his followers at length parted company, affirming that one cannot claim to be a person of culture if one declines an ethically motivated engagement with power. To refuse such ethics, they said, is to align oneself with the forces of rule, which is just what Noica did with his Romanian philosophy and his refusal of public distance from protochronism.

Having separated from Noica over the question of engagement, his followers offered a new model for linking culture with the defense of the Nation. Whereas Noica's equation of culture with the Nation's existence enabled him to defend the Nation simply by thinking, his followers came to defend it by culturally informed political action. The argument was made in an essay by Pleşu, "The Sense of Culture in the Contemporary World," reprinted in his book *Minima Moralia* (1988). The book's agenda is to discuss how one can survive decently in the gap between moral unclarity and edification, which I interpret to mean, how can one manage to live with oneself in the appalling conditions of today's Romania? Inquiring into the place of culture in such a circumstance, Pleşu answers, "Culture is the most adequate modality of subsisting in the conditions of that gap" (1988: 108), which in the context of the book means that culture is the best qualification for making moral judgments. Moreover, culture in the *absence* of such judgments is worthless:

By "wisdom" we do not mean . . . [something] beyond all worldly exigencies. We have in mind that wisdom which accepts the condition of the worldly community and of which the community has need: the wisdom that wants to radiate outward not by its simple *presence* but through discourse and public action (Pleşu 1988: 89–90, original emphasis).

In case anyone has missed the point, there is his book's dedication: "To Constantin Noica. Had I not known him, I could not have written this book. Had I listened to him, I would not have written it."

In opting for an ethics of engagement with the world rather than Noica's professed distance from it, Noica's followers and others in cultural life reproached him for many things, starting with his refusal to disown the uses to which protochronists were putting him (Liiceanu 1983: 139). They objected to his naiveté in ignoring the conditions of production that some of his grander schemes required, conditions that would ultimately compromise his ends. For example, in his quest to find and train the "twenty-two geniuses," he pleaded with political authorities for support, apparently unmindful—or worse, uncaring—of the public legitimation they would gain by association with his name;

unmindful, as well, of how accepting public funds for his "elitist" and potentially antisystemic project would necessarily compel changes in it. (The authorities were not so unmindful: they mostly refused his requests, availing themselves only of his name.) Noica always hoped to meet with Ceaușescu and plead for his program of intellectual athletics, with no thought for how that might look.

He was also derided for imagining that power would be interested in his schemes at all: "One cannot expect to go 'genius-hunting' as if genius had no historicity and no context for its realization" (Șerban 1984). "Doesn't he see that football players are preferred to philosophers, and that his efforts, justifying themselves through *Geist*, are made ridiculous by the *Zeitgeist*?" (Antohi and Petrescu n.d.: 6). Some people accused him of wanting to found a "logocracy" every bit as confining as the current regime, of regretting that it was not *his* philosophy that had been dogmatized (see Liiceanu 1987: 160–164). One of the sharpest criticisms labeled Noica's discourse "totalizing" and observed that thinkers like Foucault and Deleuze see such discourses as adjuncts to power (Antohi and Petrescu n.d.: 2). Noica made himself available, these critics objected, as an apologist of power, a prestigious annex of the propaganda machine, who carried an authority essential to a demagogic leadership. His annexation was the more likely as he vacillated in his relations with power, *because* Noica saw the ethical implications of cultural production as secondary and failed to realize that the battle was unequal, with power disposing of superior weapons available uniquely to it (ibid., 3–4).

Given the antisystemic implications of Noica's paideia and the other respects in which his work and activities did not fit with the emphases of rule, one suspects that these reproaches overconstructed Noica's relation to power. If so, the reason is probably that by defining themselves against a constructed image of political disinterest, Noica's associates were clarifying their strategy, creating a cultural resistance that was *explicit* in place of Noica's *implicit* one. Overt evidence of such explicit resistance—evidence that this School, which I called "marginal" in the introduction to this chapter as well as to this book, had consequences for Romanian society greater than the implications listed above—was to come in March of 1989, when poet Mircea Dinescu was thrown out of the Party and his job in the Writers' Union for having given a critical interview to a French newspaper. In response, seven persons signed a public letter of protest to the president of the Union—an oppositional gesture with very few precedents in Ceaușescu's Romania. Two of those seven (who included some other prominent antiprotochronists) were in what I call Noica's School. Their significance for the movement that overthrew Ceauşescu's dictatorship can be gauged from this book's Conclusion.

In departing from Noica, his followers took a path of more direct confrontation with formal authority, a path that originated in the tactics they were developing through the medium of *Letters* and their other writings. These writings not only produced an alliance among certain philosophers and certain artists, critics, and writers (the result of *Letters*). They not only instituted a new communicative style, one of "directness" and "sincerity" in place of the hieratized static communications of the authorities (see below). They not only participated in a wider movement in which pluralism was being philosophically theorized in explicit opposition to political centralization, and in which treatments of ethics emerged not from a "neutral theoretical interest but from all kinds of circumstances of daily life" (Pleşu 1988: 7) (this statement prefaces a text that treats morality as NOT a matter of obedience and that at all points opposes its pretensions and its precepts to those prevalent in the official realm). They also engaged in actions then very rare in "passive" Romania, actions the authorities felt compelled to break up.

NOICISM, POWER, AND THE QUESTION OF AUDIENCE

Although several Noicans acknowledged to me in conversation that the attempt to insulate Noica from manipulation by "the nationalists" was a conscious aim for their writings, Liiceanu's account of his motives in publishing his two books added three significant reasons to this. They were, first, with the *Journal*, to publicize Noica's paideic model; second, with *Letters*, to offer a different form of communication, one of sincerity and openness in which "truths" are told[34] and feelings clearly expressed, in place of the duplicity and ambiguity so characteristic of communications in Romania; and third, with respect to both books, an effort at popularization, at making philosophy and its issues accessible to a wider public and not simply an erudite matter for a few specialists. Using a somewhat more abstract language brings out more fully the antisystemic content of these three aims: to advocate a form of cultural reproduction different from the official one in both its institutions and its practices; to substitute for a communicative style based

upon indirection and suppression one positing directness and unmask-
ing; and to democratize exposure both to philosophy and to a particular definition of culture.

All three of these are part of what I referred to in chapter 4 as the
formation of a *cognizant public*, that is, building an audience (or maintaining one already in existence) that recognizes and supports the definitions of value upon which the cultural status of a given group of intellectuals rests. Noica's "paideic model," as already shown, employed
mechanisms for reproducing culture and values that were not those of
the regime. The attempt at greater "directness" and "sincerity" would
expand the audience to whom a communication might be comprehen-
sible, for as anyone knows who has tried to decipher a communication
in aesopic language or specialist jargon, such encoded messages presuppose a community of shared knowledge so esoteric that normally educated censors or readers do not recognize its significance. Any retreat
from aesopianism or specialist jargon opens a message to more hearers.
At the same time, however, to invoke "sincerity" as opposed to "duplicity" presupposes a contractual understanding of communication,
in which sender and hearer agree to accept the sender's account that
his or her intentions are not deceptive.[35] Thus, the sender lays claim to
somewhat more control over the reading, which may help to fend off
rival interpretations. Finally, the "democratizing" objective to which
Liiceanu referred should not be confused—especially in this case—with
a deprofessionalization of the domain in question; rather, it would increase the chance that the public would know enough to *acknowledge* a
given claim to professional competence, granting their attention to that
claim in preference to some other.

The Noicans' concern with enlarging the audience for culture, particularly for philosophy, was apparent in many activities that they also
shared with intellectuals in other fields. A good example is the con-
scientious—if much obstructed—effort to make available to Romanian
readers the important works of world culture. Noica and his followers
toiled away endlessly at translations of Plato, Heidegger, Hegel, and so
on, just as others laboriously translated Hume, Habermas, Peirce, and
Bourdieu, not to mention Shakespeare, Marquez, Eco, and hosts of
other foreign writers. (Indeed, several Romanians who read parts of the
present book objected that by focusing on marginal phenomena and
specific debates, I leave out the most common activities of many intellectuals: translating, and writing in their domains of expertise.) One
might see translations from sociology, philosophy, and so on, as the

import-based creation of "means of production" for further cultural work in Romania; yet people spoke of translation as if the issue was, rather, to create means of *consumption*, to form public tastes (generally in a pro-western direction). Because any good professional learns the languages necessary to competence in a field (Noica would say), those who benefit from a translation are people *outside* the specialty, or students with a potential interest—in philosophy, say, who can be won to it by encountering Plato's or Heidegger's thought in a form other than the canned version of university textbooks. Translations, therefore, were part of creating a larger public for culture, a sort of raising of the spiritual standard of living, parallel to the state's claims to raise the material standard of living. At the same time, however, they were like "viruses" loosed into the mechanism by which culture was officially transmitted. They were a form of political action. (Perhaps here is another motive for the protochronists' opposition to "imported techniques," which would disrupt the process whereby *their* values were instituted.) This was true of any translation but particularly true of those in fields as central as philosophy was to legitimating the Communist party.

The Noicans' concern with "raising the spiritual standard of living" received its most eloquent formulation in Liiceanu's 1985 essay, "Philosophy and the Feminine Paradigm of the Listener."[36] A skilful effort to defend Noica against accusations from various quarters and to insulate him against protochronism, the essay separates Noica's *pronouncements* from his *practices* and shows that, contrary to the "elitism" both friendly and hostile critics saw in his pronouncements, his practices were profoundly democratic and accessible. Noica claimed to be building a philosophy informed by the systematizing pretensions of mathematics, argues Liiceanu, yet his practice was closer to literature. He hoped through thought to *order* the world [recall the accusations of totalitarianism and logocracy], yet his practice showed a nonauthoritarian way of radiating into the world through an intimate relation between philosopher and listener, evident in his way of writing. Finally, Noica professed to accept the German definition of philosophy's proper goal (emphasizing its *scientific* character, via the notion of the *concept*), yet his practice toward this goal introduced the innovation of an *epic principle*: the idea that any thought worth pursuing must be *narratable*. An excellent example of this was Noica's interpretation of Hegel's phenomenology (called *Stories about Man*), whose chapter headings resemble those of an epic adventure (e.g., "The Unusual Accidents of Consciousness," "The Extraordinary Adventures of Arthur Gordon

Pym," "The Carnival of Vanities").[37] The effect of this shift was to re-position Hegel's—or any other—philosophy from the rostrum of the lecture hall to the fireplace. Thus, says Liiceanu, Noica reframed the structures of speculation by reformulating them in an epic register. Liiceanu then places this shift within the writing of philosophy beginning with Plato, whose dialogue form differentiated minimally between the expertise of teacher and student; to Aristotle, who hierarchized the relation; and on to Hegel, whose books "only God" could understand. With each such step, philosophy lost part of its audience.

In such a context, claims Liiceanu, any modification of the form in which philosophy is communicated—particularly any modification in a literary direction—will necessarily affect its audience [suddenly the reconciliation of philosophy and literary criticism in *Letters* takes on new significance]. Any reintegration of philosophy with art reestablishes lost lines of communication, restoring the possibility that philosophy might be perceived not as an arcane specialty but as something that treats the problems of *everyone*. Much of Noica's writing addressed readers directly, in a colloquial style—sometimes in the form of letters, using the second person singular (see Noica 1986)[38]—that brought them into the text and presented its problems as their own.[39] Liiceanu's own books were constructed in a similarly inviting way, breaking down the barriers between a text and its readers to engage them in a direct manner.[40] Here indeed was a style that expanded its audience and turned its readers into participants.

Why is this preoccupation with the audience significant? Partly, of course, for building the "cognizant public," which would recognize the authority and value of those who had built it and, perhaps, broaden the market for their books in the era of "self-financing."[41] The Noicans aimed to present as *everyone's* concern a set of values that were *their particular* concern and to broaden the public that would look to them for solutions. We might see this as the tactic of intellectuals whose position was being undermined and for whom it made more sense to arouse wide attention to the possibility of an irreparable loss than it did to continue thinking lofty thoughts in the presence of two or three others—even (as Liiceanu recognized [1985: 59]) at the risk that broadening the public would dilute the strictly philosophical content of the message one could transmit.

There are two other facets of Liiceanu's (and Noica's) "democratizing" impulse, however, that are more important. One is that by producing a new genre for philosophical writing, the Noica School was implementing a strongly resistant practice. Genres, Ghani suggests,[42] are defined by the characteristic ways in which they bind language, creating particular forms of closure for the reader. Any activity that changes the genre proper to a subject also challenges the kind of closure typical for that subject; it therefore holds the promise of resistance, of opening new possibilities that had been foreclosed. Turning philosophy into "stories," into a form of literature, burst the old confines set by the standard genres of philosophical writing.

This fact, and its implications for the formation of audiences, was particularly significant given that the field in question was *philosophy*. Although the *de facto* legitimation of Party rule may have shifted to nationalism, its *de jure* legitimation—and what linked Romanian socialism to the international socialist community, without which the Romanian Communist Party would not have attained and held onto power—still came from the officialized version of Marxist-Leninist philosophy. No socialist state could wholly disown its heritage in the philosophical tradition from which the Noica School also derived, and from which it departed. Any group of thinkers who claimed descent from the genealogy running from Plato through Hegel, which was also the genealogy of Marx and Engels, and who resuscitated serious creative use of that tradition (such as in Liiceanu's efforts to theorize anew the notion of "necessity" so central to Marxism), was a threat to the foundations of Party rule in a way that the antiprotochronists or the historical researches of a David Prodan or an Alexandru Zub were not. Intrinsic to Marx's heritage, for example, are the dialogues of Plato, which Noica managed to publish.[43] They inquire into the nature of the ideal society, from a position that regards the actual society of their day as not measuring up to that ideal. To this implicit subversive premise of Plato's dialogues—a critique of the forms of the present—all potential Romanian readers were already positively disposed. One had only to get their attention, to bring them into the audience.

The possibility Noica's School represented, then, was the possibility of a systematic alternative understanding—both theoretical and practical—of the world: the means through which both legitimacy (for Weber) and hegemony (for Gramsci) are threatened. As long as such alternative visions existed, they challenged the new hegemony the Party sought to impose. The alternative understandings would not themselves be sufficient for taking over the state, but they would be a major contribution to the success of other forces in society who might manage to capture state power. Noica's followers thus assumed the role—

theorized by Lukács, Gramsci, and others—of working within the confines of the existing society to broaden the visions available within it. Although this role did not itself aim at political mobilization, it might provide the bases for legitimating a change that some other mobilization would bring into being.

Perhaps this is the reason—whether consciously recognized or not—for a very peculiar feature of the protochronist reception of *Letters*. Protochronist critics gave the book several normal reviews, but in addition it was serialized virtually in its entirety in *The Week*, that central fortress of protochronism, in the column of the paper's editor-in-chief, Eugen Barbu. The serial began immediately following Noica's death (first installment December 11, 1987), and its tone was at first friendly, noting the correspondents' fine writing style, the book's interest and exemplary organization, and so forth. For months on end (the serial lasted nearly a full year[44]), perhaps 75 to 80 percent or more of Barbu's weekly column consisted of direct *but selective* quotations from the letters. The brief commentary he interpolated from time to time became more sarcastic as Noica's death receded into the past.

The Barbu-ized *Letters* had several important traits, all relevant to the question of audience. (1) Its selective quotations removed much of the sense and nearly all of the intellectual substance from the exchanges. (2) Barbu's comments dealt almost exclusively with how childish, silly, hypocritical, trivial, ignoble, and often outright ridiculous the participants were, how their punctuation left a lot to be desired, and how they quarreled constantly among themselves; the pivotal episode through which philosophy and literary criticism joined into a common front was omitted (see note 33), which meant that Barbu's readers did not know about the unity of this "quarrelsome" group. (3) By serializing the book—stringing it out a few paragraphs at a time across the space of almost a year—Barbu eliminated one of its most compelling features: its sense of urgency and passion; that is, he disarmed it of its most potent weapon and them of a major device for gaining attention. (4) Barbu reiterated time and again what terrible snobs and elitists they all were, and how much he disliked this. (He wrote in the issue for June 17, 1988, "I am not in favor of establishing classes [of readers], of ennoblements or aristocratizations in thought or in literature.")[45]

This review can scarcely have had another objective than to capture the audience sought by the Noicans. Since *Letters* was printed in only 16,000 copies and was sold out at once, it was possible that many readers eager to know what all the fuss was about would turn to the more readily available *Week* to find out. By presenting the Noicans as foolish, ignoble, petty squabblers over trifles, Barbu was undermining their pretensions to be the heirs of as grand a thinker as Noica. By calling *Letters* unworthy of philosophy and the writers hypocrites, he destroyed the book's claims as a model of dialectical philosophizing and communicative directness. By labeling them elitists and snobs, he diminished any interest "the masses" might have had in what they were saying. By continually defending Noica against these no-account rascals, he supported the protochronists' claim to being Noica's true heirs, the protectors of his name and image. And he did all this in the cultural publication with the second-largest circulation in all of Romania.[46] It does not stretch credibility to see this as an assault upon the Noicans' audience, nor to see the magnitude of this serial—which, after all, brought a lot of publicity to some people the authorities would have liked to silence—as reflecting how great a threat was perceived in the School of philosopher Noica.[47]

This chapter has presented yet another struggle over a personage, this time one who was then alive, by groups hoping to press him into the service of their different agendas for cultural production. Different claims were aired not just by Noica but through him, each set of claimants offering itself as the authentic representatives of a true, creative, and valuable Romanian philosophy and the loyal servant (if not savior) of Romanian culture. Noica was a far more suitable object for symbolic struggle in his lifetime than someone like Prodan in chapter 6, for Prodan steadfastly refused any ambiguous usage of himself and made very clear his categorical separation from the purposes of power. Noica was more malleable. Those cultural producers aspiring to power saw in him a producer of philosophical "use-values" for a Romanian state and Romanian culture (they managed to overlook his foreign imports), creator of a particularly *Romanian* philosophy that would be useful to power if severed from his unsuitable practices (his "School," his geniuses, and so forth). It makes sense that this group emphasized Noica's *production*, not his life. For his followers, in contrast, he was useful as a symbol for the creation of "true" rather than barbarized culture, transmitted outside formal institutions and through a different relation to authority; these people saw his importance in his life and not his products.

The matter of national identity, although treated less explicitly here than elsewhere in this book, nonetheless grounded the entire discussion, in two ways. First, Romania's relation with the West was itself constitutive of the entire "Noica phenomenon" at several points in its trajectory. There were Noica's ongoing relations with former rightist associates in the West, such as emigrés Cioran and Eliade, occasionally denounced by the regime and always contributing to the ambiguity of Noica's political allegiances. There was the exchange of letters with Cioran in France that brought about his imprisonment (see note 6); there was also the echo of this in his querulous 1987 "Letter to an Intellectual in the West" (Noica 1987c), which complained that Europe was neglecting both its own historical values and those people in the East who tried to uphold them. In addition, there was the East-West separation fundamental to Liiceanu's *Letters*: when the *Journal* hit Bucharest bookstores, Liiceanu and Pleşu were in Germany, and had they been at home the reverberations would have been conveyed in speech rather than on paper. The issues in *Letters* and its creation of a cultural opposition took their very life, then, from a Romanian relation to the West. There was also the support of western-based Radio Free Europe (competing with Romanians to influence Romania's image in the West), which lionized Liiceanu's books and magnified their effects and their audience within Romania. Finally, there is the fact that this oppositional group gained internal leverage through its relation to and recognition by the West. Anyone producing culture with an eye to "universal" recognition was more likely to receive invitations abroad, which would augment both leverage for their values and their cultural authority at home; the arrest of such a person was also very likely to bring down a storm of western protest upon the Romanian authorities. The group's relation to the West helped to keep them active in cultural production, rather than permanently silenced.

A second and more important reason why the matter of national identity grounded the Noica School was that Noica's followers were distinguished from their opponents precisely on the question of whether Romania is European and whether European culture is relevant for establishing one's credentials as a producer of culture in Romania, or whether one can have adequate title by indigenist means—by being born on "Geto-Dacian" soil, for example, by learning proverbs, and by thinking in the philosophically rich language Noica had shown to be Romanians' natural linguistic endowment. Arguments about Europhilia, imported values, indigenist archaism, and so on, were as much a part of relations between Noica's followers and their main opponents as in the protochronism debates. Each party to this contest over and through Noica offered a proposal for the "true" Romanian identity and "genuine" Romanian cultural values. In so doing, like the disputants in chapters 5 and 6, they implicitly built up "the Romanian people" while also supporting the position of an intellectual elite to produce values for it.

In the Noica School, however, unlike other cases presented in this book, the quarter from which such claims were made gave them special force. It was not insignificant, in the era of Gorbachev's rise, to have philosophers—of all people—speaking of pluralism, opposing centralization, democratizing their genres, and invoking a European heritage. It was unfortunate that these same philosophers said little about the masses of workers and peasants oppressed by excessive centralization, making them appear more as intellectual apologists than as champions of a more just social order.[48] Similarly unfortunate was their respectfully accepting Noica's silence about his fascist past, which left them unhelpfully vague on questions of antisemitism and intolerance that would emerge in new guises after December 1989. The moral standing these philosophers gained through their activities in the 1980s, however, gave them and those antiprotochronists with whom they were closely associated a strong platform from which to influence the democratization of Romanian society after Ceauşescu. Their public recognition in the wake of his fall shows how important their example had become.

Conclusion

For what we all are, really, is elegant scarecrows on fields of words.

—Gabriel Liiceanu

In this book I have attempted to show how Romanian intellectuals, as they produced culture, constructed politically relevant fields of discourse about the Nation, thereby reproducing national ideology through time.[1] I have grounded my analysis in the particulars of "real socialism," asking what it was in Romania's socialist society that created a special environment for cultural production and for politicking around the matter of national identity. My discussion has taken me into the company of several overlapping sets of intellectuals as they strove to define cultural values. In this process, different groups advocated standards of value that were deeply held and that were in conflict. One way of describing their conflict, I have suggested, is to see the process as occurring in a differentiated social space whose coordinates were political status and cultural authority. Some conversion was possible between these two dimensions, but there was a systemic tendency for the political dimension to engulf the cultural one.

Central to my procedure were anthropological reconsiderations of the notion of "culture," seen less as meanings and significations than as systems of action within which meanings are invoked, brought into confrontation, altered, and reproduced. From the struggles I have

302

treated, certain values and certain definitions of identity emerged temporarily "victorious": more recognized, better funded, more discussed. (This does not mean, however, that those they confronted had vanished.) The stakes in such conflicts were not only material ones—publications, travel, bureaucratic position, influence with the censor—or matters of social recognition and high status. They included the possibilities for people to view their life-activity as meaningful, through successfully promoting their preferred definition of truth, aesthetic value, scientific probity, and the identity of the people to which they belonged. Notions like this and the behavior that gave them life are "culture" in the same way as are the philosophy, literature, sociology, history, and so forth, discussed in these pages. That is, to see "culture" as practice obviates the need to distinguish between "high" culture and its other forms. Both are processes of production whose "end products" do not congeal into meanings but immediately reenter the ongoing practice of social life.

In asking why so many of these contests over the definition of cultural and scientific values occurred around "the Nation" rather than around something else, I have offered three reasons. To begin with, national identity had been central to Romanian culture and politics—both internal and external—long before the installation of the Romanian Communist Party. In addition, this historical predisposition was enhanced by the Romanian Party leadership's mode of control, which emphasized minimal remunerative incentives and a combination of coercive and symbolic-ideological controls that increasingly gave national values a major place. Furthermore, the Nation emerged as central to defining cultural values because of the way intellectuals struggled with one another. That is, the place of the Nation, and with it an ideology that was national, were reproduced not simply because the Party saw the Nation as a useful instrument but because discoursing on the Nation was how groups of intellectuals drew their boundaries and sought their advantages.

Several aspects of this were peculiar to the socialist context. First, I have argued that bargaining for resources from the center was basic to politics in command systems. For cultural producers seeking the resources to sustain their activity, much of this bargaining consisted of claims about "cultural representativeness." In part from historical predispositions, in part from preferences of the Party leadership, what was held to be culturally representative became firmly tied to definitions of the Nation and its identity in the larger world. "Representing" one's culture need not automatically entail invoking national identity, but in the Romanian context this was the form often taken by contests for attention from the center.

Second, I have proposed that one outcome of these contests over the definition of values was further to centralize culture and its means under the control of the political apparatus, the tendency several theorists see as the first "law of motion" of command-type socialist systems. Because one set of participants—those adopting the indigenist arguments I loosely refer to as "protochronism"—gained the advantage, they contributed disproportionately to this tendency: they could silence or hinder the cultural values of their adversaries, and they themselves promoted values that, being expressly national (rather than international), a national Party could readily appropriate.

Third, with respect to the economy, I have made a general and a particular argument linking these cultural struggles with socialism. The general argument is that the shortage endemic to highly centralized command systems like Romania's placed a premium on exclusionary mechanisms such as ethno-national identity. Therefore, those in the social environment of the intellectuals who produced the national ideology were not simply indifferent to its possibilities: people's daily experience made them receptive to talk of national values, as a way of coping with their own dilemmas. In particular, I have proposed that problems with Romania's command economy led to a partial recommodification of culture. More extensively felt in domains such as literature than in others such as history, this sharpened cultural-political conflict and aroused the opposition of cultural producers whose formerly secure and protected situation had suddenly become vulnerable. (The presence of poets and critics in the post-Ceauşescu government was in part a consequence.) Because their opponents and the Party leadership phrased the struggle in terms of national identity, and because of their own commitment to the national idea, these persons too were compelled to argue their alternative values in terms of what was best for the Nation. The result was to reinforce the significance of the Nation at the center of culture, in the politics of intellectual production, and, consequently, in the discursive space of ideology and legitimation.

In one final respect, I would maintain, the processes described in this book bear the stamp of a milieu that was socialist—or perhaps more accurately, of a "revolutionary" situation in which the state did not enjoy the kind of relationship with its society that has characterized western contexts. The Romanian party benefited from nothing like the decades and centuries of gradually developed practices of surveillance, manipulation, and disciplining that, in the West, have supplemented (some would say displaced [Bauman 1987b: 124]) the discursive forms of ideology. Because the political center had not yet brought under control the nondiscursive practices that, given long and stable development, became so important in forming consciousness in other social systems, struggles in the realm of discourse took on special significance in socialist societies. That is, the center's unsophisticated control over daily practice privileged the intellectual "spot" in the terrain of legitimation. These systems made the constitutive use of language in relation to political power rather more important than it is in western systems. Romania's Prodans, antiprotochronists, Noicans, and others may have felt under attack and relatively without influence; yet the space from which they spoke was nonetheless crucial for influencing the course their society would take. The Party's instant isolation of them, once they raised a protest, offers ample proof.

Although the arguments in this book are too detailed to bear further recapitulation, I cannot take leave of them without brief consideration of two final points: what if any relevance do my arguments about cultural politics in Romania have for other socialist countries, and what do the processes described in this book tell us about the role of Romanian intellectuals in perpetuating or changing their society? In connection with this second question I also ask, what was the outcome of the encounter between Romanian intellectuals and institutionalized Marxism?

National Ideology under Socialism

In this book I have discussed a case that was generally regarded as somewhat extreme within the socialist world, and at the end of chapter 3 I tried to explain why Romania displayed so much more overt nationalism than other socialist countries. By the form of my title, however, I have implied that this case can tell us something about socialism and national ideology more broadly. Is this implication of my title misleading? In what way can an extreme illuminate the norm, and what conclusions does it suggest about the link between the two phenomena I have treated?

These are huge questions, further magnified by the fact that national ideology is one of the most complicated aspects of modern societies, whether socialist or not. Ethno-national discourses have spread from multiple foci under diverse conditions over many centuries and have intersected in diverse ways with the "nation" of the western European nation-state (see Anderson 1983). In consequence, talk of nations and national values means very different things in different contexts; one cannot lightly generalize a few conclusions from Romania to other societies, and surely not to societies of nonsocialist type. Although it violates the law of parsimony to say that apparently similar phenomena require different explanations in different contexts, I am convinced that for the social world this is right, and that many false leads have come from seeking "parsimonious" accounts of social realities that are disorderly and unpredictable. It is precisely anthropology's task to puncture such illusions as that similarity of forms implies similar functions, or that socialist societies are adequately comprehended with models developed for the West or for Latin American authoritarian regimes. Therefore, I am not dismayed to find that "who-are-we?" arguments about foreign models, indigenism, cultural imperialism, and so forth, similar to those in Romania, can be found in Japan, South Korea, Mexico, South Africa, or Greece—all decidedly nonsocialist. National discourses are a common feature both of nation-building and of resistance to western domination the world over. They do not require socialism to activate them, and the explanations that would account for them will not be identical with those for cases like Romania.

Within the socialist world, I seem nonetheless to imply that national ideology has taken characteristic forms and that the Romanian case helps to clarify them. Again, one must be specific: there is national sentiment that was more or less officially promoted, as in Romania, and there is widespread national sentiment that was not publicly articulated by the Party, as in Czechoslovakia or Hungary. Both involved actions that reproduced national ideology, but the groups engaging in those actions and the motivations behind them differed. There is national feeling that has long been a response to colonial relations, as in most of Eastern Europe toward the Soviet Union, not to mention the resistance of many in the Soviet republics to the center in Moscow; and then there is the politics of identity even within the colonial center itself, as with the Pamyat' group in Russia. Are there any broader generalizations that can cut through diversities such as these?

To begin with, there appears to be a loose but not perfect association between more or less officially promoted national ideology and the persistence of a centralized, command form of socialism beyond the initial phase of "Stalinist consolidation." These command systems, such as North Korea, Bulgaria in the late 1980s, and Romania, distinguished themselves from the reformist Communist parties by persisting in a mode of control that minimized consumption and emphasized coercive and symbolic-ideological strategies. The mix of Marxism-Leninism and nationalism in these countries varied from case to case, but all strongly exhibited the latter. The Chinese leadership's return to coercive control after the June 1989 demonstrations seems also to have been accompanied by increased xenophobia and nationalism, along with some retrenchment from earlier decentralizing reforms. At the root of this association between command systems and a symbolic control that focuses at least in part on the Nation may be socialism's "weak state," whose rulers must pursue the discursive constitution of a strong, unified image. For this task, the Nation has a very long and old list of clients, satisfied and not-so-satisfied. Its implicit kinship metaphor and its subsumption of internal divisions within an image of oneness make it the premier vehicle for leaderships wishing to present their regime as the embodiment of unity and strength.

Although Party leadership strategies emphasizing the Nation are not, as I have argued throughout this book, the first cause of national ideology under socialism, it would be foolish to see them as irrelevant. This is clear from a telling comparison between the Romanian and Soviet cases, as Kagarlitsky (1988) describes the latter. Following the end of World War II, Soviet society underwent a period of Russian nationalism that lasted until Stalin's death and was encouraged, if not indeed sponsored, from the top (Kagarlitsky 1988: 128–135). Antisemitism, conflicts among intellectuals, arguments of Russia-first-in-all-things, diatribes against "cosmopolitans"—these phenomena of late Stalinism in the Soviet Union offer direct parallels with Romania during the 1970s and 1980s. Factions within the intelligentsia struggled with one another to avoid being eliminated and to praise the leader and the Russian genius. As would later be true in neighboring Romania, the sympathy of the Party leadership lay with a group equivalent to the protochronists. These events conform to the picture of "command nationalism" I have offered above.

As Kagarlitsky reports it, a second period of national revival emerged in the 1970s, virtually contemporaneous with what I have described for Romania: following a period of initiatives toward economic liberalization and reform in the 1960s, mature Brezhnevism settled in with its reaffirmation of centralized command (ibid., chap. 5). The form of symbolic-ideological control accompanying this was not, however, nationalism but a reasserted "orthodox Marxism" (later accompanied by what Aronowitz [1988] calls the ideology of the "scientifico-technical revolution"). To the extent that a national revival also occurred, it was limited to one wing within the intelligentsia, whom Kagarlitsky labels the New Right and who in many cases formed a kind of opposition (ibid., 237); the outstanding exemplar is Solzhenitsyn. As in Romania during these same years, intellectuals in a complex field of positions opposed one another and, to varying extents, the Party. Yet the Party's failure to champion national values meant that the national voice gained no privilege within the contest: those who tended to maintain the upper hand were persons employing some form of the official discourse of Marxism-Leninism. The line taken by the Party leadership clearly established the valences of the field of intellectual contention.[2]

Regardless of whether a Party leadership emphasized national ideology from the top, in socialist systems there has generally been plenty of room for national sentiment elsewhere in society. This is plain from the example just cited, as well as from the fate of the Soviet Union in the late 1980s. The Romanian instance enables us to clarify only some of the possible reasons. One, I have argued, is the elective affinity between exclusionary mechanisms, such as a widely shared ideology of ethno-national difference, and the economy of shortage endemic to socialist systems, particularly the more centralized ones. It was average citizens, not Party leaders, who felt the effects of shortage daily and might be inclined to supplement their shopping behavior with xenophobic attitudes and exaltation of their own group. Such attitudes would tighten the networks of persons who could have a claim upon one's own favors, as well as expelling potential competitors for the resources one hoped to obtain. This scenario applies chiefly to those socialist countries having multiethnic populations, particularly when territorially interspersed to some degree, rather than separate: Bulgaria, Romania, and the Soviet Union, more than Czechoslovakia, Poland, and Hungary (the latter two having few internal minorities, but even there, antisemitism has served as a telling indicator of exclusionary sentiment).

The ethno-national conflicts in the Soviet Union during the late 1980s—the high point of decentralizing reforms in the command system—would seem to contradict this hypothesized link between shortage and the effects of nonofficial national ideology, but I believe they do not. What happened during the early period of reforms in Hungary, between 1968 and 1973, showed that in that period, shortages were worse than their previous levels under the command economy. Additionally, the Romanian case suggests that reforms more thorough-going than Romania's hobbled "self-financing" may, by recommodifying culture, produce both a strong interest in "protectionism," such as we saw with the Romanian protochronists, and a readiness to pander to perceived national feelings, for market reasons. For writers in the vernacular, whom the reform periods have generally empowered, upholding the national tongue is basic to guaranteeing sales for newly market-oriented cultural production (Sherlock [1988: 28] gives specific instances of this for Soviet writers in the 1980s).[3]

Thus, reform in and of itself would not automatically eliminate the effects of shortage upon national ideology (which preexisted the socialist order throughout the region) in the behavior of socialism's elites or average citizens. How reforms affected conflicts among intellectuals, encouraged them and other elites to invoke and strengthen the national idea, or made the wider public more responsive to national appeals should be specifically investigated in any given case. So also should the historical forms taken by a given national discourse and the histories of the groups that employed it. In all the East European examples and in the Soviet Union, precommunist elites exhibited a high degree of national consciousness, and national ideologies had hegemonic or near-hegemonic force. The historical particulars of those national ideologies continued to be relevant, and not uniformly so, under socialism.

Intellectuals, Opposition, and the Power of Discourse

The second of the two questions I wish to approach concerns the role of Romanian intellectuals in transforming their society. The inclusion of poets, writers, and philosophers in the post-Ceauşescu government made it obvious that at least some people regarded these intellectuals as an oppositional force. In chapters 5 and 6, however, I tended to stress that all intellectuals, even those who considered themselves to be opposing the Party, were serving it by reproducing the national ideology that the Party had incorporated into its rule. I also observed in chapter 7 that the oppositional Noicans had spent more time in talking with and about other intellectuals than in developing an alliance with groups located further down the social structure—alliances that might have facilitated a change in society, as occurred in Poland between 1976 and 1980. In all three chapters, I called attention to rhetoric that showed intellectuals championing the privileged place of an intellectual elite. At the same time, in chapters 6 and 7 I pointed to resistant practices that I saw as impeding the purposes of the regime. Is it my intention to conclude that intellectual work was ambivalent in its effects on Romanian society? In part, yes, but the matter deserves some discussion.

If we compare their activities with those of intellectuals in Poland, Hungary, or Czechoslovakia, Romanian intellectuals—despite their opposing one another and, sometimes, the Party's dictates—appeared not to be a force for changing the increasingly inhumane rule under which they and their countrymen lived. Neither a technocratic reform faction, such as the one so influential in Hungary from the 1960s on, nor a group of intellectuals willing to subordinate their elite concerns to those of the majority, as emerged in Poland between 1976 and 1980, nor an active human rights movement such as Czechoslovakia's Charter 77, made an appearance in Romania. There was not even a movement of cultural dissidence comparable to that in the Soviet Union during the 1970s, with its extensive network of underground publications. If one remarked upon this (as I did on occasion) to Romanian intellectuals who considered themselves oppositional, the response was likely to be an impassioned defense of the values of *culture*, the support of which was seen as constituting a defense of the people against the barbarities of the regime.

Throughout the 1980s it was tempting to moralize about the failure (from a western point of view) of Romanian intellectuals to prepare the ground of "civil society," which would make Romanians better able to resist the Ceaușescu leadership and would provide the basis for a post-Ceaușescu order. Various Romanian emigrés, westerners, and Hungarians fond of showing that Romanians are "cowards" aired such views. To moralize thus was easy, from the comfort of a secure environment in which the majority of intellectuals in the West (including emigrés, as well as myself) did no more to involve ourselves in public action—and would have done so at infinitely less risk—than did the Romanians we were tempted to criticize. For most Romanian intellectuals, however, the situation in their country was such that to do anything more than they did would have been pure self-destruction.[4] The few signs that some kind of opposition might be forming in Romania, such as the Goma movement in support of Charter 77, were ruthlessly suppressed. Members of the embryonic alternative I have identified in persons associated with Noica and his followers enjoyed the constant and unpleasant companionship of the security forces, as did the few other persons in Romania who protested against conditions in their country. To retreat into veiled statements in the cultural press was about all that made sense.

The conditions surrounding cultural production and the behavior suited to academic "success" in the West may differ from those appropriate to surviving as an intellectual in Romania, but they involve every bit as much talk with and for other intellectuals, rather than broader action toward changing society. Why hold Romanian intellectuals to a different standard? This is particularly so given the role "the West" played in shoring up Ceauşescu's rule against his own population. Because Americans regarded the "maverick" Romanian party leadership as independent of Moscow, opposition to that leadership inside Romania was seen as uninteresting and, hence, unworthy of support. There was no western audience eager to construct a "dissidence" that might have entered into Romanian cultural politics, amplifying the voices that spoke against the regime. To the degree that political positions in Romania have always been defined by the intersection of more powerful forces from without (as I believe to be the case), the inefficacy of a Romanian opposition simply reflects the West's lesser interest in Romania's internal political diversity than in that of "more important" countries like "entrepreneurial" Hungary or "brave" Poland.

This conclusion is not an answer, however, to the question of whether the activities of Romanian intellectuals supported or resisted Party rule. We might begin answering the question by distinguishing between the various intellectual groups in terms of the effects of their actions. Here, I have argued that some played a more direct role than others in perpetuating the existing order and enhancing its tendencies. This was not because some were "opportunists": it would be cheap to distinguish between the opposing groups (as many of them did themselves) in terms of the presumed opportunism of one of them. There were persons acting from deep conviction on both sides, and although in 1980s Romania to be an opportunist on the side of Europeanism was difficult, it was not impossible. What distinguished the factions was rather their readiness to participate in tendencies that fed the apparatus of the Romanian party and the centralization of resources under its command. The most vocal advocates of protochronism, indigenism, and Party-serving "revolutions," as I have argued in various ways throughout this book, directly fed the political apparatus. Herein lies a basis for evaluating their actions from a moral point of view. If this had been an apparatus implementing humane values, one might less readily condemn its centralization. The Romanian party under Ceauşescu, however, became visibly antipeople and antidemocratic, indifferent to the suffering—the cold, the lack of food, the fear of police, the perpetual uncertainties, the threatened destruction of whole villages—imposed on its population in the name of massive projects glorifying its rule.

The "new indigenists" who supported this should not be applauded for their seemingly anti-imperialist stance. One can admire the genuine effort some of them mounted to develop a Romanian identity that was positive, to promote a form of "local pride" opposed to the western-based deprecation of subaltern cultures; one can acknowledge the intense passion toward this end that motivated at least some indigenists. This said, however, from the point of view of an Anglo-Saxon tradition in which opposition to "tyranny" is preferred over service to it, the agents of indigenism in politics and culture, within the Romanian context of the 1970s and 1980s, served tyranny reprehensibly.

In contrast, from the same evaluative position that prefers pluralist resistance to centralization, the practices of their opponents retarded central control—even if infinitesimally and not always visibly, and even if their somewhat self-serving defense of expertise effectively defended their own space as well. Romania's antiprotochronists, its historians such as David Prodan and Al. Zub, its Noica School, and others who struggled for their version of truth and value against the version sustained by protochronists and other allies of the Party leadership, were promoting pluralism, howsoever feebly, by refusing to accept in full the agenda set for them by the others. That they did so in part by upholding their own claims to elite status with their insistence on "professional standards" is, in the Romanian context, less important than that they were also using these standards to resist the totalization of values and activities at the political center. They impeded the construction of the "millennial state" simply by acknowledging values alternative to it; they impeded the installation of Party-mode flattened time by utilizing a different kind of time in their scholarship. They smuggled into the interior of Romanian society (through translations of Plato, "scientific" research norms, and "universal" audiences for literature) principles incompatible with the Party's direction, to disruptive effect. By these actions they kept the space for different values, for a different kind of social order, from vanishing.

To some extent, one could say that the activity of those Romanian intellectuals who thought themselves oppositional *was* ambivalent: its effects would depend on the balance of forces outside the country, more than on those within it. With the abrupt change in Soviet imperialism in the region and the consequences of Gorbachev's reformism both for western assessments of Soviet power and for reformers in the bloc, suddenly it mattered that there had been a group in Romania insisting on a European rather than an "African" identity for their country. These changes in the international balance of forces, with the resulting reassessment of Romania's "maverick" image, made it possible to see the political efficacy of an intellectual argument for a European Romania, so vivid a presence in these pages.

The above comments suggest a conclusion somewhat different from the one proposed in chapters 5 and 6. I argued there that all intellectuals were engaged in a single potentially system-reproducing endeavor, in that through arguing, they further consolidated a realm of agreement about the importance of national identity. This meant that regardless of who said what, all groups were responsible for recreating the Nation— a Nation divided between mental and manual, with internal group diversity something to be wished away rather than encouraged. Although all did indeed construct the Nation, power was served more by the uses to which some were putting it than by the national ideology itself. It is evident from chapter 1 that in the period between the two World Wars—that other major moment in recent Romanian history when the construction of unity took precedence over everything else—the national idea could be more or less categorical and rigid, more or less xenophobic, more or less intolerant. In both that period and the Ceaușescu era, all worked together to produce the Nation; their images of it and the implications of those images, however, served social tendencies of different kinds.

If these observations point to differences in the effects of one or another group's actions, at the more comprehensive level of their agreed-upon premises we see a final effect that was not the work of any one group but a veritable "coproduction."[5] It involved intellectuals, Party officials, and two other social "actors": the discourses on Marxism and the Nation, borne by the utterances of intellectuals and Party officials but to some degree independent of them, as well. Together these actors discursively ruptured the society's legitimating discourse, Marxism. As I showed in chapters 4 through 6 especially, the diligent intellectual work one or another group expended on "the Nation" deconstructed the categories and the teleologies of Marxism, substituting a push toward national unity in place of internal diversity, and replacing Marxism's progressive, discontinuous time with the continuities of the Romanian People. (Not all intellectual projects fitted this exactly: Prodan's *Horea*, for example, concentrated on *one class within* a class-differentiated society and plotted its narrative *progressively*—Prodan, remember, was analytically a Marxist. But Prodan believed as fervently as anyone in the values of the Nation, as the themes of his life's work show.)

The total effect of all these intellectuals constructing the Nation, either innovatively as with the protochronists or defensively as with the others, was that the national discourse subdued the Marxist one. The paradox is that it achieved its triumph at the initiative of the Party leadership and their protochronist allies, seconded (merely) by those who opposed them. The groups in power adopted this once-hegemonic ideology—so potently instituted beforehand—in order to overcome it, incorporate it, and profit from its strength; they were overcome by it instead. Their use of national categories, such as in their indigenizations of Marxism (chapter 4), garbled the sense of the categories of Marxism. The result was a gradual delegitimation of official Marxism, whose chief victim became Ceauşescu himself.

It was not simply intellectuals who achieved this result but they together with the Communist party leadership. Nation-loving intellectuals did not restore their preferred discourse to the public sphere single-handed. Party leaders, too, embraced it actively, having failed to constitute through Marxism a socialist state that was an effective cultural relation—having failed, that is, to establish through Marxism that mix of stabilized contention and acceptance that is hegemony. The regime's very weakness forced it into the arms of the national idea. Thus, the rupture of Marxism was not strictly speaking the work of *an intellectual opposition*, although intellectual strife was a vital element in the outcome. It was a collective product. In this light, one theoretical contribution of the present book has been to show the institutional sites, the political processes, and the concrete uses of language through which one discourse overpowered the other and undermined the social reality of a "Marxist" regime.

I wish to make two concluding points about the processes through which this took place. First, the legitimacy of Marxism was scarcely greater in most of the other East European regimes, which nonetheless mostly did not adopt the overt nationalism of Ceauşescu's rule. What is the relevance of the Romanian example to those other cases? This addresses from another angle the question raised in the preceding section. I believe an argument comparable to that for Romania could be made for them as well—that the discourse on the Nation helped to break open the discourse of Marxism, and that institutionally grounded contests among intellectuals were an important means for this. The difference was that in the other socialist states, the national agenda mostly remained more hidden, for different reasons in each of them and in different social spaces. It is obvious from the salience of national ideas in post-Kádár politics in Hungary, for example, that the absence of official nationalism in that country in no way signaled the death of national ideology there. Thus, attention to the extreme case of Romania opens a new analytic route into the more subtle ways in which Marxism was ruptured in the other Eastern European countries. The job of the social scientist will be to discover the various hidden spaces in which national discourse continued, outside the public realm, and to show how activity in those spaces entered into the language and the practices of politics.

Second, the outcome in Romania was more than simply the discursive rupture of Marxism. It was the discursive constitution of a nationalism even more powerful than before. I cannot "prove" this point: it is an intuition. With communism in 1947 there was installed an externally imposed Marxist language legitimating a monolithic political system. Its monolithism was the means of its undoing, for it effectively politicized all action within the system and made contention pervasive. Much of the contentious activity served to centralize culture within the political apparatus, as I have argued, while disabling alternative cultural foci whenever possible. The result was an increased concentration of national values and symbols, their very concentration generated by the workings of the socialist order. In a word, the monolithic Party-state produced a monolithic Nation. The indigenization (and consequent rupture) of Marxism in Romanian cultural politics was at the same time a monolithization of nationalism. This outcome—what Bateson (1936) would call a complementary schismogenesis—resulted from Stalinism's insistence on imposing its alien categories autocratically, rather than insinuating them persuasively into the categories familiar from people's experience.

On December 22, 1989, following six days of public demonstrations, rioting, and violent reprisals, the government of Nicolae

Ceauşescu fell. As the repressive apparatus sided with the demonstrators against him, he and his wife fled the capital, to be later captured and executed. An organization calling itself the National Salvation Front assumed control. Its members included signatories of the March 1989 letter of former communist officials, mentioned on the first page of this book's Introduction, along with prominent antiprotochronist writers and poets.

In subsequent weeks important administrative posts were filled, many of them with persons who have appeared (both with and without their names) in these pages. Andrei Pleşu, key Noican and signer of a second letter of protest in 1989: Minister of Culture. Mihai Şora, cosigner of that same letter and oppositionist philosopher: Minister of Education. Alexandru Paleologu, also a cosigner, antiprotochronist literary critic, and central member in the discussions of Noica's "School": Romanian ambassador to France. Gabriel Liiceanu, pivotal figure in Noica's School: editor of the Political Publishing House (rechristened "Humanitas"). The staffs of their institutions and of other newly forming organizations (such as the important Group for Social Dialogue, in Bucharest) were filled with oppositionist intellectuals, many of them active antiprotochronists of yore. The presidency of the Romanian Writers' Union went to oppositionist poet Mircea Dinescu, the editorship of the cultural magazine *Literary Romania* to its outspoken antiprotochronist literary critic, Nicolae Manolescu. The post of Minister of Religion was offered to the intransigent historian Alexandru Zub, who declined it in the interest of continuing his work in history; he accepted, however, his colleagues' mandate to become director of the Iaşi History Institute. (One of his fellow Moldavians even nominated him for president, in a gesture comparable to those that brought intellectuals Havel and Göncz to the presidencies of Czechoslovakia and Hungary.) That several of these people were later to resign or be removed is perhaps less important than their initial inclusion in the new government, testimony to the moral authority their cultural opposition had won them.

In the Transylvanian capital of Cluj, the university administration was taken over by a committee most of whose members had opposed protochronism more or less actively. Academician Prodan, by this time eighty-seven years old, had the satisfaction of seeing his rival Ştefan Pascu at long last thrown out of his many posts, including the directorship of the History Institute and the chair of History at Cluj University. In a last-ditch gesture of support for the leadership from which he had drawn so much benefit, Pascu had held a public meeting in the wake of public demonstrations and the killing of students and citizens in Timişoara (December 16–17), condemning those acts of "hooliganism" and warning the students in Cluj that they would be met with force if they followed suit. Less than two weeks later, an article over his signature lamented the profanation of Romanians' glorious history that the evil dictator Ceauşescu had imposed on the people (Pascu 1989). Vilified in the press, Pascu was not saved by this change of heart: his subordinates in the History Institute replaced him with a collective leadership, headed by a loyal follower of Prodan. Prodan himself, meanwhile, true to form, refused various invitations to take an active public role, at length capitulating only to the request that he sign a manifesto to restructure the historical profession completely, in cooperation with historians of Romania's national minorities (Prodan et al. 1989).

The spirit of national reconciliation evident in this gesture and in the early presence of Hungarians in the governing council was unfortunately short-lived. Active in resuscitating a climate of intolerance were, not surprisingly, many of the old protochronists. Some of them quickly founded new publications, from which they propagated indigenism, antisemitism, antimagyarism, and *ad hominem* attacks even worse than before. Supported in part by funds from Milan-based emigré and interwar fascist Iosif Constantin Drăgan, Eugen Barbu and Corneliu Vadim Tudor launched *Greater Romania* (*România Mare*) in press runs of 200–300,000, numbering among their contributors Dan Zamfirescu, Ion Lăncrănjan, and Edgar Papu; with the same funding, protochronist Artur Silvestri became editor-in-chief of a comparably inflammatory publication, *Nation* (*Natiune*). Within six months of Ceauşescu's overthrow, in both of these there appeared—astonishingly—articles favorable to Ceauşescu and to the infamous Secret Police, articles that pandered to the sense of dislocation felt by many Romanian citizens in the chaotic times following the dictator's fall.

The former protochronists took on varying political sympathies. Some of them sided with opposition parties, such as the National Peasants; others quickly declared their adherence to the new power, the National Salvation Front. (Antiprotochronists nonetheless blocked one such person, Ilie Bădescu of chapter 4, from attaining the university professorship he sought.) Protochronist C. Sorescu even managed to get himself on the Front's electoral lists and entered the new parliament as a senator. Whether from their strategic vantage point in publishing or from within the Front, the protochronists seem bent on infusing into the politics of whatever party they join that excess of nationalism in whose monolithization they had been so instrumental.

It is therefore unlikely that the national idea will disappear from Romanian culture in the post-Ceauşescu era. Even in the capitalist economy of the 1930s, with its combination of both state subsidies and a market for culture, the "protection" of Romanian culture and art from western imperialism had been a major theme. A similar mix of bureaucratized and marketized cultural production is likely to prevail in Romania of the 1990s; within it, cultural indigenism will continue to answer the joyous refrain of those newly empowered in 1989—"Ne întoarcem în Europa," we are returning to Europe. Whether that indigenism will be judged politically reprehensible, however, as were its forebears of the 1930s and the 1980s, will depend on the new social order that develops and the tendencies it serves within them.

The discourse on the Nation can also be expected to enter powerfully into party politics, fortified by its earlier confrontation with Marxism. There, if the political extremes prevail, the result could be to replace the socialist form of totalization with a national one, in which the patriotic celebration of Romanian values within a diverse field of possibilities loses out to chauvinism, intolerance, and a rhetoric of purification, as in Corneliu Vadim Tudor's "Ideals" (see chapter 5). For Romanians wary of such totalization, the political task of the future must be to reduce the national idea to manageable size. The best means for this might be a reversal of the procedure whereby the new monolithic nationalism arose: a determined effort to disrupt the discourse on the Nation with persuasive discourses on pluralism and democracy.

Notes

Introduction: Ideology,
Cultural Politics, Intellectuals

1. Several people generously assisted me in preparing this introduction, among them Gail Kligman, Emily Martin, Sidney Mintz, Michel-Rolph Trouillot and—most especially—Ashraf Ghani.

2. Sources for these, in order of quotation: xeroxed copy of Radio Free Europe's version of the March 10, 1989 letter (signed by Gheorghe Apostol, Alexandru Bîrlădeanu, Corneliu Manescu, Constantin Pîrvulescu, Grigore Răceanu, and Silviu Brucan); A. C. 1985: 6; Cornea 1989: 3; Paleologu 1983: 7, 13; personal communication from Romanian friends after the dictator's overthrow.

Some people were downright unsubtle in their invocations of Europe. For example, in January 1990 the London-based emigré newspaper *Românul liber* (6 [1]: 1, 4) republished an interview with Romania's exiled King Michael, which had appeared sometime earlier in *Figaro*. Inter alia, the King observed that because Romanian culture had always been influenced by that of France, it was France's job to draw world attention to Romania's tragic fate. "How can France bear to have a people, three hours' flying time away, with its eyes turned continually toward France, disappear little by little from History?"

3. Sources for these, in order of quotation: Rachieru 1985: 37, 40; Ungheanu 1985: 396, 457, 459; Deletant 1988: 77.

4. As part of a year's library research in Romania in 1985, I attempted four months of fieldwork in two villages, to see what effect elementary schooling and the public media blitz about national history had on peasants and village-based factory workers. The research was constantly disrupted by police questioning of

my informants, as I discovered only at the end. This makes me hesitate to use its results in any other than an anecdotal way.

5. Kligman's work is so close in subject and conceptualization to my own that the two ought to be seen as mutually "required reading." To avoid even greater overlap, my discussion avoids the discipline of ethnography, since it is central to her book.

6. This leads me to a comment on the form of this book. There has been a move in anthropology to reassess the form of ethnographic writing (see, e.g., Clifford and Marcus 1986; Marcus and Cushman 1982), the suggestion being made that we need "heteroglossic" texts, which give voices to the indigenes and make sense independently of the author's hegemonic frame. I see in this use of Bakhtin's notion of "heteroglossia" a misunderstanding of his intent: it was precisely in Stalin's Soviet Union, where Bakhtin was writing, that "heteroglossia" stood such a poor chance, making his whole point an inquiry into how languages relate to the phenomena of centralization and power. Thus, I present the "voices" of my research subjects as they themselves lived: in counterpoint with the centralizing discourse that sought to dominate and arrange them, and framed within my own equally dominant interpretation. This stretches them, appropriately, between the two poles—Soviet-type socialism and the West— that magnetized the entire field of Romanian intellectual discourse.

7. I am grateful to the following sources for assistance in forming my use of ideology: Jean Comaroff 1985; Friedrich 1989; Hall 1979; Lefort 1986; Therborn 1980; conversations with my colleagues at Johns Hopkins; and an oral commentary by John Comaroff. The bibliography on the subject is, of course, very large.

8. Gail Kligman argues (personal communication) that the notion of hegemony should be made specific to different kinds of social order, by which it could be said that *discursive* hegemony existed in Romania. I prefer to keep a single notion of hegemony, as necessarily a combination of discursive and practical elements, which is found in some orders at some times and not in others.

9. In general, these two words seldom show up in the same text. People who speak of hegemony usually do so from a Marxist or neo-Marxist (Gramscian) point of view, those who speak of legitimacy follow traditions of liberal political theory or Weberian sociology. My understanding of these two concepts leads me to think that they *can* be fruitfully brought together, the distinction between them being apt precisely for the socialist systems examined here.

10. Fehér rightly observes that even this minimal condition for legitimacy was not met in most East European societies, where large numbers embraced the alternative image offered by western parliamentary democracy (Fehér et al. 1983: 137–138). I choose to employ the notion of legitimacy in its "weak" sense nonetheless, as described in the text.

11. I am obliged to Ashraf Ghani for this phrasing.

12. Rolph Trouillot suggests to me that the "nation" is always and everywhere contestable, not just in Eastern Europe, for the "nation" is a crucial element in struggles for state power in most contexts.

13. Discussion with Ashraf Ghani helped to clarify both this point and those in the next paragraph.

14. For three among many statements of these reconsiderations, see Bourdieu 1977; Fox 1985; and Ortner 1984.

15. Examples include the Party's relationship to folk culture, rock music, and jazz; see, e.g., Karnoouh 1982; Kligman MS; Ryback 1990; Starr 1983.

16. A far from exhaustive list of works relevant to this subject would include Black 1956; Choldin and Friedberg 1989; Condee and Padunov 1987; Dallin and Patenaude 1988; Davies 1989; Deletant 1988; Gabanyi 1975; Gal 1988; J. and C. Garrard 1990; Georgescu 1981; Gheorghiu 1987; Ghermani 1967; Haraszti 1987; Havel 1985; Heer 1971; Hruby 1980; Kagarlitsky 1988; Kligman 1983; *Kosmas* 1984–1985; Liehm 1968; Rév 1984; Rura 1961; Shafir 1981, 1983*a*, and 1983*b*; Sherlock 1988; Shlapentokh 1987; Skilling 1984; Valkenier 1985. Most of these works deal with the relation between politics and what we might call "high culture" or scholarship.

17. Similar objections could be made of other studies of cultural politics outside socialist settings. For example, Newmeyer's (1986) work on the politics of linguistics is almost totally lacking in politics and rarely invokes anything but the content of intellectual debate. A work with which the present book shares many assumptions—as well as an express concern with national ideology—is Handler's (1988) study of the politics of culture in Quebec. His politics occur more directly within the public sphere (as opposed to the sphere of cultural producers—that is, of intellectual debate) than the cases analyzed in this book.

18. The argument is sometimes made that the "intelligentsia" is a group specific to East European societies (see, e.g., Szelényi 1982: 308), originating in nineteenth-century Russia and Poland. Others see this group as characteristic of *all* non-western societies, and as based in the need of peripheral states to force the pace of modernization (Seton-Watson 1964: 12–15). Many scholars insist on differentiating intellectuals from the intelligentsia, but a reading of definitions shows that there is absolutely no consensus on how the distinction should be drawn: for some the former is the more general category and the latter a subset of it, for others precisely the reverse. I avoid this controversy altogether by not using the word "intelligentsia" at all.

19. A small sample of the titles relevant to these and other intellectual topics would include Aronowitz 1988; Bauman 1987; Benda 1969; Bourdieu 1984 and 1988; Bové 1986; Camp 1985; Craig 1984; Coser 1965; Eyerman et al. 1987; Eisenstadt and Graubard 1973; almost the entire Foucault industry; Gella 1976 and 1989; Gouldner 1979; Konrád and Szelényi 1979; Ray and de la Lama 1981; Shils 1958—not to mention the "founding fathers" of research into this topic: Marx, Mannheim, Gramsci, Lukács, etc.

20. An approach similar to these but applied to the politics of boundary-expansion and maintenance *within* the field of professional specializations is to be found in Abbott 1988.

21. I am grateful to Rolph Trouillot for insisting on the necessity of acknowledgment as part of a definition of intellectuals. One way in which some would-be intellectuals fail to achieve that status is that their claim is unanswered and their aspirations thereby silenced. Trouillot believes this acknowledgment is so important to intellectual status that it creates contests where none might

otherwise exist, since being answered in debate is the proof *par excellence* of one's participation in the domain of intellectual activity.

22. I take this as one way of talking about the debate on "cold fusion" in 1989, as persons not recognized for their scientific authority (wrong discipline, third-rate university) made claims the "authorities" resisted.

23. This paragraph is part of an ongoing friendly battle with Ivo Banac. I hope he reads it.

24. This question of affect and interest is addressed in Latour and Woolgar's study *Laboratory Life*, in which they ask how the motivations scientists feel are related to the accumulation of scientific authority. Rather than talking, as does Bourdieu, of a sequence of "investments" and "profits" building scientific "capital," they speak of a *cycle of credibility*, which includes such phases as applying for research grants, doing the research, publishing papers, gaining recognition, and applying for more research grants. Any scientist interested in his or her work can be reasonably expected to care that this work is seen as credible. This desire presses them to good-faith research efforts within the system of scientific values and interpretations they have adopted, unmotivated by any "will to power." Nonetheless, "truth" often exists in several versions with different partisans, each striving to develop greater credibility on behalf of their version. Often what produces a successful scientific career is a good nose for a risky experiment, fortunate timing in grant applications, things that cannot be calculated "investments" but that are rewarded with greater scientific authority. One can say the same of cultural production, where I would call the cycle one not of credibility but of *creative authority*, which enables one to have one's novels or symphonies or treatises published more readily and to promote the values one espouses from a more visible platform of prizes and recognition.

25. Ashraf Ghani has encouraged me to make these points explicit (believing, with me, in anthropology's special mission—an idea my Romanian intellectuals would appreciate).

One:

1. This chapter benefited from the assistance of a number of Romanian historians and other scholars, among whom I would single out for thanks: Al. Zub, Mihai Dinu Gheorghiu, Pompiliu Teodor, Pavel Campeanu, and Ion Saizu, as well as American historians Keith Hitchins and Irina Livezeanu. I also thank Mihai Gherman for verifying several lengthy quotations. The chapter is a condensation of three other publications (Verdery 1987, 1988, 1990).

2. For more extended treatment of both the twentieth-century and earlier developments in Romanian national ideology within a framework comparable to that employed in this book, see Verdery 1987 and 1988; Gheorghiu 1985*a*, 1987, and 1990. Numerous studies treat one or another aspect of this topic from other perspectives. Among the most important in major western languages are Alexandrescu 1983, 1987; Armbruster 1977; Durandin 1987,

1989; Georgescu 1971; Heitmann 1970; Hitchins 1969, 1977, 1978, 1985; Jowitt 1978; Prodan 1971. In Romanian the number of studies defies citation within a small space. I mention particularly Cristian 1985; Gyémánt 1986; Lemny 1985 and 1986; Marica 1977; Ornea 1980; Platon 1980; Ş. Ştefănescu 1984; and Zub 1985a and b, 1989.

3. "National essence" is an approximate translation of the Romanian *specificul naţional*. Romanian translations of works on the theme often render the term as "national specificity," indicating emphasis not on the *essence* but on the *particularism*. "National specificity" does not work as well in English as "national essence," however, and since only philosophers will care about the difference between a particular and an essence, I prefer the second.

Several important words appeared in the writings I discuss. The word for "people" (*popor*) means both the ethnic "people" and people in the sense of "masses." The former is usually the sense intended, but it is shadowed (in general, helpfully, from the political point of view) by the latter. Two other words appeared often: *naţie* (sometimes *naţiune*), whose sense is clear, and more commonly, *neam* (as in *neamul românesc*). *Neam* comes from a Finno-Ugrian (and possibly Turkic) root *nem-*, having the multiple meanings of kinship group, tribe, and people or nation. It has no good English translation. My discussion reduces these meanings—and both words—to the word "nation."

To avoid placing cumbersome quotation marks around the word "nation" at each use, but to keep its particular meaning consistently in the mind of American readers likely to forget it, I will write Nation with a capital *N*. (I do not do this in quoting or paraphrasing Romanian writers.) The particular meaning I wish to signal thereby is that the Nation is not simply a "country," as in the League of Nations and the usage of "nation" common to Americans. It refers to the ethnic idea of *people*, who may or may not in fact *have* a "country."

4. This quotation and all others from Romanian are my translations, except as noted in chap. 3, n. 1.

5. For more extensive treatment of the matters raised in this section, see Verdery 1988.

6. Among the causes of Romanians' politicized historicism (see also the explanation in Prodan 1971: 436–437) was, I suspect, their having learned it from West Europeans, who had already been manipulating Romanian origins for political ends. This is a logical conclusion, at least, to be drawn from Armbruster's fascinating and understated investigation of the idea of Romanian latinity (1977). His research into the politicization of Romanians' Latin origins shows that Romanians began to appear in European scholarship at the time of the Ottoman expansion and of Hungarian-Polish rivalry for control over Moldavia; a further europeanization of knowledge about Romanians accompanied each intensification of the Ottoman problem (Armbruster 1977: 253–254). For West Europeans seeking to cement their anti-Ottoman alliance, it was very convenient to remind Romanian princes and armies at the edges of Ottoman territory that their origins lay in Rome. An excellent example is Pope Clement VIII's admonition to Muntenian Prince Michael ("the Brave," reigned 1593–1601), that as descendants of the brave Romans, his Romanians had a special duty to rally Europe against the infidel and must not shed the blood of their

own Italian kin. This was a particularly blunt appeal to a prince who had assumed the throne as a Turkish ally (ibid., 131). The Counterreformation brought additional invocations of Romanians' Latinity, as Catholic rulers pleaded with Romanian princes to protect the true (Roman) faith and encourage conversions to it (ibid., 153). It would seem that whenever major European actors decided upon a course necessitating repair of intra-European divisions, reference to Romanians' Latinity was a handy instrument.

7. Elements of an eastern origin occasionally appeared in later writings, largely by adding eastern peoples to the Daco-Roman mix. This might be done by emphasizing a Scythian origin for the Dacians, or by including settlers from among the nomadic tribes (Avars, Cumans, etc., and most importantly Slavs) that subsequently infested the area. The weight assigned to the Slavic populations has remained a matter of dispute. Following the installation of a communist government, the Slavs were suddenly given preeminence in the formation of the Romanians; the school manual by Mihail Roller (1952) shows this clearly. In more recent historiography, however, the view is that the Romanian people was essentially formed *before* the Slavic migrations, which merely added to, without fundamentally changing, the cultural, spiritual, and genetic repertory of Romanians. This fits with Romania's so-called independent line.

As is evident, there has been very little political motive for an eastern origin for Romanians since the matter of origins began to be systematized in the seventeenth century; only the period of early Soviet domination forms the exception, and the eastern origin then posited was imposed from without. Dimitrie Cantemir, seeking help from the Russians in the early 1700s, was appealing to a Czar who considered himself a *westerner*.

8. Grigore Ureche (ca. 1590–1647), Miron Costin (1633–1691), and Dimitrie Cantemir (1673–1723). All three claimed a Romanian origin in Trajan's Roman colonists, with only the most superficial reference—if that—to the Dacians. Cantemir aimed his appeal at the pro-western Peter the Great, with whose aid he hoped Moldavians might at last free themselves from the Turkish yoke. Ureche and Costin, members of a pro-Polish noble faction, probably hoped to secure assistance from Poland (as well as from the West more generally) (Armbruster 1977: 193–194). The Poles formed a powerful potential ally for seventeenth-century Moldavians, for as the self-styled "last bastion of defense for [Roman] Christendom," they might be expected to sympathize with the sons of Rome.

9. The calumnies came largely from Poles and Hungarians—both vying for control over the Romanian lands (Armbruster 1977: 193). One view particularly popular in Poland (where two of the three Chroniclers were schooled) was the "theory of exiles," according to which Romanians are descended not from Roman colonists brought by Trajan but from malefactors exiled from the Roman empire.

10. These include the Uniate Bishop Inochentie Micu and others who came after him, its most visible members being Samuil Micu, Petru Maior, Gheorghe Şincai, and Ion Budai-Deleanu. For details on this group see Prodan 1971; Lungu 1978; Hitchins 1969 and 1985.

11. Gyémánt (personal communication) says that the only people arguing

at that time for a significant Dacian mix in Romanian origins were historians of *German* nationality, for whom it was important to combat Romanians' noble bloodline by mixing in some barbarians to dilute Romanian claims to political rights (see also Gyémánt 1986: 61–62).

12. Similar reasons, I would argue, motivated the recrudescence of Dacianism in official historiography in Romania during the 1980s. See also n. 20.

13. Sugar writes (1977: 131) that at the end of the seventeenth century, the nobles were divided into turcophile, russophile, and austrophile factions, with a fourth polonophile group among the Moldavians; the dominant "philia" changed with the fortunes of the various class fractions. See also Oțetea et al. (1964: 198 ff.) for a discussion of factional processes in the Romanian Principalities.

14. Following the union of the Principalities in 1859, there developed the many organs ancillary to any state of European form. These included not only an army, expanded bureaucracy, ministries, and so forth, but also institutions of higher education, various intellectual institutions, and cultural organizations, all of which accumulated with increasing rapidity toward the century's end. Immediately after 1859, for example, were formed the Universities of Iași and Bucharest (in 1860/1861 and 1864, respectively); a centralized State Archives, in 1862; a National Museum of Antiquities, formally opened in 1864; an Academic Society, in 1866, becoming the Romanian Academy in 1879; and so forth. These institutions became vital sources of livelihood to the growing Romanian intelligentsia, spun off from the declining agricultural estates.

15. This was true also of many nobles elsewhere in Eastern Europe, such as in Hungary and Poland, who were similarly rescued by the creation of a *dirigiste* form of state.

16. This may account for why policies promoting political independence won out, in most political argumentation, whenever the choice was between that and economic independence. For example, Montias shows (1978: 57–59) that during debates on tariff policy with Austria-Hungary in the 1870s, Romanian leaders traded economic independence for higher guarantees of political sovereignty.

17. Romanian historians of the generation of 1848 developed a new theme that has remained a major preoccupation right up to the present day: the idea of Romanians' contribution to world history. Because their long centuries of war against the Turks and other Asiatic invaders had spared European civilization the devastating effects of invasion and conquest at the cost of their own freedom, they argued, Romanians were not merely the protectors of European civilization, Christendom's first line of defense: they were its sacrificial lamb, their blood the price paid to eastern barbarians for the flowering of western culture. This vital service of protection implied a European obligation to Romania in exchange (see Cristian 1985: 98–99). (One is reminded of Poland's similar self-image as the "Christ of nations.") It was sometimes even implied that Romanians had remained steadfast in Europe's defense when all around were betraying it and them. The image of gallant Romanians, obstructed in their world mission by the chicaneries and inadequacies of others, was consistent with additional images of an innocent and well-meaning people corrupted from without.

Constantly frustrated in their attempts to live lawfully by rulers who trampled on the law and subjected them to arbitrary will (Kogălniceanu's view, in Zub 1974: 487–488), Romanians were a naturally law-abiding folk whom outsiders had forced to deviate from the true path. Many other elements in medieval historiography bore the same message: but for the injustices of fate, Romanians would not now be begging for attention from the civilized world, for they would have retained the global esteem and admiration they had enjoyed in earlier times before history so wronged them.

18. Consider also the following from a note written by future Romanian statesmen Brătianu and Rosetti to their teacher Edgar Quinet in 1848: "France raised us, educated us; the spark that now lights up our country we took from the hearth of France. Here is what we ask you to tell her, in our name . . . Remind France again that we are her sons; that we fought for her on the barricades. Add that all we have done was done after her example" (cited in Babu-Buznea 1979: 197).

19. This section owes much to the fascinating and informative work by Babu-Buznea (1979).

20. This was another reason why Dacianism enjoyed a vogue under the rule of independence-minded leader Ceauşescu after 1965.

21. Without having the space to develop this argument fully, I suggest that it is not incidental that dacianism—along with several other critical discourses —was particularly associated with thinkers from or based in Moldavia. The integration of Romania into the European market proved more damaging to the economy of Moldavia (or to certain groups within it) than to Wallachia. More generally, the union of the two Principalities to form Romania soon became a union of unequals, with the major political and economic functions lodging disproportionately in the southern part (Gheorghiu 1985a: 133). This marginalization of Moldavia within Romania's political and economic life meant both a necessary specialization in cultural production and a permanent critique of the direction of politics. Not only were many "dacianists" (Hasdeu, Russo, Eminescu) Moldavian, but so also were those intellectuals who served as ideologues of the Conservative party—the Young Conservative (or "Junimea") group of the influential philosophy professor (later Minister of Education) Maiorescu. The devolution of Moldavia into a politicoeconomic backwater with a vigorous, indeed exceptional, cultural life would be felt in very contradictory ways, not the least of which was its major role in the development of both socialist and fascist movements.

22. Neither Maiorescu nor most who followed him offered very articulate ideas as to what "national essence" meant as a concept. Subsequent definitions are about as unhelpful as definitions of "culture" in American anthropology— not surprising, given that these notions are jointly rooted in German Romantic thought. The following definitions, drawn from current specialists in literature, suggest something like an artistic "national character":

The force of originality, authenticity and representativeness of [certain great] works . . . , owing to . . . organic correspondences with the essentialities of culture in their Romanian and universal modalities. This imprint, stamped upon art from the deepest level of a people's spirituality . . . is the national essence (Popescu 1977: 26).

[In] any literature there exists a characteristic vision of the world and of life, a specific *Weltanschauung*, which colors in a Romanian way the totality of the themes treated. Romanian culture has a certain unity of style. [Through it] the Romanian people expresses its own "genius" or *Volksgeist*, crystallization of a plurality of historical, social, climatic, linguistic, and cultural factors (Marino 1966: 7).

23. This matter was often not discussed as such. For example, the anti-western diatribes of Nichifor Crainic covered over his germanophilia.

24. In the pages of such magazines as *The European Idea* (*Ideea europeană*), for example, one found arguments between Transylvanians and "Regăţenii" as to what benefits the integration of Transylvania could bring (see, e.g., Rădulescu-Motru 1922 and Ghiulea 1922 for only two examples). Many Transylvanians felt that "Regăţenii" were treating their land as a colony, and others complained that the state was not active enough in their defense. Livezeanu (1986: chapter 4) provides much evidence along these lines, revealing a fundamental debate over localism and centralism between Bucharest and the provinces.

25. Those active chiefly in religious and cultural life rather than in politics were more likely to come from middling and professional families, the politicians descending more often from families of greater wealth rooted in the old landed nobility. To cite a few examples from among the influential intellectuals (several of them mentioned below): Constantin Rădulescu-Motru came from a family of medium wealth, based in both land-ownership and the professions; Lucian Blaga was the son of a village priest; Nichifor Crainic was unusual in being of poor peasant origin; Nicolae Iorga's father was a lawyer, Eugen Lovinescu's a schoolteacher, Constantin Stere's a well-to-do landowner, Garabet Ibrăileanu's a merchant. The leading political family, the Brătianus, like the Sturdzas of an earlier era, had been major landowners.

26. For example, "intellectual" Nicolae Iorga (a historian) was briefly president of the Council of Ministers; philosopher and critic Titu Maiorescu was Minister of Education, as was sociologist Petre Andrei; economist Virgil Madgearu was Minister of Commerce and Industry; and a number of well-known figures from cultural life were members of Parliament.

27. I am grateful to Pavel Campeanu for insisting on this point.

28. Those few who found the notion useless were nonetheless constrained to argue their views on it, thereby contributing to its entrenchment in intellectual parlance. The writer Mehedinţi, for example, found himself wholly unmoved by the notion that a writer should seek inspiration in the soul of the Romanian people (Călinescu 1982:641), but his was decidedly a minority view.

29. Some analysts use the labels that referred to the central publication defining a particular position on the issues: "Gîndirists," "Peasantists," "Populists," "Socialists," and so forth. Others divide the so-called "modernization" debates, which occurred primarily in sociology and political economy, from the "national-essence" debates, primarily in literature and other humanistic disciplines. Although Ornea, the most energetic Romanian student of the discussions, divides the participants into two camps, "traditionalists" and "Euro-

peanizers" or "modernists" (see Ornea 1980), a more recent anthology pointedly observes that this division is simplistic (Bucur et al. 1984: 7).

30. Because I hope this book will be read by persons other than those specializing in Romania, I use the English translation for titles of periodicals discussed in the text. Were Romanian publications as well-known as *Le Monde* or *Pravda* this would be unnecessary; the unfamiliarity and diversity of these titles poses an obstacle, however, for the nonspeaker of Romanian.

31. See n. 35, below.

32. For the former, see the 1984 reprinting of his major works, *Romanian Culture and Politicianism* and *Energetic Personalism*; for the latter, his 1936 *Romanianism: Catechism of a New Spirituality*.

33. Among the exceptions to this was Mihai Ralea, editor of *Romanian Life* after Ibrăileanu, for whom a rural Romania was necessarily passé.

34. Citations to Lovinescu's 1924–1926 *History of Modern Romanian Civilization* are from Ornea's 1972 reedition of that work in a single volume. Although the reedition eliminated a few passages, I have it from the editor that these are few and are invariably signaled by ellipses in the text.

35. Another interwar figure who became even more important than Lovinescu in the cultural politics of the 1980s is Lucian Blaga, treated briefly in the chapter. Blaga's fate is perhaps the more interesting of the two (partly in keeping with his more extensive creative output in poetry and philosophy), for he was claimed by the new indigenists and some among the new westernizers equally, whereas Lovinescu was defended only by the latter.

36. The pen-name of P. Marcu-Balş, who had begun as a collaborator with Crainic's *Gândirea* and gradually evolved to become an associate of the left.

37. For more extensive analysis along these lines, see Alexandrescu 1983 and 1987; Gheorghiu 1985a and 1990; Verdery 1990.

38. A sample of titles from several such magazines will illustrate this: "The Intellectuals," "Intellectuals and Peasantism," "Intellectuals and the Politics of Transylvania," "Appeal to All Intellectuals," "Reform of the Intellectuals," "The Scientist and Politics," "The University and Politics," "Intellectuals and My Country," "Why Are Intellectuals Cowardly," "The Situation of Romanian Intellectuals," "Writing in the Service of the Nation," "Betrayal by the Intellectuals," "In Defense of the Nation," "Scholars, Unite!" (These titles come from the magazines *Ideea europeană*, *Luceafărul*, *Societatea de mâine*, *Criterion*, and *Gând românesc*.)

39. Saizu (1984: 250–251) argues that despite differences among the political parties—greater emphasis on technical education or on agriculture, on practical education for village leaders, and so forth—all were calling for an expanded educational system. This would provide jobs for the intellectual proletariat being churned out of the overheated university system, possibilities for new school textbooks, and new positions in pedagogical institutes.

40. See the section Intellectuals and the Disciplines for details.

41. Gheorghiu (1990) examines the writings of Romania's famous Gusti School of Sociology and proposes that it was constructing itself, like the Romanian state, as above classes and parties, as tied to the Nation or people through an objective, scientific form of guidance outside the partisan realm, with the aim

of leading Romanian sociology to a place of honor in world science just as the state anticipated leading Romania to a place of honor in the world society of nations. I would add that such an argument is applicable beyond the field of Romanian sociology (Gheorghiu himself implies as much in his analysis of the Populists; see discussion later in this chapter). Rădulescu-Motru's magazine *The European Idea* was full of articles arguing for distance between intellectuals and politics.

42. According to church historian M. Păcurariu, the 1927 Concordat among Romania's churches had the effect of strengthening Roman Catholicism relative to Orthodoxy, giving Catholic parishes larger properties than they had had in Habsburg times; and it exchanged the expropriations of the agrarian reform (the Orthodox Church by and large did not have properties sizable enough to be expropriated) for rents that were worth more than the straight compensation paid other landlords. It is Păcurariu's conclusion that the Liberal government brought the Romanian Orthodox Church to a position of inferiority with respect to the other religions (M. Păcurariu 1981: 401–405).

43. This discussion took place between Minister of Religion Lăpedatu and the bishop of Rîmnic and the archbishop of Moldavia; discussion reported in *Monitorul Oficial, Şedinţe*, 13 February 1924, pp. 450–472.

44. This work was written in 1918 and published posthumously, following Andrei's suicide to avoid assassination by the fascists.

45. One notes that it was Gusti, however, who got most of the money for sociology. Whether that is to be attributed to Andrei's failure to tie his definition of sociology closely enough to the Romanian Nation or to Gusti's being related by marriage to King Carol II is impossible to say.

46. This same author gave a scathing review (1943) of a work by Rădulescu-Motru that purported to be an "ethnopsychology" or "science of the ethnic"—clearly a competitor to Pavelescu's ethnography.

47. For example, in 1908 D. Gusti was appointed head of the department of ancient philosophy and ethics, in Iaşi, to which he added sociology. He left for Bucharest in 1920 to take a chair defined as sociology, newly created as a separate department from the former department of aesthetics, ethics and sociology; the department he left in Iaşi, to be occupied by P. Andrei, was now called sociology and ethics (Popescu-Spineni 1932: 134). Through Gusti's presence and influence, I would argue, sociology achieved more independent status.

48. Herzfeld (1987) suggests that a certain kind of nationalism lay behind the rise of western European anthropology, which helped produce the notion of western superiority over other peoples. I would argue that this was the form taken by ethnography in the hegemonic nation-state, but in peripheral nation-states like Romania, disciplines such as ethnography could only promote *local* identities and shore up states that *interact* with the West, without being able to impose superiority. In such peripheral contexts, the examples I have considered here would suggest, disciplines have the Nation literally embedded into them, whereas in "core" contexts what is embedded in disciplines is a notion of a "civilizing mission" or the "scientific advance" promoted by intellectual activity in these "superior" nation-state forms.

49. Note the expressed aims of the Romanian Academy: "to promote the spiritual consolidation of national unity, to strengthen the collective forces of the nation through culture, education, and science, to civilize the ethnic territory . . . through the creative power of the national genius" (Academia Română 1937: 57). It is hard to imagine a western Academy expressing things quite like this.

Two:

1. I acknowledge with gratitude the assistance of several people who, through comment on drafts or in general conversation, have helped me formulate the points of view expressed in this chapter: József Böröcz, Pavel Campeanu, Jane Collier, Ashraf Ghani, Mihai Dinu Gheorghiu, Gail Kligman, Emily Martin, Michel-Rolph Trouillot, and my fellow scholars at the Woodrow Wilson Center, where I offered a preliminary version in 1988.

2. I use the term "real socialism," as do many others (e.g., Bahro 1978), to distinguish analysis of the actually existing forms of socialist society from utopian discussions of what a possible socialism might look like.

3. Among the works I would include in a fuller survey are Bahro 1978; Campeanu 1986 and 1988; Casals 1980; Djilas 1957; Fehér, Heller, and Márkus 1983; Hirszowicz 1980; Konrád and Szelényi 1979; Kuron and Modzelewski 1966; Simečka 1984; Staniszkis 1991; Trotsky 1937. Most of these are abstract theoretical works, to which one could add a much longer list of studies of how socialist economies function (e.g., Brus 1975; Horvat 1982; Kornai 1980; Nove 1983, etc.).

4. I am grateful to Daniel Chirot for pointing this out. All the scholars whose models I discuss were once more or less committed to the possibilities of socialism. Their critical analyses of its reality in their societies required much soul-searching, giving their models something of a harsh edge. Although this fact makes their models no less useful for my analytic purposes, it was closely tied to the loss of legitimacy of the East European regimes—so trenchantly criticized by its own subjects, including a number of "dissidents" in addition to these scholars. This is why I say that the very modeling of socialism I use in this work has itself been an element of intellectual politics in Eastern Europe. I do not regard this as a flaw: *all* social-science models have political properties, those produced by western political science at least as much so as the ones I employ here.

5. Campeanu (1988: 105) argues this point even more forcefully, contending that it is *impossible to locate* the surplus in socialism, since production is dispersed across a huge territory that the apparatus does not adequately control, and since the surplus-producing enterprises often have an interest in hoarding or hiding some of it (not to mention, I might add, the theft of considerable portions by the direct producers, as with collective farms). Moreover, assign-

ment of values from the center makes the value of the surplus impossible to determine, rendering appropriation inaccessible.

6. An alternative solution, characteristic above all of the Hungarian strategy in the mid to late 1980s, is to *coopt* other foci of production, rather than to disable them. Good examples are the formation of work partnerships in Hungarian factories (Stark 1989) and the restoration of sharecropping in collective farms.

7. Campeanu (1988: 85) offers an argument in many respects similar to this: "Incapable of controlling these [capitalist] relations, the state simply obstructed their functioning, yet without succeeding in establishing alternative, workable relations in their place."

8. The "irrationalities" of capitalist monopoly practices and government bail-outs of major firms make this, of course, a difference of degree rather than a fundamental qualitative divide.

9. That the bureaucracy of socialist systems does not conform to the Weberian image of bureaucracy is argued by a number of theorists, particularly Staniszkis (e.g., 1979: 172).

10. Campeanu says (1988: 146) that the "supreme entity" is not to be identified with *any* group *in* society, such as the Politburo, for its significance is precisely that it occupies a space *outside* the society, *above* it. He also attributes to it a strong tendency toward personification, that is, the personality cult so admirably illustrated in Romania by Ceauşescu. I read him as being evasive so as not to say precisely this.

11. Marx identified in capitalism a constant tension between capitalists' desire to accumulate by keeping workers' wages down and the necessity for workers as consumers to have enough income to purchase commodities that contribute to further accumulation. A major element in the cycles of capitalism, then, is necessary adjustments in the relationship between capital accumulation and consumption. I am looking to define a tension of comparable sort for socialism.

12. I owe a debt to Jane Collier for influencing the formulation that follows.

13. One of many inversions in the ideal-typical models of capitalism and socialism is that capitalism tends to soften the budget constraints on consuming households while leaving constraints hard for most firms, whereas socialism has soft budget constraints for firms and hard ones for consuming households.

14. This sort of behavior tends to characterize bureaucratic organizations generally, but I would hold that it is orders of magnitude higher in socialism's bureaucracies than in other kinds of societies.

15. Some readers might argue that "bourgeois" social science will always be looking for the phenomena characteristic of bourgeois societies, and that my emphasis on competition within socialism is an inappropriate displacement into that system of a problem in my own society. I disagree: my exposure to life in a socialist society convinces me that competition—in a form different from that of capitalist systems—occurs there as well, and it is my objective to describe that different form, which is central to cultural politics.

16. Decentralization, democratization, increased consumption, market, and economic efficiency have real consequences for production when they are intro-

duced into systems of the command type. Yet they also—because of this—become important constituents of social discourse, elements of a struggle for power within the apparatus. Calls for "more market" and "consumption," even before these become actual elements of economic functioning, are important rhetorical means for collecting backers among segments of the apparatus. Gorbachev's resort to such rhetoric in the mid-1980s was but the most visibly skilful use of a strategy potentially available to ambitious bureaucrats throughout the socialist world. In sum, issues concerning "markets," "decentralization," and so forth, are inscribed, albeit in a subordinate role, within both the practice of politics in socialism and its discourse, and they may be expected to reappear in the discourse of cultural production.

17. It is when they are forced by indebtedness to become linked with western economies that socialist systems can no longer remain totally indifferent to the sale of products, as they can more readily when self-contained. Thus, I would argue that the world crisis in capitalism as of the late 1960s and early 1970s, when western creditors began exporting credits and technology to the eastern bloc, can be seen as a proximate cause of the unusual amplitude of reform attempts within socialism in the 1980s.

18. This does not pretend to be an adequate account of the events of 1989, which with astonishing rapidity brought down communist rule in six countries where it had seemed impregnable. The subject of this book does not require such an account, and the recency of those events precludes one.

19. For Eastern Europe, see, e.g., Bauer 1978, Gross 1988, Rév 1987, Simmonds-Duke 1987; for the People's Republic of China, see, e.g., Anagnost 1988, Nee and Stark 1989, Shue 1988. Casals (1980: 34–35) gives a particularly pithy formulation of what was wrong with the image of socialist states as strong:

Unlimited power is only the illusion generated by conditions that the regime believes it has created all by itself, without realizing that it has become the object of those conditions. Unlimited power is a basic form of the false consciousness characteristic of Stalinist society.

20. In a somewhat different vein but to related effect, Jowitt has argued that the state in Romania was weakened by widespread "scavenging," as everyone preyed upon it to get the resources needed for daily existence. (Jowitt offered this argument in a comment at a conference in Bologna, 1986.) Points relevant to this kind of argument emerge in chap. 6, below.

21. I acknowledge a debt here to Mihai Dinu Gheorghiu, who throughout several long discussions adhered so resolutely to Bourdieu's model of cultural capital for socialist systems that he pushed my discomfort to the breaking point.

22. A similar sort of argument is made by Alvin Gouldner (1979: 75), who says that Marxism's stress on theory and scientific socialism necessarily invests theorists—i.e., intellectuals—with great authority.

23. Aronowitz argues for the Soviet scientific and technical intelligentsia (not of concern in the present book) that their revolt against Party control was to some degree responsible for the new discourse on science which came to fill Soviet official language: reference to the "Scientific-Technical Revolution" (STR) became as prevalent as reference to Marx and Lenin, if not more so

(Aronowitz 1988: 214–223). The STR presents knowledge as the foundation of civilization, as a force of production spoken of as if it had no agent; its frequent use constitutes an ongoing argument for the authority of knowledge over social life.

24. One notes a similarity in Bakhtin's characterization of authoritative discourse with Maurice Bloch's language of ritual (1975).

25. Bakhtin's discussion of the difference between the languages of poetry and the novel suggests, in this connection, why socialist regimes—at least, the Romanian one—have such a predilection for poetry: because poetic language is cleansed of the multiple intentions and meanings that are the stuff of novelistic language.

26. My thanks to Emily Martin for suggesting this point.

27. I avoid using the term capital for these dimensions, because I think it inappropriate for socialist systems. Caroline Humphrey, however, in her excellent study of two Soviet collective farms, speaks of "political capital" (Humphrey 1983: 358–362).

28. In the "laboratory life" studied by Latour and Woolgar (1979), scientists invested in building up their scientific "capital" and drawing "profits" from it through participating in a credibility cycle that involved serious research and commitments to the values and truths materialized in this research. For the socialist instances, the cycle is not one of investment and profit but of horizontal competition for allocations that will support one rather than another set of values, one rather than another version of truth, one over another form of authenticity or originality. These producers of culture are involved not in investing and profiting on a credibility market but in what we might call a cycle of authoritative cultural command, in which position is constituted not by accumulation of cultural capital but by inputs to an allocative bureaucracy that funnels resources downward.

29. This language of "accumulation" should not be seen as inappropriately imposed: it is often the language of the participants themselves, as chap. 5 will show, and as is evident in the following quotation:

[This] book puts forth a number of aspects of the material value of cultural goods—a value expressed in labour, materials and techniques, time of creation, efforts of conservation-restoration—which is permanently increasing: thus the cultural patrimony becomes an active means of storing—and therefore a part of the national wealth. . . . The author has proved the rentability of the cultural investment by the conservation-restoration of the stock of monuments and movables (Opriş 1986: 212).

Three:

1. This quotation is an amalgam of points from two key speeches Ceauşescu delivered in July 1971. The passages are from the following pages of Ceauşescu 1972: pp. 205–207, 219. A more extended version, with omissions noted, is found in chapter 5 of this book.

In quoting Ceauşescu in this chapter, I have generally used the English-language edition put out by Bucharest, rather than my own translations. These official translations are not always felicitous, and they retain Ceauşescu's characteristic punctuation—odd by English standards. I have put in parentheses after the date of the published volume the year in which the speech quoted was actually given.

2. My thanks to Michael Shafir for commenting on this chapter and to Ed Hewett and Marvin Jackson for economic information.

3. The allocation of funds to accumulation rose from 17.6 percent in 1951–1955 to 34.1 percent in 1971–1975 and 36.3 percent in 1976–1980 (Shafir 1985: 107). By comparison, figures for 1970 and 1980 in Bulgaria are 30.8 percent and 25.2 percent; for Czechoslovakia, 23.3 percent and 26.0 percent; for the GDR, 24.4 percent and 22.7 percent; for Hungary, 24.0 percent and 19.6 percent; for Poland, 26.1 percent and 20.3 percent (figures from Alton 1985: 97–98). One sees from this that the Romanian accumulation rate was far higher than that of any other socialist country, which means a consistently greater sacrifice of consumption.

4. It should be said, nonetheless, that the illegal status of the Party almost certainly made its formal membership smaller than its pool of sympathizers. The figure of a thousand Communist party members surely understates the communists' popular support.

5. Hungarians, for example, formed over a quarter of the membership in the 1930s yet only 8 percent of the overall population; Jews formed almost a fifth yet were only 4 percent overall; Russians, Ukrainians, and Bulgarians (5 percent overall) formed 18 percent of the Party, and Romanians, with nearly three-fourths of the total population, comprised less than a quarter of the Party membership (Shafir 1985: 26).

6. By contrast, in 1936 68.5 percent of Romanian exports had gone to northwestern Europe, Germany, Austria, and Italy. The average of exports to those same countries for the years 1934–1938 was 62.4 percent (Lampe and Jackson 1982: 459.)

7. Although the Romanian rebellion burst into the open in 1964, it had been subterranean for a time before this. The exact date by which one should mark Romanian "independence" is disputed; it is clear that the country was securing western credits and technology already in 1958–1959 (Montias 1967: 200–201), and resistance of other sorts was evident in the early 1960s, such as a linguistic reaction against "slavic" spellings and calls to restore the letter â (Schöpflin 1974: 82). Conditions that facilitated the "declaration" were also of long standing: the support of the Chinese, now on the far side of the Sino-Soviet split, and the greater maneuvering room that followed upon Khrushchev's secret speech of 1956. I believe that the suppression of Hungary's uprising was also a significant influence, for it would have reduced Romanian anxieties that the Soviets might have cause to favor Hungary and restore its control over Transylvania, important to Romanians both emotionally and economically.

8. Given the similarities in the evolutions of Hungary and Romania in the mid-1960s, one might wonder why the paths of the two countries had diverged

so utterly by 1971. I believe the largest part of an answer is the weak state to which the Soviet invasion of 1956 had reduced the Hungarian party, relative to other forces in society. This precluded both a Hungarian "declaration of independence" of the more limited sort made by Gheorghiu-Dej in 1964 and also a mode of control resting on national ideology.

9. The question of Ceauşescu's reversal is not well explained. Some observers, such as Georgescu (1986, 1988), speak of the defeat of a "technocratic faction" headed by Maurer or, earlier, by Miron Constantinescu, eclipsed by Dej in 1957 (Chirot, personal communication). Others, who were in the top Party apparatus during those years, find this implausible and explain Maurer's expulsion by Ceauşescu's desire to get rid of anyone he himself had not personally brought in. The latter explanation conforms with both the "sultanistic" manner in which Gheorghiu-Dej constructed his position (Crowther 1988: 55) and Ceauşescu's subsequent behavior. For my purposes, it does not matter which explanation one accepts, the major point being that reformism of the Hungarian sort was excluded from Ceauşescu's policies by 1971, if not before.

10. I owe thanks to Mrs. Anna Watkins for her lengthy summary of this work.

11. Inasmuch as the membership was determined not by Party selection but by publications and recommendations, adjudicated by an elected governing council, this was not merely a token change.

12. By the late 1960s, more than a fourth of the members of the Romanian Academy and of holders of Ph.D.s and more than half of all teachers were members of the Party (Shafir 1985: 91). That so many were accepted into the Party indicates a massive attempt to coopt the intellectual stratum.

13. For example, sociology had been revitalized and given much important work during the 1960s and early 1970s, when intensive research was carried out on the organization and functioning of collective farms (e.g., Cernea 1974), social mobility (Cazacu 1973), mass media (Campeanu 1973, 1979), and so forth. As of 1977, however, sociology departments were dismantled and their specialists merged with philosophy departments, it no longer being possible to major in sociology but only to take courses in that subject. Doctorates were no longer to be awarded in sociology, either. Research institutes in sociology still existed, but with the end of the training necessary to staff them, their demise would be only a matter of time. (See also chap. 4, especially notes 18–19.)

14. Shafir (1985: 145) gives figures that show an increase in the percentage of graduates in technical fields from 39.9 percent in 1960/1961 to 58.5 in 1980/1981; in economics for the same years the figures are 9.3 percent and 12.3 percent; in the humanities (philology, philosophy, and history) and arts 13.2 percent and 8 percent. The Central Committee announced in May 1989 that for 1990, 94 percent of ninth-grade pupils would be in industrial, agronomical, economic, and forestry high schools, and 6 percent in health and nonindustrial schools (*Lupta* no. 122, 1 June 1989, p. 2).

15. The "true" story of this scandal may never be known. As I got the story, apparently with the approval of the Ceauşescus some workshops were begun to teach Transcendental Meditation as an aid to greater productivity and con-

centration. The Party leadership became convinced along the way that people were using the workshops as a cover for plotting the government's overthrow. At least a hundred people were fired from jobs or transferred to undesirable locations; the bulk of them were intellectuals.

16. This measure has been taken advantage of by some organizations to *increase* their well-being, but not many were in a position to do this. For example, one editor of a journal explained to me that because he was not now accountable to his previous superior body for the funding of his journal, he "neglected" to go to that body for censor's approval of his articles: he simply checked them and assumed responsibility for them himself, cutting the time necessary for publication. A major means of self-financing for research institutes and academic departments was through research contracts set up with other organizations, e.g., a locality might contract with an archeological team to do a dig. Once the contract was made, however, the funds and their subsequent use were not subject to central management. See n. 22 below.

17. I have this account from a political activist who attended the Congress.

18. I have this from an Academy member who had planned to will all his savings to the Academy until he learned of this change in the status of its funds.

19. This "explanation," like so many in Romania, rests upon rumor; I accept it because I heard it from several people and because it seems plausible. Several of the institutes for historical research in Romania were headed by very powerful figures, some of them members of the Central Committee or brothers of Ceauşescu or intimately tied to that clan. Any one of these would have been able to oppose the merging of his institute with others, so as to prevent the loss of several directorial posts (including his own) that the merger entailed.

20. This argument was made to me in private concerning, for example, writer and former editor of the daily *România liberă* Octavian Paler, who by 1989 was officially a dissident, and former head of the Scientific and Encyclopedic Press, Mircea Mâciu, finally thrown out when his children requested emigration. Mâciu had continued to publish the writings of historian David Prodan despite a concerted effort by Prodan's politically powerful adversary, Pascu, to keep him out of print by blocking other publication outlets (see also chap. 6). An example from an earlier period was historian Victor Cherestesiu. Heer (1971: 128–129) gives similar examples for Soviet historiography.

21. For example, the powerful director of one important publishing house expended much effort in encouraging researchers to take up the task of reediting the opus of prior scholars whose output was enormous. His press achieved a virtual monopoly on these huge reeditions, which required substantial bureaucratic resources and endowed his operation with a prestige that enabled it to acquire other important works. Partly in consequence of all this, he was also able to run his operation more or less in the black, unlike many other presses. One thinks twice before "disembarking" a director like this.

22. I refer here specifically to a series based in Iaşi which required no central approval and in which appeared, among other officially unpublishable items, two uncensored and by no means unproblematic essays by myself—who was at the very same time being attacked in a "nationalist" magazine in Bucharest.

23. It was, I suspect, precisely the resistance of the elite guardians of "high

culture" that helped push the leadership toward redefining culture as an affair of the masses, focused on the "Song of Romania" folk festivals.

24. In some respects, the 1980s resembled the interwar years. Then, as in the 1980s, state resources flowed away from a humanist intelligentsia that lived primarily off the state budget. The Romanian leadership's attempt to free itself of foreign debt during the 1980s gave priority to the needs of industry that would generate the necessary exports. These reversals in the climate for cultural production hit at a substantial intellectual stratum, produced under earlier, less stringent budgets and resembling the new educated stratum that swollen educational budgets had pumped out in newly enlarged Romania during the 1920s. In both eras, intellectuals looking to the state for their livelihood competed with one another on grounds of who best represented national values. The cultural protectionism of the 1920s had its analogue in the 1980s, as chap. 5 will show.

25. It must be noted, however, that he also assigned the Slavs an important though not dominant role in Romanian ethnogenesis.

26. A very partial listing of some of them: *Argeș* 1970; Bratu 1983, Bucur et al. 1984; Ceterchi 1971; O. Constantinescu 1973; Florea 1982; Hurezeanu 1985; Iancu 1980; Marcea 1975; Marino 1966; F. Mihăilescu 1981; Petcu 1980; Popescu 1977; Rachieru 1985; Rebedeu 1971; Simion 1966; Tănase 1973; Vârgolici 1971.

27. I am indebted to Pavel Campeanu for insisting on these points.

28. This argument has been suggested to me by Romanian scholars, one of whom was in close contact with the Dej leadership at the time.

29. The first of these was reported to me by a kindergarten teacher as the latest disposition she had received; the second was the fate of the walls in the Cluj University philosophy department.

30. —And not only rhetorically: its 1988 membership encompassed almost one-third of the adult population. For a rhetorical example from someone other than Ceaușescu, here is nationalist poet C. V. Tudor, on the Ninth Congress that formally installed Ceaușescu as General Secretary: "I dare to affirm that it was not a Congress of the Party, only, but of the nation" (1986: 20).

31. This point will be expanded in chap. 5. Following the 1986 publication, in Budapest, of a three-volume History of Transylvania, the Romanian historiographical community was mobilized to react to the "lies" and "distortions" propagated by this treatise. The image of a truthful Romania defiled by the Great Unwashed of falsified history emerges readily from the pages of such works as Pascu and Ștefănescu, eds. 1987 (first published in 1986).

32. I have this information from a colleague who sat on his city's management council.

33. Marvin Jackson, personal communication.

34. Jowitt, personal communication.

35. The peregrinations of Blaga's statue could be used to reveal much about the politics of culture in Romania from 1960 to 1989. Commissioned in 1960 and completed in 1965, the statue stood in the inner courtyard of the Ethnography Museum in Cluj for some time, thus invisible to all but visitors to the museum. In 1966 a proposal was made and accepted in Bucharest to move the

statue to the square near the university library and student union, but the approval was then withdrawn; after a short time of sitting in the square covered by a sheet, Blaga returned to the museum. In 1971 or 1972 he was taken to the city park, where, along with a number of other figures of Transylvanian culture and letters, he enjoyed the shade. In 1986 a group of officials in the Cluj administration decided to move him to his current place of honor before the National Theater. It is claimed that approval from Bucharest was *not* sought for this, a claim I have no reason to doubt, but I also believe permission would have been granted.

36. Romanian associates in 1988 expressed to me their belief that the level of trade with the Soviet Union was heading toward 50 percent, and most of it was in foodstuffs. When asked how they know this, three of them referred to friends who were directors of food-processing plants or worked for the railway and had seen the rapid redirection of the flow of these goods from West to East.

37. I owe this phrasing to Ashraf Ghani.

38. Observers inside and outside Romania widely believe that the church was an obedient servant of the Ceaușescu regime, and indeed there is good evidence for this view. Nonetheless, in my field research I encountered several instances of the church's contesting the definition of Romanian identity—arguing, for example, that religious institutions had unified the people through centuries of foreign rule, whereas the official version held that ties among Romanians in the different provinces were maintained by economic exchanges and flows of population. I have heard these clerical counterarguments in occasional sermons, but it is nicely exemplified in two contrasting articles in church publications, which I encountered by chance (Grămadă 1978; Plămădeală 1977; the former was then a university-based historian, the latter the archbishop of Transylvania).

Another piece of anecdotal evidence concerning the church's effort to reappropriate some of the language of the Nation is that lively discussions were taking place in the late 1980s about prospective canonization of three major historical figures, hitherto appropriated by the Party and by professional historians: Prince Stephen the Great of Moldavia and Princes Constantin Brîncoveanu and Neagoe Basarab of Muntenia. These ideas excited considerable popular interest; as of 1989, their fate had not been settled.

Four:

1. Pavel Campeanu and Ștefana Steriade did me the favor of trashing an earlier version of this chapter; Susan Gal and Hy Van Luong sought to reassure me that there was nonetheless something to it. Ashraf Ghani helped me to see that the argument I was trying to make in it was even more significant than I had thought. My thanks to all of them.

2. I first read this paper in an English translation made by David Silverman

(University of London) and have employed his translation in my text. The paper was published in French, but I have been unable to find that version.

3. This somewhat cryptic statement insinuates that the writers Radio Free Europe prefers are persons who were silently complicitous with the dogmatists of the 1950s and, not being visibly compromised as are the latter, can now do dogmatism's work. As already mentioned, attacks on Radio Free Europe were a way of striking at opponents in Romania and undermining their credibility.

4. This column was for some time a regular feature of the weekly Literary-Artistic Supplement of the newspaper *Scînteia tineretului*, the young people's version of the official Party daily.

5. Mihu is one of Romania's foremost sociologists. His career has included a stint of teaching in the United States, extensive familiarity with American sociological literature of the 1960s and 1970s, a serious interest in sociological methods and the study of small-group processes, and many years as a professor (but not department head) in the department of philosophy and sociology at the university in Cluj. His relation to Marxism is not entirely clear to me, but he is too young, in any case, to have been seriously active in the socialist movement in its early days. I suspect that his use of Marxism in his writings is largely obligatory and opportunistic, rather than principled.

I ought to add a note concerning my relation to Mihu. He did me the favor of reviewing my book *Transylvanian Villagers* (see Mihu 1988*c*) after another important sociologist, Bădescu (see discussion in this chapter, and n. 11 below), had refused to review it. Although most of my associates regarded Mihu's review as negative, I was grateful for it since it allowed me the opportunity of a public reply.

6. Mihu's defense of Blaga was published in 1986 but appeared in a collection of his essays in 1988. I cite from the latter, which is more accessible.

7. Mihu describes these new communist directions as "the democratization of Romania, the dismantling of social inequality through the agrarian reform, the struggle to gain, preserve and strengthen national independence and sovereignty, the creation and promotion of the new as a special form of patriotism" (1988*a*: 48). Such a description makes it easy for Blaga not to have been anti-Marxist.

8. The plausibility of this claim rests on the fact that in Transylvania, a disproportionate number of pre-1945 communists had been Hungarians.

9. In my fourteen years of association with Romania, this was the first piece of *samizdat* identified as such with which I came into contact. Three persons from totally different backgrounds and cities mentioned it to me, which made it triply significant. Persons unfamiliar with Romania may note with surprise that a Marxist text circulated in underground form. This is indeed eloquent of the state of Marxist thought in Ceaușescu's Romania, but it was also true of other socialist countries such as Hungary, East Germany, and Poland, where leftist critics of the existing leadership became dissidents and circulated their material underground.

10. Of the less serious I would cite the effort of C. Sorescu in his polemic with "dogmatist" Z. Ornea. The argument took place in *The Week* (*Săptămîna*)

for 1982, Sorescu's first three articles dated February 19 and 26 and March 5; Ornea's replies are dated March 26, April 2, and April 9, and Sorescu's rejoinders April 16 and 23. In this polemic, Sorescu sought to show that ethnicity should be prior to class in a Marxist analysis of Romanian social history, and that such an analysis would reveal—inter alia—that Romania never had a native bourgeoisie that was fascist, hence fascism was alien to the true character of Romanians.

11. It also leaves a residue of dread in the pit of one's stomach. This, at least, was my own experience in reading the book, which I found almost impossible to put down, yet I was disturbed by its xenophobic tone. I had the feeling of having been dazzled by a performance whose underlying tendencies I could not quite fathom, and they made me uneasy.

I should add that my relation with Ilie Bădescu may color my reading of his work, for it was he above all who buried my own book on Romania (Verdery 1983) in that "eloquent silence" and the "light rain" of ridicule described in chap. 5 by literary critic Manolescu. Asked to review it early in my year's research in 1984, he found offensive to his national sensibilities the two anecdotes I had placed near the front to establish the book's analytic problem; he therefore determined to smother it, and his reaction created a number of problems for my subsequent work in Romania. Well before I learned of his role in creating difficulties for me, however, I had read his book and found it both provocative and unsettling.

12. Much of the force of this book resides in its treatment of specific features of Romanian economic and cultural history; to enter into an adequate discussion of it would require not only more knowledge of these than I myself possess but far more than the patience of the nonspecialist reader would bear.

13. Its agenda is in fact multiple, not triple. Among the goals I do not touch upon is his attack on the idea of "synchronism" associated with interwar critic Lovinescu (see chap. 1).

14. Sociologist Mihu, in an intelligent review of the book, explains this very clearly (Mihu 1988b). In the terms to be introduced in chap. 5, Bădescu's book is an excellent example of protochronism in sociology.

15. Several Romanian intellectuals with whom I have discussed Eminescu objected to my calling him antisemitic. On the basis of my admittedly limited familiarity with some of his writings, I find it difficult to accept this judgment, some of whose dubious reasoning appears below in my discussion of Bădescu. I prefer to see this passionate insistence of my friends as rooted in something else: given the attacks that were then being made on these people as "cosmopolitans" and "traitors to Romanian culture," it was vital for them to defend the great names in Romania's cultural history. How is one to defend a great poet who is a blatant antisemite? One tries to explain his antisemitism away. In Ceauşescu's Romania, it was more dangerous to speak out against tendencies in a great poet's work—lest one be branded a traitor—than it was to deny the evidence of one's intelligence as to his antisemitism.

16. It was the publication of Eminescu's political writings, full of unabashed antisemitism, that occasioned the article by C. V. Tudor discussed at the end of chap. 5 (see Shafir 1983a).

17. Bădescu offers an extensive array of quotations from Eminescu quite radical in tone and fairly persuasive of the possibility that we are dealing with an early radical thinker (or else with one of those people so conservative that his conservatism joins with the extremism of the left). Only a close and time-consuming study of his total output—the reedition of his corpus is past its thirtieth volume—could adequately establish whether Bădescu has given so selective a sample as to misrepresent Eminescu's evident intentions. I have discussed Eminescu with sophisticated and well-read Romanians who differ as to whether he was or was not a quasi-materialist, but who agree more generally that his sociopolitical writings are ragged and inconsistent, and that Bădescu has to strain to get a coherent set of notions from them.

18. Achim Mihu, mentioned above, is one instance; another, from a completely different paradigm, is M. D. Gheorghiu, cited often in this book. Mihu has on occasion said that within the possibilities open to sociologists, he saw no point in attempting positivist research on how people felt about living in high-rise apartments, when the discipline's input was restricted to this polling process. Therefore, he looked to see where something interesting was going on, found it in literature, and proceeded to make literary criticism the object of structural-functional and statistical investigation, branching off from there into consideration of the fates of major literary figures (see Mihu 1983). Gheorghiu also made literature the object of his study, attempting to found a "sociology of culture" thereby, but his approach was Bourdieuan and he maintained a much greater analytic and affective distance than did Mihu (see Gheorghiu 1987).

19. The most important sociologist inclined to history is H. H. Stahl, who cannot be accused of having chosen this orientation in response to the "crisis" of sociology because he had already been doing historical sociology for decades. Bădescu's recourse to historical sociology was doubtless more strategic than Stahl's.

20. Additional evidence of this point from another quarter concerns the case of Stahl, who published a broadside against figures he viewed as the interwar right and as an unfortunate influence on the present (1983a). His targets were Lucian Blaga, Mircea Eliade, and other lesser lights. When his book was withdrawn from circulation amid a barrage of attacks from all quarters, his reply was that he was just trying to apply a materialist analysis to the interwar political/intellectual spectrum (Stahl 1983b). This was not sufficient to restore him to anyone's good graces or secure publication of his several backlogged manuscripts.

21. That Mihu took this position may be puzzling, given the patriot-militancy of his defense of Blaga, above. It is not entirely clear to me how these two positions go together, but it does seem that Mihu's sense of patriotic militancy could encompass antisemitism and antimagyarism while stopping at the exaggerations of indigenism that denied western associations. Transylvanians on the whole seemed less prone than others to this sort of indigenism; moreover, Mihu gave every sign of pursuing a "Transylvanianist" cultural policy that looked more than a little askance at things emanating from Bucharest. Finally, I believe he could not permit the younger Bădescu to define the lineage of a discipline in which he hoped to claim preeminence.

Five:

1. A version of this chapter was greatly improved by close readings from several Romanian intellectuals in four disciplines, among whom I would single out for special thanks Sorin Antohi, Pavel Campeanu, Mihai Dinu Gheorghiu, Norman Manea, Nicolae Manolescu, Andrei and Delia Marga, Virgil Nemoianu, Marian Papahagi, Ştefana Steriade, and Alexandru Zub. They may still object to my interpretation, but it is factually more accurate and richer for their attention to it. Additionally, the chapter benefited from comments or information from Lauren Benton, József Böröcz, Andrei Brezianu, David Cohen, Jane Collier, Mihail Ionescu, Gail Kligman, Michael Shafir, Michel-Rolph Trouillot, Dorin Tudoran, and Mircea Zaciu.

2. Consider, for example, the following characterization of Ceauşescu: "[In 1965] he was an admirable knower of the principles of the struggle to affirm the new, of the *Romanian national essence*, of the ways and means of optimizing our life inside our country" (Tudor 1986: 18, emphasis added).

3. In my judgment and that of several Romanians with whom I have discusssed these matters, the most extreme protochronist statements came from such people as Ion Alexandru, Paul Anghel, Eugen Barbu, Nicolae Dragoş, Ion Lăncrănjan, Pompiliu Marcea, Ilie Purcaru, Artur Silvestri, Constantin Sorescu, Corneliu Vadim Tudor, Mihai Ungheanu, and Dan Zamfirescu. Persons who took a visible stand on the opposing side include Ovidiu Crohmălniceanu, Al. Dobrescu, Gheorghe Grigurcu, Mircea Iorgulescu, Norman Manea, Nicolae Manolescu, Z. Ornea, Alexandru Paleologu, Andrei Pleşu, Eugen Simion, Al. Ştefănescu. Persons appearing to have a position that is either more moderate or more equivocal include Adrian Dinu Rachieru, Solomon Marcus, philosopher Constantin Noica (see chap. 7), and perhaps poet Adrian Păunescu (who, in a fight with Vadim Tudor, made some public statements discrepant with those of his erstwhile protochronist allies).

I have read statements of various sorts by all these people, but those of the protochronists are especially well summarized in a set of interviews conducted and published by Ilie Purcaru (1986). To ease access for others wishing to follow this discussion, I have overcited this source in preference to the multitudinous newspaper articles in which protochronists stated their views. To simplify citations of this source in the text, I have not given the names of those who uttered a particular statement except when it is especially important to signal the author's identity. Here are the page numbers associated with particular interviews from which I have cited: Paul Anghel (35–45), Mihai Ungheanu (59–73), Edgar Papu (82–94), Al. Oprea (107–118), Pompiliu Marcea (119–130), Dan Zamfirescu (130–139), Nicolae Manolescu (140–149), Ion Lăncrănjan (149–160), Marin Sorescu (170–181), Ion Dodu Bălan (232–241), Solomon Marcus (242–252), Al. Andriţoiu (253–264), Nicolae Dragoş (319–332), Artur Silvestri (364–375).

Purcaru's collection is worth a further word of gossip. An antiprotochronist with whom I discussed it said that the originals of many of these interviews were so outrageous in their attacks on the Writers' Union, a constitutionally legitimated organization, that the press to which the book was submitted first refused it outright and then was pressured into accepting it, but only after cutting some interviews and toning down others. The collection is, therefore, censored relative to its already-published inclusions.

4. See chap. 4, concerning the protochronist column about "short-wave pseudoculture."

5. Nearly all participants in the protochronism debates were men; I therefore use the masculine pronoun throughout my discussion, with few exceptions.

6. These are English translations for the Romanian periodicals *România literară*, *Viaţa românească*, *Secolul XX*, *Luceafărul*, *Săptămîna*, and *Flacăra*.

7. According to one of my associates, the protochronists did respond, in the form of a pamphlet published in Italy by emigré Iosif Constantin Drăgan; I have not seen this pamphlet.

8. This silence infuriated protochronists, who complained that "scorn, indifference, or silence concerning protochronism indicates an attitude that is not truly intellectual" (I. Constantinescu 1977: 4) and that "silence is not . . . a sign of critical morality but is immoral and unacceptably cliquish" (Păunescu 1982*a*: 15).

9. Many of the essays in Papu 1977 do not make an active protochronist case but simply argue the merits of one or another great Romanian writer. The essays tend to presuppose a single aesthetic standard across all cultural and temporal contexts; the meaning of a work in its time and place is less important for Papu than the fact of certain stylistic or thematic priorities—-as when he argues that nine years before Vico, often seen as a precursor of Romanticism, the Romanian Cantemir wrote similar things, or that a writer of the 1840s used a "psychoanalytic" technique on his heroine decades before Freud.

Papu credited himself, incidentally, with nothing more than the label "protochronism"; he was generous in acknowledging the inspiration of others, particularly Zamfirescu (1970, 1975).

10. I have this information from a former member of the staff of that journal.

11. It seems unlikely that Papu presented his thesis with this in mind. Those with whom I discussed his theory all agreed that he was relatively apolitical, had had the idea for some time, and unwittingly got caught up in its consequences. The four antiprotochronist writers with whom I discussed Papu at length all took a surprisingly protective attitude toward him. One expressed himself vividly, as follows: "Papu is blameless in all this, a tragic figure, really. He's an old man who can't get out of the situation he finds himself in and didn't intend when he started out. He's very smart, and he had interesting ideas that were picked up and abused by others. He was a real thoroughbred before; now he's been trained to walk back and forth in a cage in the Party's zoo." He can be accused of opportunism only in that, having lost his university position in his prime, he may have resented his lack of disciples and was all too happy to find himself sought after and cited by so many admirers.

12. It is significant that this sort of statement was being made just as the

austerity program, with its restrictions on imports and on spending foreign currency for anything but essentials, was becoming a big issue in Romania. The protochronists' cultural anticolonialism thus accompanied Romania's near-total economic dependence on outside powers during the decade of the 1980s.

13. In this respect translations have a major role "as means of symbolic accumulation and impropriation, permitting in the end the accommodation of the local cultural circuit to the practices of international exchanges and indirectly easing the production of 'universality'" (Gheorghiu 1987: 25).

14. Somehow enmeshed in the question of imitations and foreign imports was the matter of plagiarism, at least three cases having been brought by anti-protochronists against protochronists: Ion Gheorghe, for plagiarizing from Lao-Tse; Corneliu Vadim Tudor, for stealing an article that appeared in the U.S. Embassy publication *Sintezis*; and Eugen Barbu, for having plagiarized from various western and Soviet writers in one of his novels.

15. Paul Hare (1988) and other economists argue that socialist systems tended to treat export—foreign trade in general—as a residual sector, which supplemented internal budgeting but was not made an integral part of economic planning from the very start. (The primary exception, Hungary, proves the rule.) This probably offers an apt characterization of Romania's economy until the debt crisis hit Romania in all its severity (about 1980), making export against foreign currency the battle-cry of the leadership.

16. This is a clear reference to the style of the mass meetings held by the one-time "court troubador," poet Adrian Păunescu, which many saw as bearing a strong resemblance to Nazi methods of mass mobilization. (Having attended one such meeting, I do not find the comparison misplaced.) Păunescu was reputed to have made fabulous sums of money through these meetings, enabling him to live in an expensive mansion and drive a Mercedes. Păunescu's was one of those faces shown on television during the 1989 rebellion, hastening his way to seek asylum (vainly) at the U.S. Embassy.

17. One might see protochronism's emphasis on priority as changing the bases for evaluating literary products from a market-based to a command style. It transformed the language of literary criticism from a language of *quality*—a cover term for marketability, which traditional command economies were not very successful at gauging—to a language of *priority*, something that command economies could more easily handle, alongside such countables as size, weight, and number (see Nove's discussion of how outputs are assessed in command economies [Nove 1980: 96–102]).

18. One writer explained to me that after years in which his novels were published in editions of 2–3000, he had unusual difficulty getting his newest manuscript through censorship; but when it was approved after months of negotiation, the press printed the novel in 26,000 copies so as to make money on it, after all the trouble it had caused. The book was sold out in three days. A story like this would not have been possible in the days before "self-financing."

19. Personal communication from Ştefana Steriade, a researcher who spent years on surveys concerning these issues.

20. My understanding of this subject has benefited from conversations with several Romanian writers, both inside and outside Romania, and from Gabanyi's useful study (1975), upon which my summary draws very heavily.

21. Attached to this, but separate, was the Literary Fund, through which writers could obtain loans for extended periods to cover times when they were engaged in lengthy projects or were having trouble publishing their works. Although the very fact of *having* a loan exerted its own form of moral pressure after a while, pushing writers to make compromises so as to publish something and earn money to pay off the loan, the existence of this cushion was a very important cause of the relatively great political independence and influence of the community of writers in socialist Romania. The fund and its contribution to writers' independence also made leadership within the Writers' Union relatively powerful, in comparison with leadership in other areas of culture. The Unions of Composers and Artists had similar funds, but neither had the membership and influence of the writers.

22. Some would call it the "reformist" faction, meaning those wishing to change the line pursued by the Party at any given time. I avoid this term, for "reformist" and "conservative" enter too readily into western judgments that are not wholly apt or helpful to understanding what was going on.

23. Shafir argues that in Ceaușescu's speeches on culture, there is good evidence for his returning to socialist realism well before 1971, as early as 1968 (Shafir 1983*b*: 417). Although I have no reason to doubt this, I—along with nearly all Romanian intellectuals with whom I have discussed these matters—use 1971 as the beginning of the change that was consolidated by 1974.

24. Writers perceived the impact of the July theses very fast, as is evident from speeches given at a Central Committee Plenum held in November of 1971, four months after Ceaușescu's speech, at which the speakers were drawn largely from education and the arts.

25. Eugen Barbu had been given *The Week* in 1970; Adrian Păunescu became chief editor of *The Flame* in 1973 and began holding his mass meetings then; Nicolae Dragoș, formerly on the board of the Party's Youth newspaper, became editor of *The Morning Star* in 1974 (Shafir 1983*a*: 229–30), following a period of unstable and collective editorships. The change was especially noticeable at *The Morning Star*, where in the early 1970s an innovative group of reformist writers challenged the literary establishment to increase the sophistication of its Marxism; under Dragoș, it soon came to resemble the main Party publications and housed elements precisely the *opposite* of those inhabiting it before.

These three magazines together had a reported weekly printing of (in the order above) 75,000, 134,938, and 9,411, in 1973 (Bălan 1975: 32–34), totaling almost 220,000 or about one copy per 100 inhabitants. In the same year, the circulation of three major national publications of the opposing side totaled about 29,500, or one per 750 inhabitants (two of these three are monthlies; I have divided their monthly totals by 4 to achieve a figure comparable to that for the others). I have no figures for later years.

26. The fascinating story of the 1977 and 1981 Writers' Conferences, as reported to me by people who were present, is longer than my account can accommodate. In brief, the insistence of Union leaders produced secret elections for conference delegates; the antiprotochronists—far more numerous than the protochronists—not only saw to it that no protochronists were elected delegates but also eliminated from the governing council all persons Ceaușescu was

known to have considered as possible presidents (until 1981, the president was always "elected" by the governing council from among its members). In 1977, not even with Ceauşescu's personal escort was Central Committee member and protochronist Eugen Barbu admitted into the hall. Ceauşescu's interference in the selection of the leadership in 1981 caused several important writers to resign from the council and the Union.

27. I take the position in this work that values are socially defined in *any* sphere; thus, I do not ask, in this discussion, how literary values relate to the production of surplus-value, in Marx's sense.

28. Gheorghiu (1987: 49) also argues that literature is the site of the largest symbolic accumulations (as compared with philosophy or sociology) because it so successfully *naturalizes* cultural production—that is, it links creative works with "the genius of the people," something to which other forms of intellectual activity are less susceptible. Perfect exemplification of this point, in my view, is the very common Romanian saying "*Românul e nascut poet,*" or "The Romanian is a born poet." One finds in the writings of specialists and nonspecialists alike endless effusions about the very special quality of Romanian poetry, its untranslatability, its superiority to the poetries of other languages, its organic connectedness with the soul of the people. To see Romanians as born poets links Romanian identity with *cultural and literary* creation, par excellence; it makes those creations a fact of nature rather than a phenomenon to be analyzed sociologically; and it sets up a nationalist standard by which accumulations of literary values may "naturally" take place.

29. This writer's reply links the concerns of 1950s "dogmatists" with the "aesthetizing" concerns of his opponents in the 1980s as if the two groups were one, thereby constructing a "dogmatism" that mixes groups and issues from different times.

30. Since juries were set by the governing council of the Writers' Union, dominated by antiprotochronists, this was a legitimate complaint.

31. Among the benefits of prize-winning were decreased problems with censorship and a degree of political immunity; by conferring visibility, prizes enabled writers to mobilize some support if they fell afoul of the regime (this may apply, for example, to former dissident Paul Goma; see his 1979 memoirs). Such is certainly the case with prizes granted outside Romania, like the Herder Prize that doubtless helped poet Ana Blândiana to weather the storm following her publication of some very critical poems in the winter of 1984–1985.

32. The subject of the Dictionary is a very sore spot with people in the literary community, several of whom volunteered their views on it to me without any provocation. I have synthesized their largely consistent opinions into a single account.

33. In Purcaru's interviews, it was generally he himself who suggested a plot against reediting certain writers; some of his protochronist interlocutors agreed with his opinions but others of them pointed to the quite objective difficulties of editing one or another writer's work. For a rejoinder to protochronist accusations about delayed reeditions, see Ornea 1985*b*.

34. In the interests of accuracy, I should note that among the first to reintroduce the full poetic corpus of Eminescu was antiprotochronist Ion

Negoițescu, and the first to discuss the problematic philosopher Blaga was old leftist ("dogmatist") Ovidiu Crohmălniceanu.

35. Reeditions also offered a substantial means of historical revisionism, which was an additional element in the "recovery of the national patrimony" of which they were part. A reedition might excise certain passages without indicating them, or add footnotes that substantially altered the hitherto accepted reading of a work. An outstanding example of this is Ilie Bădescu's reedition of historian Nicolae Iorga's 1928 *The Evolution of the Idea of Liberty* (Iorga 1987), in which a 263-page text is accompanied by 157 pages of commentary having, in the opinion of antiprotochronist reviewer Ornea, a decidedly current agenda (Ornea 1988).

36. It is impossible to quote Bakhtin on double-voiced discourses without being acutely aware of what one is doing. To remain true to the spirit of his work, therefore, I must acknowledge that I have taken the sentences following the ellipsis from a paragraph that *precedes* the first several sentences quoted. I can find no reason to think Bakhtin would disallow the last sentences as a conclusion to the others.

37. For example, the editors of the works of interwar philosopher Constantin Rădulescu-Motru and literary critic Eugen Lovinescu held very definite political positions about the way "their" authors should be regarded, positions that persons of opposed persuasion disagreed with. The matter of reeditions thus joins the question of rereadings, discussed above, both forming important elements in the accumulation of cultural authority.

38. An exchange between antiprotochronist A. Ștefănescu (1981) and protochronist Zamfirescu (1982a: 7) reveals competition to appropriate contemporary Romanian novelist Marin Preda (d. 1980) into their respective genealogies, each of the two claiming Preda as (respectively) a "modernist" and a "traditionalist." From the same exchange it appears that there was a comparable struggle to appropriate poet Nichita Stănescu (d. 1983). These examples show that it was not only precommunist cultural figures who had cultural authority it would be desirable to appropriate.

39. Purcaru added one of his rare editorial footnotes to reiterate this affirmation in italics: "[W]e congratulate him with all our hearts for the fact that— as he has declared to us—his *profession is patriotism.*" The exchange shows "patriotism" as an object of struggle among literati.

40. One very well-placed writer with whom I discussed this claimed that Ceaușescu became enthralled with protochronism by the mid-to-late 1970s and, when the energy of some of its protagonists began to flag, personally insisted on more. With this, protochronism became a part of the state doctrine, this writer said, as can be readily seen if one compares the content of Ceaușescu's major speeches on cultural themes with the content of protochronist writings. On the basis of this writer's report, it would seem that the leadership was forced to back the protochronists perhaps more fully than it might have wished, once its own man, Eugen Barbu, who had been raised up from a modest background to membership in the Central Committee and editorship of major books and publications, was proved guilty of plagiarism. The Party leadership could not afford to have its man held up as a common thief and

came to his defense, cementing protochronism to its own fate in a very direct way.

41. When an antiprotochronist's review of a protochronist text was refused, he reported to me, the reason given him by the head censor was, "The interest of the Party leadership is to have Romanian culture be as old as possible."

42. The National History Museum in Bucharest presents the visitor with numerous immense wall maps treating the history of Romanians within borders larger than any historically existing Romanian state: they run from the former Romanian-Russian border on the River Dniestr well into the territory of present-day Hungary. These same maps appear in various books published under the highest Party aegises, of which the best example is one authored by the president's brother, Ilie Ceauşescu, in 1984. See also chap. 6 below.

43. This affinity may have something to do with why the protochronists were generally rescued from above in the numerous scrapes they got themselves into. Corneliu Vadim Tudor, while writing for the paper *Free Romania*, plagiarized an article from the magazine published by the American Embassy in Bucharest; yet the editor's decision to fire him was countermanded, and he received a job at higher pay working for another paper. Protochronists Paul Anghel and Ilie Purcaru were involved in a scandal concerning misappropriation of foreign currency from a journal they edited; yet although they were fired, their careers proceeded apace. Barbu's conviction for plagiarism lost him his seat on the Central Committee but not his editorship of *The Week* or his influence with the organs of censorship.

44. I am grateful to Gail Kligman for this phrasing.

45. Shafir also suggests (1983*a*) that protochronism possibly *penetrated* high Party decision-making, rather than being *produced* by them.

46. If the group were simply reducible to the Party leadership, it would not have suffered eclipse in 1983 despite connections to the Central Committee, failed to win seats sought in Party councils in 1984, or had more than one initiative resisted by the major theoretical journal of the Central Committee (*Era socialistă*). Some antiprotochronists told me the Party leadership was actually fearful of this group, owing to the inconvenient financial consequences of the Israeli response to publication of C. V. Tudor's antisemitic articles (see Shafir 1983*a*, and discussion below). It might be more accurate to say that there remained some in the Party leadership who resisted protochronism, even if others favored it. The former group spoke out clearly over the latter in Rădulescu's (1986) attack on protochronism.

47. One is struck by the words used by some protochronists, readily open to a psychological reading—for example, the overemphasis on Romanians' self-rejection and the need to rectify it (see, e.g., Zamfirescu 1982*b*: 4). The biographies of several prominent protochronists show signs of dislocation and marginalization, but a study of antiprotochronists might well show the same.

48. An example is *Morning Star* critic Artur Silvestri, who began his career hanging out in the editorial halls of the (antiprotochronist) journal *Literary Romania*, his work published rarely because of the numbers of top-notch writers seeking to publish through this and related channels. Sooner than many, perhaps, he lost patience; *The Morning Star* offered him not just easy publication

but his own weekly column. Within two years he had become a zealous pro-tochronist, turning his pen to denouncing the emigré "traitors" in Paris and Munich, calling into question the cultural representativeness of these propaga-tors of "pseudoculture" and thereby invalidating their claims to cultural au-thority, and excommunicating its holders as "cultural terrorists" and traitors (see his interview in Purcaru 1986: 364–375). (For certain emigrés he made an exception, regarding their work as so Romanian that "one would think it had been written here among us" [Purcaru 1986: 371]. These exceptions include, most visibly, world-famous Mircea Eliade of the University of Chicago, known not only for his brilliance, not only for his association with rightist groups in the precommunist period, but also—as reported to me by Eliade's close friend, philosopher Constantin Noica—for his having urged Papu on to greater boldness in his protochronism.) Many antiprotochronists regarded Silvestri as a direct agent of the Romanian security police, since his column published infor-mation to which only the intelligence forces had access (the precise location of Radio Free Europe's broadcast towers, e.g.) and regularly named emigrés whose names the censors usually barred from print.

49. I choose this article for translation because it is the shortest of its kind. Similar to it but lengthier, and richer in religious imagery, is Tudor's introduc-tion to his set of essays (1986). Zamfirescu, as well, had numerous revealing pieces in various journals from the latter part of the 1980s.

50. The Romanian word [*tartan*] puns on an insulting term for Jews [*tîrtan*].

51. Here, for example, is the concluding paragraph of the preface to Tudor's book of essays: "He is the brow of Romania, the country invested him [with office] to guard its fullest and cleanest Ideal. Through deep roots the Romanian people prepared itself to sprout him forth, and he sprouted at the right time, in the most turbulent century. We love him and belong to him, we follow him in everything he does, through his mouth speak all the great founders who sacri-ficed themselves for the people . . . " etc. etc. (1986: 9). The organic images should be borne in mind for the analysis that follows.

52. Shafir sees the article as occasioned by the imminent issue of a volume of Eminescu's political writings that was full of antisemitic statements and was sure to stir up trouble (see Shafir 1983*a*).

53. The religious language opening the article probably aimed to make the reader's religious sensibilities more receptive to the antisemitic attack at the end, but in other pieces by Tudor and by others, especially poet Ion Alexandru, reli-gious language occurred with no such obvious explanation. One is amazed to find in the preface to Tudor's 1986 book references to the "Tree of Life," the [last] "supper," Romanians "crucified along the Carpathians," bread that "turns to blood in the mouth," etc. On the Leader's birthday, poets such as Păunescu published (unsigned) hymns full of religious language. One writer suggested to me that much of this originated with Zamfirescu, who attended theological seminary, became interested in Byzantine history, and responded to the July theses of 1971 by suggesting that more ritual of the Byzantine sort would help to produce an ideological climate suited to unquestioning obedience. The use of religious language may also have been an attempt to saturate the secular

rhetoric of nationalism with imagery from the one other institution that has long exercised a viable claim to having protected and defended Romanians over centuries of oppression by outsiders: the Orthodox Church. This would not mean "nationalizing" the great reserves of cultural authority held in religious institutions, for these have been nothing if not national for centuries, but *expropriating* or at least *devaluing* it, by broadening the contexts in which religious language appeared, beyond the religious occasions controlled by the Orthodox hierarchy.

54. An example is several articles published in 1981 and 1982 stating or insinuating that Norman Manea, a Romanian writer of Jewish descent, cannot write Romanian properly [i.e., he is a foreigner and massacres the national tongue—other critics disputed this], attacks patriotic writers, is godless [at least, not of *our* god], frequents taverns [irrelevant to his writing], and sets himself up as a grand procurator of Romanian letters. (See, inter alia, Păunescu 1982*a* and *b*; Purcaru 1982*a* and *b*; Tudor 1982; Zamfirescu 1982*b*; see also Shafir 1983*a* for other cases of antisemitism.) This attack resulted from Manea's having given public rebuttal to Tudor's "Ideals" (Manea 1981).

55. I must emphasize once again that I refer here to the most zealous partisans of protochronism. There were many Romanian intellectuals attracted to the idea who did not participate in the extremes to which some carried it. A few persons interviewed by Purcaru went out of their way to resist his attempt at dividing the literary field into warring camps.

56. Organic imagery was not the monopoly of the protochronists, but they used it continually and sometimes to excess, often also implying that their opponents were NOT organically tied to the people and the culture. One might call this a high "organic composition" of cultural capital, noting that it gave a fairly high rate of profit in Ceauşescu's Romania.

57. Whether or not identities are thought capable of change is, in fact, the basic issue distinguishing "racist" from other systems of classification. A society need not emphasize *phenotypic* differences to be racist in its implications, although virtually all societies that do so are aptly called racist. Even *cultural* differences can be thought of as inborn and immutable (Wallman 1980), a good example being nineteenth-century Hungarian attitudes toward Romanians (Hoffman 1983). By this criterion, protochronism is a racist form of national ideology.

58. Gail Kligman's work on the "Song of Romania" competitive festivals will do much to clarify and amend our understanding of the mechanisms of cultural politics discussed in this book (see Kligman MS).

59. Two examples may help clarify how this sort of exclusion proceeded: (1) Writer Paul Goma reports that during his final days as a Romanian dissident in 1977, a self-styled "patriot" took him aside and said to him, "You have a way of upsetting yourself and a way of doing things that are not specifically Romanian." To Goma's protesting that despite his having had a non-Romanian grandparent, he *feels* Romanian, the man replied, "Fine, let's grant that you are Romanian, but you act like a non-Romanian" (Goma 1979: 35). Shortly thereafter Goma was expelled from Romania. (2) Writer Norman Manea, mentioned in n. 54, gave a published interview in which he spoke his mind about

the protochronists. Their revenge came in 1986, when the Writers' Union awarded him a prize and they had sufficient power with the Committee for Culture to have the prize rescinded. They had already in effect "expelled" him from the writing community with the insinuation that he did not know the language properly. This and other forms of harassment contributed to Manea's decision to emigrate.

Six:

1. The first of these is quoted by Robert R. King (1980: 1); the second is from Nancy Heer (1971: 11).

2. This chapter draws heavily upon a paper previously published under a pseudonym (Simmonds-Duke 1987). In n. 1 of that paper I acknowledged the many friends and colleagues who so kindly contributed to it, and I will not list them again here. I add my thanks to U.S.-based Romanian historian Dinu C. Giurescu, who was good enough to read this chapter for accuracy, and to Mihai Dinu Gheorghiu, who offered some helpful comments on Simmonds-Duke 1987 and caused me to rephrase parts of the present version. I wish to affirm that the several Romanian scholars with whom I discussed the events recounted in this paper bear no responsibility for my interpretation, developed well after the fact. Unlike some of the other chapters in this book, the present one was not seen in draft by scholars in Romania, nor have I discussed its content with any of the principal characters, as I did with chaps. 5 and 7.

3. This statement holds true for Marxist-Leninist regimes in general, but different ones varied in the extent to which they attempted to control history and put it to their specific uses. The Romanian, Soviet, and East German Parties made more of an effort to direct history than did the rulers of Poland, say, or Hungary (see Heer 1971; Iggers 1975: 134–135).

4. See, for example, Kendall (1955: app. II) on revisionism in Shakespeare's portrait of Richard III, Ferro (1985: 24–25) on revisionism in debates about Joan of Arc, and Craig (1987) for a nontechnical discussion of battles within German historiography of the Third Reich.

5. A burgeoning literature on the "invention of tradition" and the "production of history" makes these points for various nonsocialist societies. See, for example, Adhiambo 1986; Breen 1989; Cohen 1986; Gathercole and Lowenthal 1990; Hobsbawm and Ranger 1983; Johnson et al. 1982; Lowenthal 1986; Trouillot 1989.

6. The literature on socialist historiography is rather large, including Black 1956; Davies 1989; Deletant 1988; Dirlik 1978; Georgescu 1981; Heer 1971; Hruby 1980; King 1973 (chaps. 9–11); *Kosmas* 1984–1985; Precan 1985; Rév 1984; Rura 1961; Sherlock 1988; Shteppa 1962; Skilling 1984; Svoboda 1985; Valkenier 1985; and Walker 1983.

7. The research project from which this book is an offshoot was originally entitled "Historians Construct the Nation" and was intended to show

how history-writing helped to form Romanian national consciousness. It is already apparent to me that the subject is too large for a single book.

8. (1) During the 1970s there was a significant and very noisy shift in emphasis from the Daco-Roman to a Dacian origin theory in certain Party and historiographical circles; it had not completely died down even in the late 1980s. It occasioned bitter disputes among historians and would make an excellent case study of the production of history in Romania. I do not pursue it here because, unlike the example I select, I was present for none of the action (indeed, one of the main players died of a heart attack the day I was to interview him!), and my experience is that one needs direct exposure to make sense of the written texts. (2) The 1980s saw moves to rehabilitate Marshall Ion Antonescu, the leader of fascist Romania during World War II, now being presented as a great and misunderstood patriot rather than as a traitor. There was also a quasi-protochronist interpretation of Romania's role in the war, which argued that owing to the 1944 coup that shifted Romania from the Nazi alliance to the other side, World War II ended six months earlier than it would have otherwise, which spared Europe much cost and bloodshed (see I. Ceaușescu et al., 1985; the Romanian edition of this work was entitled *Două sute de zile mai devreme* [*Two hundred days sooner*]).

9. These claims were not made in official rhetoric, where Hungarian politicians always scrupulously adhered to the existing boundaries. But almost any casual conversation with Hungarians, both in Hungary and living abroad, reveals widespread sentiment that Transylvania rightly belongs to them.

10. Since I do not read Hungarian adequately, I cannot offer my own assessment of this work. Those relatively neutral scholars with whom I have discussed it find it generally of high scholarly standards but feel that to expect Hungarians to accept the Romanian view is utopian: the two sides will simply never agree on this matter.

11. It is my personal opinion that we would be wrong to see this reaction as instigated first and foremost by Ceaușescu or central Party circles. I believe a considerable role was played by a historian who appears below, the director of the History Institute in the Transylvanian capital of Cluj, Ștefan Pascu, who a scant few months before had nearly lost his post. Knowing of the leadership's extreme magyarophobia, I suspect that this historian sent exaggerated word to Bucharest concerning the content of the Hungarians' *History of Transylvania*, thus positioning himself as the guardian of the Nation's honor and firmly securing his directorship thereby. His signature was prominent among the very first published articles to denounce the Hungarians' "conscious falsification of history."

12. As of 1990, to my knowledge there had been no full-scale rebuttal but some works relevant to the problem had emerged, such as Pascu and Ștefănescu 1987 and F. Păcurariu 1988. The former was a collection of articles published in the popular press even before the appearance of the Hungarian volumes, criticizing articles and reviews in Hungarian publications between 1983 and 1985.

13. Given the increasingly disastrous situation in Romania during the late 1980s, I think it not out of the question that such a mobilization of army energies may have aimed at reducing the likelihood of a military coup. The manner

of Ceaușescu's overthrow in 1989 certainly shows that such a concern would not have been misplaced.

14. A detailed description of changes in the infrastructure of history-writing can be found in Georgescu 1981.

15. There has been a long-standing division of labor, with historians based in Cluj and Iași concentrating on the histories of Transylvania and Moldavia, leaving to Bucharest the history of the third region and the organization of general syntheses. Because each region's history requires different languages, different documentary sources, and different theoretical constructs, this division makes considerable sense: only for the history of Transylvania, for example, does one absolutely have to know Hungarian and German and use the conceptual repertoire of West European feudalism. The habit of Party historians from the center to stick their fingers into matters like the Roman-Dacian wars (which "belong" to Transylvanians) or other events specific to the provinces drew considerable ire from those whose turf was being infringed.

16. Deletant (1988: 86) explains the outcome differently, also by reference to rumor, as the result of intervention by the Soviet ambassador, concerned about the possible disappearance of an Institute for Party History. Our different preferences reflect two time-worn explanatory strategies in Romania—invoke the Soviet Union, and invoke personal ambition. Deletant also suggests that interinstitutional rivalries were strong in the late 1980s. The reduced interference of the Soviet Union in Eastern Europe's internal affairs by the late 1980s causes me to prefer an internal institutional explanation.

17. I owe this interpretation to Bucharest sociologist Nicolae Gheorghe. Evidence for the redefinition of history's object and its transformation into "the entire people" is the founding in 1984 of a new historical journal, *Struggle of the Entire People* (*Lupta Întregului Popor*).

18. Because the terms used by participants are central to my argument, I have adhered strictly to the following conventions. I have narrowed the permissible translations of the Romanian word *răscoală*—which covers the meanings of the English words "rebellion," "uprising," and "revolt"—to "uprising" and will employ this word whenever I am paraphrasing someone who used Romanian *răscoală*. I employ "revolution" in paraphrasing those who used the Romanian word *revoluție*. To keep the voice of narrator distinct from that of the actors, I use "revolt" or "rebellion" when I summarize on my own account.

19. The following description is entirely of the debate *about* Horea; there is no place in my account for what "actually happened." English-language readers interested in finding out something about Horea's revolt might consult Edroiu 1978; Mușat and Ardeleanu 1985: 200–238; Shapiro 1971; and Verdery 1983: 93–106. The two works discussed in the text are found in the bibliography under Pascu 1984 and Prodan 1979.

20. The manner of my participation made it almost impossible for me to interview members of the audience, hence I cannot be sure of its composition and can only report the guesses of those around me and of the conference organizer. The numbers present were somewhat smaller on the first day; about 150 people were at the session on "Horea's Uprising in Documents of the Time," which I attended and which ran concurrently with another session on the first

day, but the audience for the plenary session on the second day was much larger.

21. The welcoming speech addressed the audience as "men of science, art, and culture, researchers into the history of the people and the Party, museum personnel, educators from around the county."

22. When this chapter was written, it seemed wise to use the names of as few persons as possible, lest my account cause people difficulty. As this book goes to press, the instability of the political situation makes it prudent to retain that strategy. In general in this book, I name only those persons whose published works I can cite; the present chapter relies on participation and on interviews more than any of the others.

23. Throughout parts of the session, the buzz of conversation in the room was growing. I learned that this did not necessarily signify inattention, however, when I overheard the exchange of three people sitting behind me, who turned out to be subengineers in mining: "Who's he citing now?" "Marx. He's saying it's a revolution if there's an ultimatum." This suggested that the outlines of the argument, if not, perhaps, all its obscure details, were obvious to at least some of the nonspecialist crowd. During the break, however, a random conversation confirmed that others in the crowd were completely unaware of the theoretical significance of the argument over uprising or revolution. (My victim was a history teacher from the nurses' aides' school, who had found Pascu's idea of revolution a convincing formula).

24. When I asked Professor Prodan why he did not offer a counterargument to his opponent in print, he replied: "If a gypsy stops you to pick a quarrel when you're on your way somewhere, do you waste time arguing with him? No." This comment illustrates perfectly the sour relations between these two longtime enemies who dominated the field of Transylvanian history, and it gives the reader a sense of why Professor Pascu might have wanted to come up with something new to say on the subject that Prodan had made his own.

25. This final Academy symposium marked what many on the "uprising" side saw as the defeat of the "revolutionary" position. Organized by Professor Pascu, the session included papers by several highly respected Cluj scholars, their papers all titled with "revolution" in the printed program (it emerged that Pascu had set the titles). Presiding over the session was the newly elected head of the Romanian Academy. To Pascu's chagrin, only his personal henchman and he himself upheld the argument for revolution, the others adhering to the other view and speaking of "uprising" despite their titles.

26. In the late 1920s, novelist Liviu Rebreanu published a fictionalized history (*Crăișorul* [*The Prince*]) about Horea's rebellion, presented from a populist point of view and showing Horea's Romanian peasantry as nationalist, much as in Pascu's view in 1984. According to Mihai Dinu Gheorghiu, to whom I owe this information, Rebreanu's objective was to provide historical legitimation for the interwar Peasant party, at the same time presenting Horea as "emperor" (true to the image of nineteenth century folk poetry). Gheorghiu believes these historical roots were very important to Pascu's manipulation of Horea as a nationalist.

27. Pascu was director of the Institute of History in Cluj, held the chair of

history at the University of Cluj (of which he was also rector for eight years), headed the National Committee of Romanian Historians, the Commission of Historians of Romania and Hungary, and the history section of the Romanian Academy, of which he was been a member since 1977. He was a candidate member to the Central Committee of the Romanian Communist Party for a number of years.

28. Some evidence for this is that Ilie Ceauşescu's 1984 book on Transylvania reproduced much of Pascu's argumentation about Transylvanian history.

29. For debates in history, the notion of "cultural authority" that is appropriate for chaps. 5 and 7 is better called "scientific authority," since writers, critics, and philosophers produce "culture," while historians produce "science." I have modified the horizontal axis of fig. 4 to reflect this.

30. In two cases, I counted as "revolutionaries" persons who also appeared in print with "uprising," the latter in contexts where I believe other usage was specifically suppressed (see Simmonds-Duke 1987: 216–217). I also counted as "uprising" one person whose public speech carefully avoided all terms but who in conversation made it clear what side he was on.

31. See Muşat and Ardeleanu 1985: 213–214 (the English translation), and compare with Pascu 1984: 27–28.

32. Arrayed in a 2x2 table—leaving off those whose usage oscillated—these data are statistically significant (chi-square 22.21, p <.001).

33. The performances of four political figures, three of them at the conference, would seem to question this proposition. The fourth, Ceauşescu, had two speeches using now one term, now the other. We cannot know whether this was simple inconsistency on his (or his speechwriters') part, his having reverted unthinkingly to the well-known older formula, or his purposely wishing to maintain two options; all are plausible explanations. But the existence of competing sacred texts created confusion and room for maneuver further down the hierarchy and illuminates the performance of the three political figures at the conference. It is likely that the first party secretary used "uprising" because Romanian politicians unanimously regarded Bucharest as the only site of ideological innovation, all others following at a respectful distance. Until it should be clear that this quite major change in the labeling of a major historical event had passed the test of acceptance, caution would be the wisest course. This speech nevertheless sat cleverly on the fence by not changing the label but accepting many points of the "revolutionary" argument. With its flanks well protected, it set the tone for the Secretary's two subordinates.

34. I made two wholly unsuccessful attempts to interview Professor Pascu about his book. Although he always treated me with exemplary courtesy, he made it clear that he did not wish to discuss this topic. I have considerably more information on the attitude of Professor Prodan, whose refusal of a public reply accompanied an agitated volubility on the subject in private.

35. Party historian Ion Popescu-Puţuri (1983: 18), in describing the remarkable contributions made to Romanian historiography by First Historian Nicolae Ceauşescu, observes that the peasant masses used to be seen as a group having no historical function, a theory aimed at calling into question the very existence of the largely peasant Romanian people. Ceauşescu has restored to

Romanians their history, he says, by showing them to have had major revolutionary possibilities. This "valuable insight" may have inspired Pascu's book.

36. East German historians argued similarly over the 1525 Peasant War, some cryptically suggesting, as in the argument over Horea, that German society was more progressive than the Soviet Union (see Walker 1983).

37. For more information on the economic context relevant to such a message, see Crowther 1988: 143.

38. See, for example, Roller 1952: 275.

39. Horea was not the only locus of anti-Hungarian scholarly activity in the 1980s; other examples can be found in the publication *România literară*, numbers 49 and 51, December 1984, and, earlier, in such writings as Lăncrănjan 1982.

40. Indeed, many historians spoke of a Calendar Strategy of publication: pick your topics by opening your calendar, not by pursuing themes that interest you.

41. To make sense of this and of the example in the next paragraph requires a reminder of what was entailed in the "self-financing" of cultural institutions in Ceauşescu's Romania. In the economic crisis, state subsidies to enterprises in the cultural field were reduced and their directors subjected to insistent financial pressure (without, however, being given the authority to make significant independent decisions). Such organizations as museums, theatres, and libraries were expected to cover at least part of their costs through their receipts. Personnel would be cut if they failed to do so.

42. Many persons made no use of the opportunities in Horea's celebration, and not all who figured in the events did so opportunistically. Prodan, it will be remembered, published his book on Horea several years before the bicentennial; he did not enter directly into the subsequent festivities. Given widespread opportunistic use of Horea, many were drawn into the fray who would otherwise have gone about their business.

43. A hilarious anecdote about the struggle to redefine history, passed on to me by Mihai Dinu Gheorghiu, makes this point very nicely. In the early 1980s, a rambunctious intellectual played a trick on a former colleague of his, who had become a high functionary in the history division of the Ministry of Education. He invented a debate—ostensibly organized by the paper for which he worked—on how Romanian history was being presented in school manuals, and he sent an official invitation to his colleague. When the latter proved unable to attend, he was promised a copy of the results of the debate (also, of course, made up). The "results" included comments by a number of very important historians, extremely critical of education in history—the domain of the victim, who now despaired that he had not been present to defend the position of his ministry and had not forewarned his superiors of this reorientation. The victim's reaction is very revealing: it shows how utterly plausible he found it that a cultural magazine could organize a debate on history at which big-time official historians criticized official history, never suspecting that the whole thing had been made up.

44. The military personnel who spoke or wrote about Horea placed special emphasis on this matter.

45. For example: "[T]he army has always been on the side of the entire people in fighting foreign aggression throughout the centuries" (I. Ceauşescu et al., 1985: 43), or "The success of the Romanian insurrection was possible through the intertwining of political-military preparedness, carefully organized and led by the Romanian Communist Party, with conditions specific to the Romanian tradition of the entire people's war" (ibid., 101).

46. I can attest to Horea's existence in peasant minds in two village communities, as well as among urban populations.

47. Although the audience most affected by this display was not large, in Horea's case, I would argue that the repetition of events such as this, involving other heroes in other places, would eventually have drawn in a fairly large number of Romanians, affecting them in a similar way.

48. See Baylis (1974: 18). The obvious contrast is, of course, with Poland in the late 1970s.

49. Because of my chance selection of texts to exemplify the views of persons I would place near the political axis of fig. 4, Prof. Ştefan Ştefănescu appears with that group disproportionate to the position I believe he in fact occupied in Romanian historiography. Historians with whom I gossiped about members of the profession generally regarded Ştefănescu as the only historian having high political status who, despite this, defended unpoliticized scientific authority, insofar as his position permitted. (As member of the Central Committee and head of the most important non-Party history institute, he was often not allowed free maneuver). I wish by this footnote to acknowledge the integrity with which I believe he sought to acquit himself, in the impossible position he was placed in during the 1980s.

50. The scholar who told me of this disposition saw it as an aspect of "romanianization" because it suppressed the Hungarian and German place-names one would normally use for Transylvanian history prior to the twentieth century. I see it also, however, as part of the flattening of time.

51. I discuss additional aspects of the flattening of time—in food lines, for example—in Verdery 1991.

52. I refer here to suppression of the works of poets Ana Blândiana and Mircea Dinescu, for example, in 1988/1989, along with interdictions on publicity for literary critic Alexandru Paleologu, aesthetician Andrei Pleşu, and others who had the effrontery to protest the leadership's policies.

53. Personal communication. The article was published in *România literară* 17 (December 20): 12–13 and was cosigned by A. Gh. Savu.

54. According to newly established anthropological canons of openly acknowledging the disruptions ethnographers introduce into their field sites, I publicly record here the fact that, having discovered by chance that the American Historical Association was electing several new honorary members, I organized the campaign for Prodan's election. My reasons for having done so were my great respect for the quality of his scholarship, my personal attachment to him, and my understanding, as argued in the text, that such acknowledgment would offer friction against the constant narrowing of the field of historical production in Romania. In other words, I interposed into the Romanian context

my American preference for pluralism over concentrations of power, a preference shared by those in whose behalf I acted. All these "political" reasons notwithstanding, by every professional standard of American history-writing, Prodan's election was absolutely deserved.

55. Both other historians and Prodan himself commented to me upon his having acquired symbolic properties.

56. As with so many things in Romania, I cannot verify this account of the nonappearance of the *Treatise*. I received very similar accounts from a number of historians, however, and have presented a composite of them here.

Seven:

1. I acknowledge here a debt to Pavel Campeanu, Mihai Dinu Gheorghiu, Claude Karnoouh, Gail Kligman, and Ştefana Steriade, who commented on drafts of this chapter, and also to Andrei and Delia Marga, who first brought Noica to my attention and who gave me copies of the two books discussed in the chapter (which were virtually impossible to find, otherwise). These persons and many others with whom I discussed the Noica School gave me not only data but also interpretations that entered into my own and cannot be adequately attributed. I am also grateful to several scholars, particularly Sorin Antohi and Al. Zub, who provided me with many of the reviews and other bibliography scattered among various magazines.

Parts of this chapter have appeared as an Occasional Paper of the Woodrow Wilson Center's East European Program.

2. My interpretation rests on Liiceanu 1983, 1985, and 1987; Pleşu 1988; Paleologu 1980; a large number of commentaries and reviews; uninformed readings of Noica 1975, 1978 and 1987*b*; and conversations with a variety of persons, both central participants in the events and interested bystanders. I also had two brief meetings with Noica in the summer of 1987, totalling about two-and-a-half hours, before I had read any of these works. At the time, I was interested in Noica's relation to the interwar national discourse, not in his contemporary significance. While these two meetings contributed little to the discussion of the present chapter, they did give me a feel for this fascinating and elusive personage and for his link with the problem of national identity.

3. In the circle closest to Noica I count Gabriel Liiceanu, Andrei Pleşu, and Sorin Vieru; those in particularly significant relations with them include Alexandru Paleologu, Thomas Kleininger, Vasile Dem. Zamfirescu, and Victor Stoichiţa (now living in Germany), most of whom figure in *Letters*. It is to these people, despite differences among them, that I refer with the terms "Noica School" or "Noicans," for all were touched in transformative ways by their exposure to Noica and to the others. My lumping of these persons under a single label obscures many important differences among them in style, politics, and relation to Noica. In the circle of persons relatively well disposed to the project of the group I include Ştefan Augustin Doinaş, Radu Enescu, Andrei Pippidi,

N. Steinhardt (despite a nasty review), and a number of the "antiprotochronists" of chap. 5, such as Nicolae Manolescu, Mircea Iorgulescu, etc. Among those favorably disposed to Noica but hostile to the purposes of the others are a number of protochronists, such as Eugen Barbu, Paul Anghel, Ion Coja, Dan Zamfirescu, and Ion Stroe. I do not deal with commentaries from the Romanian emigré community, which helped to bring more attention to the Noicans and thereby broadened their internal and external audience.

4. Eliade, now deceased, emigrated from Romania in the 1940s and ended his days as a world-renowned philosopher of religion at the University of Chicago; Cioran became the epigone of a skeptical philosophy in Paris.

5. Alexandru Paleologu, who knew Noica intimately, insists that Noica was never in fact as much under the spell of Ionescu as were the rest and that his association with fascism (mentioned below) was brief and impulsive, rather than a matter of conviction. Others will, of course, contest this view.

6. The story told me by Noica's friend N. Steinhardt was that during the period of forced domicile, Noica occasionally escaped to Bucharest, where he met with a group of friends to read and discuss prohibited works, such as the writings of the by-then-emigré Eliade and Cioran. During this time Cioran published in Paris a "Letter to a Distant Friend," addressed to Noica, who wrote a reply that he sent out to the West together with some manuscripts. The package was intercepted and the entire group was arrested, tried, and given prison terms of up to twenty-five years.

7. Because so much of cultural interpretation in Ceaușescu's Romania—and especially that concerning Noica—was politicized to greater or lesser degree, one should situate Marga himself in relation to the Noica group. Marga is what I would call a "friendly outsider," a philosopher with extensive training in western philosophical thought (like Noica and his followers) but strongly influenced by lines in contemporary German philosophy different from those of the main Noicists: the Frankfurt School and Habermas (with whom he has worked extensively), rather than Heidegger and hermeneutics, so influential in Noica's circle. This affiliation leads Marga to accentuate the critique of modernity in Noica's work. The intellectual genealogy Marga compiles nevertheless conforms well with that suggested by Noica's published works and by his own presentation of himself (see Noica 1987a). Despite the differences in their basic concerns, Marga acknowledges Noica as Romania's most systematic and deep philosophical thinker of the postwar period.

8. Marga refuses, however, to see Noica's refuge in Plato as a return to premodern times but interprets him, rather, as a *postmodern* thinker, his solutions differing from both the second wave of postmodern thinkers (such as Heidegger) and the most recent wave (such as Derrida and Lyotard) (Marga 1988: 47).

9. I am grateful to Claude Karnoouh for this phrasing.

10. When I asked Noica how the interwar questions concerning the "national essence" had found their way into his present work, he gave the following account: after he emerged from prison, he realized that the new climate precluded what he had hoped to contribute to metaphysics, and then in musing over problems of language (a direction having ample precedent both in Heideg-

ger and in Romanian scholarship), he discovered that interesting philosophical problems could be put via linguistic means. Attention to ethnic questions thus enabled him to publish his metaphysics in a disguised form, and he soon found that this form brought him far greater success than he had ever imagined possible. His reply accords with his remark in his *Jurnal de Idei* (forthcoming) that Romanianness was simply a pretext, for him. Given how crafty Noica showed himself in other contexts, however, we should bear in mind that he knew enough about western scholarship to know what sort of answer to give a westerner. His answer also conveniently omitted his having written on questions of Romanianness in the 1930s and 1940s, before the conjuncture of the Ceauşescu period forced this choice on him.

11. Although one occasionally found a short piece by Noica in *Morning Star*, he most commonly wrote for *Romanian Life* and *Literary Romania*, both of which generally excluded protochronist writings.

12. On the walls of the philosophy department in Iaşi and Cluj were a series of portraits of such persons as Aristotle, Plato, Lao-Tse, Confucius—but not Marx. (These portraits were later replaced in some locations by those of Ceauşescu and Dacian leaders.) One of the most unusual exchanges in *Letters* occurs between Liiceanu and his former professor Ion Ianoşi, who argues for a tolerant climate in which the validity of Marxist philosophy will be accepted along with the claims of other approaches!

13. The *Journal* was published in 8,000 copies and *Letters* in 16,000 (the usual specialist work in philosophy might expect a run of 5,000; novels generally have much larger ones, often exceeding 75,000 copies). Since in Romania any book that gets as much attention as these did will be read much more widely than the size of its press run—one of my associates guessed that any copy would pass through at least ten sets of hands—these figures indicate at best what the press was prepared to risk (politically) in choosing to publish these books. Both were published by Cartea Românească, the press of the Writers' Union, which had somewhat greater editorial independence in its selections than did the majority of presses.

14. My count of seventeen reviews of the *Journal* did not include several that appeared early or a number that appeared within the context of articles on other subjects, such as obituaries following Noica's death in 1987. Although the number of cultural publications in Romania was quite large, to obtain this many reviews was unusual; it meant that most regional magazines and the entire spectrum of the political/cultural field found the book worth comment. Some magazines published more than one review (e.g., *Literary Romania*).

15. Reference to the Ninth Congress was a fundamental move in the rhetoric of those who wished to participate in Ceauşescu's personality cult, for it was at this congress that he was formally installed as General Secretary.

16. This term does not appear in any of the writings I have consulted; I am coining the expression so as not to prejudge the analysis by using a term like *protochronist*, even though there was some overlap between persons who espoused protochronism and those who defended Noica's national writings or argued for what I call ethnophilosophy. In speaking of "ethnophilosophy," I am creating a composite that did not exist as such; it had ample precedent, how-

ever, in the writings of earlier thinkers such as Vasile Pârvan and Ovidiu Densuşianu.

17. A good example of what passed for "normal" philosophy in the 1970s is a volume published in 1979 called *Philosophical Thinking in Romania Today* (Ghişe et al. 1979), the articles containing a multitude of references to western thinkers and only the most perfunctory mention of Marxist problems, never in a sloganizing manner.

18. Although I have not sufficient space to emphasize it here, accusations of "dogmatism" did more than merely oppose Noicans and materialists, having played a major role in forming the Noica School itself. Liiceanu claims to have discovered the beauty of philosophy only after leaving the stultifying form of it encountered in university, and his accusations against his "materialist" mentors are among the sharpest in *Letters* (1987: 282–292). That "dogmatism" was a weapon in the hands of *both* sets of adversaries clarifies once again, as I argued in chap. 4, its importance as a categorical excluder bearing little relation to the concrete details of a person or work.

19. My thanks to Mihai Gherman for providing me with this text.

20. This accounts for the significance of the *paideic model* in Noica's and his followers' program; see my discussion later in this chapter.

21. Noica shared his missionarism with the intellectual generation in which he had participated before World War II, and a similar missionaristic spirit had flourished in the Romania of the late nineteenth century. In the process of transforming the nature of the intelligentsia, I would argue, something like a form of messianism has often been produced, usually by that fraction of it whose position was being challenged by other groups and whose expertise re-quired reassertion. But the messianism of Romania's nineteenth-century intel-lectuals and of the interwar period were not motivated by quite the same pro-cesses as that of the 1980s, nor by exactly the mechanisms signaled in Bauman's argument, inapplicable to societies such as socialist Romania in which legit-imating functions were not assumed by a consumer-oriented market.

22. It is tempting to see in this eulogy the church's joining the contest to control Noica, but although something of that sort may have been going on, another explanation offered me is more to the point. The archbishop was a good friend of Noica's, and he had accepted the task of trying to fulfill Noica's request for burial in the hermitage even though by normal monastic practice Noica had no right to be there. His strategy was to present Noica as a Christian, as leading a life close to that of a good monk—something his highly ascetic lifestyle facilitated. Without making such an argument, the archbishop would have been sorely exposed with his own religious hierarchy—and could not, in any case, have justified his presence at the burial of an ordinary philosopher with no claims upon the church.

23. My point of view here resembles that of Burawoy in his *Politics of Pro-duction* (1985), where he tries to understand why consciousness of exploitation is so much less veiled in socialist systems.

24. As of 1980—the beginning of the economic crisis in Romania—I no-ticed far more frequent references to the Biblical Apocalypse among my village respondents than I had in my earlier visit in 1974. I would also say impression-

istically that the sense of urgency among intellectuals increased then as well, but I have no "proof" of this.

25. I am aware that the "strategies" and "tactics" in the discourse of persons influenced by Bourdieu and Foucault are understood not as subjectively planned by the individuals who execute them but as properties of a field of culture or power—actorless requirements that remind one of Pirandello's characters in search of an author. I myself am still irremediably mired in the idea of subjectively relevant social action, however, as this paragraph shows.

26. Here I take issue with a point of view Bourdieu has not (to my knowledge) expressed in print but stated in a conference I attended. Following a presentation in which he talked of the symbolic market for linguistic exchanges, he was asked what sort of sense an analysis resting on a market analogy had for societies in which markets were systematically suppressed. His reply was that this made no difference. I cannot agree.

27. Although it was Liiceanu's phrasing that made this a matter of public discussion, there is no doubt that the paideic ideal was part of Noica's original intent—see the quotation about his "School" at the head of this chapter. He had also attempted on at least two prior occasions to set up relations of tutelage similar to those he instituted at Păltiniş.

28. This is not to say that Noica's relation to his disciples was egalitarian, which it surely was not. I emphasize, rather, the manner in which his authority was defined and exercised, in contrast to the manner of the regime.

29. One manifestation of the debate over philosophy and literary criticism was an argument as to whether Liiceanu was really more of a writer than a philosopher, whether his books were not more exemplary as literary than as philosophical texts (e.g., Dobrescu 1987: 12; Paleologu in Liiceanu 1987: 79; Marino 1987: 6); one reviewer even analyzed *Letters as a novel*, pointing out its literary structure and so forth (Breban 1988).

30. Liiceanu came closest to expressing something like this when he suggested that necessary to cultural creation is some sort of *theory*, and literary critics do not for the most part work with or produce their own theories: they have to borrow from disciplines that do produce theory (see 1987: 146–147). To rephrase Liiceanu's argument in a familiar metaphor: he and Noica both tended to see philosophy as the "heavy industry" of cultural production, an industry that employs the raw materials of certain other fields and creates machines ("theory") that are essential to production within other domains. In making an argument of this kind, they follow directly in the tracks of certain philosophers from the interwar years, most notably Vasile Băncilă (1927), whose view I presented in chap. 1. The irony of the Liiceanu-Noica variant of this, however, is that they were proposing to construct this heavy machinery through a sort of cottage production, on a mountaintop, involving only a few workers, precisely *avoiding* the main urban centers of philosophical manufacture.

31. A writer with whom I discussed these books said that if Noica were in Ceauşescu's shoes, things would be just the same as under Ceauşescu because Noica's was the same totalitarian spirit. Some might add that Ceauşescu's personality cult created a suitable environment for Noica's cult of himself.

32. Note again the emphasis signaled above, a defense of a kind of expertise based on advanced study of western cultural traditions.

33. *Letters* has an aesthetic elegance that my discussion cannot adequately honor. It seeks to achieve its aim through the idea that "from often-impassioned conflicts a purer truth is born" (Liiceanu 1987: 7)—that is, the book's message will be structured through discord pursued with passion. A certain emotional tension is set up at the outset by recording Liiceanu's anxiety over how the *Journal* is being received, then following the criticisms and enthusiasms communicated to him. The letters provide two emotional climaxes, in the form of heated accusations and generous reconciliations (between Liiceanu and two persons his *Journal* presented in an unfavorable light), and a series of intellectual climaxes partly linked with these emotional ones. Within this structure, argument for a pluralist strategy emerges by making the parties to a personal quarrel also represent different positions on the question of philosophy versus literary criticism. As Gheorghiu observed in a penetrating review, the first quarrel and its reconciliation reconfigure the whole field of forces, both reequilibrating the personal relations of two men and restoring the relations of philosophy with literature and art (1988*a*: 5). The argument about philosophy and literature is taken up more explicitly somewhat later between Liiceanu and Vieru, and then a second quarrel and reconciliation (with a "lapsed" philosopher become poet) confirms Liiceanu's adherence to the reconfigured field.

34. Contributing to this idea is not only the fierce honesty of the correspondents but also the editor's statement at the beginning that "The omission of passages of strictly personal nature or otherwise unacceptable has been marked with [. . .]" (p. 8)—as overt a statement of censorship as one was likely to find in Romania, and a solace to readers accustomed to wondering where something had been left out. Liiceanu was proposing, in a word, a "German" style of communicating in place of Romania's usual "Byzantine" one.

35. I am grateful to Frances Ferguson for pointing out to me this contractual premise, rooted in concerns of the Romantic period, as well as for an inspiring discussion on the question of audiences.

36. Although published before *Letters*, this essay was completed at about the same time and shows the effects of the unification of philosophy and literature in the latter work. Despite my attempt to remain somewhat distant from the phenomena discussed in this chapter, I have to confess that I have rarely taken as much delight in an essay—in any field or any language—as I did in this stunning piece.

37. For readers who may wonder what is meant by "creating an audience for philosophy," it may be helpful to note that Noica's exegesis of Hegel was published in a printing of 30,000 copies (Liiceanu 1983: 123)—in a country having one-tenth the population of the United States. His *Romanian Sentiment of Being* was printed in 10,700 copies, and his 1987 edition of *Romanian Ways of Speaking Philosophically* (Noica 1987*b*) in 60,000.

38. The first sentence of Noica's preface to his book *Letters about the Logic of Hermes* reads thus: "These letters are addressed to someone, in the hope that when they reach the border-crossing of culture, they will be intercepted and

perhaps read by a few mathematicians, logicians and other magicians of naked forms." His first chapter begins: "To your confession that you do not know what logic is, I reply that I don't know either." (See Noica 1986: 5, 11.) It is difficult not to feel that one could get somewhere with this treatise on logic, even if one knew little about the subject.

39. I have omitted from my already-long summary the matter of the "feminine paradigm," which Liiceanu ties to gender divisions in the creation and transmission of knowledge.

40. When I discussed *Letters* with people who had given it a general rather than a philosophical or sociological reading, several said they had found the book unusually gripping because *all* the contradictory points of view were so persuasive. "I'd read one letter and I'd say, 'He's right!' and then I'd read the reply and say 'He's right too!'" said one woman in the library I frequented.

41. Books of philosophy resembled those in history in having somewhat more institutional protection from the market than did literature or literary criticism. Because the chief Noicans' institutional situation was marginal within philosophy, however, they resembled literary critics—in whose press their works primarily appeared. In chap. 3 I suggested that vulnerability to the market may have accompanied greater tendencies to opposition, by which argument the Noicans' constitution of a united front among critical philosophers and literati makes sense.

42. This point, as well as the one in the subsequent two paragraphs, was suggested to me by Ashraf Ghani.

43. I have it on good authority that these would never have been published without the assistance of persons highly placed in the Party—one of the few respects in which Noica's appeals to authority bore fruit.

44. An uncharitable account of this serial was that the "incredibly lazy Barbu" saw a way of having his column written for him for a whole year with minimal effort and with certain increases in the sales of his magazine.

45. These several features of Barbu's serial meant that even those readers with well-developed "bracketing practices" (in Ghani's phrase) would not get much out of the serial—that is, one could not simply ignore Barbu's comments (bracket them off) and get the true sense of *Letters*.

46. Figures for its circulation are hard to come by, as I reported in chap. 5; although it was printed in 100,000 copies in the 1970s, some people told me that it was down to 50,000 in the late 1980s. This was, in any case, larger than any other literary publication and was exceeded in size only by the major dailies and by the more general cultural magazine *The Flame*.

47. One might ask why the books of the Noicans were published, if they were such a threat to power. The fate of those who signed the March 1989 protest made it clear that one could go too far, for these authors were at once placed under interdiction (they were "disabled" as foci of cultural production). Liiceanu himself often wondered whether he ought to allow his writings to be used by power, as he assumed must be the case if his books were permitted to appear—and his productivity suffered, in consequence (he "disabled" himself anticipatorily). Although I cannot answer the question of why the books were published, I would guess that it had to do with hidden support from persons

high up in the Party leadership, with struggles between the bureaucracies of culture and propaganda, and/or with the efforts of publishers to promote values (and salable works) that strengthened positions they wished to defend. Defenders of the books could always point to ambiguities in the texts that made them acceptable or even desirable—such as that the *appearance* of opposition would make people think that the climate was not, after all, so oppressive, or that the Party was strong enough to afford the publication of an occasional provocative text. Only in the case of persons who had clearly gone too far (such as by signing public protests) would editors not try such a defense.

48. Indeed, the problem of creating a worker-intellectual alliance that had never been forged was one of the first to emerge after December 1989. A long interview with Liiceanu in February 1990 shows him preoccupied with precisely this problem (see Pavel 1990).

Conclusion

1. Grateful thanks to Ashraf Ghani, Mihai Dinu Gheorghiu, and Gail Kligman for ideas that entered into this concluding chapter.

2. The Party line cannot itself be readily predicted, however. It is not simply that the *command* form of socialism inclines toward an official preference for national ideology; other things may affect the leadership's mode of control even within the command form. In the Soviet case, it is likely—the experience of the late 1940s notwithstanding—that the Soviet Union's multinational composition made official nationalism dangerous as long as a mono-ethnic entity, the "Soviet Nation," had not been successfully constructed. While national ideology has certain clear affinities for "command" leaderships, no law dictates it of necessity. Reliance upon it will be influenced by such things as preexisting ideological fields, the other options available to a Party leadership, the balance of social forces, and the prior mobilization of a socialist (or other) consciousness.

3. The Soviet nationalisms that result not from such "cultural" causes but from efforts to unseat entrenched high bureaucrats were another very important form of national phenomena in Gorbachev's Soviet Union, but the material presented in this book does little to illuminate them.

4. In the absence of factional splits within the Romanian party, which might have given internal critique some leverage, in the absence of a more highly developed working-class consciousness with its own "practical movement for democracy" (cf. Kagarlitsky 1988: 215), in the absence of institutional foci with some independence of the center, such as Poland's Catholic Church or uncollectivized peasantry—in the absence of all these, no dissenting voice in Romania had much chance of becoming a chorus. Not one of the conditions that promoted the formation of Solidarity in Poland obtained in Romania, including, as I observe in the text, western support for those willing to speak out against the regime.

5. I owe these final points to a discussion with Ashraf Ghani, who encouraged me to push my argument to its limit.

Bibliography

A. C.
1985   Prezenţe româneşti: "Scriitorii români împotriva idiocraţiei." *Lupta* nr. 49 (December 15): 6.

Abbott, Andrew
1988   *The system of professions: An essay on the division of expert labor.* Chicago: Univ. of Chicago Press.

Academia Română
1937   *Anale*, vol. 56 (1935–1936). Bucharest: Monitorul Oficial şi Imprimeriile Statului.

Adhiambo, Atieno
1986   The production of history in Kenya: The Mau Mau debate. MS.

Alexandrescu, Sorin
1983   "Junimea": Discours politique et discours culturel. In *Libra: Etudes roumaines offertes à Willem Noomen*, ed. J. P. Culianu, 47–79. Groningen: Presses de l'Université.

1987   Populisme et bourgeoisie: La Roumanie au début du siècle. In *Populismes d'Europe Centrale et Orientale: restauration et utopie.* Cahiers du Centre d'Etude des Civilisations de l'Europe Centrale et du Sud-Est 6: 11–46.

Alton, Thad P.
1985   East European GNP's: Origins of product, final uses, rates of growth, and international comparisons. In *East European economies: Slow growth in the 1980s*, vol. 1: 81–132. Selected Papers of the Joint Economic Committee, U. S. Congress.

Anagnost, Ann
1988   Defining the socialist imaginary: The "civilized village" campaign in post-Mao China. Paper presented at the Annual Meeting of the American Anthropological Association, Phoenix.

367

Anderson, Benedict
1983   *Imagined communities: Reflections on the origin and spread of nation-
        alism.* London: Verso.
Andrei, Petre
1945   *Filosofia valorii.* Bucharest: Fundaţia Regele Mihai I.
Anghel, Paul
1970   Săptămîna: Rostirea românească. *Contemporanul* nr. 33 (August
        14): 1–2.
1977   O precizare legată de noţiunea de tezism. *România literară* 10
        (35): 8.
Antipa, Gr.
1923   *Paralizia generală progresivă a economiei naţionale şi remedierea ei.*
        Bucharest: Cultura Naţională.
1940   *Necesitatea institutelor de cercetări ştiinţifice pentru satisfacerea ne-
        voilor actuale ale ţării.* Bucharest: Monitorul Oficial.
Antohi, Sorin, and Dan Petrescu
n.d.   Dialoguri. Unpublished MS. (Published with pseudonyms in
        Agora 2 (2): 36–73, under the title "Noica, Denker in dürftiger
        Zeit," 1989.)
Antonesei, Liviu
1987   Rar şi iradiant, Noica. *Opinia studenţească* 14 (6–7): 20.
Argeş
1970   Spiritul muntean în cultura română de azi. *Argeş* 5 (11): 3, 6–8.
Arghezi, Tudor
1928   Epistola Dlui Sabin Drăgoi. *Bilete de papagal* nr. 246: 1–2.
Armbruster, Adolf
1977   *La romanité des Roumains: Histoire d'une idée.* Bucharest: Ed.
        Academiei.
Aronowitz, Stanley
1988   *Science as power: Discourse and ideology in modern society.* Minneap-
        olis: Univ. of Minnesota Press.
Babu-Buznea, Ovidia
1979   *Dacii în conştiinţa romanticilor noştri: Schiţă la o istorie a dacismului.*
        Bucharest: Ed. Minerva.
Bădescu, Ilie
1984a   Cultură şi sociologie. *Luceafărul* 27 (22 December): 2.
1984b   *Sincronism european şi cultură critică românească.* Bucharest: Ed.
        Ştiinţifică şi Enciclopedică.
1988   Un Iorga pitoresc? *România literară* 21 (February 18): 19.
Bahro, Rudolf
1978   *The alternative in Eastern Europe.* London: Verso.
Bakhtin, Mikhail
1981   *The dialogical imagination.* Austin: Univ. of Texas Press.
1984   *Problems of Dostoevsky's poetics.* Minneapolis: Univ. of Minnesota
        Press.
Bălan, Ion Dodu
1975   *Cultural policy in Romania.* Paris: UNESCO Press.

Bălcescu, Nicolae
1974   Opere, vol. 1, ed. G. and E. Zane. Bucharest: Ed. Academiei.
Băncilă, Vasile
1927   Autohtonizarea filosofiei. Gândirea 7 (11): 273–280.
1937   Lucian Blaga: Energie românească. Gând românesc 5: 121–156,
        194–210, 283–317, 505–538; 6: 38–60, 113–135.
Barbu, Eugen
1988   O paranteză: Între filosofi. Săptămîna (weekly rubric, December
        11, 1987, through October 28, 1988. Portions cited in text are
        from 1988.)
Bateson, Gregory
1936   Naven. Cambridge, Eng.: Cambridge Univ. Press.
Bauer, Tamás
1978   Investment cycles in planned economies. Acta Oeconomica 21:
        243–260.
Bauman, Zygmunt
1987a   Intellectuals in East-Central Europe: Continuity and change. East-
        ern European Politics and Societies 1 (2): 162–186.
1987b   Legislators and interpreters: On modernity, post-modernity, and intel-
        lectuals. Ithaca, N.Y.: Cornell Univ. Press.
Baylis, Thomas A.
1974   The technical intelligentsia and the East German elite: Legitimacy and
        social change in mature communism. Berkeley, Los Angeles, Lon-
        don: Univ. of California Press.
Benda, Julien
1969 [1928]   The treason of the intellectuals. New York: W. W. Norton.
Bialer, Seweryn
1988   Gorbachev and the intelligentsia. In Soviet scholarship under Gor-
        bachev, ed. Alexander Dallin and Bertrand M. Patenaude, 73–85.
        Stanford: Stanford University Russian and East European Studies
        Publications and Reprints, no. 3.
Binns, C. A. P.
1979–1980   The changing face of power: Revolution and accommodation
        in the development of the Soviet ceremonial system. Man 14:
        585–606; 15: 170–187.
Black, Cyril E.
1956   History and politics in the Soviet Union. In Rewriting Russian his-
        tory: Soviet interpretations of Russia's past, ed. Cyril E. Black, 3–31.
        New York: Praeger.
Blaga, Lucian
1921   Revolta fondului nostru nelatin. Gândirea 1: 181–182.
1966   Gîndirea românească din Transilvania în secolul al XVII-lea. Bu-
        charest: Ed. Ştiinţifică.
1980 [1937]   Elogiul satului românesc. In Discursuri de recepţie la Academia
        Română, pp. 250–262. Bucharest: Ed. Albatros.
Bloch, Maurice
1975   Political language and oratory in traditional society. New York: Aca-
        demic Press.

Böröcz, József
1989   Mapping the class structures of state socialism in East-Central Europe. *Research in Social Stratification and Mobility* 8: 279–309.

Bourdieu, Pierre
1975   The specificity of the scientific field and the social conditions of the progress of reason. *Social Science Information* 14 (6): 19–47.
1977   *Outline of a theory of practice.* Cambridge, Eng.: Cambridge Univ. Press.
1980   The production of belief: Contribution to an economy of symbolic goods. *Media, Culture and Society* 2: 261–293.
1984   *Distinction: A social critique of the judgement of taste.* Cambridge: Harvard Univ. Press.
1985   The social space and the genesis of groups. *Theory and Society* 14: 723–744.
1988   *Homo Academicus.* London: Polity Press.

Bové, Paul A.
1986   *Intellectuals in power: A genealogy of critical humanism.* New York: Columbia Univ. Press.

Brăescu, Mariana
1982*a*   Confesiuni esenţiale: Sabin Bălaşa. *Scînteia tineretului, supliment literar-artistic* 2 (March 21): 5.
1982*b*   Confesiuni esenţiale: Eugen Barbu. *Scînteia tineretului, supliment literar-artistic* 2 (March 28): 3.
1982*c*   Confesiuni esenţiale: Mihai Bardac. *Scînteia tineretului, supliment literar-artistic* 2 (April 2): 3.
1982*d*   Confesiuni esenţiale: Ion Lăncrănjan. *Scînteia tineretului, supliment literar-artistic* 2 (April 11): 3, 10.
1982*e*   Confesiuni esenţiale: Al. Oprea. *Scînteia tineretului, supliment literar-artistic* 2 (May 9): 3, 10.
1982*f*   Confesiuni esenţiale: Radu Theodoru. *Scînteia tineretului, supliment literar-artistic* 2 (May 23): 3, 10.
1982*g*   Confesiuni esenţiale: Dan Zamfirescu. *Scînteia tineretului, supliment literar-artistic* 2 (June 20): 5, 10.

Brătescu, Gh.
1988   Exigenţe ale gîndirii filosofice româneşti în actuala etapă. *Magazin* 31 (August 13): 2.

Bratu, Florin
1983   *Cultura populară sau virtuţile permanenţei.* Iaşi: Junimea.

Breban, Nicolae
1988   Tinerii corifei. *Viaţa românească* 83 (2): 48–63.

Breen, T. H.
1989   *Imagining the past.* Reading, Mass.: Addison-Wesley.

Brus, Wlodzimierz
1975   *Socialist ownership and political systems.* London and Boston: Routledge and Kegan Paul.

Brym, Robert
1980   *Intellectuals and politics.* London: George Allen & Unwin.

Bucur, Marin, et al.
1984   *Atitudini şi polemici în presa literară interbelică.* Bucharest: Institutul de Istorie şi Teorie Literară "G. Călinescu."
Buduca, I.
1987   Hermeneutica ghilimelelor. *Amfiteatru* 21 (2): 2.
Bugnariu, Tudor
n.d.   Untitled samizdat, typescript, arguing against A. Mihu's articles on L. Blaga (Mihu 1988*a*).
Burawoy, Michael
1985   *The politics of production.* London: Verso.
Calendar
1988   Proverbele, prima filozofie a românilor. *Calendar* 27 August 1988. Ed. Litera.
Călinescu, G.
1982   *Istoria literaturii române de la origini pînă în prezent.* 2d ed., rev. and enlarged. Bucharest: Ed. Minerva.
Camp, Roderic A.
1985   *Intellectuals and the state in twentieth-century Mexico.* Austin: Univ. of Texas Press.
Campeanu, Pavel
1973   *Oamenii şi teatrul.* Bucharest: Ed. Meridiane.
1979   *Oamenii şi televiziunea.* Bucharest: Ed. Meridiane.
1986   *The origins of Stalinism: From Leninist revolution to Stalinist society.* Armonk, N.Y.: M. E. Sharpe.
1988   *The genesis of the Stalinist social order.* Armonk, N.Y.: M. E. Sharpe.
Casals, Felipe Garcia
1980   *The syncretic society.* White Plains, N.Y.: M. E. Sharpe.
Cătineanu, Tudor
1985   Intre idei şi mituri dominante. *Steaua* 36 (3): 46–47.
Cazacu, Honorina
1973   *Mobilitate socială.* Bucharest: Ed. Academiei.
Ceauşescu, Ilie
1984   *Transilvania: Strǎvechi pǎmînt românesc.* Bucharest: Ed. Militarǎ.
Ceauşescu, Ilie, Florin Constantiniu, and Mihail E. Ionescu
1985   *A turning point in World War II: 23 August 1944 in Romania.* Boulder, Colo.: East European Monographs.
Ceauşescu, N.
1969*a*   *Romania on the way of completing socialist construction,* vol. 1. Bucharest: Meridiane.
1969*b*   *Romania on the way of completing socialist construction,* vol. 3. Bucharest: Meridiane.
1969*c*   *România pe drumul desǎvîrşirii construcţiei socialiste,* vol. 3. Bucharest: Ed. Politicǎ.
1972   *Romania on the way of building up the multilaterally developed socialist society,* vol. 6. Bucharest: Meridiane.
1983*a*   *Istoria poporului român: Culegere de texte.* Bucharest: Ed. Militarǎ.
1983*b*   *România pe drumul construirii societǎţii socialiste multilateral dezvoltate,* vol. 24. Bucharest: Ed. Politicǎ.

1988   *Nicolae Ceauşescu's exposition on the current stage of Romanian socialist society*, etc. November 28. (Brochure).

Cernea, Mihail
1974   *Sociologia cooperativei agricole.* Bucharest: Ed. Academiei.

Ceterchi, Ioan
1971   Naţiunea în epoca contemporană. In *Naţiunea şi contemporaneitate*, ed. I. Ceterchi, D. Hurezeanu, et al., 5–81. Bucharest: Ed. Ştiinţifică.

Chirot, Daniel
1976   *Social change in a peripheral society: The creation of a Balkan colony.* New York: Academic Press.

Choldin, Marianna Tax, and Maurice Friedberg, eds.
1989   *The red pencil: Artists, scholars, and censors in the USSR.* Boston: Unwin Hyman.

Ciachir, Dan
1983   Intre cultură şi utopia ei. *Scînteia tineretului, supliment literar-artistic* 3 (December 11): 5.

Ciocârlie, Livius
1988   Iniţiere în despărţire. *Viaţa românească* 83 (6): 23–29.

Ciopraga, Constantin
1981   *The personality of Romanian literature.* Iaşi: Junimea.

Clifford, James, and George Marcus, eds.
1986   *Writing culture: The poetics and politics of ethnography.* Berkeley, Los Angeles, London: Univ. of California Press.

Cohen, David William
1986   *The production of history.* MS.

Coja, Ion
1984   Cîteva precizări. *Luceafărul* 27 (February 25): 6.

Colceriu-Leis, Maria
1968   Mici însemnări pe marginea unei probleme mari—*Naţiunea. Analele* 14: 270–277.

Comaroff, Jean
1985   *Body of power, spirit of resistance: The culture and history of a South African people.* Chicago: Univ. of Chicago Press.

Condee, Nancy, and Vladimir Padunov
1987   *Soviet cultural politics and cultural production.* IREX Occasional Papers. December 1987.

Condurache, Val
1981   Spiritul critic şi conştiinţa literaturii. *Convorbiri literare* 87 (12): 3.

Constantinescu, Ion
1977   De ce protocronism? *Ateneu* 4 (182): 4.

Constantinescu, Olga
1973   *Critica teoriei "România—ţara eminamente agricolă."* Bucharest: Ed. Academiei.

Constantinescu, P.
1929   Creştinismul folcloric. *Kalende* 1 (5): 132–137.

Contemporanul
1987   Texte şi contexte: Eroare. *Contemporanul* nr. 38: 14.

Cornea, Doina
1989   Ţara astăzi este într-o nemărturisită stare de asediu. *Lupta* nr. 125 (15 July): 1, 3.

Corrigan, Phillip, and Derek Sayer
1985   *The great arch: English state formation as cultural revolution*. Oxford and New York: Basil Blackwell.

Coser, Lewis A.
1965   *Men of ideas: A sociologist's view*. New York: Free Press.

Craig, Gordon A.
1987   The war of the German historians. *New York Review of Books* (January 15): 16–19.

Craig, John E.
1984   *Scholarship and nation building: The universities of Strasbourg and Alsatian society, 1870–1939*. Chicago: Univ. of Chicago Press.

Crainic, Nichifor
1929   Sensul tradiţiei. *Gândirea* 9: 1–11.
1936   *Puncte cardinale în haos*. Bucharest: Ed. Cugetarea.

Cristian, Vasile
1985   *Contribuţia istoriografiei la pregătirea ideologică a revoluţiei române de la 1848*. Bucharest: Ed. Academiei.

Croan, Melvin
1989   Lands in-between: The politics of cultural identity in contemporary Eastern Europe. *Eastern European Politics and Societies* 3 (2): 176–197.

Crowther, William
1988   *The political economy of Romanian socialism*. New York: Praeger.

Dallin, Alexander, and Bertrand M. Patenaude, eds.
1988   *Soviet scholarship under Gorbachev*. Stanford: Stanford University Russian and East European Studies Publications and Reprints, no. 3.

Davies, R. W
1989   *Soviet history in the Gorbachev revolution*. Bloomington: Indiana Univ. Press.

Deletant, Dennis
1988   The past in contemporary Romania: Some reflections on current Romanian historiography. *Slovo* 1 (2): 77–91.

Dinescu, Mircea
1986   Cîteva cuvinte despre ghetrele lui Constantin Noica. *Scînteia tineretului, supliment literar-artistic* 6 (June 28): 5.

Dirlik, Arif
1978   *Revolution and history: Origins of Marxist historiography in China, 1919–1937*. Berkeley, Los Angeles, London: Univ. of California Press.

Diţă, Alexandru V.
1988   Un vis al înaintaşilor. *Luceafărul* 31 (February 13): 1–2.

Djilas, Milovan
1957   *The new class: An analysis of the communist system*. New York: Praeger.

Dobrescu, Al.
 1979   *Foiletoane*, vol. 1. Bucharest: Cartea Românească.
 1981   Preliminarii. *Convorbiri literare* 87 (12): 2–3.
 1984   *Foiletoane*, vol. 3. Iaşi: Junimea.
 1987   Jurnalul şi epistolarul. *Convorbiri literare* 93 (10): 12.
Dobridor, Ilarie
 1935   Trădarea intelectualilor. *Gând românesc* 3: 216–223.
Dobrogeanu-Gherea, Constantin
 1976   *Opere complete*, vol. 2. Bucharest: Ed. Politică.
Doinaş, Ştefan Aug.
 1984   Un scenariu al formării de sine. *România literară* 17 (March 15): 8.
Durandin, Catherine
 1987   Le populisme roumain ou un romantisme démocratique. In *Populismes d'Europe Centrale et Orientale: Restauration et utopie*. Cahiers du Centre d'Etude des Civilisations de l'Europe Centrale et du Sud-Est 6: 47–97.
 1989   *Revolution à la francaise ou à la russe: Polonais, Roumains et Russes au XIXe siècle*. Paris: Presses Universitaires de France.
Editura Institutului Biblic şi de Misiune Ortodoxă
 1957   *Istoria Bisericii Romîne: Manuel pentru Institutele Teologice*, vol. 2. Bucharest: Editura Institutului Biblic şi de Misiune Ortodoxă.
Edroiu, Nicolae
 1978   *Horea's uprising: The 1784 Romanian peasants' revolt of Transylvania*. Bucharest: Ed. Ştiinţifică şi Enciclopedică.
Eidlin, Fred
 1987   Comment. Presented at panel on "The uses of history in legitimating Communist regimes," Annual Meeting of the American Association for the Advancement of Slavic Studies, Boston.
Eisenstadt, S. N., and S. R. Graubard, eds.
 1973   *Intellectuals and tradition*. New York: Humanities Press.
Eliade, Mircea
 1934   De ce sînt intelectualii laşi? *Criterion* 1 (2): 2.
Elias, Norbert
 1978   *The history of manners*. New York: Pantheon.
Emerson, Rupert
 1962   Power-dependence relations. *American Sociological Review* 27: 31–41.
Enescu, Radu
 1987   Despărţire de Noica? *Familia* 23 (December 12): 8.
Eyerman, Ron, Lennart G. Svenson, and Thomas Söderqvist, eds.
 1987   *Intellectuals, universities, and the state in western modern societies*. Berkeley, Los Angeles, London: Univ. of California Press.
Fabian, Johannes
 1983   *Time and the other: How anthropology makes its object*. New York: Columbia Univ. Press.

Fehér, Ferenc, Agnes Heller, and György Márkus
1983   *Dictatorship over needs: An analysis of Soviet societies.* New York: Basil Blackwell.

Ferro, Marc
1985   *L'Histoire sous surveillance: Science et conscience de l'histoire.* Paris: Calmann-Levy.

Filotti, Eugen
1924   Gândul nostru. *Cuvântul liber* (ser. II) 1: 2–4.

Fischer, Mary Ellen
1989   *Nicolae Ceauşescu: A study in political leadership.* Boulder, Colo.: Lynne Rienner.

Florea, Elena
1982   *Naţiunea: Realităţi şi perspective.* Bucharest: Ed. Ştiinţifică şi Enciclopedică.

Foucault, Michel
1972   *The archaeology of knowledge and the discourse on language.* New York: Pantheon.
1977   *Language, counter-memory, practice: Selected essays and interviews,* ed. Donald Bouchard. Ithaca, N.Y.: Cornell Univ. Press.
1978   *Discipline and punish: The birth of the prison.* New York: Pantheon.
1980   *Power/knowledge: Selected interviews and other writings 1972–1977.* New York: Pantheon.
1982   *The subject and power.* In *Michel Foucault: Beyond structuralism and hermeneutics,* ed. Hubert L. Dreyfus and Paul Rabinow, 208–228. Chicago: Univ. of Chicago Press.

Fox, Richard
1985   *Lions of the Punjab: Culture in the making.* Berkeley, Los Angeles, London: Univ. of California Press.

Friedrich, Paul A.
1989   Language, ideology, and political economy. *American Anthropologist* 91: 295–312.

Gabanyi, Anneli Ute
1975   *Partei und literatur in Rumänien seit 1945.* Munich: R. Oldenbourg.

Gal, Susan
1988   Bartok's funeral: Representations of Europe in Hungary. Paper presented at the Annual Meeting of the American Anthropological Association, Phoenix.

Garrard, John and Carol
1990   *Inside the Soviet Writers' Union.* New York: Free Press.

Gathercole, Peter, and David Lowenthal
1990   *The politics of the past.* London: Unwin Hyman.

Gavrilă, Ana
1968   Naţiunea socialistă—etapă superioară în viaţa naţiunilor. *Analele* 14: 101–108.

Geană, Gheorghiţă
1986   Paradigma freudiană a paideii. *Viaţa românească* 87 (8): 84–96.

Gella, Aleksander
1976   *The intelligentsia and the intellectuals: Theory, method and case study.* London: Sage Studies in International Sociology, 5.
1989   *Development of class structure in Eastern Europe: Poland and her Southern neighbors.* Albany: SUNY Press.
Georgescu, Vlad
1971   *Political ideas and the Enlightenment in the Romanian Principalities (1750–1831).* Boulder, Colo.: East European Quarterly.
1981   *Politică şi istorie: Cazul comuniştilor români 1944–1977.* Munich: Jon Dumitru-Verlag.
1983   Politics, history and nationalism: The origins of Romania's socialist personality cult. In *The cult of power: Dictators in the twentieth century,* ed. Joseph Held, 129–142. Boulder, Colo.: East European Monographs no. 140.
1986   Romania 1985: Round table organized by Professor Vlad Georgescu. *Journal of the American Romanian Academy of Arts and Sciences* 8–9: 42–60.
1988   Romania in the 1980s: The legacy of dynastic socialism. *Eastern European Politics and Societies* 2 (1): 70–93.
Ghani, Ashraf
1987   Islam in Pakistan: The production and reproduction of a universe of discourse. Paper presented at the Spring Meeting of the American Ethnological Society, Santa Fe.
Gheorghiu, Mihai Dinu
1985a   La stratégie critique de la revue "Viaţa românească" (1906–1916). In *Culture and society,* ed. Al. Zub, 127–136. Bucharest: Ed. Academiei.
1985b   Un filosof în particular. *Viaţa românească* 80 (3): 75–80.
1987   *Scena literaturii.* Bucharest: Ed. Minerva.
1988a   Filosofiile Bucureştilor. *Dialog* 19 (4): 5.
1988b   Specificul naţional în viaţa literară interbelică: Schiţă unei istorii. Colloquium, Institutul de Istorie şi Arheologie, Iaşi.
1990   Specificul naţional în sociologia românească. In *Cultură şi societate,* ed. Al. Zub. Bucureşti: Ed. Ştiinţifică şi Enciclopedică (in press).
Ghermani, Dionisie
1967   *Die kommunistische Umdeutung der rumänische Geschichte unter besonderer Berücksichtigung des Mittelalters.* Munich: R. Oldenbourg.
Ghibu, Onisifor
1924   Rostul politic al vizitei patriarhului dela Ierusalim în România. *Societatea de mâine* 1: 555–557; 579–580.
Ghiulea, N.
1922   Ardealul în viaţa noastră politică. *Ideea europeană* 3 (89): 2–3.
Ghişe, Dumitru, et al.
1979   *Philosophical thinking in Romania today: An anthology.* Bucharest: Ed. Ştiinţifică şi Enciclopedică.
Gilberg, Trond
1990   *Nationalism and communism in Romania: The rise and fall of Ceauşescu's personal dictatorship.* Boulder, Colo.: Westview.

Goma, Paul
1979   *Le tremblement des hommes*. Paris: Seuil.
Gouldner, Alvin W.
1979   *The future of intellectuals and the rise of the new class*. New York: Continuum.
Grămadă, Ilie
1978   De la conştiinţa de neam, la conştiinţa naţională—trăsătură distinctivă a istoriei românilor. *Mitropolia Moldovei şi Sucevei* 54 (5–8): 501–520.
Grigurcu, Gheorghe
1981   Autoritate şi falsă autoritate. *Convorbiri literare* 87 (12): 2.
Gross, Jan T.
1988   *Revolution from abroad: The Soviet conquest of Poland's western Ukraine and western Byelorussia*. Princeton: Princeton Univ. Press.
1989   Social consequences of war: Preliminaries to the study of imposition of communist regimes in East Central Europe. *Eastern European Politics and Societies* 3 (2): 198–214.
Gusti, Dimitrie
1968 [1937]   Ştiinţa naţiunii. In D. Gusti, *Opere*, vol. 1: 492–507. Bucharest: Ed. Academiei.
Gyémánt, Ladislau
1986   *Mişcarea naţională a românilor din Transilvania 1790–1848*. Bucharest: Ed. Ştiinţifică şi Enciclopedică.
Hall, Stuart
1979   Culture, the media and the "ideological effect." In *Mass comunication and society*, ed. James Curran, Michael Gurevitch, and Janet Woollacott, 315–348. Beverly Hills: Sage.
Handler, Richard
1988   *Nationalism and the politics of culture in Quebec*. Madison: Univ. of Wisconsin Press.
Hann, C. M., and Steven Sampson
MS   Politics in Eastern Europe.
Haraszti, Miklos
1987   *The velvet prison: Artists under state socialism*. New York: Basic Books.
Hare, Paul G.
1988   Industrial development of Hungary since World War II. *Eastern European Politics and Societies* 2 (1): 115–151.
Havel, Václav
1985   *The power of the powerless: Citizens against the state in central-eastern Europe*. Armonk, N.Y.: M. E. Sharpe.
Heer, Nancy Whittier
1971   *Politics and history in the Soviet Union*. Cambridge: M.I.T. Press.
Heitmann, Klaus
1970   Das "rumänisches Phänomen": Die Frage des nationales Spezifikums in der Selbstbesinnung der rumänischen Kultur seit 1900. *Südost Forschungen* 29: 171–236.

Herseni, Traian
  1941   *Probleme de sociologie pastorală.* Bucharest: Institutul de Științe
          Sociale.
Herzfeld, Michael
  1984   The horns of the Mediterraneanist dilemma. *American Ethnologist*
          11: 439–454.
  1987   *Anthropology through the looking glass: Critical ethnography in the
          margins of Europe.* Cambridge, Eng.: Cambridge Univ. Press.
Hirszowicz, Maria
  1980   *The bureaucratic leviathan: A study in the sociology of communism.*
          New York: New York Univ. Press.
Hitchins, Keith
  1969   *The Rumanian national movement in Transylvania, 1780–1849.*
          Cambridge: Harvard Univ. Press.
  1977   *Orthodoxy and nationality: Andreiu Șaguna and the Rumanians of
          Transylvania, 1846–1878.* Cambridge: Harvard Univ. Press.
  1978   *Gîndirea*: nationalism in a spiritual guise. In *Social change in
          Romania, 1860–1940*, ed. Kenneth Jowitt, 140–173. Berkeley:
          Univ. of California, Institute of International Studies.
  1985   *The idea of nation: The Romanians of Transylvania, 1691–1849.*
          Bucharest: Ed. Științifică și Enciclopedică.
Hobsbawm, Eric
  1983   Mass-producing traditions: Europe, 1870–1914. In *The invention
          of tradition*, ed. Eric Hobsbawm and Terence Ranger, 263–307.
          Cambridge, Eng.: Cambridge Univ. Press.
Hobsbawm, Eric, and Terence Ranger
  1983   *The invention of tradition.* Cambridge, Eng.: Cambridge Univ.
          Press.
Hoffmann, Richard C.
  1983   Outsiders by birth and blood: Racist ideologies and realities
          around the periphery of medieval European culture. *Studies in Me-
          dieval and Renaissance History* 6: 1–34.
Horvat, Branko
  1982   *The political economy of socialism: A marxist social theory.* Armonk,
          N.Y.: M. E. Sharpe.
Hruby, Peter
  1980   *Fools and heroes: The changing role of communist intellectuals in
          Czechoslovakia.* Oxford: Pergamon Press.
Humphrey, Caroline
  1983   *Karl Marx collective: Economy, society and religion in a Siberian collec-
          tive farm.* Cambridge, Eng.: Cambridge Univ. Press.
Hurezeanu, Damian
  1985   Psihicul românesc și individualitatea creatoare a figurilor exponen-
          țiale ale culturii noastre. *Argeș* 20 (10): 1, 4.
Iancu, Adela Becleanu
  1980   *Spiritualitatea românească: Permanență, devenire.* Bucharest: Ed.
          Politică.

1988   Elemente de filosofie nescrisă în cultura românească. *România lite-*
          rară 21 (June 23): 19.
Ibrăileanu, Garabet
1909   *Spiritul critic în cultura românească.* Iaşi: Ed. Viaţa Românească.
1933   După 27 de ani. *Viaţa românească* 25 (1): 8.
Iggers, Georg
1975   *New directions in European historiography.* Middletown, Conn:
          Wesleyan Univ. Press.
Ionescu, Nae
1937   *Roza vânturilor.* Bucharest: Cultura Naţională.
Iorga, Nicolae
1987   *Evoluţia ideii de libertate.* Bucharest: Ed. Meridiane.
Iorgulescu, Mircea
1987   Proba dialogului. *România literară* 20 (September 10): 11.
Jackson, Marvin
1981   Perspectives on Romania's economic development in the 1980s. In
          Romania in the 1980s, ed. Daniel Nelson, 254–305. Boulder,
          Colo.: Westview.
Janos, Andrew C.
1978   Modernization and decay in historical perspective: The case of Ro-
          mania. In *Social change in Romania, 1860–1940,* ed. Kenneth
          Jowitt, 72–116. Berkeley: Univ. of California, Institute of Inter-
          national Studies.
Joja, Athanase
1965   Profilul spiritual al poporului român. *Steaua* 16 (9): 3–12.
Johnson, Richard, Gregor McLennan, Bill Schwarz, and David Sutton, eds.
1982   *Making histories: Studies in history-writing and politics.* Minneapolis:
          Univ. of Minnesota Press.
Jowitt, Kenneth
1971   *Revolutionary breakthroughs and national development: The case of*
          Romania, 1944–1965. Berkeley, Los Angeles: Univ. of California
          Press.
1978   *Social change in Romania 1860–1940: A debate on development in a*
          European nation. Berkeley: University of California, Institute of
          International Studies.
1983   Soviet neo-traditionalism: The political corruption of a Leninist
          regime. *Soviet Studies* 35 (3): 275–297.
1987   Moscow "Centre." *Eastern European Politics and Societies* 1 (3):
          296–348.
Kagarlitsky, Boris
1988   *The thinking reed: Intellectuals and the Soviet state 1917 to the*
          present. London and New York: Verso.
Karnoouh, Claude
1982   National unity in Central Europe: The state, peasant folklore, and
          monoethnism. *Telos* 53: 95–105.
1987   Constantin Noica: Metaphysicien de l'ethnie-nation. *Cahiers du*
          Centre d'Etude des Civilisations de l'Europe Centrale et du Sud-Est 6:
          125–158.

1990   "L'invention du peuple": Chroniques de Roumanie et d'Europe orien-
         tale. Paris: Ed. Arcantère. ⁻

Kendall, Paul Murray
1955   Richard the Third. London: George Allen and Unwin.

Kideckel, David
1982   The socialist transformation of Romanian agriculture, 1945–
         1962. American Ethnologist 9: 320–340.

King, Robert R.
1973   Minorities under communism: Nationalities as a source of tension
         among Balkan communist states. Cambridge: Harvard Univ. Press.
1980   A history of the Romanian Communist Party. Stanford: Hoover In-
         stitution Press.

Kirițescu, Constantin
1935   Suprapopulația universitară: Proporții—cauze—remedii. Revista
         generală a învățămîntului 33 (5–6): 3–16.

Kleininger, Thomas, and Gabriel Liiceanu
1987   Exigența lucrului bine făcut: Pe marginea a două traduceri din
         Heidegger. Revista de istorie și teorie literară 35 (12): 85–96.

Kligman, Gail
1983   Poetry and politics in a Transylvanian village. Anthropological
         Quarterly 56: 83–89.
MS   Cultural policy and the body politic in Romania.

Kogălniceanu, M.
1940   Opere alese. Bucharest: Cugetarea.

Konrád, George, and Ivan Szelényi
1979   The intellectuals on the road to class power: A sociological study of
         the role of the intelligentsia in socialism. New York: Harcourt Brace
         Jovanovich.

Kornai, János
1980   Economics of shortage. Amsterdam: North-Holland Publishing Co.
1982   Growth, shortage, and efficiency: A macrodynamic model of the socialist
         economy. Berkeley, Los Angeles, London: Univ. of California
         Press.

Kosmas
1984–1985   Kosmas: Journal of Czechoslovak and Central European Studies
              3–4.

Kundera, Milan
1984   The tragedy of Central Europe. New York Review of Books 31 (8):
         33–37.

Kuron, Jacek, and Karol Modzelewski
1966   An open letter to the Party. New Politics 5 (2): 5–47.

L. B.
1982   Ne-au mirat . . . versurile săptămînii. Viața studențească (June 2).

Laclau, Ernesto
MS   Politics as the construction of the unthinkable (trans. David
         Silverman).

Lampe, John, and Marvin Jackson
1982   *Balkan economic history, 1550–1950*. Bloomington: Indiana Univ. Press.

Lăncrănjan, Ion
1982   *Cuvînt despre Transilvania*. Bucharest: Ed. Sport-Turism.

Latour, Bruno, and Steve Woolgar
1979   *Laboratory life: The construction of scientific facts*. Beverly Hills: Sage.

Lefort, Claude
1986   *The political forms of modern society: Bureaucracy, democracy, totalitarianism*. Cambridge: M.I.T. Press.

Lemny, Ştefan
1985   La critique du régime phanariote: Clichés mentaux et perspectives historiographiques. In *Culture and society*, ed. Al. Zub, 17–30. Iaşi: Ed. Academiei.
1986   *Originea şi cristalizarea ideii de patrie în cultura română*. Bucharest: Minerva.

Lévi-Strauss, Claude
1966   *The savage mind*. Chicago: Univ. of Chicago Press.

Liehm, Antonin J.
1968   *The politics of culture*. New York: Grove Press.

Liiceanu, G.
1983   *Jurnalul de la Păltiniş*. Bucharest: Cartea Românească.
1985   Filozofia şi paradigma feminină a auditorului. *Viaţa românească* 80 (7): 55–69.
1987   *Epistolar*. Bucharest: Cartea Românească.

Linden, Ronald
1986   Socialist patrimonialism and the global economy: The case of Romania. *International Organization* 40 (2): 347–380.

Linke, Ulrike Hildegard
1986   Where blood flows, a tree grows: The study of root metaphors in German culture. Ph.D. diss., Univ. of California, Berkeley.

Livezeanu, Irina
1986   The politics of culture in Greater Romania: Nation-building and student nationalism, 1918–1927. Ph. D. diss., Univ. of Michigan.

Lovinescu, Eugen
1927   Etnicul. *Sburătorul* 4, seria noua (11–12): 2.
1972   *Istoria civilizaţiei române moderne*. Bucharest: Ed. Ştiinţifică.

Lowenthal, David
1986   *The past is a foreign country*. Cambridge, Eng.: Cambridge Univ. Press.

Luceafărul
1984   Modernitatea valorificării tradiţiei cultural-ştiinţifice. *Luceafărul* 27 (October 27): 4–5.
1985   Noua geografie a literaturii române contemporane: Evoluţia valorilor. *Luceafărul* 28 (5) (February 2): 4–5; 28 (6) (February 9): 4–5.
1987   O problemă uitată. *Luceafărul* 30 (February 7): 2.

Lungu, Ion
    1978   *Şcoala Ardeleană: Mişcare ideologică naţională iluministă.* Bucharest:
            Ed. Minerva.
Macoviciuc, Vasile
    1986   O variantă a "orgoliului" elitist. *Luceafărul* 28 (April 26): 2.
Madgearu, Virgil N.
    1921   Intelectualii şi ţărănismul. *Ideea europeană* 3 (75): 1–2.
Manea, Norman
    1981   De vorbă cu epoca: "Scriitorul—acea dreaptă conştiinţă în care se-
            menii săi să poată crede." *Familia* 17 (12): 6.
Mannheim, Karl
    1955   *Ideology and utopia.* New York: Harcourt Brace.
Manolescu, Nicolae
    1977   Tezism şi spontaneitate. *România literară* 10 (August 11): 9.
    1984   Sociologie şi cultură. *România literară* 17 (December 13): 9.
Marcea, Pompiliu
    1975   *Naţional şi universal.* Bucharest: Ed. Eminescu.
Marcus, George E., and Dick Cushman
    1982   Ethnographies as texts. *Annual Review of Anthropology* 11: 25–69.
Marga, Andrei
    1988   Raţiune şi creaţie (asupra filosofiei lui Noica). *Steaua* 34 (4):
            44–47.
Marica, George Em.
    1977   *Studii de istoria şi sociologia culturii române ardelene din secolul al
            XIX-lea,* vol. 1. Cluj-Napoca: Ed. Dacia.
Marino, Adrian
    1966   Specificul naţional în literatura română: Subiectul sau unghiul de
            percepţie? *Gazeta literară* 13 (14): 7.
    1987   Sensul "epistolarului." *Tribuna* 31 (November 5): 6.
Márkus, György
    1981   Planning the crisis: Remarks on the economic system of Soviet-
            type societies. *Praxis International* 1 (3): 240–257.
Marx, Karl
    1964   *Insemnări despre români (manuscrise inedite).* Bucharest: Ed.
            Academiei.
McNeill, William F.
    1964   *Europe's steppe frontier, 1500–1800.* Chicago: Univ. of Chicago
            Press.
Meyer, Alfred G.
    1969   The comparative study of Communist political systems. In *Com-
            munist studies and the social sciences,* ed. F. J. Fleron, 188–198. Chi-
            cago: Rand McNally.
Mihăilescu, Florin, ed.
    1981   *Aesthesis Carpato-Dunarean.* Bucharest: Ed. Minerva.
Mihăilescu, Vintilă
    1985   Rostul cuvintelor umile sau trădarea paideei. *Luceafărul* 28 (No-
            vember 2): 1, 6.

Mihu, Achim
1983   *Meandrele adevărului*. Cluj-Napoca: Ed. Dacia.
1984*a*   Maestrul şi iedera. *Tribuna* 28 (January 5): 5.
1984*b*   Problematica naţiunii române în sociologia interbelică. (Trei socio-
        logi, trei concepţii despre naţiune). In *Naţiunea română*, ed. Ş.
        Ştefănescu, 518–546. Bucureşti: Ed. Ştiinţifică şi Enciclopedică.
1988*a*   Lucian Blaga în Clujul postbelic. In Achim Mihu, *Maestrul şi
        iedera*, 33–84. Cluj-Napoca: Ed. Dacia.
1988*b*   Sincronism şi protocronism. In *Maestrul şi iedera*, pp. 224–254.
1988*c*   Transylvanian Villagers. In *Maestrul şi iedera*, pp. 198–216.
Montias, John Michael
1967   *Economic development in Communist Rumania*. Cambridge: M.I.T.
        Press.
1978   Notes on the Romanian debate on sheltered industrialization:
        1860–1906. In *Social change in Romania, 1860–1940*, ed. Ken-
        neth Jowitt, 53–71. Berkeley: Univ. of California, Institute of
        International Studies.
Muşat, Mircea, and Ion Ardeleanu
1985   *From ancient Dacia to modern Romania*. Bucharest: Ed. Ştiinţifică şi
        Enciclopedică.
Nee, Victor, and David Stark
1989   *Remaking the economic institutions of socialism: China and Eastern
        Europe*. Stanford: Stanford Univ. Press.
Newmeyer, Frederick J.
1986   *The politics of linguistics*. Chicago: Univ. of Chicago Press.
Nistor, V.
1935   Les cultes minoritaires et l'église orthodoxe roumaine dans le
        nouveau budget de la Roumanie. *Revue de Transilvanie* 2: 7–40.
Noica, Constantin
1944   *Jurnal filosofic*. Bucharest: Ed. Publicom.
1975   *Eminescu sau gînduri despre omul deplin al culturii românesti*.
        Bucharest: Ed. Eminescu.
1978   *Sentimentul românesc al fiinţei*. Bucharest: Ed. Eminescu.
1986   *Scrisori despre logica lui Hermes*. Bucharest: Cartea Românească.
1987*a*   Autoprezentare. *Tribuna* 31 (December 12): 6.
1987*b*   *Cuvînt împreună despre rostirea filosofică românească*. Bucharest:
        Cartea Românească.
1987*c*   Prefaţă la modelul european: Scrisoare către un intelectual din Oc-
        cident. *Viaţa românească* 82 (7): 54–55.
1988   Ce nu se vede. *Viaţa românească* 83 (3): 10–12.
Nove, Alec
1980   *The Soviet economic system*, 2d ed. London: George Allen & Unwin.
1983   *The economics of feasible socialism*. London: George Allen & Unwin.
Novick, Peter
1988   That noble dream: The "objectivity question" and the American
        historical profession. Cambridge, Eng.: Cambridge Univ. Press.

Opriş, Ioan
1986   *Ocrotirea patrimoniului cultural: Tradiţii, destin, valoare.* Bucharest: Ed. Meridiane.

Ornea, Z.
1980   *Tradiţionalism şi modernitate în deceniul al treilea.* Bucharest: Ed. Eminescu.
1985*a*   *Actualitatea clasicilor.* Bucharest: Ed. Eminescu.
1985*b*   Din nou despre "integrala-Eminescu." *Revista de istorie şi teorie literară* 33 (2): 134–139.
1988   N. Iorga despre ideea de libertate. *România literară* 21 (January 14): 8.

Ortner, Sherry
1984   Theory in anthropology since the sixties. *Comparative Studies in Society and History* 26: 126–166.

Oţetea, A., D. Prodan, M. Berza
1964   *Istoria Romîniei, vol. 3: Feudalismul dezvoltat în secolul al XVII-lea. Destrămarea feudalismului şi formarea relaţiilor capitaliste.* Bucharest: Ed. Academiei.

Păcurariu, Francisc
1988   *Romînii şi maghiarii de-a lungul veacurilor.* Bucharest: Minerva.

Păcurariu, Mircea
1981   *Istoria Bisericii Ortodoxe Române,* vol. 3. Bucharest: Institutul Biblic şi de Misiune al Bisericii Ortodoxe Române.

Paleologu, Alexandru
1980   Amicus Plato . . . sau: "Despărţirea de Noica." In Al. Paleologu, *Ipoteze de lucru,* 7–67. Bucharest: Cartea Românească.
1983   A fi european. In Al. Paleologu, *Alchimia existenţei,* 7–14. Bucharest: Cartea Românească.

Pandrea, Petre
1931   Specificul naţional şi moment istoric. *Adevăr literar şi artistic* 10 (561): 1.

Papahagi, Marian
1987   Exerciţii de sinceritate. *Tribuna* 31 (September 3): 4, 6.

Papu, Edgar
1974   Protocronismul românesc. *Secolul XX* (5–6): 8–11.
1976   Protocronism şi sinteză. *Secolul XX* (6): 7–9.
1977   *Din clasicii noştri: Contribuţii la ideea unui protocronism românesc.* Bucharest: Ed. Eminescu.

Pascu, Ştefan
1984   *Revoluţia populară de sub conducerea lui Horea.* Bucharest: Ed. Militară.
1989   Apel către toţi istoricii români. *Adevărul în libertate* 1 (December 29).

Pascu, Ştefan, and Ştefan Ştefănescu
1987   *The dangerous game of falsifying history: Studies and articles.* Bucharest: Ed. Ştiinţifică şi Enciclopedică.

Pătrăşcanu, Lucreţiu
1946   *Poziţia Partidului Comunist Român faţă de intelectuali.* Bucharest:
        Ed. P.C.R.
Păun, Paul
1935   Elitele conducătoare. *Cuvântul liber* 2 (43): 4.
Păunescu, Adrian
1982*a*   Pentru totalitatea şi unitatea culturii române. *Flacăra* 31 (January
          29): 15, 17.
1982*b*   Valoarea prin adăugire. *România liberă* 40 (June 9): 2.
Pavel, Dan
1990   Intre chilie şi agora: Interviu cu filosoful Gabriel Liiceanu. *22* 1
        (February 23): 12–13, 15.
Pavelescu, Gh.
1939   Etnografia românească din Ardeal în ultimii douăzeci de ani
        (1919–1939). *Gând românesc* 7: 449–462.
1943   *Review of* Etnicul românesc: Comunitate de origine, limbă şi des-
        tin, by C. Rădulescu-Motru. *Saeculum* 1 (5): 72–75.
Pecie, Ion
1984   Balada unui jurnal. *Ramuri* nr. 235 (January 15): 11.
Pelin, Mihai
1983   Repere pentru o gîndire dialectică, antidogmatică a literaturii şi
        artei. *Scînteia tineretului, supliment literar-artistic* 3 (April 24): 4.
Petcu, Dionisie
1980   *Conceptul de etnic: Eseu metodologic.* Bucharest: Ed. Ştiinţifică şi
        Enciclopedică.
Plămădeală, Antonie
1977   Biserica Ortodoxă Română şi războiul de independenţă. *Biserica
        Ortodoxă Română* 95 (5–6): 536–550.
1987   A plecat şi Constantin Noica. *Telegraful român* 135 (December
        1–15): 7–8.
Platon, Gheorghe
1980   *Geneza revoluţiei române de la 1848.* Iaşi: Junimea.
Pleşu, Andrei
1981   Rigorile ideii naţionale şi legitimitatea universalului. *Secolul XX*
        (1-2-3): 189–196.
1985   Intre filosofie şi înţelepciune. *Ateneu* 20 (5): 5.
1988   *Minima moralia: Elemente pentru o etică a intervalului.* Bucharest:
        Cartea Românească.
Poovey, Mary
1986   "Scenes of an indelicate character": The medical "treatment" of
        Victorian women. *Representations* 14: 137–168.
Popescu, Ion Mihail
1987   *Personalităţi ale culturii româneşti.* Bucharest: Ed. Eminescu.
Popescu, Titu
1977   *Specificul naţional în doctrinele estetice româneşti.* Cluj-Napoca: Ed.
        Dacia.

Popescu-Puţuri, Ion
1983   Istoria poporului român în opera Preşedintelui Nicolae Ceauşescu. In N. Ceauşescu, *Istoria poporului român*, 7–50. Bucharest: Ed. Militară.
Popescu-Spineni, Marin
1932   *Instituţii de înaltă cultură*. Vălenii-de-Munte: Datina Românească.
Popovici, Aurel
1908*a*   Demagogie criminală. *Convorbiri literare* 42: 296–307.
1908*b*   Idei anarhice. *Lupta* 2 (86): 1–2; (87): 1–2.
Precan, Vilem
1985   Some problems of Czechoslovak history after 1968. Paper presented at World Congress of Soviet and East European Studies, Washington, D.C.
Prodan, David
1971   *Supplex Libellus Valachorum*. Bucharest: Ed. Academiei (English ed.).
1979   *Răscoala lui Horea*. 2 vols. Bucharest: Ed. Ştiinţifică şi Enciclopedică. (2d ed. 1984.)
Prodan, David, et al.
1989   Declaraţia Comitetului istoricilor liberi din România. *Adevărul în libertate* 1 (December 31): 2.
Purcaru, Ilie
1982*a*   Elucidări necesare. *Flacăra* 31 (February 5): 16–17.
1982*b*   N.M. şi noua ordine literară. *Flacăra* 31 (January 22): 20.
1986   *Literatură şi naţiune*. Bucharest: Ed. Eminescu.
Rachieru, Adrian Dinu
1985   *Vocaţia sintezei: Eseuri asupra spiritualităţii româneşti*. Timişoara: Facla.
Rădulescu, Gheorghe
1986   Profesorii mei de limba şi literatura română. *România literară* 19 (August 16): 12–13.
Rădulescu-Motru, Constantin
1921   Apel către toţi intelectualii. *Ideea europeană* 2 (61): 2.
1922   Scandal European? *Ideea europeană* 3 (88): 1–2.
1936   *Românismul: Catehismul unei noi spiritualităţi*. Bucharest: Fundaţia Regală.
1984   *Personalismul energetic şi alte scrieri*. Bucharest: Ed. Eminescu.
Ralea, Mihai
1943   *Intre două lumi*. Bucharest: Cartea Românească.
Raul-Teodorescu, A.
1919   Reforma intelectuală. *Ideea europeană* 1 (12): 2.
Ray, S. N., and Graciela de la Lama
1981   *The role of the intelligentsia in contemporary Asian societies*. [Mexico City]: El Colegio de Mexico.
Rebedeu, I.
1971   Cu privire la fizionomia spirituală a naţiunii. In *Naţiunea şi contemporaneitatea*, ed. I. Ceterchi, D. Hurezeanu, et al., 273–320. Bucharest: Ed. Ştiinţifică.

Rév, István
1984   Local autonomy or centralism—when was the original sin committed? *International Journal of Urban and Regional Research* 8: 38–63.
1987   The advantages of being atomized. *Dissent* 34: 335–350.
Riza, Adrian
1985   Sociologia eminesciană, I-IV. *Luceafărul* 28 (March 3, 9, 30, and April 13): 6, 7, 6, 6.
Roberts, Henry L.
1951   *Rumania: Political problems of an agrarian state*. New Haven: Yale Univ. Press.
Rodden, John
1989   *The politics of literary reputation*. Oxford: Oxford Univ. Press.
Rogger, Hans, and Eugen Weber
1965   *The European Right: A historical profile*. Berkeley: Univ. of California Press.
Roller, Mihail, ed.
1952   *Istoria R. P. R.: Manual pentru învăţămînt mediu*. Bucharest: Ed. de Stat Didactică şi Pedagogică.
România literară
1977   Colocviul naţional de critică şi istorie literară. *România literară* 10 (December 22): 3–11.
Romanian Communist Party
1975   *Congresul al XI-lea al Partidului Comunist Român, 25–28 noiembrie 1974*. Bucharest: Ed. Politică.
Rura, Michael J.
1961   *Reinterpretation of history as a method for furthering communism in Rumania: A study in comparative historiography*. Washington, D.C.: Georgetown Univ. Press.
Ryback, Timothy W.
1990   *Rock around the bloc: A history of rock music in Eastern Europe and the Soviet Union*. New York: Oxford Univ. Press.
Saizu, I.
1981   Relaţia ştiinţă-societate în gîndirea românească interbelică. *Revista de istorie* 34 (5): 799–819.
1984   Menirea învăţămîntului în modernizarea României contemporane (puncte de vedere din perioada interbelică). *Anuarul Institutului de Istorie şi Arheologie "A. D. Xenopol"* 21: 277–302.
Săptămîna
1980   Idealuri. *Săptămîna* (September 5): 1.
Schöpflin, George
1974   Romanian nationalism. *Survey* 20 (2–3): 77–104.
Scott, Joan
1988   "Ouvrière, mot impie, sordide": Women workers in the discourse of French political economy, 1840–1860. In Joan Scott, *Gender and the politics of history*, 139–163. New York: Columbia Univ. Press.

Şerban, George
    1984   Alternativa compensatoare. *Tomis* 19 (3): 13.
Seton-Watson, Hugh
    1964   *Nationalism and communism: Essays 1946–1963.* New York: Praeger.
Seton-Watson, Robert W.
    1922   *The historian as a political force in Central Europe.* London: School of Slavonic Studies, Univ. of London.
Shafir, Michael
    1981   The intellectual and the Party: The Rumanian Communist Party and the creative intelligentsia in the Ceauşescu period 1965–1972. Ph.D. diss., Hebrew University, Jerusalem.
    1983a   Men of the archangel revisited: Anti-semitic formations among communist Romania's intellectuals. *Studies in Comparative Communism* 16 (3): 223–243.
    1983b   Political culture, intellectual dissent, and intellectual consent: The case of Romania. *Orbis* 27: 393–420.
    1985   *Romania: Politics, economy, and society.* Boulder, Colo.: Lynne Rienner.
    1989a   Romania and the reburial of Imre Nagy. *Radio Free Europe Background Report* no. 117, June 30, pp. 1–6.
    1989b   Xenophobic communism: The case of Bulgaria and Romania. *Radio Free Europe Background Report* no. 112, June 27, pp. 1–11.
Shapiro, Paul A.
    1971   *The Horia rebellion in Transylvania, 1784–1785.* Columbia Essays in International Affairs, 65–93.
Sherlock, Thomas
    1988   Politics and history under Gorbachev. *Problems of Communism* 37: 16–42.
Shils, Edward
    1958   The intellectuals and the powers: Some perspectives for comparative analysis. *Comparative Studies in Society and History* 1: 5–22.
Shlapentokh, Vladimir
    1987   *The politics of sociology in the Soviet Union.* Boulder, Colo.: Westview.
Shteppa, Konstantin F.
    1962   *Russian historians and the Soviet state.* New Brunswick, N.J.: Rutgers Univ. Press.
Shue, Vivienne
    1988   *The reach of the state: Sketches of the Chinese body politic.* Stanford: Stanford Univ. Press.
Silvestri, Arthur
    1985   A study of the ethnic. *Romanian News* 8 (June 21): 8.
    1986   Protocronism şi antidogmatism. *Luceafărul* 29 (July 9): 3.
Simečka, Milan
    1984   *The restoration of order: The normalization of Czechoslovakia, 1969–1978.* London: Verso.

Simion, E.
1966   Specificul naţional în literatura română: Perspectivă istorică. *Gazeta literară* 13 (14): 7.
1983   Indîrjirile filosofului. *România literară* 16 (November 10): 11.
Simmonds-Duke, E. M.
1987   Was the peasant uprising a revolution? The meanings of a struggle over the past. *Eastern European Politics and Societies* 1 (2): 187–224.
Skilling, H. Gordon
1984   The muse of history, 1984: History, historians and politics in Communist Czechoslovakia. *Cross Currents* 3: 29–47.
Skinner, G. William, and Edwin A. Winckler
1969   Compliance succession in rural Communist China: A cyclical theory. In *A sociological reader on complex organizations*, ed. Amitai Etzioni, 410–438. New York: Holt, Rinehart and Winston.
Şoimaru, Tudor
1925   De vorbă cu dl. Nichifor Crainic. *Mişcarea literară* 2 (June 20–27): 1–2.
Solacolu, Ion
1988   Conştiinţa pericolului ce vine din noi. *Dialog* (Dietzenbach) 85 (March): 25–28.
Sorescu, Constantin
1982   Cum polemizează Z. Ornea? (I). *Săptămîna* (April 16): 3.
1983   Alţi protocronişti fără voie (1). *Luceafărul* 26 (June 4): 6.
1984   Antiprotocronism de-a gata. *Scînteia tineretului, supliment literar-artistic* 4 (January 29): 4.
Stahl, Henri H.
1937   Satul românesc: O discuţie de filozofie şi sociologie culturii. *Sociologia românească* 2 (11–12): 489–502.
1938   Filosofarea despre filosofia poporului român. *Sociologia românească* 3 (4–6): 104–119.
1983*a*   *Eseuri critice despre cultura populară românească.* Bucharest: Ed. Minerva.
1983*b*   Notă despre valorificarea tradiţiilor noastre culturale. *Revista de istorie şi teorie literară* 31 (4): 122–123.
Stăniloae, Dumitru
1942   *Pozitia dlui Lucian Blaga faţă de creştinism şi ortodoxie.* Sibiu: Tipografia Arhidiecezană.
Staniszkis, Jadwiga
1979   On some contradictions of socialist society: The case of Poland. *Soviet Studies* 31 (2): 167–187.
1991   *The ontology of socialism.* Oxford: Oxford Univ. Press (forthcoming).
Stark, David
1988   Work, worth, and justice in a socialist mixed economy. MS (forthcoming in French translation in Actes de la Recherche en Sciences Sociales).

1989   Coexisting forms in Hungary's emerging mixed economy. In *Re-making the economic institutions of socialism: China and Eastern Europe*, ed. Victor Nee and David Stark, 137–168. Stanford: Stanford Univ. Press.

Starr, Fred
1983   *Red and hot: The fate of jazz in the Soviet Union, 1917–1980*. New York and Oxford: Oxford Univ. Press.

Ştefănescu, Alex.
1981   Un raft de bibliotecă. *Convorbiri literare* 87 (12): 2–3.
1984   Un nescriitor. *Pagini bucovinene (supliment)* 3 (1): 3.

Ştefănescu, Ştefan
1978   Istoria—puternic factor de educaţie partinică şi patriotică. *Era socialistă* 58 (2): 37.
1984   *Naţiunea română: Geneză, afirmare, orizont contemporan*. Bucharest: Ed. Ştiinţifică şi Enciclopedică.

Steinhardt, N.
1983   Catarii de la Păltiniş. *Familia* 19 (12): 7.
1988   Puţine cuvinte despre singurătatea lui Noica. *Tribuna* 32 (Sept. 29): 3.

Stroe, Ion
1984   Un personaj pretext. *Luceafărul* 27 (March 31): 10.

Sugar, Peter F.
1977   *Southeastern Europe under Ottoman rule, 1354–1804*. Seattle: Univ. of Washington Press.

Sugar, Peter, Iván Berend, Charles Gati, and Josef Brada
1985   *Eastern Europe: A question of identity*. Occasional Paper no. 2, East European Program, Woodrow Wilson Center, Washington, D. C.

Svoboda, George
1985   Frantisek Kutnar and the advancement of Czech social history. Paper presented at World Congress of Soviet and East European Studies, Washington, D.C.

Szelényi, Ivan
1982   The intelligentsia in the class structure of state-socialist societies. In *Marxist inquiries*, ed. M. Burawoy and Theda Skocpol. American Journal of Sociology Special Supplement, vol. 88: 287–327.

Tănase, Al.
1973   Naţional-universal în cultură (I-II). *Cronica* 8 (15): 9 and (18): 8.

Tăslăuanu, Octavian
1908a   Două culturi. *Luceafărul* 7: 59–64.
1908b   O lămurire. *Luceafărul* 7: 305–6.

Teodorescu, Alin
1987   Timpul operei sau restituirea prin gîndire. *Amfiteatru* 21 (December 12): 8.

Therborn, Goran
1980   *The ideology of power and the power of ideology*. London: Verso.

Tismăneanu, Vladimir
1984   The ambiguity of Romanian national Communism. *Telos* no. 60: 65–79.

1989   The tragicomedy of Romanian Communism. *Eastern European Politics and Societies* 3 (2): 329–376.

Trotsky, Leon
1937   *The revolution betrayed.* Garden City, N.Y.: Doubleday, Doran & Co.

Trouillot, Michel-Rolph
1989   The three faces of Sans Souci: Glory and silences in the Haitian Revolution. Paper presented at Sixth Roundtable in History and Anthropology, Bellagio, Italy.

Tudor, Corneliu Vadim
1981   Cine îi educă pe dascăli. *Săptămîna* (December 4): 7.
1982   Împărăţia cărţilor. *Săptămîna* (4 June): 3, 7.
1986   *Mîndria de a fi români (eseuri, recenzii, medalioane).* Bucharest: Ed. Sport-Turism.

Tudoran, Dorin
1982   Să rămînem tineri şi înţelepţi! *Steaua* 33 (2): 26–27.

Turnock, David
1986   *The Romanian economy in the twentieth century.* New York: St. Martin's Press.

Ungheanu, Mihai
1970   Rostirea filozofică românească (C. Noica). *România literară* 3 (September 3): 14–15.
1982   *Interviuri neconvenţionale.* Bucharest: Cartea Românească.
1985   *Exactitatea admiraţiei.* Bucharest: Cartea Românească.

Ungureanu, Cornel
1983   Zeul şi oglinzile. *Orizont* 34 (December 9): 2.

Valkenier, Elizabeth Kridl
1985   The rise and decline of official Marxist historiography in Poland, 1945–1980. *Slavic Review* 44 (4): 663–680.

Vârgolici, Teodor
1971   *Comentarii literare.* Bucharest: Ed. Eminescu.

Verdery, Katherine
1983   *Transylvanian villagers: Three centuries of political, economic, and ethnic change.* Berkeley, Los Angeles, London: Univ. of California Press.
1987   The rise of the discourse about Romanian identity: Early 1900s to World War II. In *Românii în istoria universală*, vol. II-1, ed. I. Agrigoroaiei, Gh. Buzatu, and V. Cristian, 89–138. Iaşi: Universitatea "Al. I. Cuza."
1988   Moments in the rise of the discourse on national identity, I: Seventeenth through nineteenth centuries. In *Românii în istoria universală*, vol. III-1, ed. I. Agrigoroaiei, Gh. Buzatu, and V. Cristian, 25–60. Iaşi: Universitatea "Al. I. Cuza."
1990   The production and defense of "the Romanian Nation," 1900 to World War II. In *Nationalist ideologies and the production of national cultures*, ed. Richard G. Fox, 81–111. American Ethnological Society Monograph Series, Number 2.

1991   The "etatization" of time in Socialist Romania. In *The politics of time*, ed. Henry J. Rutz. American Ethnological Society Monograph Series (forthcoming).

Vetişanu, Vasile
1982   Filosofia lumii româneşti, i-iii. *Flacăra* 31 (March 12): 15, (March 26): 13, (April 2): 13.

Viaţa românească
1906   Către cititori. *Viaţa românească* 1 (1): 5–7.

Vrancea, Ileana
1965   *E. Lovinescu: Critic literar*. Bucharest: Ed. pt. Literatură.
1975   *Confruntări în critica deceniilor IV-VII (E. Lovinescu şi posteritatea lui critică)*. Bucharest: Cartea Românească.

Walker, Mack
1983   Recent historical writing in the D.D.R. Unpublished lecture, presented at the Wissenschaftskolleg zu Berlin.

Wallman, Sandra
1980   The boundaries of race: Processes of ethnicity in England. *Man* 13: 200–217.

Williams, Raymond
1982   *The sociology of culture*. New York: Schocken Books.

Zamfirescu, Dan
1970   Studiu introductiv. In *Invăţăturile lui Neagoe Basarab către fiul său Theodosie*, ed. Florica Moisil and Dan Zamfirescu, 5–55. Bucharest: Ed. Minerva.
1975   *Istorie şi cultură*. Bucharest: Ed. Eminescu.
1979   *Via Magna*. Bucharest: Ed. Eminescu.
1982*a*   Sensul tradiţiei şi al protocronismului, I: Răspuns unui critic. *Săptămîna* (January 15): 7.
1982*b*   Sensul tradiţiei şi al protocronismului, II: "Provizoratul" unei retrospective. *Săptămîna* (February 5): 7.
1983   *Accente şi profiluri (1968–1983)*. Bucharest: Cartea Românească.

Zub, Al.
1974   *Mihail Kogălniceanu istoric*. Iaşi: Ed. Junimea.
1981   *A scrie şi a face istorie (istoriografia română postpaşoptistă)*. Iaşi: Ed. Junimea.
1983   *Biruit-au gîndul (note despre istorismul românesc)*. Iaşi: Junimea.
1985*a*   Critical school in Romanian historiography: Genetic model and strategy. In *Culture and society*, ed. Al. Zub, 113–126. Iaşi: Ed. Academiei.
1985*b*   *De la istoria critică la criticism*. Bucharest: Ed. Academiei.
1989   *Istorie şi istorici în România interbelică*. Iaşi: Junimea.

Index

396   INDEX

Decebal (Dacian king), 36
Deletant, Dennis, 353 n. 16
Deleuze, Gilles, 292
Densuşianu, Ovidiu, 361 n. 16
Descartes, René, 261
Dialectics (as rhetorical weapon), 145, 160, 162, 268–269, 270–271, 285. *See also* Indigenization of Marxism
Dictionary of Romanian Literature, 193
Dinescu, Mircea, 3, 292, 316, 357 n. 52
Discourse: as constitutive of reality, 91, 131, 139, 305, 307, 314; defined, 8–9; double-voiced, 201; overlapping fields of, 11, 28–29; under socialism, 89–91, 139, 305, 333 n. 25. *See also* Ideology; Indigenization of Marxism; National ideology, and Marxism
Dissidence. *See* Opposition
Dobrescu, Al., 342 n. 3
Dobrogeanu-Gherea, Constantin, 53, 148, 163
Dogmatism, 111, 112; history of, as idea, 120–121, 133, 146; as rhetorical weapon, 112, 138, 140, 142, 145–156, 168, 171, 195, 196, 200, 211, 267, 270–271, 274, 276, 279, 339 n. 3, 346 n. 29, 361 n. 18. *See also* Elitism; Fascism; Foreign; Proletcultism
Doinaş, Ştefan Augustin, 358 n. 3
Domination, mode of, 85–86. *See also* Control, modes of
Dragoş, Nicolae, 342 n. 3, 345 n. 25
Drăgan, Iosif Constantin, 170, 317, 343 n. 7
Dumas, Alexandre, 183

East Germany, 86, 105, 334 n. 3, 339 n. 9, 351 n. 3, 356 n. 36; and national ideology, 131
Eco, Umberto, 294
Economy, developments in, 42, 337 n. 24; interwar, 42, 60, 334 n. 6; to nineteenth century, 34–35, 40, 325 n. 16, 326 n. 21; under socialism, 73, 100, 104–107, 130, 334 n. 3, 343–344 n. 12, 344 n. 15. *See also* Autarchy; Romanian Communist Party, "independence" of
Economy of shortage, 78–79; and historiography, 248; and national ideology, 126–127, 209–213, 304, 308. *See also*

Second economy; Shortage; Socialist system, "laws of motion" of
Education. *See* Romanian Communist Party, educational policy of
Eliade, Mircea, 2, 49, 125, 258, 284, 300, 341 n. 20, 359 nn. 4, 6
Elias, Norbert, 16, 94
Elitism, as rhetorical weapon, 138, 140, 142–144, 155, 194, 196, 198, 211, 274, 285, 298. *See also* Dogmatism; Fascism; Foreign; Proletcultism
Emigrés, Romanian, 110, 132, 170, 172, 310, 317, 343 n. 7, 349 n. 48, 359 nn. 3, 6. *See also* Cultural representativeness; Radio Free Europe
Eminescu, Mihai, 38–39, 326 n. 21; in 1970–80s cultural politics, 124, 125, 148, 150, 157–164, 181, 192, 199, 200, 202, 209, 340 nn. 15–16, 341 n. 17, 349 n. 52. *See also* Genealogical appropriation; Reeditions
Enescu, Radu, 358 n. 3
Epistolar. See Letters
Ethnic identity. *See* National identity; National ideology
Ethnology/ethnography: form of, in core vs. peripheral states, 329 n. 48; and Romanian identity, 63, 66, 69
Ethnophilosophy, 269–277, 360–361 n. 16. *See also* Marginality, institutional; Philosophy; Protochronism
European Idea, The (Ideea europeană), 50, 327 n. 24, 328 n. 38, 329 n. 41. *See also* Rădulescu-Motru
Expertise. *See* Science; Scientific authority

Fascism, 48–49, 144–146, 211, 248, 326 n. 21, 339–340 n. 10, 352 n. 8; as rhetorical weapon, 137, 138, 140, 145–146, 168, 173, 196. *See also* Dogmatism; Elitism; Foreign; Interwar period; Proletcultism
Fehér, Ferenc, 9, 74–76, 79, 320 n. 10
Fieldwork. *See* Anthropology
Filotti, Eugen, 51
Flacăra. See Flame, The
Flame, The (Flacăra), 172, 176, 343 n. 6, 345 n. 25, 364 n. 46
Foreign, as rhetorical weapon, 34, 54, 61–63, 138, 140–143, 147, 150, 160, 211, 274. *See also* Dogmatism; Elitism; Fascism; Proletcultism

Designer: UC Press Staff
Compositor: G & S Typesetters, Inc.
Text: 10/13 Galliard
Display: Galliard
Printer: Edwards Bros., Inc.
Binder: Edwards Bros., Inc.